In Search of Self

In Search of Self

INTERDISCIPLINARY PERSPECTIVES
ON PERSONHOOD

Edited by

J. Wentzel van Huyssteen *&* Erik P. Wiebe

WILLIAM B. EERDMANS PUBLISHING COMPANY
GRAND RAPIDS, MICHIGAN / CAMBRIDGE, U.K.

Published 2011 by Wm. B. Eerdmans Publishing Co.
2140 Oak Industrial Drive N.E., Grand Rapids, Michigan 49505 /
P.O. Box 163, Cambridge CB3 9PU U.K.

Printed in the United States of America

17 16 15 14 13 12 11   7 6 5 4 3 2 1

Library of Congress Cataloging-in-Publication Data

In search of self: interdisciplinary perspectives on personhood /
    edited by J. Wentzel van Huyssteen & Erik P. Wiebe.
        p.   cm.
    ISBN 978-0-8028-6386-7 (pbk.: alk. paper)
    1. Philosophical anthropology.   2. Self.   3. Theological anthropology — Christianity.
    4. Theological anthropology.   I. Huyssteen, J. Wentzel van.   II. Wiebe, Erik P.
    III. Title: Interdisciplinary perspectives on personhood.

BD450.I5   2011
126 — dc22

2010052133

www.eerdmans.com

Dedicated to our lovely wives,

Hester and Katherine

Companions in life, partners in thought

Contents

Part Two: The Self and Multiplicity

Part Three: The Self and Identity

Part Four: The Self and Emergence

Acknowledgments

The idea for a multidisciplinary anthology on "notions of self" gradually emerged over the past few years from our ongoing conversations about, and a shared fascination with, some of the most salient themes in contemporary theological anthropology. As time went by, this journey increasingly exposed us to the multiple interdisciplinary perspectives on the "self" now impacting theology — perspectives from disciplines as diverse as philosophy, archeology, primatology, anthropology, psychology, neuroscience, and cognitive science of religion, to name just a few. Many hours of conversation over as many months always brought the impact of these multiple disciplinary voices back to the heart of the matter: the human condition, and what it is that really makes us human. In this way the idea of self, and the idea of personhood, quickly emerged as a natural overarching theme, a kind of interdisciplinary forum, that enabled us to invite scholars from very diverse disciplines to present their views on the self and personhood.

For us this shared journey has been not only deeply rewarding and gratifying but also immensely fulfilling — in both an academic and a personal sense. We therefore honor and thank our collaborators, all twenty-five of them, for their challenging and remarkable contributions to this anthology. Not only did each and every one instantly accept our invitation to collaborate on this volume, but each and every author supported this project with great enthusiasm by meeting every deadline and by providing us with exactly the kind of engaging, high-level essays we were hoping for. We are proud to have shared in this remarkable team effort, and for the way in which our colleagues have taken time out of their busy schedules to devote to this project, which has been so important to us. We have been enriched by the process, and by the quality of our authors' work. We trust that our readers will share in this experience and will see in this volume a one-of-a-kind resource for the fascinating interdisciplinary conversation on notions of self that is alive and well in our academic culture today.

We are very grateful to Princeton Theological Seminary, which provided us with tangible support in the form of a research grant, without which this project would not have been possible. This grant enabled the two of us to collaborate fully, to meet at the Stead Center for Ethics and Values at Garrett Evangelical Seminary in Evanston, Illinois, and in Tampa, Florida, for editorial meetings in which this volume could be planned, executed, put together, edited, and provided with an extensive written Introduction that sets the stage for the eighteen essays of our authors. We also want to express our gratitude to C. J. Dickson, our editorial assistant at Princeton Theological Seminary, for successfully creating the two outstanding and comprehensive indexes at the end of this book.

We are proud and happy to be part of the William B. Eerdmans Publishing Company's ongoing effort to provide the broader public with the very best of intellectual material that will keep stimulating both the ongoing theological conversation and the current exciting interdisciplinary context of philosophical theology. We are especially grateful to Mr. Bill Eerdmans (President) and Ms. Linda Bieze (Managing Editor) for their ongoing, unqualified, and enthusiastic support.

We thank, with much appreciation, our spouses Hester van Huyssteen and Kate Wiebe, for their unwavering loyalty and loving support for a project that has meant so much to the two of us. We are thrilled to dedicate this anthology to the two of them.

As editors of this exciting project we are grateful for the exceptional privilege of working together so effortlessly, and with so much pleasure, on a project and topic that has not only been crucially important to both of us, but also rewarding and gratifying in every sense of the word.

J. WENTZEL VAN HUYSSTEEN AND
ERIK P. WIEBE

Introduction

J. Wentzel van Huyssteen and Erik P. Wiebe

Theology today finds itself in the middle of one of the most salient interdisciplinary academic discussions of our time, namely, the search for the self, which for a wide array of disciplines translates into a profound quest for the understanding of self-identity and personhood. At the heart of this quest is the remarkable human phenomenon of self-awareness or self-consciousness, that is, the introspective, reflexive ability that enables us to reflect on our motives and reasons, our likes and dislikes, our character traits and our relationship with others.[1] At the deepest level of this quest, however, is the search for self and the haunting conviction that if there were no self, how could my thoughts and my conscious experiences belong to *me?* This is also the reason why we so often speak, quite innocuously, of "my former self," "my better self," or "my true self," or say, after someone has recovered from illness, "she is quite her old self again."[2] It is, of course, this materiality of our embodied existence that has come about through the process of biological evolution and has given us what seems to be a unique human sense of self. Cognitive archeologist Steven Mithen puts it well: one's self-identity is intimately related to the feeling that one has a suite of beliefs, moods, desires, and feelings that are quite unique to oneself.[3]

Precisely the notion of "self," however, has undergone fierce questioning

1. Cf. M. R. Bennett and P. M. S. Hacker, *Philosophical Foundations of Neuroscience* (Oxford: Blackwell, 2003).

2. Bennett and Hacker, *Philosophical Foundations of Neuroscience*, 334.

3. Cf. Steven Mithen, *The Singing Neanderthals: The Origins of Music, Language, Mind, and Body* (Cambridge, MA: Harvard University Press, 2009), 214.

at the hands of pressing contemporary discussions. In a very comprehensive essay, four co-authors have reviewed a number of recent deconstructions and reformulations of the self, and myths about the self that have lost or gained credibility.[4] In this "brief history of the self," a large, if not bewildering number of notions of self emerge that are still at the very heart of interdisciplinary discussions today: the premodern self, the modern self, and the postmodern self — the latter of which includes relational notions of self as diverse as the hermeneutical self, the plural self, the empty self, the multiple self, the emergent self, the saturated self, the erotic self, and the posthuman self. What emerges from this, and from the history of the idea of self, as Jerrold Seigel has shown in his magisterial work,[5] is the remarkable fluidity of the self, the elusiveness of the self, and the many ways to think of the self as socially constructed. In addition, a wide variety of approaches to the self include existential notions of self, the Buddhist idea of No-Self, notions of paradoxical selves, process approaches to the self, and *Gestalt* and Jungian notions of the self, which are just a handful in a long list of approaches.[6]

It is precisely this plurality of approaches then, that makes the "self" difficult to locate, define, or describe. In fact, many feel that even the scientific study of the self has been slow to mature because the nature of the self appears to be so complex. The self indeed draws on several psychological and neuropsychological domains, such as autobiographical memory, emotional and evaluative systems, sense of agency, self-monitoring, bodily awareness, mind-reading of others' mental states, subjectivity, and finally the sense of unity conferred on consciousness when it is invested with the subjective perspective. It seems that any account of the psychology and neurology of self should be at least consistent with most or all of these properties. No wonder, then, that progress in understanding the self has been slow.[7]

The confusing number of notions of self that are alive and well in interdisciplinary discussions today adds to the plausibility of the idea that the self in some important sense is socially constructed and thus can indeed be conceived of in many ways. The idea of a socially constructed self, and therefore

---

4. Cf. Louis Hoffman, Sharon Stuart, Denise Warren, and Lisa Meek, "Toward a Sustainable Myth of Self: An Existential Response to the Postmodern Condition," *Journal of Humanistic Psychology* 49: 135ff.

5. Cf. Jerrold Seigel, *The Idea of Self: Thought and Experience in Western Europe since the Seventeenth Century* (Cambridge: Cambridge University Press, 2005).

6. Cf. Hoffman, Stewart, Warren, and Meek, "Toward a Sustainable Myth of Self," 135ff.

7. Patrick McNamara, *The Neuroscience of Religious Experience* (Cambridge: Cambridge University Press, 2009), 60.

also the increasingly popular idea of multiple selves, does not necessarily mean that that there is not a "real self," or that this real self cannot be experienced. Rather, it could indicate that the self is something that cannot be definitively known, that cannot be isolated from its context and studied in a reductionistic manner.[8] The idea of socially constructed, multiple selves does, however, pose significant challenges for Christian theology. One challenge of moving toward a conception of multiple selves or notions of no-self is the difficult problem of evil: if there is no self, or if there are only multiple selves, it would be easy to disregard what we might call "the potential for evil" inherent in every person. Would not the reality of multiple selves, therefore, enable us to relegate evil to particular selves, or aspects of the self, and so help us avoid taking full responsibility for dangerous evil acts?[9] For those of us who are theologians, at least, might it be that the problem of evil by itself may necessitate a stronger argument for maintaining a notion of an integrated self?

For many of us who are philosophers and/or theologians, and confronting the difficult challenge of finding a viable way into the extreme complexity of contemporary discussions of self, it will be important to show that this multidisciplinary conversation has without question been shaped — sometimes directly, sometimes indirectly — by the work of French philosopher Paul Ricoeur. Ricoeur's work spanned several decades and, especially in its later phase, managed to set the tone and lift up dimensions of the self and of personhood that had great influence on a vast body of scholarship. Because of this, it would be appropriate to introduce an interdisciplinary anthology about the self — the self in all its elusiveness and complexity — by briefly noting the many dimensions of "self" and "personhood" that Paul Ricoeur has brought into focus and that will emerge very pointedly in the diverse interdisciplinary voices represented in this volume, even if he is not always referred to directly.

In his most recent body of work, Ricoeur develops a striking notion of the self as defined, at the deepest level, by time and narrative. What is more, as Ricoeur links narrative directly to empathy, he advances the understanding of the self and of its multivalent relationship to the other.[10] For Ricoeur, the narrative dimension of human self-awareness and consciousness not only enables us to envision new projects, to evaluate motivations, to initiate

---

8. Cf. Hoffman, Stewart, Warren, and Meek, "Toward a Sustainable Myth of Self," 135ff.

9. Cf. Hoffman, Stewart, Warren, and Meek, "Toward a Sustainable Myth of Self," 135ff.

10. Cf. Paul Ricoeur, *Oneself as Another* (Chicago: University of Chicago Press, 1992), 3.

viable courses of action, but also enables us to deeply empathize and identify with others. Ricoeur claims that a narrative understanding provides us with an ethics of responsibility that then propels us, precisely through empathy, beyond self-reference to relationships with others.[11] It is this extension of the "circle of selfhood" that involves an enlarged mentality ultimately capable of imagining the self in the place of the other. In this way Ricoeur has revisioned the notion of narrative understanding — where one represents oneself as another — to the extent that it ultimately liberates us from an all-consuming narcissistic interest without liquidating our identity as selves. Narrative understanding thus generates a basic act of empathy whereby the self flows from itself toward the other in a free variation of imagination. Thus narrative imagination transforms self-regarding into a self-for-another.[12]

In his Gifford Lectures,[13] Paul Ricoeur argued that our sense of self, our personal identity, should be understood precisely in terms of this narrative identity. Through the power of imagination we are able to weave together various elements of a life into a single story, just as we also maintain a sense of personal identity when we stay true to our promises over time.[14] For Ricoeur there is a direct connection between this notion of personal identity and self, which we model on the unity of various narratives and our imaginative capabilities. As he strikingly puts it: "in many narratives the self seeks its identity on the scale of an entire life."[15] By directly linking memory and imagination,[16] Ricoeur could argue that in this sense our memories retain within themselves a claim to faithfulness to the past and serve an integral role in shaping personal identity in the present and into the future. Ricoeur claims, then, that memory is the "gateway to the self" and to personal identity, and since there is always a narrative component to memory, our remembering always implies narrative experience.[17] However, since memory is so

---

11. Cf. Ricoeur, *Oneself as Another*, 113-39.

12. Cf. Richard Kearney, *On Paul Ricoeur: The Owl of Minerva* (Aldershot: Ashgate, 2004), 173.

13. Cf. Ricoeur, *Oneself as Another*, 3.

14. Cf. Ricoeur, *Oneself as Another*, 118-25.

15. Cf. Ricoeur, *Oneself as Another*, 115.

16. Cf. Paul Ricoeur, *Memory, History and Forgetting* (Chicago: University of Chicago Press, 2004), 1-55.

17. Cf. Paul Ricoeur and Peter Homans, "Afterword: Conversations on Freud, Memory, and Loss," in *Mourning Religion*, ed. William B. Parsons, Diane Jonte-Pace, and Susan E. Henking (Charlottesville: University of Virginia Press, 2008), 222.

directly associated with imagination, our recollections of our own past are liable to distortions, and by implication our personal identities are fragile.[18] The fragility of these identities is due, in part, to the continual help that is needed to express our memories and to grow in self-esteem. Memory is not always directly or readily accessible on our own, so we need the encouragement of the other. It is in this sense that the other, as Ricoeur claims, authorizes the act of remembrance, and of the cognitive intention of memory as faithful.[19] It is also in this way that self-esteem and self-respect together represent the most advanced stages of the growth of selfhood.

Ricoeur builds on these salient notions of the interdependence of the self and the other, and in both his books, *Oneself as Another* and *Memory, History and Forgetting*, memory and imagination are also closely tied to conscience: the voice of conscience within us should also be understood as the remembered voices of other persons coming to us from the past, those who have come before us.[20] At least in part, then, the voice of conscience within us should be understood as the voice of persons in the past, which is accessible only through memory. What is more, insofar as I as a self exist within a particular people who share a common memory, the voice of those who precede me lives on in this collective memory. It goes into shaping my identity, my sense of where I am coming from, and thus my sense of self.[21]

In the philosophical framework that Ricoeur builds, then, memory serves as the ultimate mediator between time and narrative, while imagination leads the way in forging an understanding of the human self as *oneself* only in and through the other person. As such, personal identity, or "self," is both articulated *and* constructed solely through the temporal and relational dimensions of embodied human existence. On this view, self-identity rises out of our narrative identities, and in many narratives the self as a lived body seeks its identity for the duration of an entire lifetime.[22] In this way Ricoeur could anticipate contemporary multiple-selves theories and could explicitly state: "to be a human being is to live at the same time at several levels of self-structuring, of the constitution of self-identity."[23]

18. Cf. C. J. Dickson, "Paul Ricoeur and Theological Anthropology" (unpublished doctoral paper, Princeton Theological Seminary, 2009), 11.

19. Cf. Ricoeur, *Memory, History and Forgetting*, 414.

20. Cf. Ricoeur, *Oneself as Another*, 318f., 341-356.

21. Cf. Ricoeur, *Memory, History and Forgetting*, 93-132; Dickson, "Paul Ricoeur and Theological Anthropology," 11f.

22. Cf. Ricoeur *Oneself as Another*, 115.

23. Cf. Ricoeur and Homans, "Afterword," 229.

It is in this way, then, that the defining role of narrative understanding in Ricoeur's work clearly points to the important role of interpretation as it participates in the construction of the hermeneutical self. Interpretation for Ricoeur can be said to engage us in a hermeneutical circle of historical intersubjectivity, precluding any idealist claim to occupy an absolutist, totalizing standpoint as a rational self. On the contrary, to interpret meaning, for Ricoeur, is to arrive in the middle of an exchange that has already begun and in which we seek to orient ourselves in order to make sense of it. It is in this sense, then, that for Ricoeur the "self-as-another" is attained only after complex interpretative detours of experience. Hermeneutical selfhood is not that which initiates understanding, but that which terminates it: it exists at the end, not at the beginning, and in this sense the retrieval of selfhood lies at the far end of the hermeneutical circle.[24] It is exactly in this sense that the shortest route to the self is through the other: the self only returns to itself after numerous hermeneutical detours through the embodied language of others, to find itself enlarged and enriched by the journey. Finally, it is the embeddedness of the self in time through memory and imagination that reveals the link of a sense of self to the future: insofar as my personal identity is dependent on keeping my word, the act of promising binds me to the future.

As Ricoeur developed the striking notion of the self as ultimately defined at the deepest level by time and narrative, the notion of *attestation*[25] became increasingly central to his conception of the emerging self. For Ricoeur attestation defines the kind of certainty that a hermeneutics of the self can claim as deeply embedded in one's own flesh, one's body.[26] Ricoeur even calls attestation the password for this entire book.[27] For Ricoeur it is attestation that ultimately reveals and enables the assurance of being oneself in acting and suffering. This definition includes three key elements of self as attestation unfolds in assurance, action, and suffering.

First, *assurance* is the only kind of certitude that is proper to claims of selfhood. In contrast to the *cogito* of Descartes and its static, substantialist, and singular notion of self, the claim to selfhood is not one that is irrefutable or one that might serve as its own foundation. Instead, for Ricoeur the claim to selfhood is not a matter of truth, but is rather a matter of veracity. This is a radical epistemological shift in adjusting to what it is we can know about

---

24. Cf. Kearney, *On Paul Ricoeur*, 5ff.
25. Cf. Ricoeur, *Oneself as Another*, 21ff., 318 ff.
26. Cf. Ricoeur, *Oneself as Another*, 30-55.
27. Cf. Ricoeur, *Oneself as Another*, 289, note 82.

ourselves as selves: the best I can offer by way of affirming my identity is an attestation, an assurance, a testimony, which is not a matter of definitive proof but rather a matter for belief and credibility.[28] This allows for a critical assessment of my claims to selfhood, a continuing critical inquiry into the question of whether I am who I say I am.

Second, *action* provides us with the specific content and confirmation of the assurance. The attestation I provide in my claim to be an authentic self is the assurance of a consistency in acting, an assurance that I will keep my word. In arguing in this way Ricoeur wants to move us away from thinking of the self, and thus of personal identity, in terms of sameness, as though it were on the basis of some unchanging characteristics that we would be able to identify the same person across time. The self, and personal identity, is not based on an unchanging character. Rather, the self is based on my doing in the future what I said I will do. In this sense my claim to be an authentic self is fundamentally based on the promises I make.

Third, to speak of *suffering* is to attest to our fragility as persons; the fact that our sense of self is formed at the very point of interaction with others. Being enjoined with the other in a dialectic with the other is internal to my very sense of self, but also reveals why the self is fragile and vulnerable.[29] It is in this way that Ricoeur pulls together assurance, testimony, and promise, making them central and indispensable to our understanding of what it means to be a self. Moreover, Ricoeur's epistemological shift, from thinking about the self in complete proofs and indubitable certitude, to thinking of the self in terms of assurances, promises, and critical engagement with one another, provides a compelling framework for a fuller interdisciplinary understanding of the self.

In this way we begin to understand the invaluable contributions of Ricoeur for an interdisciplinary understanding of the self. Some theologians in direct conversation with the neurosciences and psychology, in a remarkable convergence with Ricoeur's central themes, are developing these questions by focusing on the most basic dimensions of human self and self-identity and also exploring the way that we observe, remember, and imagine.

In a bold interdisciplinary move, theologian David Hogue, in his book *Remembering the Future, Imagining the Past: Story, Ritual, and the Human Brain*,[30] brings pastoral theology into direct conversation with cognitive

28. Cf. Dickson, "Paul Ricoeur and Theological Anthropology," 15.

29. Cf. Dickson, "Paul Ricoeur and Theological Anthropology," 15.

30. Cf. David A. Hogue, *Remembering the Future, Imagining the Past: Story, Ritual, and the Human Brain* (Cleveland: Pilgrim Press, 2003).

neuroscience and thus manages to provide a biological/neurological explanation for our narrative perspectives on the self, and for how we go about constructing the self. In developing the central themes of his book, Hogue focuses precisely on memory and imagination and explains how current research on these two mental functions has revealed their creative, constructive nature. Memory in particular is a constructive act and depends on a variety of neurological, psychological, and cultural variables. The task of the pastoral theologian is to support memory through scripture and ritual, and to help persons who suffer from blocked or distorted memory. Closely interwoven with memory is imagination, which is even more obviously a creative mental faculty. Hogue's reflections on the role of imagination in the Christian life and in theology converge with his research on imagination in brain-mind research. Hogue especially focuses on the way that neuroscience has argued that human consciousness is a thoroughly embodied phenomenon. In doing so, Hogue seeks a retrieval of Christian teachings that valorize the human body, and he uses neuroscience as a conceptual leverage against simplistic soul-body dualisms. At the heart of David Hogue's project is his explaining how the brain contributes to time-consciousness and to the foundational ability of the human self to remember the past and imaginatively anticipate the future, and on this view the rationality, emotionality, and spirituality of the human self are deeply rooted in biological processes. In this regard Hogue's project, by providing us with a neurological explanation for constructive and narrative perspectives on the self, not only shows affinities with Ricoeur's work, but also with feminist and more postmodern studies of the human self.[31]

In the work of theologian Marjorie Hewitt Suchocki also, we find strikingly similar themes emerge when she argues that human beings construct our selves socially and temporally not only through memory and imagination, but in relation to others, through deep attachment and empathy. In her book *The Fall to Violence: Original Sin in Relational Theology*,[32] Suchocki develops a distinct notion of self by arguing for what she calls *empathetic transcendence:*[33] a form of empathetic existence that does not make the self, or the other, absolute. For Suchocki, this model avoids the overreaching of self-transcendence that precipitates a loss of self. Instead, self-transcendence

31. Cf. Kelly Buckeley on David Hogue's, *Remembering the Future, Imagining the Past: Story, Ritual, and the Human Brain,* in *Journal of Religion* 85, no. 2 (2005): 331-32.

32. Cf. Marjorie Hewitt Suchocki, *The Fall to Violence: Original Sin in Relational Theology* (New York: Continuum, 1999).

33. Cf. Suchocki, *The Fall to Violence,* 40.

through empathy emerges when one relates to the other as the *related other,* who is also at the same time a subject. Such self-transcendence is the enrichment of the self as well as the enrichment of the other. On this dynamic relational view both the self and the other are at the same time transformed and preserved. And it is in fact *empathy,* through the mutuality that it creates, that retains an appreciative differentiation between self and other and thus honors the subjectivity of each: one brings another's experience into one's own, and one offers one's experience to another. Self-transcendence through empathy, then, entails a regard for the other as other, an openness to the other as subject, and ultimately a transformation of the self.

It is in this sense that for Suchocki self-identity is constituted by time: self-transcendence through self-consciousness as *memory* evolves through one's relation to one's past, one's own historicity. Self-transcendence through *empathy* is a living of the present created through the relation to the other as subjective other. Self-transcendence through *imagination* calls upon the creative, rich possibilities of the future. Also on this view empathy and imagination can richly condition one another, and the human person emerges as a self in and through relationship to the other.[34] But Suchocki puts it even stronger: through the self-transcendence of empathy and imagination, the ontological connectedness to the other is lifted up into consciousness. For Suchocki, then, this is compassion, a "feeling with" that at the same time longs and works for the well-being of the other and therefore for the self. One becomes "one" with the other for the sake of transformation toward an inclusive well-being. Empathy is, therefore, the de-absolutization of the self and therefore the transcendence of the self by knowing the self as one center among many centers. Empathy requires a "feeling-with" that mediates exactly this sense of interconnectedness.[35] It is, however, through the *transcendence of memory* that one differentiates oneself from a pathological absorption in the past by allowing the past to *be* past. Strikingly convergent with Ricoeur, then, it is through the transcendence of *empathy* that one gains the ability to separate self from other and to see the other as fully other in relation to the self. Through the transcendence of *imagination,* one receives release for the past through openness to a new future. Also for Suchocki then, memory, empathy, and imagination constitute the movement into transformation, the healthy self.[36]

---

34. Cf. Suchocki, *The Fall to Violence,* 41.
35. Cf. Suchocki, *The Fall to Violence,* 147.
36. Cf. Suchocki, *The Fall to Violence,* 153.

In other contemporary literature, the problem of the "self" or personhood begins to take shape around the various attempts to find different ways of balancing and connecting notions of multiple, narrative selves with "being a body" and the central importance of being one's own flesh. This is one reason why contemporary interdisciplinary discussions of notions of the self, personhood, the "soul," consciousness, self-awareness, and imagination have today risen to an unprecedented level of intensity. For Christian theology this intense inquiry into notions of self focuses the crucial question on the many dimensions of human personhood, and underpins the greatest challenge of all: How do we maintain a notion of an *integrated* self, and, more important, *should* we even pursue a notion of an integrated self? This is what psychologist of religion and theologian Léon Turner, in his recent *Theology, Psychology, and the Plural Self*,[37] has referred to as "the problem of the self." In this work Turner has argued persuasively that we are today still deeply affected by the same enigmatic paradoxes and contradictions that have plagued the subject of the "self" for centuries. Simultaneously, it seems, the self is both "me" and "I"; it is both the object of experience and the experiencing subject; it is both the source and product of identity; it is immanent and physiological yet transcendent and immaterial; it is unique, singular, and individual, but also universal, plural, and relational.[38] Turner's book focuses on a single aspect of these paradoxes, namely, the unity and the multiplicity of the self. The intuition that we have of ourselves as a unified and continuous person over time is basic to almost all human experience and has a long history and is always associated with normality, but a complete explanation of self-unity eludes us. At the same time, increasingly, the sense of the self-multiplicity is increasingly disentangled from what is regarded as abnormal and there seems to be an emerging acquiescence that a certain degree of multiplicity may actually be the norm.[39] In this sense, as carefully traced in Charles Taylor's *Sources of the Self*,[40] the contemporary self has become destabilized, both theoretically and experientially, as modernity's individualism continues to retreat from the postmodern world.

Léon Turner has persuasively argued that now, in most psychological

---

37. Cf. Léon Turner, *Theology, Psychology, and the Plural Self* (Aldershot: Ashgate, 2008).

38. Cf. Turner, *Theology, Psychology, and the Plural Self*, 1ff.

39. Cf. Turner, *Theology, Psychology, and the Plural Self*, 1ff.

40. Cf. Charles Taylor, *Sources of the Self: The Making of Modern Identity* (Cambridge, MA: Harvard University Press, 1989).

theorizing and phenomenological explanations of the self, concepts of self-multiplicity and unity are not necessarily polar opposites but are being combined in various degrees of coherence with nonpathological concepts of self-multiplicity. In this sense a divided self is not always a troubled self, and by distinguishing between representational and experiential theories of self, and between synchronic and diachronic forms of self-multiplicity and unity, Turner suggests that a single person can form a broad array of self-presentations that are not unified at any given time, and also do not merge into unity over time.[41]

This idea that we humans have the potential to experience ourselves in a variety of ways at any given moment, and that a person's sense of self can be radically different from one moment to the next, has also been argued persuasively by pastoral psychotherapist and theologian Pamela Cooper-White. In her *Many Voices: Pastoral Psychotherapy in Relational and Theological Perspective*,[42] Cooper-White argues strongly against any notion of self or subjectivity that is static or monolithic, and stresses that multiplicity of self is indeed a sign of health. The self is not bounded or singularly unique, but is rather a conglomerate of self-states, subject-moments, intersubjectivity, and social constructions, where even the subjective state of being oneself is just another self-state. On this view contemporary psychoanalytic theory is increasingly replacing Freud's vertical "depth" model of consciousness/unconsciousness with an even more sweeping reconception of the mind as a multiplicity of mental states: a normal "nonlinearity of the human mind" that is conceived of as more horizontally dispersed and existing on various levels of conscious awareness. Our subjectivity, therefore, is not monolithic, but is nonunitary in origin, a mental structure that begins and continues as a multiplicity of self-states, maturing over time into a feeling of coherence that overrides the awareness of discontinuity.[43] As such, the challenge for theological anthropology would be a theology of multiplicity. Both Turner and Cooper-White take on this challenge and thus present contemporary theological anthropology with serious questions: If the true and unified self is replaced by a multiplicity of divergent self-images, who or what exactly bears the image of God? If identities are transitory and fragmented, who and what is burdened by sin, and who is finally redeemed by Christ?[44]

41. Cf. Taylor, *Sources of the Self,* 179ff.

42. Cf. Pamela Cooper-White, *Many Voices: Pastoral Psychotherapy in Relational and Theological Perspective* (Minneapolis: Fortress Press, 2007).

43. Cf. Cooper-White, *Many Voices,* 54ff.

44. Cf. Turner, *Theology, Psychology, and the Plural Self,* 4f.

A markedly different approach to these multiple-selves theories is found in Patrick McNamara's recent *The Neuroscience of Religious Experience*.[45] As a neuroscientist McNamara wants to develop his own central conviction that religion is a defining mark of what it means to be human, as emblematic of its bearer as the web for the spider.[46] The special focus of McNamara's work, however, is to examine the phenomenon of religion through the eyes of the self. Strikingly, in spite of the self's great dignity and worth, it is still treated by religions as divided, conflicted, and in need of salvation. Most important, McNamara argues that there is a considerable anatomical overlap between the brain sites implicated in religious experience and the brain sites implicated in the sense of "self" and self-consciousness. This accounts for the crucial conclusion that religious practices often operate to support a transformation of self such that the self becomes more like an "ideal self" that the individual hopes to become.[47] In this sense religious practices directly contribute to the creation of a unified self-consciousness, and what McNamara calls an ideal "executive self." So, when religions are operating normally they tend to create a healthy, unified, and integrated sense of self. Religions accomplish this feat by promoting a cognitive process that McNamara calls decentering,[48] where religious practices help to build up a centralized executive self by reducing the discrepancy between an "ideal self" and a current, divided self.

McNamara thus wants to study religions "through the eyes of the self" precisely because so many religious forms and practices are about transformations of the self. Another benefit of looking at religion through the eyes of the self is that the method will require that due regard is given to the role of the brain in the shaping of religious experiences. There is no human self that is not embodied, and because no body can function without a brain, there is no human self without the brain.[49] McNamara thus wants to use notions of self to probe potential core properties and functions of religion, while at the same time explaining the ways in which religion helps to produce and shape the self. Crucial here is the fact that religious practices create a decentering effect that transiently relaxes central control but ultimately leads to greater self-control. At the heart of this argument is the idea that all religions, in one form or another, ultimately address and solve the problem of the "divided self." In

45. McNamara, *The Neuroscience of Religious Experience*.
46. McNamara, *The Neuroscience of Religious Experience*, ix.
47. McNamara, *The Neuroscience of Religious Experience*, xi.
48. McNamara, *The Neuroscience of Religious Experience*, 44f.
49. McNamara, *The Neuroscience of Religious Experience*, 2.

this sense the conscious experience of "free will in a divided self" lies at the center of the human religious experience. This divided self, therefore, is not just a psychological or emotional problem, but also a cognitive, intellectual problem; and divided consciousness, because it is easier to achieve than the more challenging sense of unified consciousness, is in fact the default state of the human mind.[50] Religions solve the problem of the divided self by enlarging the sense of self so that inner divisions are reconciled, information-processing capacities are enhanced,[51] and the self is transformed into a higher, better, more mature self. On this view religion emerges as a bio-cultural system that facilitates maturation of autonomous individuals, each of whom is capable of experiencing a unified sense of self. To that extent religion is an engine that enhances consciousness and self-consciousness in particular.[52] McNamara's bold claim, then, is that religion constructs this centralized, executive self. For the evolutionary status of religion this implies that religion is not, as is often argued, an unfortunate by-product of more useful cognitive capacities of the human mind. On the contrary, this implies that religion is an adaptation, which is confirmed by the fact that the practice of religious rituals and belief in supernatural agents occur in virtually all human cultures.[53] But it is precisely religion's impact on the problems associated with the self and consciousness that could be seen as adaptive. The self and its default position, the divided self, should thus be taken into account when discussing the evolutionary history of religion.[54] This feeds into the fact that the self is a biocultural and social construct: the self is certainly rooted in genetically shaped biological potencies, but these biological roots are in turn manifested in and shaped by social and cultural interactions. In this sense one could also say that the self is an accomplishment of the individual and of his or her social milieu. One way the "executive" self is constructed is via editing of autobiographical memories, the retrieval of sets of memories or episodes that can match one's current self-model and its goals. From an evolutionary perspective this evolution of a central, executive self with a unified consciousness clearly presupposes the acquisition of a full-blown grammar and language by early humans.[55] For Patrick McNamara, finally, the self is also more than just a psychological and cultural construct that heals inner divisions and allows

---

50. McNamara, *The Neuroscience of Religious Experience*, 30.
51. McNamara, *The Neuroscience of Religious Experience*, 23f.
52. McNamara, *The Neuroscience of Religious Experience*, 246.
53. McNamara, *The Neuroscience of Religious Experience*, 249.
54. McNamara, *The Neuroscience of Religious Experience*, 250.
55. McNamara, *The Neuroscience of Religious Experience*, 254ff.

for greater social cooperation. The human self is also a highly sophisticated and very delicate cognitive system that is capable of handling greater computational and information-processing demands than any comparable system based on consciousness.[56]

During the past decade the ever-expanding interdisciplinary conversation about the "self" has indeed been especially enriched by the brain sciences as neurologists and psychiatrists have focused on emerging discoveries in the brain sciences that are offering us new ways to understand the way our brains operate when as selves we perceive, remember, and imagine. In his groundbreaking book *The Feeling of What Happens: Body and Emotion in the Making of Consciousness*,[57] neuroscientist Antonio Damasio has led the way in investigating the neurobiology of consciousness and the experience of self, in an attempt to address more carefully the mystery of consciousness and how it creates the self. Already in his earlier book, *Descartes' Error*,[58] Damasio argued over against Descartes that reason and emotion are not separate entities. In his later work Damasio would argue persuasively that consciousness cannot only be the result of the operations of those brain centers most closely related to working memory, reasoning, attention, or language.[59] In fact, the normal functioning of such faculties rests upon a foundation that they do not create. For Damasio that foundation is core consciousness: core consciousness is the transient but constantly updated awareness of the "here and now," and a necessary component of this core consciousness is the *core self*. The core self is the nonverbal "sense of self in the act of knowing," requires little in the way of memory or anticipation, and is present in a great number of animals.[60] From an evolutionary point of view the core self is phylogenetically quite old, begins extremely early in life, and remains intact in individuals who have suffered severe impairments of the higher cognitive capacities.

Layered over this core consciousness and its core self is what Damasio calls an emerging *extended consciousness*, which correlates with a reflexive *autobiographical self*: a robust conception of oneself that results from the

---

56. McNamara, *The Neuroscience of Religious Experience*, 258.

57. Cf. Antonio Damasio, *The Feeling of What Happens: Body and Emotion in the Making of Consciousness* (New York: Harcourt, 1999).

58. Cf. Antonio Damasio, *Descartes' Error: Emotion, Reason, and the Human Brain* (New York: Harper, 1994).

59. Cf. Damasio, *The Feeling of What Happens*, 107-35, 184-89.

60. Cf. Kenneth Williford, review of Antonio Damasio's *The Feeling of What Happens: Body and Emotion in the Making of Consciousness*, in *Minds and Machines* 1 (2004): 391-431.

memorial accumulation and constant interpretation and reinterpretation of information regarding one's own history, one's future, one's longstanding desires, and one's relationship with others.[61] In this sense, the sense of self is generated in consciousness as a kind of mental image, as a "feeling of what happens,"[62] and the sense of self is revealed as an ineradicable feature of human consciousness. Self-consciousness, then, is indeed an introspective, reflexive ability that enables us to reflect on our motives and reasons, our likes and dislikes, our character traits and our relationship with others,[63] all of which make up our sense of self.

Neuroscientist Daniel Siegel has fine-tuned notions of self and self-awareness by asking a further question: How is it that our relationships with others and our brains interact to actually shape who we are? In his book, *Developing Mind,* Siegel develops and further integrates John Bowlby's attachment theory and asks how human experience shapes the information that enters the mind, while also shaping the way the mind develops the ability to process this information.[64] This integrative function relies heavily upon the dynamic of memory and imagination and allows us to explore the way in which interpersonal relationships may form the drive toward a coherent sense of self as memory and imagination inform the process of knowing. Indeed, neural pathways are forged in interpersonal relationships that are then revealed as deep attachment relationships. For Siegel, human beings find our most intimate personal processes such as "self" are actually created by our neural machinery, that is, by evolution, designed to be altered by relationship experiences.[65] Thus, practices of interpersonal communication, not only psychologically, but neurologically, become infinitely important for the self and for the narrative development of selfhood.

In his book *The Neuroscience of Human Relationship: Attachment and the Human Brain,*[66] Louis Cozolino has developed similar themes and ar-

---

61. Cf. Damasio, *The Feeling of What Happens,* 222f.

62. Cf. Damasio, *The Feeling of What Happens,* 19. See also Williford, review, 391-431.

63. Cf. Bennett and Hacker, *Philosophical Foundations of Neuroscience,* 323f.

64. Cf. Daniel Siegel, *The Developing Mind: How Relationships and the Brain Interact to Shape Who We Are* (New York: Guilford, 1999).

65. Cf. Daniel Siegel, "An Interpersonal Neurobiology of Psychotherapy: The Developing Mind and the Resolution of Trauma," in *Healing Trauma: Attachment, Mind, Body, and Brain* (New York: W. W. Norton, 2003), 9.

66. Cf. Louis Cozolino, *The Neuroscience of Human Relationships: Attachment and the Human Brain* (New York: W. W. Norton, 2006).

gued for a social neuroscience that understands we have evolved as social creatures with brains and biologies that interweave in deeply constitutive ways. While individuality is cherished, we know that our constant relationality with others plays a defining part in our emotional and social behavior. In fact, for Cozolino the human brain itself is a social organ, and to understand human individuality and interrelated sociality, we need to know what it means that our brains exist in relationship to other brains. This interpersonal neurobiology enables Cozolino to provide for us a compelling narrative of exactly how our brains — and ultimately our selves — develop in the context of our relationships and how that development can become derailed, but also how healing interactions can trigger neurological changes in our brains that promote healing. For Cozolino, then, it is in the architecture of the brain, through the role of mirror neurons and the brain's neural plasticity, that we find the beginning of an answer to the kind of biology of attachment that ultimately yields a notion of self.

Another fascinating study of the self and its social brain emerging from social neuroscience has been John T. Cacioppo's recent work, *Loneliness: Human Nature and the Need for Social Connection*.[67] In this book he explores the impact of loneliness/social isolation on the human self, and thus finds a new way to talk about the importance of social connections and interpersonal relationships. Relying on studies of brain imaging, analysis of blood pressure, immune response, stress behavior, and even gene expression, Cacioppo argues that human selves are neurologically far more interdependent than we might have realized before. Cacioppo traces the evolution of these traits by showing how, for our primitive ancestors, survival depended not only on physical strength and cleverness, but especially on greater commitments to and from one another. The pain of loneliness encountered in fear response is so powerfully disruptive that even now, millions of years later, a persistent sense of rejection or isolation can impair DNA transcription in our immune cells. It also limits the ability of the self to internally regulate emotions, all of which reinforces the very isolation and rejection that we dread.

While neuroscientists like Daniel Siegel, Louis Cozolino, and John Cacioppo have argued for a deep neurological basis for interpersonal attachment, neuroscientist and anthropologist Terrence Deacon has taken a different direction in developing theories about the emergent self and the symbolic human mind by focusing on the remarkable co-evolution of the brain and

---

67. Cf. John T. Cacioppo, *Loneliness: Human Nature and the Need for Social Connection* (New York: W. W. Norton, 2008).

language.[68] Andrew Newberg and Eugene d'Aquili[69] and archeologist David Lewis-Williams[70] each in their own way developed different conceptual frameworks for these neurological processes and their connection to the complex spectrum of human consciousness, embodied emotions, and the unmistakable fact that all humans are significantly "wired," not only for attachment, but for alternate states of consciousness. In addition, cognitive scientists like Harvey Whitehouse[71] and Justin Barrett[72] focus on the evolution of the human brain's natural disposition for metaphysical and religious questions, and primatologists like Frans de Waal[73] are specifically looking at emotionally empathetic experiences in primates, linking the emergence of the self directly to the evolution of moral imagination. And as we saw earlier, this conversation gains new depth through the work of constructive psychologists/theologians Pamela Cooper-White and Léon Turner, who want to move away from monolithic notions of selfhood to the malleability of psychological processes that give reality to nonpathological notions of multiple selves. Neuroscientific ideas of spectra of consciousness, combined with ideas of constructive, multiple selves, indeed pose a very serious but ultimately exciting challenge to Christian-theological notions of person and the *imago Dei*. This challenge is deepened by evolutionary epistemologists like Franz Wuketits,[74] and archeologists and paleontologists like Steven Mithen,[75] Ian Tattersall,[76] and Richard Potts,[77] who all argue that hominid and human brains, and therefore human selves, have evolved over hundreds of thousands

68. Cf. Terrence Deacon, *The Symbolic Species: The Co-Evolution of Language and the Brain* (New York: W. W. Norton, 1997).

69. Cf. Andrew Newberg, Eugene d'Aquili, and Vince Rause, *Why God Won't Go Away* (New York: Ballantine Books, 2001).

70. Cf. David Lewis-Williams, *The Mind in the Cave: Consciousness and the Origins of Art* (New York: Thames & Hudson, 2002).

71. Cf. Harvey Whitehouse, *Modes of Religiosity: A Cognitive Theory of Religious Transmission* (Lanham, MD: Altamira Press, 2004).

72. Cf. Justin L. Barrett, *Why Would Anyone Believe in God?* (Lanham, MD: Altamira Press, 2004).

73. Cf. Frans de Waal, *Primates and Philosophers: How Morality Evolved* (Princeton: Princeton University Press, 2006).

74. Cf. Franz M. Wuketits, *Evolutionary Epistemology and Its Implications for Humankind* (Albany: SUNY Press, 1990).

75. Cf. Steven Mithen, *The Prehistory of the Mind: A Search for the Origins of Art, Religion, and Science* (London: Thames & Hudson, 1996).

76. Cf. Ian Tattersall, *Becoming Human: Evolution and Human Uniqueness* (New York: Harcourt Brace, 1999).

77. Cf. Richard Potts, *Humanity's Descent* (New York: Morrow, 1996).

of years to make physical, emotional, and spiritual sense of their environment. Scholars like Maxine Sheets-Johnstone have pushed even deeper into the roots of these questions by embedding notions of self, self-identity, and intersubjective communication, in the embodied prehistoric evolution of human sexuality, communication, and morality.[78]

The interesting question for us, as interdisciplinary theologians, is whether these multiple disciplinary perspectives might afford some degree of convergence on the intriguing, multilayered question of what it means to be human, and what the implications of this for theological anthropology might be. Human nature and the idea of self have, of course, always been at the heart of theological reflection, but these interdisciplinary themes have not yet been dealt with adequately. It is precisely because the horizon of interdisciplinary possibility contains such opportunities for collaborative understanding that we take up this approach in this volume.

*   *   *

Against the background of this introductory sketch from the current interdisciplinary dialogue on notions of self, we are happy to present to our readers a state-of-the-art interdisciplinary discussion on "the problem of self," the elusive nature of the human self and all of its complex dimensions, traditionally represented by concepts like creative imagination, self-awareness, consciousness, soul, religiosity, and personhood. In doing so, we hope this anthology will constructively add to a much-needed interdisciplinary dialogue between theology and the sciences, and to a much-needed revisioning of anthropological themes in contemporary theology. To enhance exactly this interdisciplinary spirit, we have invited eighteen prominent multidisciplinary voices to present to us their very diverse perspectives on notions of self. We have organized these essays into an interpretative grid consisting of four themes or sections:

- The Self and Origins
- The Self and Multiplicity
- The Self and Identity
- The Self and Emergence

---

78. Cf. Maxine Sheets-Johnstone, *The Roots of Thinking* (Philadelphia: Temple University Press, 1990); *The Roots of Morality* (University Park: Pennsylvania State University Press, 2008).

These themes are neither designed to "box in," as it were, the contributions of our authors nor to attempt to exhaustively define each contribution in terms of one theme only. On the contrary, each essay relates to most of the four themes in multiple ways, and we present these four organizational themes as a dynamic, interactive presentation that should enable creative, transversal readings of essays in any number of comparative combinations.

In Part One, "The Self and Origins," we present five essays.

In "Origin of the Human Sense of Self," Ian Tattersall argues that, although humans are not unique in their ability to recognize themselves in mirrors, the emergence and acquisition of a fully developed sense of self had to await the attainment, in one hominid lineage only, of the symbolic consciousness that ultimately allowed internalized mental self-representation. In fact, while indicating an episodic increase in the complexity of hominid interactions with the outside world over the last 2.5 million years, behavior preserved in the material, tangible archeological record suggests that this cognitive state, this remarkable state of symbolic consciousness, was achieved only subsequent to the emergence of *Homo sapiens* as a recognizable anatomical entity. The neural substrate that allows symbolic reasoning clearly had to be in place before such reasoning could be adopted, and whatever that substrate is, it was most plausibly acquired in the major genetic and developmental event that allowed for the invention of language, which in many ways could be seen as the ultimate symbolic activity. The modern sense of self and individual identity as we experience it today had its roots in this symbolic capacity: it is this that gives us our ability to objectify ourselves, and to see ourselves, as well as others, from the "outside" as actors with complex motives and intricate interior existences. In this sense we could argue that *a fully developed sense of self*, of the kind with which we are familiar today, and which depends on internalized mental representation of self, is a recent acquisition in the human lineage that indeed postdated the arrival of *Homo sapiens* on earth.

In "An Archeology of the Self: The Prehistory of Personhood," Ian Hodder explores debates concerning the relationships between self and the object world, the world of "things." Hodder argues that archeologists can in fact demonstrate transformations in self and personhood as related to major social and economic changes in prehistory. This essay focuses in particular on transformations in self and personhood as related to the emergence of farming, settled life, and ownership. Hodder uses evidence from Çatalhöyük, a 9000-year-old city in central Turkey, to show that this early time period sees the emergence of new forms of agency, as well as changed notions of self and personhood. Changes in notions of self, and the gradual emergence of a clearly defined sense of a separate, individual self, are tied up in the new materialities and modes of life that emerged as people settled down and molded identities and personal histories in stable houses, plastered forms, and longer-term social entanglements. And along with an increased sense of exclusive property, the sense of self became more marked, both personally, in terms of bodily decorations and burial, and collectively, as in communal ritual enclosures. At Çatalhöyük, then, the sense of self was directly tied to the houses and thus situated in complex webs of memories, which suggests that individual lives were distinctly remembered.

In "Are Apes and Elephants Persons?" Barbara J. King analyzes and effectively deconstructs the pervasive dichotomy by which humans have recognizable selves and animals do not have selves. The blurring of animal-human identity goes beyond the obvious fact that *Homo sapiens* is an animal too, as King shows through fascinating examples of cross-species communication. King also moves beyond purposeful communication and clearly demonstrates the case of primates and elephants by arguing for these animals as distinct beings with emergent selves with emotion, memory, and imagination. In this sense every great ape, as well as every elephant, is a unique, self-aware, thinking and feeling self, a long-lived, highly social, and intelligent creature. Moreover, these selves are defined through relationships, and like humans, are ultimately created in relational plurality. This fact has implications for animal rights issues, and calls upon us to understand each species in its environmental, social, and emotional context. For King this understanding of animal selves should inspire human communities, including religious communities, to accept greater responsibility for the conditions in which animals live. In fact, human personhood depends on moving beyond the strict human-animal dichotomy and realizing that we become fully human only through our relationship with other animals.

In "Neuroscience and Spirituality," Eric Bergemann, Daniel J. Siegel, Deanie Eichenstein, and Ellen Streit discuss the integration of ideas from the fields of neuroscience and spirituality in those fields' efforts to expand our knowledge of what it means to be human. Utilizing the words of Albert Einstein regarding the "optical delusion of our consciousness," they explore the ways in which the human brain creates a cortically constructed view of a separate self, which spiritual practices strive to deconstruct in a variety of ways. The universal teachings of wisdom traditions and religions throughout the ages reveal the powerful ways in which our species has struggled to create a way of being in which we can find a deep sense of meaning in realizing the true nature of our interconnected relationships with one another and with the larger world in which we live. Interpersonal Neurobiology is used to discuss the ways in which definitions of mind tend toward understandings of the body, including the brain and nervous system, in which the mind is an embodied and relational process that regulates the flow of energy and information. Discussing the open probability of quantum physics, the plane of possibility itself becomes like a field of open potential before material and mental phenomena arise on either side. Because of this, energy, a physical property, and information, a mental property, flow together in patterns to shape both spatial and experiential emergence simultaneously. Greatly important for this wider project is the issue that our nervous system's very origins begin and continue at the interface of the outer and the inner. This function of connecting the inside and outside places of our nervous system is the important position of linking "us" to "them." In the end, we are hard-wired to connect to one another.

In "In Search of 'Folk Anthropology': The Cognitive Anthropology of the Person," Emma Cohen and Justin L. Barrett start out by noting that everyday notions about personhood exhibit considerable cross-cultural variability, as documented in the vast anthropological literature on the subject. However, a growing corpus in developmental psychology also suggests that naturally emerging, panhuman constraints and biases inform the ways in which humans reason about persons and the social world in general. Despite the obvious potential for constructive dialogue and theory refinement across these two perspectives, there has been little such engagement to date. In this essay, Cohen and Barrett seek to develop an ethnographically and psychologically informed interdisciplinary understanding of personhood that bridges nativist and cultural-relativist or "blank slate" approaches. Species-specific, naturally emerging cognitive predispositions constrain the range of variability in person-related concepts cross-culturally (e.g., to do with what is intuitively recognizable as an intentional agent/action, how individual identity is construed, how people think about the relation between biological and psychological properties of the person, etc.). It does not follow, however, that no interesting variability exists. Patterns of systematic variation can be explained with reference to the interaction between specific cognitive capacities and unique features of specific cultural and historical settings. Against this background this essay wants to answer the question: Where does our conceptual category of the *person* come from, and what aspects of it are cross-culturally relevant? The balanced approach advanced here aims to establish a nascent comparative cognitive anthropology of the person upon an empirically and theoretically sound foundation.

In Part Two, "The Self and Multiplicity," we present five essays.

In "Disunity and Disorder: The 'Problem' of Self-Fragmentation," Léon Turner surveys how, alongside postmodern philosophical critiques of the unified continuous self, psychologists and sociologists began to embrace complex dynamic theories of the plurality of the self. Throughout the human sciences, self-multiplicity is now commonly lauded as a positive cognitive and social adaptation to the constant fluctuations, novelty, and uncertainty of life. Many Christian theologians, by contrast, have continued staunchly to defend the unity of the self. They have rejected the autonomous self-creating subject of modernity, and thereby embraced notions of socially constructed personhood. But they have also challenged postmodern philosophy's fragmentation of the individual subject, and railed against the existential angst that they believe accompanies contemporary culture. Turner therefore explores and explains the discrepancies between recent theological and human scientific accounts of the multiplicity of the self, and argues that self-multiplicity can be understood in a variety of ways, not all of which can be considered psychopathological. He claims that unqualified theological antipathy toward self-multiplicity, both theoretically and existentially, arises both from ethical commitments to the principle that people can and should experience themselves as singular and continuous beings under ideal conditions, and from the failure to acknowledge an important psychological distinction between the singularity and continuity of the self and the experiential singularity and continuity of the person. Acknowledging the difficulties that arise from theologians' tendency to treat all types of self-disunity as pathological, he aims to develop broader theoretical and ethical implications of a more nuanced conception of the plural self.

In "Reenactors: Theological and Psychological Reflections on 'Core Selves,' Multiplicity, and the Sense of Cohesion," Pamela Cooper-White argues that the notion of a core, nuclear, true, or essential self is ubiquitous in psychotherapy, including pastoral counseling. Each of these terms — core, true, and essential — has its own (often unacknowledged) intellectual lineage, which she traces back to the Enlightenment. Here our personal anthropologies have been saturated with the notion that there is, finally, a true, core self at the heart of each person and that this core self is the defining factor in human personality. This idea of a core self, together with its moral overtones, has been revealed to be highly problematical, a social construction, and as such can be interrogated about its cultural, political, and social purposes. The problem with any notion of a core or essential self is not so much what it contains, but what it excludes, i.e., the inherent relationality and interdependence of persons.

Cooper-White champions the rapidly growing movement to acknowledge, explore, and unpack theories of multiple selves. Along with other relational analysts, she distinguishes between multiplicity (as normative fluidity, mutability, and diversity of the self) and fragmentation (a pathological sense of being in pieces without any reliable cohesiveness). The challenge here is whether both multiplicity and a sense of self-cohesion can be retained as mutually dependent constructs that operate in dialectical tension. She argues that only if both constitute subjectivities can they be mutually compatible. As constructs representing different experiences of one's own solidity or complexity, they can be represented as "existing" not in binary opposition, but on a continuum of experience. This would allow for a notion of "core self" only in the most minimal sense and only if understood as an *aspect* of all one's subjectivities, and not as an actual definitive locus of identity, agency, and purpose. In the end, therefore, multiplicity is the overarching paradigm, which leads toward a concept of multiple selves as a powerful bridge toward empathy, especially toward others we perceive to be different.

In "The Existential Self in a Culture of Multiplicity: Hubert Hermans's Theory of the Dialogical Self," Hetty Zock discusses the relevance of Hubert J. Hermans's theory of the dialogical self for understanding religious identity processes in a radically pluralist, globalized context. Since the "turn to the subject" in modernity, authentic individual experience has been a prerequisite for establishing a meaningful personal identity. However, identity theorists now wrestle with the question of how such a unique, personal sense of identity is established by way of increasingly diverse cultural traditions and collective identities. Against this background, and in dialogue with Hubert Hermans and Léon Turner, Zock argues that the seminal importance of the self as a unified core of meaning-making today is both emphasized and contested, and in this essay specifically asks how multiplicity and unity, discontinuity and continuity of the self go together. The self is no longer seen as an unalterable essence, something that is "really there": the self is plural and dynamic, changing in time and according to circumstances, and is a process that is socially constructed by language, culture, and power relations. And yet, the experiential sense of self, the self as an experiencing, coherent agent, is not only crucial for all psychosocial identity development, but is also the basis of all human meaning-making, and of moral and religious development in particular. In this sense the theory of the dialogical self is a useful tool to further intercultural and interreligious dialogue, but it also explains how easily religious traditions and collective identities may be defensively used to restrict dialogical capacities.

In "The Multiple Self," Helene Tallon Russell and Marjorie Hewitt Suchocki examine the self with special attention to its structure and form. Over against the Western philosophical and theological tradition that has constructed the self as ideally a hierarchical unity of internal parts, singular in form, Russell and Suchocki argue that this formulation is inadequate to a contemporary understanding of personhood because it does not adequately account for the multiple forms of relationality that are essential for the becoming of human selfhood. Russell and Suchocki then argue that in the human self, multiplicity and unity are not hierarchical, with unity always trumping multiplicity. Rather, multiplicity and unity are continuously negotiated realities within the complex relationality of the self. For their argument that the self as relational is necessarily multiple, Russell and Suchocki utilize the thought of Kierkegaard and Whitehead and suggest a vision of personhood in which the person is comprised of multiple internal and external relations, with changing forms of relating these relations to self and others. This, in turn, argues against settled notions of personhood in favor of continual openness to the richness of relation. As such the human self is composite, not singular, and is constituted through multiple relationships. This multiplicity is essential to the self, and is also, through dialectic, the basis for the common experience of the self as a unity.

In "On the Elusive Nature of the Human Self: Divining the Ontological Dynamics of Animate Being," Maxine Sheets-Johnstone claims that methodological and experiential similarities exist between Husserl's phenomenology and vipassana (Buddhist) meditation. Against this background, this essay spells out the elusive nature of the self in terms of the nature of animate being, in particular the nature of animate mind or consciousness. In so doing, it does not equate the self with consciousness, but views the self in the context of the lived and living temporal dynamics of consciousness. It addresses the tendency to regard the self as something spatial rather than temporal. In so doing, it highlights the inverse relationship of constitution as phenomenologically defined, to impermanence as defined in Buddhist thought. It furthermore explains on the same basis how and why a singular continuously impermanent self exists, but how it is also possible, as some researchers maintain, to have multiple selves. For Sheets-Johnstone the self ultimately is elusive and is nowhere to be found in experience. What is found in experience are cognitive-affective-kinetic habitualities that are experientially evident in our preferences, dispositions, styles of movement, ways of feeling, and patterns of thinking. The self, in short, is a construct, and this construct is based on animate realities but has no reality in and of itself. This construct is obviously fortified by language, by "myself," "oneself," "our-selves," and so on. As such, an empirically sound methodology reveals the living temporal dynamics of being and the impermanent nature of all that is. The "self" is no exception: it is no more than the sum of habitualities evident in what Husserl describes as "personal character," and that vipassana monks describe as "habits of mind."

In Part Three, "The Self and Identity," we present four essays.

In "The Quest for Self-Identity," Calvin O. Schrag chooses as his point of departure a critical revisiting of the Kantian vocabularies of "transcenden-tal" and "ego" and its relation to self through a hermeneutical reading, and tracks the epistemic descent of the transcendental ego into the density of a concretely experienced lifeworld. In his search for self-knowledge and the seeking of traces for a vibrant, embodied self-identity through perception, imagination, and conception, Schrag explores time and space as marking out our horizons of experience in its lived concreteness. In this herme-neutical holism, understanding is seen to function within a holistic web of pre-theoretical percepts, feelings, desires, emotions, and thoughts that are already meaning-laden. This idea of self, as a subject descended from its epistemic transcendental status into the thick of embodied, lived-through experiences, reveals time and space as part of the lived experience of the self as much as they are transcendental conditions for the experience of the self. This praxis-oriented and life-experiencing self announces its presence more like an event than like an object for inspection; an event of speaking that does not originate language but always speaks *from* a language. Arguing against foundationalist epistemic principles and irreducible traits of mind (either mentalist or materialist), this hermeneutical self is implicated in its discourse and action and appears on the scene of experience as an *emergent* from the history of communicative praxis rather than an impermeable *foun-dation* of it. Thus the ego descends as an avatar into lived time and space and is revealed as an incarnation in a lived body that bridges the chasm between mind and matter, culture and nature.

In "Posthuman Selves: Bodies, Cognitive Processes, and Technologies," Jennifer Thweatt-Bates surveys the history of conceptions of self construc-tion and identity construction through the use of technology, namely, cyber-netics, that have inaugurated the various forms of posthuman and transhuman projects. The contrasts between a cybernetics that is meant to extend liberal humanism and a cybernetics that at its heart is dehumanizing expose the tension inherent in the posthuman and transhuman projects:

whether the faculties of human being are enhanced, or whether they are ultimately supplanted. Narratives of the self figure heavily in the manifold potential response to either scenario; and whether the self embraces narratives
of apprehension or narratives of hope determines in large part the perceived
or real loss of subjectivity and agency. Articulating a conception of the self
that weaves together individual agency with a complex systems approach to
an anthropology of hyper-relationality, the location of cognitive processes
and states of mind provides the occasion for questions of self and identity
constitution. The line between technological tool and subjective user becomes thin indeed. From a posthuman point of view, neither relationships,
ontologies, nor particularities of embodiment can be regarded as organic
givens. For this reason, the unity of the subjective in the self becomes the
core of self-identity and self-ownership. Because the self is always intrinsically relational and acts with indubitable agency, the theological level of autonomy and agency becomes a continual invitation to the collaboration of
divine agency to intertwine with our own.

In "The Erotic Self and the Image of God," Jan-Olav Henriksen claims
that the intimate link between eros and desire manifests itself not only in
the realm of sexuality, where eros and desire are most commonly depicted
in current culture, but is also expressed in a child's longing for its mother's
love, as well as in our desire to be recognized. As a result of this link, we not
only feel that we are valuable and lovable, but we also have the desire to love
someone. Henriksen claims that love and our love stories are part of what
define us as human, and that our lost as well as our fulfilled love is, as part
of the relational web with others that eventually defines us, part and parcel
of who we turn out to be. Hence love — eros — is central to the development of the self and self-perception. Love is what is desired, and love also
expresses itself in desire. The self is shaped by the erotic and by our struggle
with and desire for eros. These experiences of struggle for love and for becoming a self permeate our lives, and thus require a theological interpretation. Henriksen develops an understanding of how eros and desire may be
interpreted in a theological framework that takes into account the understanding of the development and constitution of the self as relational, in a
manner that interprets desire and the erotic dimension of human life in
light of what it means to be created in the image of God. Exploring the resources of philosophical theology, he seeks to develop an understanding of
how basic phenomena of human life may be seen as integral to what shapes
the content of important theological constructions like the *imago Dei*.

In "Human Pharmakon: The Anthropology of Technological Lives,"

João Biehl discusses the pharmaceuticalization of mental health care in Brazil and charts the social and subjective side effects that come with the un-regulated encroachment of new medical technologies in urban poor settings. Biehl tracks the development and dissolution of identity as an abandoned young woman named Catarina talks about psychopharmaceuticals — the drug constellations that she was brought into — and how she tries to find, mainly through writing, an alternative to the deadly experiment she literally became. Catarina's life thus tells a larger story about shifting value systems and the fate of social bonds in today's dominant mode of subjectification at the service of global science and capitalism. However, significantly critical aspects of Catarina's identity remain intact, and language and desire continue as she integrates her drug experience into her new self-perception and her literary work. Her "minor literature" grounds an ethnographic ethics and gives us a sense of becoming that dominant health models would render impossible. While the figure of the *pharmakos* (the human figure excluded from the political body) in philosophical thought is quite pertinent, speaking of Catarina as a modern-day *human pharmakon* accentuates her story as paradigmatic of a contemporary familial/medical/political structure that operates like the law. The questions and tensions of Catarina's identity are explored regarding how she became the object of a logic and sociality in which people were no longer worthy of affection and accountability, and yet they were remembered. Through attempting to trace the ambiguous lines of causation, a constellation of forces is discovered that reveals Catarina's identity as neither free from nor totally determined by this machinery, dwelling instead in the luminous lost edges of human imagination that she expanded through writing.

In Part Four, "The Self and Emergence," we present four essays.

In "Enigmatic Experiences: Spirit, Complexity, and Person," Catherine Keller creatively revisions the well-known Pauline text, "Now we see in a mirror, in an enigma, but then, person to person" (1 Cor. 13:12), and argues that its hermeneutical puzzle surprises us by theologically revealing the concept of the embodied human person as a transdisciplinary concept. Most important, the eschatological deferral ("but then") does not imply the standard guarantee of afterlife, but rather the outer edge *(eschaton)* of personal emergence where personhood already reflects an inescapable interdependence and the personal is always already the interpersonal. Through this interpersonality the self is always situated as a field of interdependence, which then marks at once both the irreducible uniqueness as well as the constituent multiplicity of the self. In this way the enigma of the Pauline text reveals complex relationality and at the same time lures into the very emergence of self in and among others, where the self becomes other than what it was. Here emergent complexity as the dynamic of the spirit becomes an alternative to both reductionist and inflationist understandings of the self/person. Against this background Keller explores five criteria for the emergence of the spirited self as transdisciplinary potentialities or sites of articulation of its becoming: counter-reductionist in its recourse to complexity theory; pneumatological as a theological construction; biblical in its theopoetic reading strategy; feminist in its specular gender, and as far as the complexity of the person goes, irretrievably enigmatic. Personal agency should thus be understood as a cooperative autopoiesis. Ultimately spirited selves emerge inasmuch as they participate in the system-opening transpersonality of the spirit. But in the enigmatic looking glass of the embodied self, gender cannot be separated from sex, but emerges entangled with sex, class, race, and ecologies, as never separated from the incarnate specificities of our racial, cultural, bodied transpersonalities.

In "The Emergence of Self," James W. Haag, Terrence W. Deacon, and Jay Ogilvy are concerned with the very possibility of explaining the existence of selves. In doing this, they do not follow the traditional options of David Hume's disavowal of the self (the self as a useful fiction), nor do they emphasize the experience of having a self and assuming it to be a brute fact of the world (the self as a phenomenological experience). These are both approaches that reflect a failure to adequately deal with issues of teleology, since selves are ultimately defined by their teleological properties. This means that human consciousness is not the only relevant exemplar of the self in the cosmos. Selves are associated with life and are not only limited to organisms like humans with complex brains and subjective experiences. The authors thus want to develop an emergence-based account of the physical basis for true teleological relationships and then apply this to a basic conception of the organism's self. Thus a conception of the self emerges that can be described as a system capable of acting on its own behalf. The critical features of the self can thus be seen as autonomy and agency. This core property that links the selves of even the simplest life forms with that of the human experience of self is a special form of dynamical organization. On a human level, however, having a brain contributes fundamentally to experiences of subjectivity and higher-order properties emerging from lower-order reflexive dynamics. Rather than relying on introspection to provide us with a window on selfhood, agency, or subjectivity, the authors construct an account of self that is based on simpler selves than those of the human. Instead of a continuous grayscale of degrees of self, the evolution of brains and symbolic communications clearly marks transitions to higher-order forms of selves.

In "Neurononsense and the Soul," Roger Scruton takes to task the popular conviction that neurobiology is destined to replace all the many vague studies of the human mind and its cultural by-products with precise neurological sciences. In doing so, he challenges the idea that we are constantly getting closer to explaining consciousness by locating it as a physical process and by removing the final mystery from the human condition, which is the mystery of the self. "Neurononsense" is described then as a translation into the jargon of neuroscience of some highly contentious philosophical arguments and as such violates the proper discussion of two important features of the human condition: consciousness and first-person awareness. For Scruton, the idea of "folk psychology" as a proto-science, and one that could be replaced by a sophisticated theory of the nervous system, deeply misrepresents the way in which people relate to their environment and to each other. Scruton proceeds to distinguish two modes of understandings: science, which aims to explain experiences; and "intentional understanding," which aims to interpret. By intentional understanding he means the kind of understanding that forms the basis of reciprocal exchanges between creatures with a first-person point of view. By critiquing "neurononsense," Scruton aims to expose the fallacy of assuming that an event in the *brain* is identical with the decision of a *person*. To remedy this, Scruton wants to return to the traditional concept of the soul, a concept that was meant to identify the target of those thoughts and emotions that are alive in our dealings with one another. He suggests that we understand the person as an emergent entity rooted in the human being, but belonging to another order of understanding than that which is explored by biology. Central to personhood as an emergent feature of the human being are consciousness and the first-person perspective, which are now revealed as beyond the reach of reductionist sciences of the mind. This does not require a denial of the truth of empirical psychology, neurobiology, or cognitive science, but rather to see these truths as belonging to another level of analysis.

In "Persons at Home in the Universe: Openness, Purpose, and Transcendence," Philip A. Rolnick explains the rough outlines of Gödel's incompleteness theorems, Michael Polanyi's account of crossing logical gaps, and quantum physics in order to display certain family resemblances with the narrative, historical thread of human decisions, and what the notion of self or person *might* mean theologically. Just as the intrusion of an observer's measurement brings about the "collapse of the wave function," so too does a human decision "collapse" various possibilities into a clearly defined datum and into a past event. In one sense, history is what we live. We do not merely write histories; instead, each of us *is* a history. In another sense, history is the epistemological attempt to graph the lived data along the axis of meaning. Whatever else human persons are, we are ineluctably historical, narrative beings. Our words, deeds, relationships, suffering, and overall experiences have a freshness about them — the "freshness of the finite." Given the arrow of time, each situation in which we find ourselves is new and presents an opportunity to actualize the potential of the given conversation, activity, or decades-long relationship. As we attempt to do so, we inscribe something new in the cosmos and something new in ourselves. In this sense persons possess an inherent excess, something that is neither determined by laws of cause and effect, nor violates those laws. Theologically human identity is defined by something that greatly exceeds our current status: we humans are created in the *image of God,* and to pursue the true, good, and beautiful is to pursue manifestations of the intellect and will of God in our own sphere of activity. Human uniqueness is thus found in the actualization of these transcendent potentials that distinguish human persons. In this sense the fate of the human person hinges on the issue of transcendence, and "transcendence" becomes another name for the "person." The personal is what is unique, nontransferable, what the theological tradition from Boethius to Aquinas has called *incommunicabilis.* Functioning through the unique combination of intellect and free will, human persons, in the narrative possibilities of our lives, behave neither randomly nor by a program of cause and effect. Instead, human uniqueness can be detected among the complexities of cause and effect patterns, probabilities, and the interrupting applications of human intellect and will.

The Self and Origins

Origin of the Human Sense of Self

Ian Tattersall

Introduction

In the very broadest of meanings, every organism has a sense of itself. From the simplest unicellular creature on, all living things have mechanisms that allow them to detect and react to entities and events beyond their own boundaries. As a result, every animal may be said to be self-aware at some level, however rudimentary such responsiveness might appear. In sharp contrast, complex human self-awareness is a very particular possession of our species. We human beings experience ourselves in a very specific kind of way — a way that is, as far as we know, unique in the living world. We are able to take a step backwards, as it were, and to conceptualize and characterize ourselves as objects distinct from the rest of Nature — and from the rest of our species. We consciously *know* we have interior lives. The intellectual resource that allows us to have such knowledge is our symbolic cognitive style, whereby we mentally dissect the world around us into a huge vocabulary of intangible symbols that we can then combine and recombine in our minds, according to rules that allow an unlimited number of statements to be formulated from a finite set of elements. Using these rules we are able to generate alternative versions or explanations of the world — and of ourselves. It is this unique symbolic

I thank Wentzel van Huyssteen and Erik Wiebe for their kind invitation to contribute to this fascinating volume.

ability that underwrites the internalized self-representation expressed in the peculiarly human sense of self.

In between the two ends of the spectrum, between the primordial and the symbolic styles of self-awareness, the vast diversity of the living world presumably harbors a near-infinity of states of self-knowledge. Yet because alien cognitive states are among the few things human beings find it impossible to reconstruct accurately and fully in their imaginations, any discussion of such "intermediate" forms of self-knowledge is fraught with all the risks of anthropomorphizing. When trying to understand how other organisms comprehend particular situations, or their place in society or indeed the world, our tendency is always to impose our own constructs. The temptation is to assume that they are seeing and understanding the world somehow as we do, just not as well. Yet the truth is that we simply cannot know, still less *feel*, what it is subjectively like to be a bat (Nagel 1974), or indeed any organism other than ourselves, modern *Homo sapiens*.

The extraordinary human cognitive style is the product of a long biological history. From a nonsymbolic, nonlinguistic ancestor, itself the outcome of an enormously extended and eventful evolutionary process, there emerged our own unprecedented symbolic and linguistic species, an entity possessing a fully-fledged and entirely individuated consciousness of itself. This emergence in itself was an extraordinary event, one that involved bridging the most profound cognitive discontinuity of them all. For there is a *qualitative* difference here; and, based on any prediction from what preceded us, the only reason for believing that this gulf *could* be bridged, is that it *was*.

Explaining the event itself is, of course, something that continues to elude us at the level of function. We simply do not know at this point just what it is about our neural wiring that allows us to transform a mass of electrochemical discharges in our brains into what we subjectively experience as human consciousness — although speculations abound (e.g., Coolidge and Wynn 2005; Lieberman 2007). From the vantage point of paleoanthropology we can currently hope, at best, to sketch in the larger context within which our remarkable information-processing ability was acquired — and I hope at least to establish a framework for this here. However, going beyond such broad generalities to the question of what kind of subjective experience of self even our most immediate ancestor enjoyed is immensely more difficult; and for the reasons already given it may, indeed, prove ultimately impossible for us to objectify and describe such "other" cognitive conditions.

In the following I will glance at some attempts to characterize states of self-awareness in species other than *Homo sapiens,* and will then summarize what can be said of cognitive evolution within the human lineage over the past several million years, for the most part using the frequently murky evidence of past cognitive states and putative symbolic behaviors that is furnished by the Old Stone Age archeological record. This record, which covers the entire period from the invention of the earliest documented technology through the emergence of fully modern human consciousness, is a remarkable register of changes in the material productions of extinct hominids, especially in the stone implements that provide the most durable and continuous testament to past hominid activities. However, it must always be remembered that the stone tool record is a selective and highly incomplete reflection of the full spectrum of ancient hominid behaviors, and that until a very late stage all potential material proxies for the internalized sense of self are highly debatable.

The Mirror Test

Back in the mid-nineteenth century, Charles Darwin (1872) placed a mirror on the floor between two orangutans housed at the London Zoo. He recorded a variety of reactions, but was rather vague as to what, if anything, he had specifically concluded from the experiment. There the matter rested for almost a hundred years, until the cognitive psychologist Gordon Gallup (1970), noting that the norm among animals was to treat mirror images as other individuals, carried out a more controlled test. Gallup exposed two juvenile chimpanzees to full-length mirrors for several days, and watched how they responded to the images of themselves they saw in them. Over this period self-directed behaviors increased, while social reactions to the mirror images declined, suggesting that the individuals were learning to recognize the images as themselves. The chimpanzees were then anesthetized, and red marks were applied to their faces. Once they were reintroduced to the mirrors self-directed behaviors intensified, many of them mark-oriented. In contrast, marked chimpanzees without prior mirror experience failed to respond in this way, suggesting that self-recognition had indeed been learned by the others during the habituation period. Similar testing of macaques produced contrary results, implying to Gallup that these monkeys lacked the chimpanzees' capacity for self-recognition.

Since Gallup's pioneering study, the "mirror test" has become the standard yardstick for the issue of self-recognition among vertebrates, and a wide variety of species has been tested. Human beings naturally need to learn mirror self-recognition (MSR) just as the chimpanzees did, but sight-restored adults do so quickly (Archer 1992). Most human infants are able to recognize their own features in a mirror following about 18-20 months of age (Brooks-Gunn and Lewis 1984), although delayed recognition of video images may be more problematic as late as the age of three (Povinelli and Simon 1998). Young apes develop more rapidly than human children in many respects, but studies building on Gallup's original have shown that among chimpanzees mirror self-recognition is rare before eight years of age (de Veer et al. 2002). Interestingly, in the same longitudinal study a sample of chimpanzees showed peak self-recognition by the age of 15, with significant decline in this ability thereafter (de Veer et al. 2002). In humans such loss occurs only in association with specific disease states.

By now, MSR has been demonstrated not only in chimpanzees but also in bonobos, orangutans, and gorillas, although invariably not all tested individuals have shown it. Outside the human–great ape group, however, MSR is evidently extremely rare among vertebrates. It even appears to be absent among lesser apes, as a recent marking study of gibbons has strongly suggested (Suddendorf and Collier-Baker 2009). As just noted, Gallup (1970) encountered negative results in a small sample of macaque monkeys; and in subsequent monkey studies the nearest thing to MSR has been found in capuchins, by a group of researchers who concluded that these monkeys "possibly . . . reach a level of self-other distinction intermediate between seeing their mirror image as other and recognizing it as self" (de Waal et al. 2005: 11140). Other MSR studies of capuchins (e.g., Roma et al. 2007) have, however, yielded entirely negative results; and even if the de Waal group is right, its finding exemplifies the difficulties we encounter in characterizing states of consciousness other than our own, for to us the difference between "self" and "other" is probably the most fundamental one we ever make. It is virtually impossible to imagine what an intermediate state might consist of; and if such a thing does exist, it calls into question the very experimental concept and design at issue here.

MSR has been widely investigated beyond the order Primates. However, it has only been plausibly documented in three nonprimate species: two mammals and a bird. The avian case is equivocal. Epstein et al. (1981) reported that pigeons pecked at white spots on their feathers that they could see only in mirrors, but noted that such pecking was specifically trained, and denied that this behavior had cognitive significance. On the other hand, Prior et al. (2008) demonstrated spontaneous pecking at marks by one or two magpies within a larger test group. They interpreted this pecking as true

MSR, independently evolved in a nonmammal. In 2001 Reiss and Marino reported behaviors consistent with MSR in a pair of bottlenose dolphins and pointed out that, like apes and humans, cetaceans are highly encephalized. They thus suggested that self-awareness might occur not only as a result of structures specifically present in the brains of large-bodied hominoids, but also as a by-product of encephalization. Finally, MSR was recently demonstrated (Plotnick et al. 2006) in three Asian elephants, although only one of their subjects passed the mark test. These huge mammals are, of course, famously large-brained; but the authors in this case attributed the MSR ability to their complex sociality and cooperativeness.

Human beings and, to a lesser extent, the great apes show both high encephalization and complex sociality and cooperation; but it seems pretty clear that, in all of the cases of nonhuman MSR so far reported, different underlying structural mechanisms are at work. Only in the human–great ape case does it seem plausible that MSR abilities are homologous, the greater facility shown by humans being due to some additional neural structure or function that was acquired subsequent to the ancestral split. What's more, it's not at all clear what it means when only some individuals in a test group show behaviors consistent with MSR. In almost every domain of experience there are some exceptionally talented individuals; but until those talents become the property of a significant portion of the species, they have little evolutionary significance over the long haul. Then there is the issue of relevance. MSR abilities have little consequence in the lives of animals that are predominantly olfactory — even if, as in the case of dogs, those animals are highly cooperative and social. And even where animals *are* highly visual, the fact remains that mirrors are not big features in any animal's environment except (very recently, and not everywhere) our own. What is more, whatever the capacity is that allows us to recognize our own image in a mirror, it probably plays only a strictly limited and compartmentalized role in the overall sense we have of ourselves as individuals. Ultimately, then, tests with mirrors cannot reveal exactly which aspects of consciousness are being explored, although whatever they do disclose is clearly limited to "perception of the body" (Tomasello and Call 1997: 337).

Alternative Approaches to the Self in Nonhuman Primates

An alternative approach to the sense of self in nonhuman primates was taken by Seyfarth and Cheney (2000). These researchers adopted William

James's distinction between the "spiritual" (one's "psychic faculties and dispositions") and "social" (knowledge of being one of many distinct individuals embedded in a group) components of self-awareness (James 1892). Cercopithecoid monkeys, like human beings, are intensely social, and Seyfarth and Cheney looked at what could be discerned of the understanding by individual vervets and baboons of their places in the social hierarchy. The reasonable assumption here was that animals cannot exhibit a sense of "them" without also possessing a sense of "I." Looking at kin relations, and at individuals' appreciation of their own and others' positions in the dominance hierarchies to which they belonged, Seyfarth and Cheney concluded that these monkeys do indeed recognize other group members as individuals, behave toward them in appropriate ways, and hence appreciate their own individuality vis-à-vis their fellows.

Clearly, then, on some level monkeys have a sense of the social self. On the other hand, this kind of self-awareness is clearly different from that of human beings. For, while being able to behave appropriately in complex social settings, vervets and baboons are as far as can be told unaware of the knowledge that allows them to do so. In Seyfarth and Cheney's (2000: 902) words, they "do not know what they know, cannot reflect on what they know, and cannot become the object of their own attention."

No observer would deny that great apes possess more complex cognitive and behavioral repertoires than monkeys do. Still, it is far from clear just how far they exceed cercopithecoids in these respects, and particularly in the ability for self-reflection. Some great apes, at least, are adept users of symbols in experimental situations (Savage-Rumbaugh 1994). But whether this means that they are able to manipulate those symbols mentally in such a way as to produce objective images of themselves is rather doubtful. For in general, the apes' use of symbols seems to be additive: they can comprehend short strings of concepts ("take," "red," "ball," "outside"), but they do not recombine them according to mental rules to produce new concepts, ideas of the possible rather than of the observed. The chimpanzee manner of dealing with symbols is thus inherently limited, since lengthening series of symbols rapidly become confusing, and ultimately meaningless.

Daniel Povinelli, a distinguished researcher of chimpanzee cognition, has recently proposed that a fundamental distinction between the ways in which chimpanzees and humans view the world is that, while humans form abstract views about other individuals and their motivations, "chimpanzees rely strictly upon observable features of others to forge their social concepts. If correct, [this] would mean that chimpanzees do not realize that there is more to others than their movements, facial expressions, and habits of behavior. They would not understand that other beings are repositories of private, internal experience" (Povinelli 2004: 33). And it would also imply that individual chimpanzees do not have such awareness of themselves, either. They *experience* the emotions and intuitions that arise in their own minds; and they may act on them, or suppress them, as the social situation demands or permits. But, just as they "do not reason about what others think, believe and feel . . . because they do not form such concepts in the first place" (Povinelli 2004: 33), it seems legitimate to conclude that this exclusion also applies to self-reflection. For if individual chimpanzees are deficient in the ability to develop accounts of the internal lives of others, it is highly probable that they lack equivalent insight upon their own interior existences.

Profound as it is, this cognitive difference between us and them may not always produce radically distinctive observable behaviors; and indeed the ways in which chimpanzees and humans behave sometimes appear strikingly similar (e.g., de Waal 1998). Still, we should be wary of overstating these similarities. The behavioral resemblances we perceive are readily explained by an enormously long shared evolutionary history and the resulting structural similarities; but as Povinelli would doubtless point out, similar observable behaviors may also hide ratiocinative processes that differ greatly in form and complexity.

So, despite the fact that hardly a day passes during which it is not announced that an ape does something that we once thought only we did (most spectacularly, spear-hunting by chimpanzees: Pruetz 2007), the cognitive gulf still yawns. Among all those organisms that we can study in the world today, it appears that only modern human beings show "spiritual self-awareness" in William James's sense; and even his "social self-awareness" appears to differ dramatically in quality between humans and nonhuman primates. Still, even though there has doubtless been a lot of evolutionary water of one kind or another under the bridge on both sides since human beings shared an ancestor with any ape, most authorities find it reasonable to conclude that cognition of the kind we see among chimpanzees (and, generally speaking, among other great apes too) provides us with a reasonable approximation of the cognitive point from which our ancestors started some seven million years ago. To use Povinelli's (2004: 34) words, one may reasonably assume that those ancestors were "intelligent, thinking creatures who deftly attend[ed] to and learn[ed] about the regularities that unfold[ed] in the world around them. But . . . they [did] not reason about unobservable things: they [had] no ideas about the 'mind,' no notion of 'causation.'" In the human sense, they had as yet no idea of self. This is a very plausible characterization of our lineage's starting point, and at the same time it exhausts what can usefully be said on this subject based on existing studies of comparative cognition. To follow the story from there, we need to turn to our fossil and archeological records.

The Human Fossil Record

All of our extinct relatives who shared a common ancestor with us more recently than with any of the apes are grouped together with us in the primate family Hominidae (or the subfamily Homininae, or whatever: the exact terminology is of no consequence here). For the first few million years of the family's existence the hominid record is confined to Africa and consists uniquely of the fossils of "bipedal apes": small-brained, large-faced, short-statured creatures (often referred to in later stages as "australopiths") whose main claim to hominid status is showing adaptations in the cranium, pelvis, leg, and foot to bipedality: upright walking on two legs when on the ground. The adoption of this very rare form of locomotion by primates with an unquestionably arboreal ancestry is thought to have been spurred by ecological changes that took place in Africa following about 10 million years ago (10 mya), consequent on the initiation of a trend to climatic drying and greater seasonality of rainfall. With these environmental shifts the formerly monolithic African forests began to break up, giving way to woodland and occasionally open grassland. This was a slow process, and it was not until well after 2 mya that true open savannas began to appear. But once the climatic change was under way forest-living great ape populations began to find themselves deprived of their ancestral habitat, and it seems likely that many such populations would have responded by exploration, tentative at first, of the new opportunities available along the expanding forest edges and woodlands.

Some of those populations of formerly arboreal apes evidently adopted bipedality when they descended to the ground. There has been a great deal of discussion over just why primitively quadrupedal forms would have chosen to move on two legs terrestrially, and the argument has usually been couched in terms of a "key advantage" (efficiency of locomotion on the new substrate, freeing of the hands, more effective heat loss, and so forth) that favored the new way of moving around. But the plain fact remains that these ancient hominids would not have adopted this unusual way of getting around unless they had been most comfortable doing it; and the only reason they would have been comfortable is that they were already accustomed to holding their trunks erect in the trees, as some primates do today.

The earliest reported hominids are a motley assemblage of mostly fragmentary fossils dating to between about 7 and 4 mya. What they have in common is that bipedality has been claimed for all. If they *were* all hominids (and more than one hominoid lineage might well have adopted bipedality as a solution to the new environmental problems faced by many of them) they show that at this early stage a persistent theme in hominid evolution had already been established: a theme of diversity. Our species is accustomed today to being the only hominid on the planet, and through familiarity this seems entirely natural to us; but it is evidently very much the exception rather than the rule.

By about 4 mya the record begins to pick up, and we start to find australopiths quite abundantly in the African fossil record. The most familiar of them is the species *Australopithecus afarensis,* most famously represented by the 3.2 myr-old Ethiopian fossil "Lucy." Like other australopiths, Lucy would have walked upright on the ground, but was still well equipped, especially in her upper body, for moving in the trees. This "have it both ways" adaptation was evidently very successful, for we see no major departure from this primitive hominid body form until after 2 mya.

Throughout this long early period we have no reason to suspect any significant departure from the cognitive state exemplified by modern apes, and these early hominids presumably remained cognitively much like the hypothetical human ancestor described by Povinelli. Until, that is, the first stone tools start to show up in the record around 2.5 mya. Evidently, the first stone toolmakers were small and archaically bodied; and if so, we have good evidence from the very beginning of a theme that has characterized human evolution ever since: new technologies do not coincide with the appearance of new physical types.

Yet the cognitive innovation represented by the invention of stone tools was a radical one. Even with intensive coaching, ape subjects have been reluctant to grasp the idea of hitting one stone with another at the precise angle necessary to detach a sharp flake (for more details of this and other features of the hominid record, see discussion and references in Tattersall 2009a). What's more, from the beginning the early stone toolmakers carried suitable raw materials around with them for considerable distances in evident anticipation of needing them, thereby showing substantially more foresight than is typical of today's apes. Sadly, though, we have no idea how this radical innovation may have affected the broader lives of these early hominids, beyond permitting them to butcher carcasses and carry off body parts for consumption in safer places. And neither do we have any idea about exactly how it might have reflected the toolmakers' changing views of themselves.

Following its introduction, stone-working technology barely changed for a million years, until well *after* a radically new kind of hominid, *Homo ergaster,* had come on the scene. Best exemplified by the 1.6 myr-old "Turkana Boy" skeleton from Kenya, *Homo ergaster* was the first hominid of essentially modern body proportions and stature. Below the neck, it represented a huge departure from its predecessors, although its brain was only modestly enlarged compared to the australopiths'. But for all its biological innovations, *Homo ergaster* remained technologically conservative, producing simple sharp flakes from fist-sized "cores" that were sometimes also used for pounding.

It was not until about 1.5 mya that a new kind of tool was introduced. This was the "handaxe," a larger implement carefully and symmetrically shaped, with many blows on both sides, to a standard teardrop form that evidently existed in the knapper's mind before toolmaking started. Again, we see here evidence for an increase in the toolmakers' cognitive complexity, but we are frustratingly unable to relate it to innovations beyond the technological sphere. However, there is absolutely no reason at this stage to suspect that symbolic processes were developing in the handaxe makers' minds: what we see is at most a refinement of the intuitive mental processes that governed early hominid behavior.

A little under 2 mya hominids began to spread beyond Africa. Since the émigrés were small-brained and still wielded very simple stone tools, their new mobility is most plausibly attributed to the new body form, which announced our precursors' final emancipation from wooded habitats. Once out of Africa, hominids diversified locally all over the Old World, but the archeological record shows little evidence of significantly increasing technological complexity until around 800 thousand years (800 kyr) ago, when we find the first firm evidence for the control of fire in hearths at a site in Israel (Goren-Inbar et al. 2004). The domestication of fire was doubtless a momentous event for hominids, with significant implications on the social front as well as for cooking, which would have rendered a whole variety of foodstuffs more digestible. Yet it was not until less than 400 kya that fire control began to become a regular feature at hominid sites. This is also the time from which the first deliberately constructed shelters are known, and from which the earliest wooden spears are recognized. Miraculously preserved in a peat bog at Schöningen in Germany, these long spears are shaped like modern javelins and were clearly missiles, suggesting that ambush-hunting techniques had been developed at this time. Such hunting practices are more complex than one might have guessed from the stone tool record, for it was not until under 300 kya that a new kind of stone implement began to be made.

This was the "prepared-core" tool, whereby a stone "core" was elaborately worked until a single blow would detach from it a more or less finished tool of predetermined shape. Together with the earlier innovations, this conceptual advance in toolmaking technology must imply a corresponding increase in cognitive complexity; but again, it is hard to specify exactly what this would have meant in behavioral and experiential terms. The identity of the first prepared-core toolmakers is uncertain, but this innovation occurred within the timespan of the first cosmopolitan hominid species, *Homo heidelbergensis*. Known from sites widely scattered in China, Africa, and Europe, this new kind of hominid possessed a brain that lay comfortably within the modern size range, although it was well below modern average volume.

It is worth noting that from around 2 myr onward, fossils attributed to the genus *Homo* show a pretty consistent brain size increase over time, after hominids had essentially flatlined in this respect for the first 5 myr of their existence. In view of this, paleoanthropologists have tended to assume a steady process of brain enlargement within a single lineage of *Homo* that eventually culminated in *Homo sapiens*. However, the record shows a strong signal of diversity throughout this period, and a more realistic assessment appears to be that this was a time during which larger-brained *Homo* species were outcompeting smaller-brained ones. Since there seem to have been independent tendencies toward brain enlargement in diverse lineages, there was clearly some general property of species of the genus *Homo* that predisposed them toward (metabolically expensive) brain size increase. Other things being equal, at basically static body sizes enlarging brains might be expected to indicate increasing "intelligence" in some sense; but exactly what this implies about cognitive style remains obscure.

So what can we say about the cognitive status of *Homo heidelbergensis?* It turns out that it's easier to say what it probably wasn't than what it was. The materials preserved in archeological deposits give us a highly incomplete notion of the full range of behaviors and material products of any hominid; but a strong argument can be made that we cannot reliably deduce symbolic mental processes from any Old Stone Age technological products (Tattersall 2009b). Only in the presence of unambiguously symbolic artifacts can we confidently impute such mental processes to their makers; and the archeological record offers us nothing to suggest a symbolic form of consciousness in *Homo heidelbergensis.* In which case, we can reasonably conclude that, intellectually complex as these hominids evidently were, they still lacked the capacity for self-reflection.

The same is probably true for *Homo neanderthalensis,* a species that came on the scene in Europe about 200 kya, and had brains fully as large as our own today. Neanderthals are incomparably better known both physically and behaviorally than any other extinct hominids, and provide us with the best mirror in which to perceive our own uniquenesses. They were probably the most skilled practitioners ever of prepared-core toolmaking, but they made beautiful tools unimaginatively, with a notable lack of significant local variety. They did at least occasionally bury their dead, but they did so simply, without the grave goods typically left by their modern successors in Europe. Long-term survival of handicapped individuals suggests high sociality and advanced empathy and cooperativeness, but their sites lacked the complexity and density of those left by the first modern *Homo sapiens* who entered Europe about 40 kya and within 10 kyr entirely displaced them. Only arguably did Neanderthals ever produce any putative material evidence of symbolism, and what such evidence there is comes very late, in the "post-contact" period, and is susceptible to diverse explanations.

The Origin of *Homo sapiens*

The earliest evidence for hominids with effectively modern bony structure comes from sites in Ethiopia dating to 195 and 160 kya. Associated with remarkably crude stone tools these fossils, together with slightly later evidence from other sites, confirm that anatomically modern *Homo sapiens* emerged in Africa in the period following 200 kya. Fossils from the site of Jebel Qafzeh in Israel show that this anatomically distinctive entity had spread beyond its natal continent by about 93 kya. Significantly, Neanderthals had occupied the Levant considerably earlier, and persisted in the region until about 40 kya, indicating some form of partitioning between *Homo sapiens* and *Homo neanderthalensis* of the Levantine environment for upwards of 50 kyr: a very different scenario from the one that had played out in Europe, where the Neanderthals became extinct in short order following the arrival of moderns. Significantly, throughout this time of coexistence (or possibly alternating existences) the two species made virtually identical stone tool kits and showed few if any signs of symbolism. There is no reason to suspect any cognitive differences between the two species during this period.

The earliest clearly symbolic artifacts come from significantly later in time, and are again found in Africa, sadly not in association with any human fossils. The site of Blombos Cave, near the continent's southern tip, has produced two geometrically engraved ochre plaques dated to about 77 kya. These are the earliest material products that most observers would accept as the product of a symbolic sensibility, and their interpretation as symbolic is enhanced by the finding in adjacent deposits of small pierced invertebrate shells, apparently intended for stringing into body ornaments — again, plausibly symbolically important items. Similar "beads," possibly even older, have been found at a couple of other African sites, and even possibly at one in the Levant. By a little under 100 kya, perhaps as much as 100 kyr after *Homo sapiens* had come into existence as an anatomical entity, the symbolic capacity was stirring in Africa.

For evidence of the full flowering of that capacity, however, we currently have to wait until the period following 40 kya. At around that time *Homo sapiens,* from an ultimately African source, finally invaded the European peninsula, evicting the resident Neanderthals by about 30 kya. The lives of these "Cro-Magnons" were drenched in symbol. By 35 kya they were painting powerful images on cave walls, producing exquisite carvings and engravings, developing elaborate notational systems on plaques of bone, and even eventually firing clay figurines in kilns. These hunter-gatherers occupied the landscape in larger numbers than any hominid had ever achieved before, implying an unprecedented ability to exploit the natural resources around them. In intellectual attainment, these people were truly us. Cognitively, as well as anatomically, they were fully modern *Homo sapiens.* The picture we see here stands in stark contrast to what had been seen in the Levant some 60 kyr before, where the earliest *Homo sapiens* penetrating the region had apparently behaved just as the Neanderthals did, and failed to drive them to extinction.

The Human Identity

Big brains evidently do not necessarily equate with symbolic mental processes. Not only did the almost certainly nonsymbolic Neanderthals have large brains, but so did the equally nonsymbolic earliest *Homo sapiens.* Evidently, the intellectual ability to form and manipulate symbols was acquired well subsequent to the origin of our species as an anatomical entity. This acquisition continued the earlier pattern of disassociation between physical and technological innovations in the hominid record, and provides an excellent example of "exaptation," whereby features are initially acquired in a context other than the one in which they later become familiar. Exaptation is a routine phenomenon in evolutionary history: tetrapods, for example, acquired their limbs in water, well before employing them to walk on land; and birds possessed feathers for millions of years before using them to fly.

The neural substrate that allows symbolic reasoning clearly had to be in place before such reasoning could be adopted; and whatever that substrate is, it was most plausibly acquired in the major genetic and developmental event that gave rise to *Homo sapiens* as a distinctive anatomical entity. In which case, it must initially have lain fallow, awaiting the "discovery" by some necessarily cultural agent of the unprecedented new use to which it could be put. Most plausibly, this agent was the invention of language, which in many ways is the ultimate symbolic activity. And it should be borne in mind that, in another example of exaptation, a peripheral vocal tract of the kind required to produce the sounds of articulate speech had been present since the origin of *Homo sapiens* as an anatomical entity. Earlier hominids, including the Neanderthals, almost certainly possessed complex forms of vocal and gestural communication. But to have language you need to be symbolic, able to create and recombine a vocabulary of mental symbols; and, if the Neanderthals were indeed symbolic, it is at the least highly remarkable that, in the huge expanse of time and space they inhabited, they should not have left some unarguable material evidence of that fact.

The "release" of the symbolic faculty by the intellectual exigencies of language places the altogether unprecedented human capacity in the realm of emergence, whereby a chance coincidence of acquisitions creates a product with entirely new potential. The human symbolic ability was clearly the endproduct of a long chain of neural acquisitions, stretching back hundreds of millions of years to the very earliest vertebrate brain; and it would have been impossible to attain it in the absence of any one of those acquisitions. But it was not *predicted* by any of them. Apparently, *Homo sapiens* was not driven across that seemingly unbridgeable cognitive gulf by the inexorable pressure of natural selection over the eons; instead, it leapt across, recently and in two distinct and short-term biological and cultural events, as the result of an accretionary but entirely adventitious concatenation of innovations.

What do these conclusions mean for the human sense of self? It seems reasonable to suppose that individual identity as we modern human beings experience it has its roots in our symbolic capacity. It is this that gives us our ability to objectify ourselves, and to see ourselves, as well as others, as it were from the outside, as actors with complex motives and intricate interior existences.

As Povinelli points out, this ability appears lacking in chimpanzees, and it was equally certainly absent in the ancient hominid ancestor. For the first five million years of hominid history, nothing much seems to have changed. Two million years ago, however, hominid brain sizes began to increase; and over the long haul technologies, almost the only proxy we have for more general behaviors, became more complex. Did this imply that the sense of self was becoming more refined (or better defined) among hominids over this period? Possibly. But even if it did, given our inability to imagine cognitive states differing significantly from our own, it is hard to know what that actually meant. All we can say with confidence is that the pattern of highly episodic innovation continued until very recently, and that it was only with the advent of demonstrably cognitively modern *Homo sapiens* that it changed. Previously, hominids had accommodated to constantly fluctuating climates and environments by adapting old technologies to new purposes; but over the past fifty millennia or so, the typical response to such challenges has been the invention of new technologies. At the same time, art, representation, and notation were introduced, each of them exemplary of a fully developed symbolic sense. All of this points to the conclusion that, by this juncture, a truly new kind of organism, a ratiocinative being with insight into itself, was on the scene.

The limits of our perception unfortunately allow us only to speculate rather emptily about "intermediate" states of self-awareness. But we can be on fairly firm ground in proposing that a *fully developed* sense of self, of the kind with which we are familiar today, the kind that depends on internalized mental representation of self, is a recent acquisition in the human lineage. Indeed, it seems to have postdated the arrival of *Homo sapiens* itself on Earth.

REFERENCES

Archer, J. 1992. *Ethology and Human Development*. Lanham, MD: Rowman & Littlefield.

Coolidge, F. L., and T. Wynn. 2005. Working memory, its executive functions, and the emergence of modern thinking. *Cambridge Archaeological Journal* 15: 5-26.

Darwin, C. R. 1872. *The Expression of the Emotions in Man and Animals.* London: John Murray.

de Veer, M. W., G. G. Gallup, L. A. Theall, R. van den Bos, and D. V. Povinelli. 2002. An 8-year longitudinal study of mirror self-recognition in chimpanzees *(Pan troglodytes).* NeuroPsychologia 1493: 1-6.

de Waal, F. 1998. *Chimpanzee Politics,* revised ed. Baltimore: Johns Hopkins University Press.

de Waal, F. B. M., M. Dindo, C. A. Freeman, and M. J. Hall. 2005. The monkey in the mirror: Hardly a stranger. *Proceedings of the National Academy of Science USA* 102: 11140-147.

Epstein, R., R. P. Lanza, and B. F. Skinner. 1981. "Self-awareness" in the pigeon. *Science* 212: 695-96.

Gallup, G. G. 1970. Chimpanzees: Self-recognition. *Science* 167: 86-87.

Goren-Inbar, N., N. Alperson, M. E. Kislev, O. Simchoni, Y. Melamed, A. Ben-Nun, and E. Werker. 2004. Evidence of hominin control of fire at Gesher Benet Ya'aqov, Israel. *Science* 304: 725-27.

James, W. 1892. *Psychology: Briefer Course.* Cambridge, MA: Harvard University Press.

Lieberman, P. 2007. The evolution of human speech: Its anatomical and neural bases. *Current Anthropology* 48: 39-66.

Nagel, T. 1974. What is it like to be a bat? *Philosophical Review* 83: 435-50.

Plotnick, J. M., F. B. M. de Waal, and D. Reiss. 2006. Self-recognition in an Asian elephant. *Proceedings of the National Academy of Science USA* 103: 17053-57.

Povinelli, D. J. 2004. Behind the ape's appearance: Escaping anthropocentrism in the study of other minds. *Daedalus,* Winter issue.

Povinelli, D. J., and B. B. Simon. 1998. Young children's understanding of briefly versus extremely delayed images of the self: Emergence of the autobiographical stance. *Developmental Psychology* 34: 188-94.

Prior, H., A. Schwarz, and O. Güntürkün. 2008. Mirror-induced behavior in the magpie *(Pica pica)*: Evidence of self-recognition. *PLoS Biology* 6: 1642-50.

Pruetz, J. D., and P. Bertolani. 2007. Savanna chimpanzees, *Pan troglodytes verus,* hunt with tools. *Current Biology* 17: 412-17.

Reiss, D., and L. Marino. 2001. Mirror self-recognition in the bottlenose dolphin: A case of cognitive convergence. *Proceedings of the National Academy of Science USA* 98: 5937-42.

Roma, P., A. Silberberg, M. Huntsberry, C. Christensen, A. Ruggiero, and S. Suomi. 2007. Mark tests for mirror self-recognition in capuchin monkeys *(Cebus apella)* trained to touch marks. *American Journal of Primatology* 69: 989-1000.

Savage-Rumbaugh, S. 1994. *Kanzi: The Ape at the Brink of the Human Mind.* New York: John Wiley & Sons.

Seyfarth, R. M., and D. L. Cheney. 2000. Social awareness in monkeys. *American Zoology* 40: 902-9.

Suddendorf, T., and E. Collier-Baker. 2009. The evolution of primate visual self-recognition: Evidence of absence in lesser apes. *Proceedings of the Royal Society B* 276: 1671-77.

Tattersall, I. 2009a. *The Fossil Trail: How We Know What We Think We Know about Human Evolution,* 2nd ed. New York: Oxford University Press.

Tattersall, I. 2009b. Human origins: Out of Africa. *Proceedings of the National Academy of Science USA* 106: 16018-21.

Tomasello, M., and J. Call, 1997. *Primate Cognition.* Oxford: Oxford University Press.

An Archeology of the Self:
The Prehistory of Personhood

Ian Hodder

This paper explores debates concerning the relationships between self or personhood and the object world. Archeologists can demonstrate transformations in self and personhood related to major social and economic changes in prehistory and history. This paper focuses in particular on transformations in self and personhood related to the emergence of farming and settled life. It uses evidence from Çatalhöyük, a 9000-year-old town in central Turkey, to show that this early time period saw the emergence of new forms of agency, as well as changed notions of self and personhood. The latter are themselves tied up in the new materialities and modes of life that emerged as people settled down and molded identities in stable houses, plastered forms, and longer-term social entanglements.

Many nonhuman species engage with things in elaborate and magical ways. Among some forms of Bowerbird in Papua New Guinea and Australia the male attracts its mate by building a hut of sticks and placing in it brightly colored objects such as shells, flowers, stones, berries, coins, nails, and pieces of glass. There is a continually expanding understanding of the ranges of tools used by other species, and particularly by chimpanzees. The evolution of hominids is closely linked to the production and use of stone tools from 2.6 mya onwards. There is a gradual increase in the range of tool use by hominids through time, and by 70-50 kya material things are being embellished by *Homo sapiens* as art objects — certainly by this time humans too are doing magical things with the material world.

It is possible to argue that the emergence of a human sense of self was also a gradual process, closely tied to the increasing entanglement between humans and things. Throughout the social sciences and humanities there has been a "return to things" (Preda 1999), and there is widespread recognition that human sociality, cognition, psychology, bodily well-being, and spiritual awareness depend on human relations with things. We go to things, and as humans we often seem continuous with the things we identify with. But there is also a process whereby we recognize our difference from things, our separate identity from inanimate or nonhuman things. This "to and from" things is described by Freud. When Freud observed his grandson Ernst say "Fort!" and "Da!" as he pushed objects away and brought them back, repetitively, he interpreted this in terms of the child dealing with and mastering absence from people (such as his mother), and this incident has been the subject of much debate by Klein, Winnicott, Lacan, and others. We can generalize from such debates to talk about the ways in which our sense of self emerges from our relations to and separation from objects.

There has been much discussion in archeology, anthropology, and related disciplines of the extended mind and the distributed self (Bird-David 1999; DeMarais et al. 2005; Fowler 2004). In anthropology there has been a long tradition of study, going back to Mauss, of the extension of self into the material world in gift economies. For Mauss (1954: 25-26), "Souls are mixed with things; things with souls. Lives are mingled together, and this is how, among persons and things so intermingled, each emerges from their own sphere and mixes together." For Strathern (1988), in Polynesian and Melanesian cultures, persons are "dividuals" or "partible persons" — that is, persons are the product of chains of socially reproductive acts or enchainment, so there is no division between the social and individual persona. Every person is a product of others, or has an identity that is produced from all the social actions that were involved in marriage, giving birth, nurturing, etc. Enchainment is created because of the "hau" of things — that is, their need to be moved on, to be mobile (see also Weiner 1992). Strathern describes the Papua New Guinea Highlands where "continuities of identity between persons and things may be taken for granted" (1999: 180). But at the same time she notes (180) that in PNG people talk a lot about how one cannot tell by looking at a thing (e.g., a motorbike) whose it is or what power mobilizes it. There is thus, even here where human and thing are so mixed together, a recognition of the difference and separateness of humans and things.

This to-ing and fro-ing from things underpins much of our moral and spiritual sense. Many religions struggle with the tension between going toward images of the divine and ascetically going away from things. As human beings we discover ourselves as we labor, and we find our spiritual and moral sensitivities in our interactions with the world, but this self-discovery always seems to involve a tension — a simultaneous movement toward and away from things. Another way of conceiving of this relationship between humans and things is in terms of property. As humans have increasingly engaged with things they have produced, notions of property have developed and have become increasingly well defined. Given the to-ing and fro-ing between humans and things, subjects and objects, it seems reasonable to argue that as humans increasingly came to own things, and to struggle with that ownership, they simultaneously developed a greater sense of self. As they increasingly separated off objects that they owned from other objects, it seems likely that they would have increasingly separated off themselves from others. Is there any ethnographic and archeological evidence to support such a hypothesis? And what is the role of the spiritual and religious in such a process?

Humans Owning Things: A Long-Term Perspective

Barnard and Woodburn (1988: 23) argue that in all societies there is a principle that "whatever I, as an individual, obtain from nature or make by myself using my own labor is residually recognized as in some sense my property" unless some other principle overrides this. The basic principle is that "work . . . transforms material things into property" (1988: 24). These rights are overlain by others. Thus, a mother's labor in reproducing a child also confers rights that can be overridden by male rights of control of bridewealth, etc. Ritual work may also confer rights.

A property right is "a particular type of association between a person and a 'thing.' The type of association is one which involves a measure of socially recognized control over the 'thing' and which necessitates some restrictions on other people's control of the same 'thing'" (Barnard and Woodburn 1988: 13). These restrictions lead to controversy and challenge, so there have to be rules and sanctions and justifying ideologies (1988: 14).

Barnard and Woodburn (1988: 14) define five categories of rights that often occur in hunter-gatherer societies: (1) rights over land, water sources, and other fixed assets such as ritual sites, dwelling sites, dams, weirs, pit traps, etc.; (2) rights over movable property such as tools and weapons, clothing, pots, ornaments, and beads; (3) rights over hunted carcasses and harvested vegetable foods; (4) rights over the capacities of specific people — over their hunting labor, their domestic labor, their sexual capacity, their reproductive capacity; (5) rights over knowledge and intellectual property — songs, sacred knowledge, ritual designs, etc.

Among immediate-return hunter-gatherers, there are low production targets, little difficulty in meeting nutritional needs, and strong social pressures for immediate use of food and artifacts so that "not many material things are held and even fewer are accumulated over time" (Barnard and Woodburn 1988: 12). Woodburn (1998) discusses the Hadza of Tanzania as an example of immediate-return hunter-gatherers. He makes the point that the sharing of meat is not a form of reciprocity that is returned by later gifts. The donor is obligated to share and has little influence over who gets it. People expect and demand a share. "Storing meat for later private consumption is unacceptable" (Woodburn 1998: 52). Personally owned objects such as arrowheads, knives, bead necklaces, and clothes are shared. People are demanded to pass things on and people do not hold on to anything for very long. Gambling is a major way these objects are passed around. "Objects are distributed without binding people together" (1998: 53). In receiving goods there are no obligations. A few objects are not transferred — such as a man's bow or his leather bag. But these objects are seen as worthless as they are not transferable.

Ownership among another immediate-return hunter-gatherer group, the !Kung, has some similarities to the Hadza but here there is also a system of exchange called *hxaro* — this is a system of gift-giving in which property is used to develop symmetrical ties of friendships. These exchanges are of "personally owned objects such as beads, arrows, clothing or pots, but not food" (Woodburn 1998: 57). These gifts are then reciprocated. But the *hxaro* is not a fully developed gift exchange in that little emphasis is placed on the objects themselves or their parity, or on competitive showing of status. There is "no Maussian mystical notion that gifts embody the donor" (1998: 58) such that reciprocation is necessary.

Delayed-return hunter-gatherers differ in that there are corporate households of clans, lineages, and other extra-domestic forms of social grouping, and sets of binding social relationships so that people are dependent on each other, connected to the control of assets (the delayed returns on labor). Delayed-return systems and agricultural societies "usually limit sharing much more" (Woodburn 1998: 61), for example, by confining sharing to the household or a restricted group of kin. A central issue becomes the control of women (and young men). Women (and young men) are fully incorporated into household units led by household heads who come to control women's and young men's labor.

Even in agricultural societies the control of things and assets may be complex and very unlike our own notions of ownership. Giving a thing often involves giving a part of oneself — so a gift has to be repaid or returned, as it contains the spirit or essence of the donor. The previous possessor of an object has a continued claim on the object. So each object is unique with its own history. An example of this for Mauss was the *kula* exchange in Papua New Guinea. As Annette Weiner (1992) argued, to acquire another person's valuable object such as a *taonga* is to acquire that person's rank, name, and history. In Melanesia, things are inalienable — an object bears the identity of those in the past. However, Carrier (1998) explores the nature of property itself in Melanesian societies and shows that in terms of land, while rights are traced back to patrilineal ancestors, in fact usufruct rights are given to others, and then to others, so that ownership questions can be very complex, messy, and contested. According to Carrier, Melanesian societies do have some exclusive property and commodities, just as Westerners have gifts and inclusive properties.

So is it possible to take these ethnographic insights back in time and argue that property rights came to be more marked and more exclusive during the Paleolithic and Neolithic? And is it possible to further suggest that as property rights came to be more clearly defined a sense of separate self gradually emerged? It may be helpful in considering this question to distinguish two aspects of self and personhood. The first is the question of whether the self is coincident with the body boundary. The second is whether the self is seen as an autonomous agent. These two aspects of self may be closely linked, but there is some value in distinguishing them since, wherever the self may be seen as located, it may have more or less ability to act autonomously.

Among the more immediate-return hunter-gatherer societies of the Middle and Upper Paleolithic, the ethnographic parallels would suggest that there was some degree of property ownership in the senses outlined above, and it is indeed possible to argue that there is already some evidence of an awareness of self or personhood. The occurrence of the first burials associated with Neanderthals and with *Homo sapiens* from about 100 kya and the appearance of bodily adornment and human figuration (the Venus figurines and representations of humans in the Franco-Cantabrian art) from 40 kya onwards all suggest a gradually increased concern with self, however continuous that self may have been with worlds around it. Some social groups at this time were becoming increasingly invested in long-term relationships and well before the domestication of plants and animals there was some degree of investment in memory construction on particular sites (Hodder 2007). Thus at Ein Gev 1 in the Jordan Valley in Israel there is a fourteenth-millennium BC Kebaran site on the eastern side of the Sea of Galilee (Arensburg and Bar-Yosef 1973). A hut was found dug into the slope of a hill and periodically occupied as indicated by six successive layers of flooring. At "Ain Mallaha in the following Natufian, even more marked evidence of continuity of housing is found" (Perrot 1966), associated with possible evidence of storage. Thus by the eleventh millennium BC at least, there is good evidence of long-term investment in place, the construction of "histories" through time, some evidence of storage, and a major extension of the human engagement with things — antler and bone tools, groundstone grinders, pounders, axes, more stable housing.

And indeed as we go through this late Paleolithic and Epi-Paleolithic period in Europe and the Middle East we increasingly see signs of greater use of burial, greater elaboration of the human body in the proliferation of beads and ornaments, and more depiction of humans (Cauvin 2007). Ownership at this time must have been both individual and collective. The composite stone-tipped arrowheads typical of the Epi-Paleolithic are more likely to have been personal items, as many of the items of personal decoration, but there is much evidence of collective action. This in the Pre-Pottery Neolithic in the Middle East, following on from the Natufian in the tenth and ninth millennia BC there emerge large round buildings at sites such as Göbekli, Jerf el Ahmar, and Djade that are clearly ritual in content and collective in scale (Mithen 2004).

The site of Göbekli is of particular interest because here massive stone pillars encircle ritual enclosures (Schmidt 2006) in a society still without fully developed domestication of plants and animals. These four- to six-meter-high stones are carved with an array of wild animals, but the pillars also have engraved arms, indicating that they "represent" or "are" humans in some form. We can talk here of a new sense of human agency — at least in relation to the animals engraved on the sides of the pillars. In the Franco-Cantabrian cave paintings, humans are not shown dominating or interfering with wild animals. At Göbekli humans or human-like beings dominate the setting and the animals carved on their bodies. As Cauvin (2007) argued, here we see the sort of domination of animals that was a prerequisite of their domestication. The increased human agency here may have been collective, and it may have been associated with a greater sense of ownership as people invested in longer-term relationships with things and each other. It may also have been linked to an increase in exchange. While long-distance exchange of stone artifacts occurred in the Paleolithic, there is a great expansion of such interaction as obsidian, chert, shells, ochres, and baskets come to be exchanged throughout the Middle East from the late Epi-Paleolithic onwards. It is likely that during this time, things came to act as gifts that tied people to each other.

So, in summary, it is possible to argue that as humans came to be more and more entangled with things through the Pleistocene and into the early Holocene, and as their relations with things turned toward an increased sense of exclusive property, so the sense of self became more marked, both personally, in terms of bodily decoration and burial, and collectively, as in communal ritual enclosures. At the same time, that sense of self may have become very tied to things and to other humans. As gift exchange increased, the human person may increasingly have been seen as partible and distributed. As people became more entangled with things, so the tensions between self and other in human relations with things may have been more marked.

The Self at Çatalhöyük

I have so far been able to talk only in the most general of terms. It is at particular sites where different types of data can be explored in relation to each other that a fuller sense of the early Holocene construction of self can be gained. So I wish now to turn to the particular case of Çatalhöyük, a Neolithic "town" of between 3500 and 8000 people in central Turkey dated to 7400-6000 BC. The houses of the settlement (Figure 1) were clustered together to such an extent that there was no room for streets, and people moved about the settlement on the rooftops (Hodder 2006). The subsistence economy was fully agricultural in terms of domesticated plants, and domesticated sheep and goats were utilized, but wild resources were also exploited including cattle and pigs. There was small-scale storage within houses but also evidence of sharing of food between houses. Although much production, of bone tools, beads, bricks, and stone tools, was organized at the scale of individual houses, there is no evidence that houses owned their own land. For example, the clays used to make the sun-fired mud-bricks used to construct houses were not derived from distinct and consistent sources.

In contrast to earlier sites in central Turkey and the Middle East, Çatalhöyük brings many more activities into the house. Not only is there no

Figure 1. Reconstruction of the 9000-year-old settlement at Çatalhöyük in central Turkey. Drawing by John Swogger.

evidence for large collective ritual structures as noted above from sites in the PPNA/B (Pre-Pottery Neolithic A and B) in the Middle East, but the houses are more heavily used for a range of domestic activities than at, for example, the earlier site of Akl Höyük, and burial occurs only in houses — unlike the situation in the PPNB to the east. So one might expect to see a greater emphasis on house-based identities in contrast to these earlier sites and regions. On the other hand, there is much restraint and much focus on larger-scale community organization at Çatalhöyük. Overt expressions of individual house differences were clearly not sanctioned, and there is very little in the way of individual burial variability. Houses are grouped into small clusters associated with ancestral houses in which people from the group are preferentially buried — in one case, Building 1, sixty-two people had been buried beneath the floors of one house, and some of these people had been previously buried in or had lived in other houses. These small groupings of houses were also organized into sectors of maybe ten to sixty houses separated from other sectors by areas of midden or discard. In addition, the main East Mound at Çatalhöyük is organized into two halves, or moieties.

We know that people spent much of their lives, especially in the snow-driven winters, in these small, seven-meter by four-meter houses (Figure 2). There are many micro-traces of activities on the floors, and we have found evidence of soot from the fire that built up in people's lungs and got deposited on the insides of their ribs. The different floor segments were constructed of different materials, and they were associated with different types of matting and activity. The houses contain, on their south sides, hearths and ovens, and much daily productive activity took place near these hearths and ovens. This southern part of the main room was also where neonates and young infants were buried. In the northern part of the main rooms there were whiter and higher platforms on which people may have slept and under which adults were buried. We know that people in the houses remembered where they had placed individual bodies as they were able with great precision to dig down and retrieve bodies, and indeed to retrieve skulls from bodies (see below). So in these houses the self was situated in complex webs of memories. As a person moved around the house he or she would have known about who was buried where and what activities were to be done where and who was to sit or sleep where.

The link between humans and things in the house at Çatalhöyük is rather nicely demonstrated by the clay ball shown in Figure 3. The ball has been bitten into by a child. By studying the pattern of teeth impressions Simon Hillson has been able to demonstrate that the child was two to three years old. Such clay balls, often initially unfired, were baked and used to heat liquids and were usually kept by the oven, and the taste and feel of clay, rather like Proust's "petite Madeleine," must have linked the growing child to a particular site of memories. The identity of the child was indissolubly linked, through such physical sensations, to clay, hearth, and house. The child was here able to start a narrative identity, embodied and linked to circulation around the house.

But if the sense of person was mixed with the house at Çatalhöyük, it also seems to be the case that this self was partible. In Building 49 at the site, a grave was found in which a fully articulated torso was discovered, without legs, arms, or scapulae. The fact that the remaining parts of the body were in perfect anatomical position and that no cut or hack marks were found suggests that those who had removed the arms and legs had very detailed anatomical knowledge of the human body. Presumably the arms and legs circulated, creating links with this body and this Building 49. But it is mainly head removal that is practiced at Çatalhöyük. One of the most distinctive aspects of the Neolithic in the Middle East is head removal after burial. Head

Figure 2. Building 65 at Çatalhöyük seen from above. South is at the bottom of the photograph. Photograph Jason Quinlan.

Figure 3. A clay ball from Çatalhöyük showing the marks of human milk teeth, as identified by Simon Hillson.

removal is common in the PPNB in the Middle East, and it often has a collective character there in that groups of three or more heads are frequently found together in the Levant (Kuijt 2008) and a large number of skulls were found together in a building at Çayönü in southeastern Turkey. But at Çatalhöyük skull removal is very rare and the heads are usually deposited individually. In one case the face was modeled in clay and painted red and deposited with a woman in a grave. This latter case seems not to have been a normal burial beneath a floor, but was a foundation burial — one placed beneath a house as it was being constructed. In another case, a skull was found placed at the base of the post holding up the walls of a house. Several of the individual heads that have been found were painted, and in one house (VII.10) discovered by James Mellaart in the 1960s the entire head had been coated in red ochre "and two large sliced cowries of Red Sea type had dropped out of the eye sockets" (Mellaart 1966: 183).

There is some continuity between the removal and circulation of human heads and animal heads. The installation of bull and ram heads in the houses is a feature of Çatalhöyük. Wild animals such as bulls, rams, wild boar, and bears seem to have been teased, hunted, killed, and used to provide meat in feasts of various sizes. The skulls of the animals were often then kept, sometimes placed on walls and pedestals in houses, with the facial features modeled in clay, or just the horns, claws, and teeth were installed in the house. In at least one case a pit was dug down to retrieve an earlier installation, perhaps so that it could be reused in a later house. The pot shown in Figure 4 rather nicely reinforces this continuity between the removal and circulation of human and animal heads. At either end of the pot is shown a human head. The eyes are not shown and the image may represent a dead person. On both sides of the pot are shown bull heads. Looking at the ends of the pots, the lines of the bull horns appear to be the hair of the human, but as the pot is turned around they transform into the horns of the bull.

The removal and placing of heads is also a theme in the small clay figurines found at the site (Meskell et al. 2008). As shown in Figure 5, many of these figurines have dowel holes and a missing head, and separate individual heads have been recovered at the site. Perhaps heads were interchangeable or perhaps these figurines simply allowed the reenactment of the head removal process in the burials. It should also be mentioned that the art on the house walls at Çatalhöyük shows headless bodies associated with vultures — it is possible that head removal was associated with myths/stories in which vultures were involved in the removal of heads and flesh from bodies.

The removal of heads suggests a nonintegrated and partible self. It is rea-

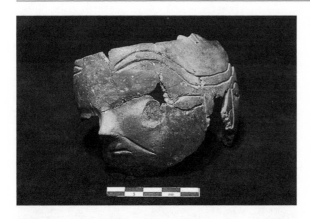

Figure 4. Pot
reassembled from
fragments found
in a midden in the
4040 Area at
Çatalhöyük, with
a human face at
both ends, and
a bull head on both
sides. Photograph
Jason Quinlan.

sonable to argue that at Çatalhöyük individual heads became transformed into the heads of ancestors that were then used to hold up and found houses. The transformation from life into death is also seen in the headless figurine shown in Figure 5. Looked at from the front, the woman seems healthy and perhaps pregnant, but as one turns the figurine around one notices the skinny arms and then from behind the figurine shows the ribs, vertebrae, scapulae, and pelvic bones of a very thin or dead individual. There are other intimations of transformation of the self at Çatalhöyük. The wall paintings include one panel in which two vultures both seem to have human feet, and we have found the bones of a crane wing on which there are wear traces suggestive of being used in a costume (Russell and McGowan 2003). So the overall evidence of personhood gained at Çatalhöyük from burials, figurines, and other imagery suggests not the atomized individual and bounded self of our own world. This is more a self that can be divided up, that can transform, that can become ancestors and perhaps birds and animals.

Thus at one level we can argue that at Çatalhöyük the self was bound up with the house and was continuous with ancestors and other beings and things. But at another level we seem to see the increasing emergence of a personhood coincident with body boundaries, as indeed we would expect given the increased tensions over ownership at a densely packed agricultural settlement such as Çatalhöyük. One possible way in which we can examine this idea is to study bodily functions — of which archeologists have special ability to monitor defecations preserved as coprolites. There is a possibility that the northeast corner room in Building 1 was used as a latrine, perhaps laid with straw and periodically cleaned out. Recent chemical analysis of the bile acids in coprolites in the midden areas around and between houses has

Figure 5. Figurine found in the IST Area at Çatalhöyük. Gratitude to Mihriban Özba'aran. Photograph Jason Quinlan.

shown that they include human markers. The careful cleaning of the spotless floors inside the houses, and the cleaning out of fecal material, contrasts with the dense concentrations of hearth and floor sweepings, butchery debris, and human excretions immediately outside. Presumably the fecal material in the house was swept up, taken up the stairs onto the roof, and discarded on a nearby midden. Such practices draw attention to the physical boundaries of self. The daily to-ing and fro-ing of bodily excretions perhaps draws attention to body boundaries and to the boundaries of an individual self.

There is other evidence to support this idea that there was a distinct or emerging sense of self as individualized at Çatalhöyük. In her account of the bone tools from the site, Nerissa Russell describes the occurrence of whole pendants in burials. She shows that they were at least sometimes worn around the neck. Together with their variability of form, this suggests that the pendants were a part of personal identities. Russell also notes the striking frequency of repair of these items in contrast to other bone artifacts. There is evidence of use after repair, and in some cases pendants that had lost their perforation and could no longer be worn were kept, perhaps as amulets. All this suggests that the pendants were linked to individual and shorter-term memories, and that they would have contributed to a sense of individual self.

Possible evidence of a stronger sense of self is provided by the obsidian mirrors found at the site. Experimental work by Jim Vedder has shown that these do not function well as signaling devices, and would not be useful to start fires, but that they do reflect images well. They may have been used to "see" and "divine" the spirit world, but it is tempting to suggest that, whatever their specific function, they could have been used to look at one's own body. There is a new technology of the body seen in a set of equipment related to bodily decoration (grinding stones used to grind ochre, and shells containing ochre associated with a small spatula in graves, although we cannot be sure these were used for body painting). Some of the skulls have red paint that may parallel painting of the face in life. We know from the figurines that people had elaborate hairstyles and hat styles (although the faces of the figurines themselves do not seem highly individualized). All this attention to facial and bodily presentation fits well with a focus on individual self-image.

The main things that we find in burials are items of bodily adornment or bodily preparation. These are mainly things closely associated with the body and its skin. It is in burials that we find boar tusk necklaces, belt hooks, huge numbers of beads from necklaces, pendants, finger rings (in some cases still on the fingers), bracelets (often still on the arms). We find obsidian mirrors and bits of cloth from clothing and binding. It is true that we also sometimes find baskets in which bodies are placed, and we sometimes find obsidian points and tools — but at least in some cases the obsidian is closely associated with the skeleton as if it was tied to the leg or placed on the back or shoulder. So people were mainly buried with material that was closely associated with the bodies and skin — things that were close to them. What seems rare or absent from burials is material that was less close but might have been thought to be part of what one owned — things like pots and figurines. In the burials the focus is on the individual body boundary, even if body parts can then sometimes be removed and transformed into a more social and partible self.

There is some evidence to suggest that at Çatalhöyük individual lives were remembered. It is difficult to say how individualized the "portrait" of the plastered skull described above is. The face is finely executed, showing the details of nostrils, for example. And the nose is very distinctive in shape, although there has been some movement due to the pressure of the earth in the grave and disturbance by an animal burrow. But it is clear that the locations of individual heads and bodies were remembered with such accuracy that people were able to dig down and remove heads and body parts with little disturbance to the rest of the body.

I argue, therefore, that people at Çatalhöyük were very strongly and immediately socialized into social rules and roles, and that their sense of self was primarily associated with the house and other social groups. This was a distributed and transformable self. But as part of this process, some sense of individual self, and the construction of individual bodily boundaries, became more marked. The seeds of individual selves were being sown.

In fact, there is some evidence that this process of individuation increases through time in the upper levels of the site. There is more adornment of burials in the upper levels. There are stamp seals from the site that are not well understood as to function, but the most likely explanation is that they were used in some way to identify individuals — either by stamping cloth and clothes or by stamping bodies. Stamp seals become common in the upper levels of the site (especially from Level V onwards), and again they are found in burials, supporting the notion that burial goods concentrate on things close to the body. In the upper levels of the site, there are changes in the subsistence economy to focus more on secondary animal products, and we also see houses getting larger and more separate from each other. It is reasonable to argue that as this happened there would have been increased emphasis on the ownership of the resources in which one was more intensively investing.

I suggested earlier that it might be helpful to distinguish the issue of body boundaries from the question of whether persons were seen as autonomous agents, however difficult such a distinction might be. Certainly at Çatalhöyük there are strong images of agency that seem to be largely collective and social. Some of the most telling scenes in the wall art show large groups of humans dancing toward and then teasing, baiting, or otherwise interacting with wild bulls, stags with erect penises, wild boars, and bears. As noted above, this type of domination of animals can be read in terms of the fact that humans at the site were about to turn to domesticated cattle and pigs. Yet the paintings can be interpreted in other ways. For example, Lewis-Williams and Pearce (2005) see them as showing humans touching and obtaining the spirit power from the wild animals. Whatever the specific interpretation, the scenes suggest a collective action that must have been important in establishing group positioning and interactions. It seems likely that these interactions with wild animals were associated with the provision of feasts from which a social group gained prestige in relation to other groups.

But once again there also seem to be very distinctive acts at Çatalhöyük that are suggestive of a more individualized agency. One of the most distinctive experiences of digging at the site is that as we start to dig each house we know from the start what it will look like, where we will find the oven and the hearth, where the burials will be, what the floors and fills will look like. We know that posts will have been removed from walls leaving scars, and we know that we will find little on the floors, and that there will be multiple layers of plaster on the walls. But we are always also surprised by the individuality of what we find. We are always coming across odd, unique things or actions that have no parallel anywhere on the site. For example, the face pot discussed above and shown in Figure 4 is just wrong. This pot comes from middle levels at the site when all pottery, every sherd, remains undecorated. Then suddenly, out of nowhere, someone decides to make this beautiful and fascinating object that resonates so well with the themes of human and bull head removal that are so common at Çatalhöyük. Of course we cannot be certain that the pot was made by only one person, but it certainly has a distinctive and unique individual style that suggests individual action. Another example is the figurine of the woman with the skeletal back shown in Figure 5. Again, this is an entirely unique and individual object, even if it plays on themes widely found at Çatalhöyük. There are no other figurines remotely like it. We also find strange burials. For example, humans are never buried with animals during the main sequence at the site. But in one building found in the South Area of the site we discovered a whole sheep had been laid in an extended position across the grave of a man with whom was buried a possible bone flute or whistle. In another burial, in Building 17, the body had been laid out with its legs wide apart and a wooden plank placed over the body before the head was removed. More recently a burial has been found with obsidian and chert blades stuck upright around the head.

These strange and idiosyncratic things and actions suggest the ability of persons to make individual decisions and to express an individual agency. A further category of such acts consists of odd collections of objects either worn as bracelets and necklaces or cached as special deposits. In her study of these collections of things, Nakamura (2010) notes provocative groupings such as:

- [Unit 4401] a badger mandible, tooth pendant, green rubbing stones, an ax point, and one piece each of obsidian and flint deposited in a scoop under an oven in Building 6

- [Unit 14522] animal bone, figurine, baby leg, stone, obsidian, and crystal deposited in southeast corner of Building 65 under preconstruction makeup of a platform

Nakamura interprets these clusterings of assorted objects as magical in tone, contrasting with the regularized rituals and symbolic associations that dominate at the site. Again, these suggest a very personalized set of associations brought together and indicating a more individualized symbolic agency.

Overall, then, the evidence from Çatalhöyük suggests that personhood and agency were strongly tied to and distributed within social collectivities, especially the house, but that increasingly a more individualized self began to emerge. There is evidence of storage within houses at the site, and through time investment in animals and plants led to increased separation of houses, possibly associated with a greater sense of ownership. As the emphasis on ancestry and memory construction in house sequences decreased in the later levels of the site, there may have been more opportunity for individual selves to be asserted.

In such a dense and intensely occupied site, there must have been all sorts of tensions and conflicts, both group and individual, underpinning varied senses of self and of self in relation to others and things. One example may have been the ownership of women. In recent work using the phenotypic variation of teeth as proxies for genetic distance between individuals buried beneath house floors, Marin Pilloud has found differences between the variability of men and women, suggesting that women may have been married into the settlement from outside while men stayed within the site and showed less variation of genetic markers. The evidence suggests a virilocal or patrilocal society in which women were exchanged as objects between male-centered groups. Such practices may have promoted a sense of a separate self, as women were torn from one group to another.

Conclusion

The Neolithic of the Middle East saw a major expansion of the entanglement between people and made things. It has long been argued, at least since Rousseau, that the domestication of plants and animals led to an increased sense of ownership, of bounding of resources. As people invested more in things, so they became more concerned with exclusive rights.

The overall archeological evidence from the Middle East, but in particular the detailed results from Çatalhöyük, suggest that as human entanglement with things increased, a greater sense of agency emerged, at least in relation to animals, together with a stronger sense of both dividual and individual selves.

The shifts were not solely concerned with a self-representational capacity of the brain. It is possible that the mirrors used at Çatalhöyük encouraged self-reflection, and I have noted the increased focus on representing the skin of the body in plaster, and the great expansion of necklaces, beads, rings, and other body ornament. But much of the changed conception of personhood that I have described emerges from the practices of an embodied engagement with the entanglements of daily life. As humans became more entangled in the things they had invested in, as they were trapped into the tending of plants and animals that had come to depend on them, so notions of an exclusive relationship with things, objects separated from other objects, became pronounced, and in these daily relations to separated things humans too became more bounded and separated, more attuned to various forms of self. In the practices of creating memories and histories in house sequences, heads and body parts were circulated — thus partitioning and dispersing the body. And yet these circulated parts were from identifiable bodies whose locations beneath the house floors were remembered. There were both dividualizing and individualizing practices in daily life.

It is notable, however, how many of the practices I have been able to discuss at Çatalhöyük relate to interactions beyond the immediate practical world. So many of the examples I have given seem to involve constructions of persons in relation to ancestors, to animal spirits, or to birds associated with the mythical removal of flesh. They involve apparently magical depositions and collections of things. They involve burial, figurines, and the depictions of a narrative wall art. They involve feasts and festivals. It seems then that the emergence of a stronger and more complex sense of personhood at this time was intimately bound up with the self as a transcendent category.

I argued at the start of this chapter that humans define themselves through a continual to-ing and fro-ing, to and from things. The self is always a social category, bound up in the entanglements of daily life. But this dependence on things seems to require a transcendence. The more the self is dragged into things, the more it seems to seek for some transcendent meaning. The self seems produced by things while seeking to transcend them. The self tries to deal with the tension and contradiction of both being defined by and separate from things.

67

REFERENCES

Arensburg, B., and O. Bar-Yosef. 1973. Human remains from Ein Gev 1, Jordan Valley, Israel. *Paléorient* 1: 201-6.

Barnard, A., and J. Woodburn. 1988. "Introduction." In *Hunters and Gatherers 2: Property, Power and Ideology,* ed. T. Ingold, D. Riches, and J. Woodburn, 4-32. Oxford: Berg.

Bird-David, N. 1999. "Animism" revisited: Personhood, environment, and relational epistemology. *Current Anthropology* 40 Supplement: 67-90.

Carrier, J. G. 1998. "Property and social relations in Melanesian anthropology." In *Property Relations: Renewing the Anthropological Tradition,* ed. C. M. Hann, 85-103. Cambridge: Cambridge University Press.

Cauvin, J. 2007. *The Birth of the Gods and the Origins of Agriculture.* Cambridge: Cambridge University Press.

DeMarais, E., C. Gosden, and C. Renfrew, eds. 2005. *Rethinking Materiality: The Engagement of Mind with the Material World.* Cambridge: McDonald Institute.

Fowler, C. 2004. *The Archaeology of Personhood: An Anthropological Approach.* London: Routledge.

Hodder, I. 2006. *The Leopard's Tale: Revealing the Mysteries of Çatalhöyük.* London: Thames & Hudson.

Hodder, I. 2007. Çatalhöyük in the context of the Middle Eastern Neolithic. *Annual Review of Anthropology* 36: 105-20.

Kuijt, I. 2008. The regeneration of life. *Current Anthropology* 49: 171-97.

Lewis-Williams, D., and D. Pearce. 2005. *Inside the Neolithic Mind: Consciousness, Cosmos, and the Realm of the Gods.* London: Thames & Hudson.

Mauss, M. 1954 [in French 1950]. *The Gift.* Oxford: Routledge.

Mellaart, J. 1966. Excavations at Çatal Hüyük, 1965: Fourth preliminary report. *Anatolian Studies* 16: 165-91.

Meskell, L. M., C. Nakamura, R. King, and S. Farid., 2008. Figured lifeworlds and depositional practices at Çatalhöyük. *Cambridge Archaeological Journal* 18, no. 2: 139-61.

Mithen, S. 2004. *After the Ice.* Cambridge, MA: Harvard University Press.

Nakamura, C. 2010. "Magical Deposits at Çatalhöyük: A Matter of Time and Place?" In *Religion in the Emergence of Civilization: Çatalhöyük as a Case Study,* ed. I. Hodder. Cambridge: Cambridge University Press.

Perrot, J. 1966. Le gisement Natoufien de Mallaha (Eynan), Israel. *L'Anthropologie* 70: 437-84.

Preda, A. 1999. The turn to things: Arguments for a sociological theory of things. *The Sociological Quarterly* 40, no. 2: 347-66.

Schmidt, K. 2006. *Sie bauten den ersten Tempel. Das rätselhafte Heiligtum der Steinzeitjäger.* Munich: C. H. Beck.

Strathern, M. 1988. *The Gender of the Gift: Problems with Women and Problems with Society in Melanesia.* Berkeley: University of California Press.

Strathern, M. 1999. *Property, Substance and Effect: Anthropological Essays on Persons and Things.* London: Athlone Press.

Weiner, A. 1992. *Inalienable Possessions: The Paradox of Keeping While Giving.* Berkeley: University of California Press.

Woodburn, J. 1998. "'Sharing is not a form of exchange': An Analysis of Property-sharing in Immediate-return Hunter-gatherer Societies." In *Property Relations: Renewing the Anthropological Tradition,* ed. C. M. Hann, 48-63. Cambridge: Cambridge University Press.

Are Apes and Elephants Persons?

Barbara J. King

In Gabriel Garcia Marquez's masterpiece *One Hundred Days of Solitude,* José and Ursula Buendía, matriarch and patriarch of the Buendía family, living in the now-famed fictional city of Maconda, worry about what their marriage may produce. They are cousins; might their love result in a child born with a pig's tail? This anxiety springs up again and again in the family members' consciousness down through the generations.

In his introduction to the novel, Carlos Fuentes notes that *One Hundred Days* speaks to "the desolation and fear of reverting to an anonymous and inhuman nature, the terror of giving birth to a son with a pig's tail and initiating a regression" (1995: xi).

An anonymous and inhuman nature. Here is the idea that animals live dumbly, en masse, and without individual distinction. Humans, by contrast, live expressively and with individual distinction. By extension, humans have selves. Animals are without selves. To become animal is to revert to some primitive, indeed, "anonymous," state. It mustn't happen — at least not outside the special contexts within certain religious traditions, where shamans or other spiritual masters transform at will (though not without dangers) into animals and then back into humans (for examples see King 2007, 2010).

We all recognize this idea of the animal-human boundary. Far from dwelling only in literary worlds, it formed the basis of Descartes' views in the seventeenth century that animals lack reason and language, and thus are soulless, nonthinking organic machines. This stark summation of what it is to be animal is by no means dead. To take just one example, in 2008 the

Washington Post published an op-ed whose author contrasted reasoning humans with "irrational and immoral" animals, including apes (La Valle 2008; for a response see King 2008; and for related reviews see Bekoff and Pierce 2009, Bradshaw 2009).

Increasingly, scientists and theologians, as well as philosophers, are pushing back against this supposed dichotomy. This blurring of animal-human identity goes beyond the obvious fact that we *Homo sapiens* are animals too. It goes further because animals refuse to toe the line. They live neither dumbly nor en masse. Rather, they live vocally, with individuality, and with self-awareness. They always have, but more and more this fact rises to humans' notice.

A Quintet of Squid

In the book *Kinship with Animals* (2006), Anthony L. Rose retells a story offered by his friend Randy Harwood. Harwood went diving in the waters off the Solomon Islands, accompanied by one other person. In shallow water, the pair encountered five squid — possibly, judging from their sizes and behaviors, a mother and her offspring.

As the two divers approached, the squid began to change colors. (Cephalopods such as squid and octopus communicate through color change.) Over some minutes, a parade of hues came to life before the divers' eyes, with the smaller animals matching the bigger one in sequence. The divers "hung motionless, unable to respond." At one point, the larger squid broke off and communicated directly with the smaller ones.

Then — and here I quote Harwood's words as written by Rose — "All five went transparent and slowly, tentacles first, approached us. At four feet distance they stopped and as a group, large and small, repeated the brilliant displays of the first encounter. It was incredible! They had discussed us and decided to try again. In all the colors of their rainbow, five self-aware aliens from another world talked to us. As they repeated the inquiry with exquisite precision, the message boiled down to a simple one — *Hey stupid, who are you?* It was magical — if only we could have replied."

Harwood's frustration at the trans-species communication barrier seeps through his words. With a chimpanzee, or with a dog, we may look a fellow mammal straight in the eye and offer words and other gestures that have a reasonable chance of being comprehended, at the level of voice tone or content or both. By comparison, squid and other cephalopods, though undeniably intelligent, really fit that word *alien* so well. How can we possibly communicate with them?

I have no idea if squid can feel frustration, but if they can, this quintet may have experienced it. Given the level of nonresponse from the divers, in Harwood's judgment they "got bored and slowly drifted off." Despite its unsatisfactory nature, that close encounter affected Harwood deeply. He felt a connection with animals that normally don't connect with humans. He concluded that the squid "have individual feelings [and] personalities."

I love this story and urge reading it in the original; it encourages us to imagine how active, how alive, how purposefully communicative other creatures may be as they go about their daily lives, even beyond the loyal dog or the cuddly panda, beyond the apes and elephants that form the focus of this chapter. Yet, as a scientist, I find no evidence within the story to conclude that squid have individual feelings and personalities that they express as self-aware creatures. We may find ourselves wishing to map those things onto the squid, because of the evidence for purposeful communication the story contains — and because of the story's magic.

Yet to seek animal selves — to seek evidence of the expression of individual feelings and personalities in other self-aware species — we need to look for more than purposeful communication. We need to discover which self-aware animals express preferences, or show emotions, in different ways, one from the other. This point is not a taxonomic one; it may well be that squid and other cephalopods indeed do those things. But we need to look.

A Quintet of Apes

As a biological anthropologist, I turn naturally to the consideration of our closest living relatives, the great apes, when thinking about animals' selves. To some, this turn will smack of speciesism. Yet for me it's a natural reach and makes no statement about where else we might — indeed, where else we should — look to find animal selves.

Chimpanzees, bonobos, gorillas, and orangutans are highly intelligent, self-aware, and social creatures who recognize each other as individuals, who relate emotionally with each other, and who communicate in ways that are dynamic and creative. It is now beyond question that they intersect with the world as creatures who are aware of their existence. These great apes express grief and empathy, and they may take into account another's perspective even when it differs from their own; they make meaning together in ways that go beyond simple exchange of survival-related messages; and they solve problems using abstract reasoning. In other words, they consciously feel and think about their social world (Boesch and Boesch-Achermann 2000; Byrne 1995; Goodall 1990; King 2004; Russon, Bard, and Parker 1996; Segerdahl, Fields, and Savage-Rumbaugh 2006; de Waal 2006). Some scholars see morality (Bekoff and Pierce 2009) or even incipient spirituality (Goodall 2006) in ape behavior.

A paragraph of scientific summary conveys facts about various ape species, and their capacities, but it tells us nothing about ape selves. For that, we need data and, especially, narratives about ape selves. For this reason, I invite you to meet five apes.

(1) In Gombe, Tanzania, lived a chimpanzee named Flo. She was brought to the world's attention by Jane Goodall, and, upon her death, she merited an obituary in the *London Times*. Flo was a calm, caring mother; she raised her offspring with a sure hand and passed along her maternal competence to her daughter Fifi. The Flo-Fifi pair became famous, especially because they brought home in concrete terms the notion of the chimpanzee personality. These confident and effective mothers made a vivid contrast with other chimpanzee females who were neglectful of their offspring or even outright violent with others' infants (Goodall 1990).

Flo's last offspring, called Flint, became well known in his own right for a sad reason. When Flo died, Flint, age 8, became ill and died as well. Grief was, Goodall feels sure, a major reason for that premature death, for Flint was old enough to care for himself. What he couldn't survive was his own tide of emotion at his loss.

(2) Across the continent, at the Tai National Park in Cote d'Ivoire, lived an equally illuminating chimpanzee called Brutus. Brutus was a hunter of exceptional skill, who carried out what Christophe Boesch and Hedwige Boesch-Achermann (2000) call *double anticipations*. That is, he was able to anticipate not only the movements of the monkeys he hunted as they fled through the trees in advance of a chimpanzee hunting party but also those of his fellow chimpanzee hunters. Over and over again, Brutus subtly adjusted his own moves to those of his prey and his hunting confederates; in this way, he drove up the rate of hunting success and affected the entire chimpanzee community.

For years now I have written or spoken about Brutus for another reason. When a young chimpanzee of his community died of a leopard bite, Brutus headed the community contingent that stayed near the body. As community leader, he kept away all infants except one: the dead female's juvenile brother.

The brother was allowed to sit at the body, and he pulled at the hand of his dead sister. This anecdote moves me because it illustrates not only the depth of chimpanzee emotion, but also the ability of one ape to recognize and act upon emotion in another ape. Can it have been a coincidence that Brutus allowed only the dead female's brother through to the body? Is it not more likely that Brutus grasped the emotion the youngster felt and enabled him to express it?

(3) Washoe was a chimpanzee pioneer in the study of ape language. Studies in teaching aspects of American Sign Language to an infant named Washoe graced the pages of the journal *Science* over four decades ago; Washoe went on to make scientific history when she used elements of ASL effectively with other chimpanzees as well as with her human caretakers.

When Washoe died in 2008 at the age of 42, I was asked to write an appraising article for the journal *Sign Language Studies* and an obituary (though it was termed a "death notice" upon publication) for the American Anthropological Association's *Anthropology Newsletter*. These two requests hint at Washoe's impact on academe, but perhaps more significant were the numerous newspaper articles and online tributes dedicated to Washoe's impact on how people thought about apes.

In the ways she expressed her language skills — which were by any measure significant — Washoe led people to recognize apes as animals with individual feelings and personalities. Washoe routinely made up new terms for objects for which she had no term in her gestural vocabulary. Confronted with a refrigerator, for instance, she created the term "open food drink." She taught some signs to her adopted son, in some cases by molding his hand into the appropriate shape as she herself had been taught, a feat no other ape has been seen to do. She signed with empathy ("Hurt there, come" — followed by a kiss to the injury) when her closest human friend broke his arm. When she sneaked into a room she was forbidden to enter, she signed "quiet" to herself.

Washoe signed, too, to her dolls. This self-chatter shows that language became part of her interior life; it meant far more to her than a mere technique for pleasing her human caretakers and thus obtaining some reward (Fouts 2001). Washoe used her language skills to express her likes and dislikes. Famously, she was persistently intrigued by shoes, and even shoe catalogs!

(4) Michael was a western lowland gorilla who, like his well-known companion Koko who lived at the same facility, also communicated by using elements of American Sign Language. Michael was seized from his wild

home in Cameroon at age 2. Until his death at age 28, he lived a life in the United States enriched by "synergistic relationships, multi-species communications, and artistic enrichment" (Patterson, Tanner, and Rose 2009).

Here I will remark upon a single aspect of Michael's life, his intense pleasure in rhythm and music (Tanner 2009). Michael enjoyed listening to classical music and visibly relaxed as he listened; Pavarotti was a favorite. He participated with others in music-making in a variety of ways, as when he coordinated his foot-tapping in sync with a human companion's or when he hit sticks together and hit sticks on PVC pipe.

Most intriguing, Michael developed a penchant for creating gorilla guitars! They were quite definitely guitars, in fact, and these objects showed Michael's inventiveness and creativity. He didn't merely make one sort of instrument and strum it in the same way over and over again. Instead, at different times he employed materials of rope, branches, or blanket strips; he stretched the strings from teeth to feet, from hand to hand, from chin to foot, or from foot to foot; he fashioned two variations in string length and thus in pitch; and he vibrated the strings in different ways, by finger-strumming, fist-hitting, and teeth-plucking.

Gorillas' proclivities for percussive rhythm in the wild and in captivity — including their iconic chest-beating — have long been known, but with observations of Michael, our understanding of apes' capacity for pleasure in music listening and music-making has taken a leap. His enriched or, as the term goes, "enculturated" life has apparently allowed this basic sensitivity to rhythm and sound to flourish.

(5) The bonobo Panbanisha enjoys music too; a bit of her — and her brother Kanzi's — music-making behavior is included in a seventeen-minute video: http://www.ted.com/talks/susan_savage_rumbaugh_on_apes_that_write.html.

Panbanisha is a bonobo who — like Kanzi — was raised to converse with humans using not ASL but computer symbols called lexigrams. Panbanisha understands a fair amount of spoken English as well. Along with all the apes I have so far considered, she expresses her distinctive self through her behaviors. When I met her, Panbanisha suggested (through lexigrams) that I hide behind a large pile of debris, and she didn't seem particularly eager for me to emerge again! She enjoyed, too, asking me for ice on a hot day and watching me serve her. The philosopher Per Segerdahl has woven into an account of Kanzi and Panbanisha's language skills his own encounters with Panbanisha's forceful personality (Segerdahl et al. 2006).

Flo, Brutus, Michael, Washoe, and Panbanisha — each of these five apes is a distinct being, an emergent self with emotion, memory, and imagination at work. Flo's case is a little different than the other four, for my description of her, unlike my description of the other apes, includes no direct evidence for emotion, memory, or imagination at work. This is an important point, for it is the totality of what we know about apes in the wild and captivity that allows us to interpret Flo's personality fully, to understand that her behavior isn't just an example of statistical variation around a mean of maternal behaviors. The accumulated data point us toward an inescapable conclusion, a conclusion we are in no position to reach with squid: *every great ape is a unique, self-aware, thinking, and feeling self.* Apes live in protected reserves in Africa and Asia, or out in forests under attack by loggers and poachers; apes live in research centers and sanctuaries and excellent zoos where their welfare is paramount, and in roadside zoos and biomedical centers where their welfare is anything but a priority compared to tourist or research dollars (Siebert 2009). Wherever they live, these apes collectively and individually are the antithesis of *an anonymous nature.*

Elephants

Like apes, elephants are long-lived, highly social, intelligent, self-aware, and emotional creatures. Matriarch-led elephant groups are highly charged social units, marked by joy trumpeted when individuals reunite, and an emotional response we don't entirely understand when kin or companions die. Stories of elephant graveyards are apocryphal, but at least some of the stories of elephant mourning are true. Elephants recognize the bones of their dead kin and companions, and caress them — whereas they don't do this with strangers' bones (Moss 1988).

Elephants illustrate in an exceptionally clear way the costs that come along with living as distinctive selves. What elephants may feel is connected to elephant history at the hands of humans and goes beyond grief at the natural cycle of life and death, to include felt pain, both physical and emotional, at the infliction of great trauma. Gay Bradshaw (2009) has described the pain endured by young elephants who watch their mothers killed by poachers or farmers, or by wildlife managers who wish to thin a herd. These accounts make for gut-wrenching reading.

Ndume was a baby elephant living wild with his family in Kenya. When the family wandered from the forest into an area seeded with crops, the elephants were attacked and many were killed by angry farmers wielding spears and arrows. Ndume himself managed to flee. However, he witnessed a smaller calf near him hacked into pieces and suffered from shock and from the knife gashes he himself experienced.

Ndume was brought to an elephant sanctuary outside Nairobi called the David Sheldrick Wildlife Trust. Three months of age at the time of the attack, he began to cry and bellow for his dead mother after his arrival at the Trust. He could not sleep well. Sanctuary experts believe he was reliving the trauma of the attack in his dreams. Then Ndume became depressed.

Because of the Trust's patient and healing routines, during which he was bottle-fed and encouraged to enjoy the company of other elephants, Ndume began to regain some joy in life. As Bradshaw puts it, "Interacting with other elephants worked like an elixir" (2009: 139). She explains: "The free-ranging elephant self is defined through relationships; infant elephant cognition, emotion, behavior, and values are created in plurality" (2009: 137). Bradshaw's book makes clear that elephants recover from trauma (or sadly, sometimes fail to recover) in ways as individual as their personalities. Each elephant is as unique as any ape.

The Relational Self

What's most striking about the apes and elephants considered here — and by extension their brethren in wild and captive settings across the globe — is how they bring to life the idea of *the relational self.* African apes and all elephants live communally, as we have seen; infants develop in the midst of a thriving and socioemotionally structured society. Infants become selves only through interaction; their situation is reminiscent of the pediatrician D. W. Winnicott's famous dictum about our own species: there's no such thing as a baby — only a baby and someone (Small 1999). When, as adults, Brutus the chimpanzee responds with empathy to the grief felt by another self, Michael the gorilla makes music with another self, and Ndume the elephant recovers with elephant and human selves, they are embodying their developmental histories.

During this socioemotional development, young apes' and elephants' brains are sculpted by experience in ways related to what happens with young children's brains (Greenspan and Shanker 2004). In one sense, this biocultural fact is a cause for worry, because negative experiences will have substantial consequences developmentally. Bradshaw's (2009) data show, for example, that traumatized young elephant males living wild may become hyperaggressive. They kill other elephants and may even kill rhinoceroses in bizarre acts of violence that are inconsistent with what we understand to be elephant culture. Yet the brain-sculpting is also a cause for hope, because it means that when healing action is taken for traumatized elephants and apes, chances of recovery are substantial, as Ndume's case demonstrates.

Humans share our relational selves, and the attendant joys and sufferings that go with them, with other creatures. To be seen to have selves, animals need not express individual emotions, self-awareness, and preferences in ways identical to our own. Indeed, human selves differ in pronounced ways from the selves of apes or elephants or other creatures. We express, and indeed shape, our relational selves in unique ways. We alone create and tell each other sweeping narratives of our past, present, and future; we alone not only feel but also anticipate or revel in or regret or mourn the wonder, compassion, anxiety, and terror with which we act toward others and are acted upon by others.

The statements in the paragraph just above about unique human capacities may seem obvious, but in a chapter on animal selves they must be said. Before I explain why this is so, let us consider a question that follows from the consideration of animal selves.

Are Apes and Elephants Persons?

Apes and elephants are selves — vibrant, thinking, and feeling selves distinct from one another — that come about in relation to other creatures. Does this mean that apes and elephants are persons? This question is hotly debated. Certainly it has been embraced by some who work on behalf of ape or elephant welfare. Rogers Fouts, in writing about the chimpanzee Washoe, does not hesitate to break the link between humans and persons: "I have to accept the Darwinian fact that Washoe is a person by any reasonable definition and that the community of chimpanzees from which she was stolen [in West Africa] are a people" (Fouts 2001; see also Fouts and Mills 1997). Similarly, Bradshaw considers elephants to be persons; she refers to one elephant as "a young woman," for example.

The question of personhood is often closely linked to legal goals involving animal rights. Readers interested in legal challenges may consult Steven Wise's books *Rattling the Cage* and *Drawing the Line* and search online for news articles about ongoing court battles, such as the ongoing one concerning Matthew the chimpanzee, who lives in Vienna, and whether he will be declared a person by the European Court of Human Rights.

Fouts and Bradshaw don't write about ape persons and elephant persons in direct linkage to legal goals, however. They write instead in order to re-shape our thinking about other animals, so that we may reshape our actions toward other animals. Apes and elephants are only the leading edge. They invite us to observe, film, study, and think differently about the possibility of dolphin selves and whale selves, about mice selves and cat selves, about bird selves and turtle selves — indeed, about squid selves (see Bekoff 2007; Bekoff and Pierce 2009). Not all of these species will show the same *degree* of personality differentiation or of emotional subtlety as apes and elephants do, but that isn't the point. We will not know about the other animal selves on Earth until we look hard for them.

My call for comparative research may still worry some people, who may ask: Why should animals who look to us to have distinct relational selves be more entitled to our care than animals who do not? Let me speak to this point with an example. I don't know if spiders have distinct relational selves. I suspect they do not. But even if I am right about that or even if I never find out, I still won't kill a spider (in our house, we usher spiders outdoors and set them free). As many centuries of religious traditions teach us (Armstrong 2006; King 2010), compassion for all animals may be unmoored from an animal's brainwaves or personality or emotional capacities.

Yet comparative analysis does matter in the real world, as much as academic or legal debates about whether some animals should be declared persons. To understand each species in its environmental, social, and emotional context is crucial as we make decisions about wild and captive management with limited resources. To house an elephant in a zoological park is not the same as to house a spider.

Human Uniqueness and Human Responsibility

Bradshaw (2009) compares elephants who have survived trauma to people who survived the concentration camps of the Holocaust. One of many such passages in her book *Elephants on the Edge* reads:

> While life in the circus or zoo has taught wariness — to view change with suspicion — what elephants may feel when coming to the [Elephant Sanctuary in Tennessee] is closer to weariness. Elie Wiesel describes the evolution of such weariness and the focused numbness that creeps up as time goes by under the grinding violence of captivity and the past life begins to recede into an unfamiliar reality. (2009: 154)

79

Bradshaw then quotes a long paragraph from Wiesel's book *Night*. It includes this sentence: "I thought of us as damned souls wandering through the void, souls condemned to wander through space until the end of time, seeking redemption, seeking oblivion, without any hope of finding either."

And with this stunning passage about human torment, we are brought back to a point I made earlier: elephants are not humans. Elephants have distinct selves — and the joys and sufferings that go along with those selves. This fact exists and is not incompatible with another series of facts: elephants cannot think about souls, redemption, or oblivion; they cannot grasp what it means to live with a reality that not only their selves but also their extended society is under threat of planned extermination under the cruelest conditions possible. It does no one — suffering elephants included — a service to force elephant trauma and Holocaust trauma into a framework where they are made to become the same phenomenon. Elephants needn't be rendered in Holocaust terms to deserve freedom from suffering.

Bradshaw conflates elephants and humans for a reason. When she writes that we may understand an elephant "much like we would a person from a different culture" (2009: 117), she launches her case for animal rights: "To address elephant breakdown, we must accept that elephants, and other animals, have rights comparable to those of persons" (2009: 127).

Working toward animal rights is one path through which we may reshape our thinking about animals and our actions toward animals. Another, the one I embrace, is to use an understanding of animal selves as inspiration to motivate human communities, including religious communities, to accept — and to act upon — greater responsibility for the conditions in which animals live. If every ape and every elephant were magically anointed "persons" by the courts tomorrow, it would still be humans, and only humans, who could bring about meaningful change in their lives.

Concluding Note

To recognize animal selves is to recognize human responsibility for other animals' lives — in the wild and in captivity. We become fully human — fully vibrant, thinking, and feeling selves — only through our relationship with other animals (King 2010). *Our* personhood depends on moving beyond a strict human-animal dichotomy, on moving toward a view where compassion for the world's creatures depends neither on a necessary superiority (where we make ourselves entirely different from other animals) nor on claims of identity (where we make animals entirely like us). Animals are neither dumb anonymous creatures nor humans in some alternative guise. Far more critical than deciding whether to consider them persons, we need to see their relational selves as they are and act on that vision.

References

Armstrong, K. 2006. *The Great Transformation.* New York: Knopf.

Bekoff, M. 2007. *The Emotional Lives of Animals: A Leading Scientist Explores Animal Joy, Empathy and Sorrow — and Why They Matter.* Novato, CA: New World Library.

Bekoff, M., and J. Pierce. 2009. *Wild Justice: The Moral Lives of Animals.* Chicago: University of Chicago Press.

Boesch, C., and H. Boesch-Achermann. 2000. *The Chimpanzees of the Tai Forest: Behavioural Ecology and Evolution.* Oxford: Oxford University Press.

Bradshaw, G. A. 2009. *Elephants on the Edge: What Animals Teach Us about Humanity.* New Haven: Yale University Press.

Byrne, R. 1995. *The Thinking Ape: Evolutionary Origins of Intelligence.* Oxford: Oxford University Press.

de Waal, F. 2006. *Our Inner Ape: A Leading Primatologist Explains Why We Are Who We Are.* New York: Riverhead.

Fouts, R. S. 2001. "Darwinian Reflections on Our Fellow Apes." In *Great Apes and Humans,* edited by Benjamin Beck et al. Washington, DC: Smithsonian Institution Press.

Fouts, R. S., and S. T. Mills. 1997. *Next of Kin: My Conversations with Chimpanzees.* New York: William Morrow.

Goodall, J. 1990. *Through a Window.* Boston: Houghton Mifflin.

Goodall, J. 2007. "The Dance of Awe." In *A Communion of Subjects: Animals in Religion, Science, and Ethics,* edited by Paul Waldau and Kim Patton. New York: Columbia University Press.

Greenspan, S. I., and S. G. Shanker. 2004. *The First Idea: How Symbols, Language, and Intelligence Evolved from Our Primate Ancestors to Modern Humans.* New York: Da Capo.

King, B. J. 2010. *Being with Animals: Why We Are Obsessed with the Furry, Scaly, Feathery Creatures Who Populate Our World.* New York: Doubleday.

King, B. J. 2004. *The Dynamic Dance: Nonvocal Communication in African Apes.* Cambridge, MA: Harvard University Press.

King, B. J. 2007. *Evolving God: A Provocative View on the Origins of Religion.* New York: Doubleday.

King, B. J. 2008. Op-ed, "What Binti Jua Knew." *Washington Post,* August 23.

LaValle, P. R. 2008. Op-ed, "Why They're Human Rights." *Washington Post,* July 27.

Marquez, Gabriel Garcia. 1998. *One Hundred Years of Solitude*. New York: Knopf (Everyman's Library). With introduction by Carlos Fuentes.

Moss, C. 1988. *Elephant Memories: Thirteen Years in the Life of an Elephant Family*. New York: William Morrow & Co.

Patterson, F., J. Tanner, and A. L. Rose. 2009. "Remembering Michael: A Gifted Gorilla." Paper presented at American Society of Primatologists meeting, September.

Rose, A. L. 2006. "On Tortoises, Monkeys & Men." In *Kinship with Animals*, edited by Kate Solisti and Michael Tobias. San Francisco: Council Oaks Books.

Russon, A., K. Bard, and S. T. Parker, eds. 2006. *Reaching into Thought: The Mind of the Great Apes*. Cambridge: Cambridge University Press.

Segerdahl, P., R. Fields, and S. Savage-Rumbaugh. 2006. *Kanzi's Primal Language*. London: Palgrave Macmillan.

Siebert, C. 2009. *The Wauchula Woods Accord: Toward a New Understanding of Animals*. New York: Scribner's.

Small, M. 1999. *Our Babies, Ourselves: How Biology and Culture Shape the Way We Parent*. New York: Anchor.

Tanner, Joanne. 2009. Unpublished PowerPoint presentation, American Society for Primatologists meeting, September.

Wise, S. 2000. *Rattling the Cage: Towards Legal Rights for Animals*. New York: Perseus.

Wise, S. 2006. *Drawing the Line: Science and the Case for Animal Rights*. New York: Basic Books.

Neuroscience and Spirituality

Eric Bergemann, Daniel J. Siegel,
Deanie Eichenstein, and Ellen Streit

A human being is a part of the whole, called by us "Universe," a part lim-
ited in time and space. He experiences himself, his thoughts and feelings as
something separated from the rest, a kind of optical delusion of his con-
sciousness. This delusion is a kind of prison for us, restricting us to our
personal desires and to affection for a few persons nearest to us. Our task
must be to free ourselves from this prison by widening our circle of com-
passion to embrace all living creatures and the whole of nature in its
beauty. Nobody is able to achieve this completely, but the striving for such
achievement is in itself a part of the liberation and a foundation for inner
security.

Einstein 1972

This chapter focuses on the integration of ideas from the fields of neuroscience and spirituality in their efforts to expand our knowledge of what it
means to be human. Utilizing the words of Albert Einstein regarding the
"optical delusion of our consciousness," we will explore the ways in which
the human brain creates a cortically constructed view of a separate self that
we propose spiritual practices strive to deconstruct in a variety of ways. The
universal teachings of wisdom traditions and religions throughout the ages
reveal the powerful ways in which our species has struggled to create a way
of being in which we can find a deep sense of meaning in realizing the true
nature of our interconnected relationships with one another and with the
larger world in which we live.

Part I: Spirituality and the Self

At a recent education conference, we asked dozens of people about their definition of spirituality. Though each person gave a different answer to the question, "What is spirituality?" we found that people consistently spoke about an awareness of being connected to something larger than their individual skin-defined body. Parallel to Einstein's statement, the conference participants' responses suggest that spirituality can be defined as a knowing or awareness of the interconnectedness of all things in nature. Yet, as will be defined more thoroughly in the next section on neuroscience and the self, our brains are hardwired to experience ourselves as separate individuals contained within our own skin who exist for a finite amount of time, or, "a part limited in time and space." Perhaps our notion of spirituality moves our conceptualizing minds farther along an evolutionary path toward what science has recently begun to show — that at the quantum level, reality exists not as finite, separately quantifiable matter, but as open possibility that is "part of a dynamic web of interactions" (Wallace and Hodel 2008: 50).

When we define ourselves as limited by time and space, we embrace a perspective that constrains us spatially to our skin and temporally to about 100 years of existence. Spirituality can be viewed as an attempt to expand that sense of identity beyond just the physical aspect of our bodily selves. Neuroscience provides us with new insights into how neural processes shape our mental life and in turn influence the developing sense of self. In this chapter, we will attempt to show how these two ways of knowing, the fields of spirituality and neuroscience, intersect to offer a revised view of the self.

Neuroscience and spirituality have often existed in disharmony, with neuroscience taking the material view of reality and spirituality taking a more mystical perspective. Both have frequently fallen short in offering a complete view of existence. For example, Thompson (2007) states that "a complete science of the mind needs to account for subjectivity and consciousness" (2007: 3), yet we have no explanation from a material perspective of how these phenomena arise. Likewise, spirituality has often been ungrounded and vaguely defined in its attempt to explain reality based on mystical beliefs frequently lacking in measurable physical properties.

However, a perspective that takes a more integrative approach to mental reality, or the mind, comes from Interpersonal Neurobiology (IPNB; Siegel 1999, 2007, 2010a, 2010b). IPNB defines the mind, in part, as an embodied and relational process that regulates the flow of energy and information. This flow occurs within the body, including the brain and extended nervous system. Energy and information are also shared between people. In this way, the mind uses both the brain and relationships to create itself. This is an important starting point for our discussion of spirituality. Since spirituality is a widespread human phenomenon, it is important to explore how the mind of *Homo sapiens sapiens,* the one who knows it knows, creates its drive toward becoming aware of being part of a larger whole.

One Plane of Reality

We can consider a model where there are two distinct elements or sides of human reality. The first, the material element, exists in the spatial dimension, or the visible, tangible material world. This realm includes physical matter that can be seen, touched, heard, and manipulated. The second, the mental element, exists in the experiential dimension, or the subjective world. This realm includes our internal sense of life, our thoughts and emotions which, while having neural correlates, can only be known directly through reflective experience. No one has ever visibly seen a thought or a feeling of happiness, yet we do have a subjective experience of what they are.

Dualism would tell us that there is an unbridgeable gap between the physical and the mental. We could accept this gap as a fact of dualism, or we could remove the gap by the reductionist approach of scientific materialism, saying that the brain is primary. We could also bridge the gap by adding an empirically unprovable magical ingredient through ungrounded incarnations of spirituality (Thompson 2007). In any of these cases, we are leaving out the possibility of mutually developing phenomena that exist because they arise together. Searle (2004) refers to this co-arising as conscious states that are biological processes with a subjective ontology. That is, they only exist if they are experienced by a conscious subject.

To elucidate this latter perspective, we can begin to think of a single plane of reality that has two sides, the spatial material side and the experiential mental side (see Figure 1). Both are integral to the human experience, and one is not more real than the other. Energy manifests itself in the physical properties of the material domain, and information coalesces as mental activity in the experiential domain. Each side influences the other, but neither exists in the other's domain. That is, matter is distinct from experience, but they arise together in parallel processes.

How and where do physical matter and subjective experience meet? We might be asking the same question if we queried, what is the meeting point

Figure 1. The Plane of Possibility

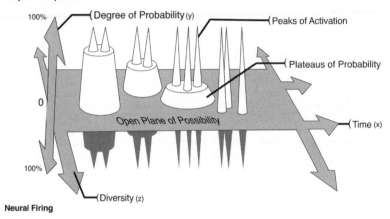

This is a visual metaphor for embracing several dimensions of human experience. (1) We can envision that our primes of neural firing (below the plane) and mental subjective experience (above the plane) reflect one another — and sometimes one "leads" the other, as brain drives subjective experience or the focus of attention drives neural firing across time (the x-axis). (2) Based on degrees of probability, the y-axis (vertically above and below the plane) graphs when open possibility exists in the plane (as in open mindful awareness), or certainty manifests at a peak of activation (a particular thought, feeling, memory — and their parallel in neural firing). (3) The diversity of mental experience or neural firing possible is symbolized along the z-axis (away and toward you in the plane) so that the wider the zone in this axis, the more variety of neural firing/mental experience possible. The plane is wide open; the plateau is broad or narrow, but limited in its diversity; a peak of activation is singular in its array of mental experience or neural firing. (4) A peak represents a specific activation of mind or brain instantiated in that instant — activations that are committed to manifest as that particular activity in that moment of time. A plateau represents a state of mind or profile of neural firing that may have various shapes and degrees of height and broadness: lower means less certainty of which firings might be possible and wider signifies more variety, a wider set of propensities; higher indicates more probability of firing of those options that are "primed" to occur in that state or profile, and narrower indicates a more restricted set of choices of which peaks might arise from that particular plateau. The open plane of possibility reveals a zero probability that any particular peak or plateau will arise and thus represents an open state of mindful awareness and a receptive neural profile at that moment. Used with permission from *The Mindful Therapist*, by Daniel J. Siegel, M.D. Copyright 2010 Mind Your Brain, Inc.

of neuroscience and spirituality? Neuroscience is typically concerned with the physical neural properties of reality, and spirituality is concerned with our subjective experience in life. How and where do these two perspectives arise together?

Quantum physics shows us that before particles become actualized as matter, they first exist only as infinite possibility, a sort of open probability. We can view this in our model in the following manner. The closer we are to the open plane of possibility on the physical side, the more broad a range of possibilities exists. Matter becomes actualized as it moves away from the plane, up into the spatial side of existence. Similarly, an infinite combination of possible mental experiences exists initially on the experiential side of the plane. Mental subjective states become experienced as specific thoughts or emotions the farther away one moves from the plane. Simultaneous to these experiences, neural firing patterns arise on the physical side of the plane. The plane of possibility itself is like a field of open potential before material and mental phenomena arise on either side.

Within this theoretical framework, the two sides of the one plane of reality meet at the common ground of time. That is, both physical properties of a material nature such as neural firing patterns and the subjective side of mental properties of our internal experiences both happen in time. Changes in one domain are correlated temporally with changes in the other. Energy, a physical property, and information, a mental property, flow together in patterns to shape both spatial and experiential emergence simultaneously. We can define these patterns of energy and information flow as emerging from regulatory processes that bridge the spatial and experiential sides of human reality. These regulatory processes happen in time, and serve to bind matter and experience. We use the term "correlation" in science to express this temporal synchronization of experience and the emergence of changes in measurable matter.

A useful term that might be used to illuminate patterns of activity in matter and in experience is "integration," defined as the linkage of differentiated elements. Through integration, the correlated interweaving of the material and mental sides of reality results in harmonious functioning. Complexity theory tells us that when integration is blocked from occurring, systems develop rigidity and/or chaos. In our model, a lack of integration would involve disruptions in the energy and information flow of both the material and mental sides of reality. In an unintegrated state, the material domain moves toward rigidity as inflexible neural firing patterns are experienced as habitual states. Similarly, chaos can ensue and random neural firing patterns can be experienced as untethered thoughts and emotions.

This brings us to the intersection of neuroscience and spirituality. Recall our earlier definition of spirituality as a connection to a larger whole beyond our spatially and temporally defined selves. When fully realized, that membership in the interconnected whole we seek can be viewed as attunement. In attunement, bodily resonance circuits produce the material manifestation in which neural states and signals are aligned and approximated in reciprocal time-based and spatially manifest ways. For example, interpersonal attunement results in what Ed Tronick has called "dyadic states of expanded consciousness" (Tronick 2007). This material attunement of shared neural signaling in space is coupled in time with the other side of the reality plane, the mental experience of a subjective sense of harmony, peace, connection, and at-one-ness.

An example of this is mutual eye-gazing between mother and infant. Neuroscience research has shown that bodily resonance circuits allow the mother to serve as regulator of the developing infant's internal homeostasis (Ovtscharoff and Braun 2001). Through these neural circuits, the attuned mother matches her infant's internal state and offers bodily based regulation. The mother's body temperature, for example, automatically changes to accommodate the needs of the infant. In this integrated state — the linkage of differentiated elements into a functional whole — the mother may also simultaneously have the experience of feeling a connection to something that is beyond her view of self as limited by space and time. Higher degrees of integration lead her to an experience that expands her sense of self: the whole is truly greater than the sum of the parts. This is the deep nature of expansion that accompanies integration.

In other words, when the material side of the plane of reality begins to involve an attunement with others that has resonance beyond our skin-defined selves, when we become aware of being a part of a larger whole, we have the mental experience of spirituality. Spirituality is the experience; resonance is the spatial correlate. Spirituality and resonance are the temporally coupled elements of high degrees of integration within the wholeness of reality.

Neuroscience offers a systematic approach to identifying material elements and studying their properties and interactions. Spirituality is also a way of knowing, but rather than the knowing of science that begins in the quantifiable spatial/material domain, spirituality begins in the equally real, yet different, often nonquantifiable experiential domain. Spirituality (the state of experience in which we are aware of a larger interconnectedness of all things) and science can find common ground through the framework of integration, the linking of disparate elements into a functional whole. With this, the felt experience of spirituality can be studied by the systematic methodologies of neuroscience, and the self can begin to be viewed and experienced in an expanded way beyond the boundaries initially defined by cortically constrained notions of neurally identified limits in time and space.

Part II: Neuroscience and the Self

Cultural Factors Supporting an Optical Delusion

Modern westernized culture emphasizes and encourages separateness, not interconnectedness. It can often feel as if, every step of the way, youth are entering into a new competition. In high school, there is often a quiet battle between students, a Cold War of sorts, in which it seems as though many are fighting to have the highest grades, the largest number of extracurricular activities, and the most leadership positions in order to get accepted to the highest-ranked university. In college, many students fight to beat the grade curve, rack up the largest number of internships, and gain the most work experience in order to be accepted to the best medical, graduate, or business school, or to be chosen for the highest-paying entry-level job. Then in the workplace, colleagues are often trying to prove that they have worked hard enough for the promotion everyone is hoping for, and neighbors want to have the most square feet on the block. We are literally programmed to focus on the "I," the "me," and the "mine." We are taught to believe that if we don't, if instead we invest our time in building a strong sense of "we," we will not succeed.

But how do we go from "you versus me" to "we"? How can we remove the optical delusion of our separateness?

Einstein addressed this notion of the self when he said, "He [a human being] experiences himself, his thoughts and feelings as something separated from the rest, a kind of optical delusion of his consciousness." From the moment we learn to recognize our reflection in a mirror, to see the face staring back at us and know it to be our own, we begin to see ourselves as a separate and unique entity. And why shouldn't we? Each of us has our own physical body, our own fingers, eyes, and mouths. We are not physically literally linked to anyone, and we each have our own thoughts, opinions, and feelings. Naturally we build relationships with friends, family, and even enemies, but ultimately, we see ourselves as separate: "We are born alone, we die alone." As it turns out, this self-centered view is not solely a product of societal norms, but in fact has a neurological basis behind it. The human neo-cortex constructs its own vision of reality. And one of those realities is the il-lusion of a continuous and a separate self. Rather than seeing the interconnected role we play in a larger whole — as one specialized cell in a complex living organism where each organ system depends on the others for their survival as a whole — we instead have neural patterns that create a sense of our isolation, independence, and, ultimately, one-of-a-kind notion of a "me." What hope, then, is there in fighting a natural proclivity for this neural delusion?

The Plastic Brain

Contrary to what neuroscientists for many years believed to be true, our brains are not fixed and rigid entities. Rather, culture actually provides us with experiences that alter the structure and therefore the function of the brain itself. Neural networks made up of millions of neurons throughout the brain are formed through experiences and learned associations, and with each new experience, new connections are made. This neural molding, known as "neuroplasticity," occurs each and every time we have a new experience (see Doidge 2007). With each new experience, patterns of neurons fire, and with each instance of neural firing there is the potential to create new synapses linking neurons to one another, to strengthen old synaptic connections, and to stimulate the growth of new neurons that enable even more connections to be made, processes called synaptogenesis and neuro-genesis.

The way we act and behave and the way each of us views situations is in-fluenced by past experiences. Neuroplasticity and prior learning allow for "top-down processing" that is different from the "bottom-up processing" we rely on as small children when experiencing everything for the first time. We allow our associations created by our past experiences and embedded in the neural networks of our memory stores, the "top," to influence the way we fil-ter our perception of things, the "down." Whereas a four-year-old child navi-gates through her senses — sight, taste, touch, sound, and smell — from the "bottom up," she subsequently learns to consolidate these perceptions into learned ideas and to store those ideas in her memory. Top-down processing emanates from these consolidated learned events, and in modern culture can give us an identity of a self that is separate from everyone else, that exists as a unique and self-sufficient entity, because it uses our past experiences within contemporary society, yet unique to each of us, to dictate our reactions to future experiences.

Brain Structure

Before overall brain structure can be reviewed, let us first offer a brief overview of cortical architecture. In fetal development, the brain develops from the lower areas first. At the lowest level within the skull rests the brainstem, which connects the top of the spinal cord to the limbic area. The brainstem carries out our most basic survival processes, including regulating heart rate and respiration, monitoring internal body temperature, and controlling certain visceral aspects of the fight-or-flight-or-freeze response. Moving farther up we find the limbic area, which is involved in the creation along with the brainstem in generating motivational states and the processes of emotion, attachment, and memory. The limbic area, brainstem, and body-proper are each below the cortex and therefore are called the subcortical regions, which serve as vital connections between our nonrational somatic and emotional input and our consciousness-generating cortical regions above (Siegel 2007). The brainstem and limbic areas are fundamentally responsible for our survival in that they drive our motivational states, causing us to seek more oxygen when we are deprived of it, find a source of food when malnourished, and run from life-threatening danger.

However, our lives are about much more than simply surviving, and this is where the modern neocortex comes in. The cortex, or outer bark, of the brain is responsible for more complex processes, including perception, planning, and attention. The last part of the brain to develop in both individual development and our human evolutionary history, the cortex is not yet well developed at birth, so it is the most susceptible to influence by experiences. It comprises six layers, starting at the bottom of the cortex and moving toward the top (see Figure 2). The bottom (layers 6, 5, and 4) carries information forward from our basic sensations from the outside or inner world. The top (layers 1, 2, and 3) is in charge of our perceptual filters from prior learning, motor plans, and thought. The frontmost part of the frontal lobe of the cortex, just behind the forehead, is the prefrontal cortex. This prefrontal region is responsible for carrying out the processes that make us uniquely human. The side of this area controls our working memory, often called the "chalkboard of the mind." The middle prefrontal areas receive information from a wide array of neural zones — from the cortex itself, the limbic zones, the brainstem, and the body-proper. The insula cortex is one part of this middle region that serves as an information superhighway relaying data from the body upward into the prefrontal area and enabling a sense of self-awareness. This middle area of the prefrontal cortex is also involved in making neural firing patterns that represent others' minds, vital for social communication and self-observation (Siegel 2010a). The middle aspects of the prefrontal region essentially link the body, brainstem, limbic areas, and even the social signals from other brains with the cortex.

One view of the way the six layers function within the cortex is that incoming data streams "bottom-up" to enable us to have sensations of our outside or inner world. At the same time, memory processes trigger a "top-down" flow in which prior learning influences the flow of data from layer 1 to 2 to 3. As top-down at layer 3 meets bottom-up at layer 4, the two streams collide and the outcome of this mingling directly influences our experience of awareness in that moment in time. How we shape the balance of top-down and bottom-up determines our experience of consciousness (see Siegel 2007, 2010b). In this way, experiences in our families and our larger cultural milieu will influence how top-down perception shapes and filters our ongoing conscious experience of the world and of the self. As there is no "immaculate perception," our sense of an "I" will be sculpted by the neural top-down views we've learned earlier in our lives.

Spiritual practices may work at this very basic level of freeing our bottom-up from the potential prisons of top-down.

From Toxic to Awakened Top-Down Processing

Recall that Einstein stated that the view that each of us is separate from the rest is an "optical delusion of his consciousness." He continued: "This delusion is a kind of prison for us, restricting us to our personal desires and to affection for a few persons nearest to us." The truth is, the separate and distinctive "I" we each tend to see ourselves as may merely be a construct of our plastic cortex, shaped by external and internal experiences. Our society places tremendous emphasis on the individual, and we find ourselves following a "survival of the fittest" ideology of sorts. The first three layers of our cortex learn to see the world through an "I-centric" lens. If *I* waste my time connecting and resonating with the world around me, allowing myself the time to build deeper connections with my friends and even those I do not know, *I* am wasting precious moments that could be better spent finish-

Figure 2. A Schematic of the Six-Layered Neocortex and the Bottom-Up and Top-Down Flow of Information.

Layer	Top-Down	Top-Down Dominance	Top-Down
1	⇓⇓⇓⇓	⇓	
2	⇓⇓⇓⇓	⇓	
3	⇓⇓⇓⇓	⇓	
AWARENESS	⇒→⇒→	→⇒⇒⇒	⇒→→→→→
4	↑	↑	↑↑↑↑↑
5	↑	↑	↑↑↑↑↑
6	↑	↑	↑↑↑↑↑
	Bottom-Up	Bottom-Up	Bottom-Up Dominance

Information from sensation flows "bottom-up" from the lower layers of the cortex streaming from layers 6 to 5 to 4. Information from prior learning, called "top-down," streams from layers 1 to 2 to 3. Awareness is thought to emerge by the co-mingling of these two streams. In the first condition, bottom-up and top-down are balanced and the resultant awareness blends the two streams. In the second condition, top-down input is dominant and prior expectations and categorizations overshadow incoming sensory streams within awareness. In the third condition, sensory input in the here-and-now is dominant, and awareness reflects a predominance of input from this sensory flow. Mindfulness may enable layer 3/4 intermingling to disentangle these two streams by at first practicing enhancement of the bottom-up flow of present sensory experience. Used with permission from *The Mindful Therapist*, by Daniel J. Siegel, M.D. Copyright 2010 Mind Your Brain, Inc.

ing my errands so that *I* can return home, meet *my* deadlines, and advance *my* career. I, me, and mine form the top-down filter through which I appraise what has merit and warrants my focus of attention. Family and society provide the experiences and knowledge that influence the way our top-down processing filters incoming information. Needless to say, a society that provides for experiences that teach the importance of the individual will create a constrained form of top-down processing that ignores the opportunity to encourage people to connect and nurture the development of others. We are taught to see ourselves as separate and thus have a cortically embedded top-down view of ourselves as "separate from the rest."

The potential exists, however, for us to intentionally create a top-down view that sees us as interconnected rather than individual, and this is precisely where we can see the intersection of neuroscience and spirituality becoming essential in shaping the course of cultural evolution and therefore the personal development of identity. In the previous section, we defined spirituality as "the state of experience in which we are aware of a larger interconnectedness of all things." Achieving a degree of spirituality that creates a sense that we are part of a greater whole is directly linked to neural circuits involved with attunement and resonance. When we allow the mind, or the process that regulates the flow of energy and information that occurs within the body and our relationships with one another, to embrace the reality that this flow interconnects us all, we expand our constrained sense of a separate self to an awakened sense of an interdependent whole self. When a mother uses her neural circuits to resonate with her baby, she no longer feels like a separate entity, but rather feels deeply interconnected with her child. And let's say for a moment that that same mother also allowed her body and mind to resonate with everyone else around her, including friends and even strangers. She would then find herself feeling deeply interconnected with the world around her, and thus part of something much larger than a single body limited to her skin. This is both the nature of mother, and mother nature.

Spiritual practices have the power to reimmerse us in bottom-up processing so that we can become freed from the top-down optical delusion of our separateness. They expose us once again to the bottom-up experiences and feelings of resonance we relied on as children so that we can see the true nature of reality. This is spirituality writ large. Spirituality is a tool we can use to expand our top-down view of the self to one that allows for resonance and recognizes that we are truly a part of a larger whole. If our prior experiences repeatedly push us to see ourselves as separate and unique, they become the filter that our top-down processing uses to bias how we see the world and our "selves." Spiritual practices offer to help us construct a very different story, one that defines us as belonging to something much larger, something not constrained by the limitations of time and space. Spirituality essentially opens us up to much of the bottom-up processing we lost in leaving our youth because it loosens the filter our top-down processing uses to experience the world around us. The good news for all of us is that while our society may train us to see ourselves as separate, our brains have the capacity and incredible ability to change: this may be the reason why, for thousands of years, our human ancestors have found the need for the liberation that spiritual disciplines offered. New experiences facilitate neuroplasticity, so with repeated spiritual practices our brains can adjust to new ways of thinking about the self. We have the power to use our awakened minds to train our brains to see ourselves as part of an interconnected whole.

Part III: The Neuroscience of Spirituality and the Spirituality of Neuroscience

With a working definition of spirituality including the awareness of the interconnected nature of reality and our realization that we are a part of a larger whole beyond the boundaries of a skin-defined self, we can explore the ways in which our nervous system plays a fundamental role in spiritual life. We can also dive deeply into how studying the connections among brain, mind, and relationships within interpersonal neurobiology is imbued with a "spiritual dimension" as we come to realize, through science, that the sense of a separate self is in fact an illusion of the brain's own making. Dissolving this neural creation may be an essential outcome of a variety of contemplative and mindfulness practices.

As we step back from our individual experience of having personal histories, separate bodies, and continual endeavors to survive and try to thrive in these modern times, we see that throughout the continuum of recorded history people have explored the nature of reality. We are a storytelling, meaning-making species. Questions about how the physical universe is created, what the fundamental forces of nature are, how we play a role as human beings in the world, and where we go after death may have been essential questions that plagued our ancestors as much as they are part of our contemporary concerns. By viewing the differences between the right and the left hemispheres, we can come to see that the logical, linguistic, linear, and literal processing left side of the brain has the drive to tell the story of our lives — to make logical, linear sense out of what we perceive. One distinction between our brains and those of the great apes is that the left and right sides of the cortex are even more isolated from one another in our human neural architecture (Semendeferi 2009). This anatomical finding makes potential separations in function even more pronounced in our human experience. The right side of the brain has a dominant mode of processing, for example, that is in contrast to the left as it takes things in as they are, generates visual imagery, sends and receives nonverbal signals, and creates maps of the whole body and our autobiographical memory. Faced with existential inquiries into reality, we do the best we can to weave stories that make sense of our right hemisphere perceptions and recollections with our left hemisphere drive to explain the world with our own invented brand of logic and reasoning.

When we also realize that the human cortex has evolved to have both maps of our perceptions that create self-awareness of our bodies in space as well as maps that correlate with the emergence of a complex self-knowing awareness in which we connect past, present, and future, we can see that a "self" may also be an elaborate cortical construction. As our most forward region of the brain, the prefrontal area, enables us to have a perception of the future and contemplate the past, we come to perceive the existential realities of our finite existence: where we are now is not where we will be in the far, or even near, future. We learn that time undoes us all — that life is a death sentence. The challenge of being human is to somehow feel at ease with an awareness of our transience, to appreciate the present and not become obsessed with the future, or the past. This prefrontal challenge also entails not taking the "self" too seriously, or, ironically, not taking it too personally. The self is just another notion, a perceptual construction, an idea, an organizing sensibility, which serves as a center of narrative gravity around which the story of "me" and of "you" unfolds. But this story, too, is just a construction.

The Neuroscience of Spirituality

The neuroscience of spirituality offers us a clue as to the universal practice of encouraging some intentional mental training outside the norm of everyday living to find peace in life. These are mindfulness practices that liberate us from the prison of cortical contraptions that limit our living in the present moment. Not only are mindfulness practices found across cultures and eras, but across all major forms of religion we find that the teaching that we are a part of "one" interconnected whole is a fundamental lesson. Sometimes buried beneath the rules and regulations of specific religions, this universal teaching of the interconnected nature of all beings is the essential element of what we can call contemplation or spirituality. These practices unite us, rather than dividing us into separate and sometimes warring camps. With spirituality there is an invitation for all to participate, whatever their background. The neuroscience of this realization of our interconnectedness is perhaps something that requires effort to awaken the mind to the nature of reality beyond cortical construction: the natural "delusion of our separateness" is a by-product of the modern human cortex that imprisons our lives and necessitates an antidote from its inherently toxic and dividing effects. Top-down experience reinforces culturally shaped neural proclivities that incline the brain to structure the mental experience of self as separate. The result may be a near catastrophe that only awakening the mind to this entrapment might turn into a far and distant memory of a brush with annihilation. Now more than ever in our overcrowded and warming planet we need to embrace the interdependent nature of our collective lives.

The Spirituality of Neuroscience

Likewise, the spirituality of neuroscience may hold a promise for such human enlightenment. Though it is often stated that science is essentially value-free, it is possible to actually consider the notion that our drive for the understanding of truth actually contains within it a secular morality that places kindness and compassion at the heart of well-being. By viewing health as a universal value, we can see that modern studies of a life well-lived in areas of positive psychology and wisdom traditions reveal that treating others as you would have them treat you is not only a common teaching in various religions, but it may have a scientific underpinning. Here is how we can come to a view that kindness is at the heart of neuroscience and spirituality. In the field of interpersonal neurobiology we look toward the function of systems — of neurons, body organs, people, families, communities, and societies — to help us gain insights into flexible and adaptive ways of living. In this perspective, the process of linking differentiated elements into a functional whole emerges as perhaps a universal way in which systems move toward the most adaptive, energized state. The linkage of differentiated elements at the core of this coherent self-organization is called integration. When we experience the harmony of a choir in which the singers come together yet maintain their own unique contribution, we are immersed in the vitality of an integrated system. As mentioned earlier, without integration — when linkage and/or differentiation are not present — a system moves to chaos or rigidity, or both.

The notion of our interconnectedness also begins during the embryological development of the nervous system. After the sperm and egg merge and one cell is formed, we soon have two, then four, eight, sixteen, thirty-two, and then sixty-four cells. On and on, the growing conceptus finally becomes so large that some cells are located on the inside, and some are on the outer layer. The outer cells, the ectoderm, will go on to become our skin. But some of these ectodermal cells will invaginate and become the neural tube. The important issue is that our nervous system's very origins were to be at the interface of the outer and the inner. This function of connecting the inside and the outside places our nervous system in the important position of linking "us" to "them." We are hardwired to connect to one another.

This essential interpersonal nature of the brain is revealed further in the social nature of our mirror neuron and resonance systems — that from the very beginning of life outside of the womb, they enable us to perceive the intentional states of other people. We come to perceive others' nonverbal signals, ready ourselves to carry out similar actions in behavioral imitation, and also simulate their internal states in emotional resonance. Our nervous systems are constructed to connect.

Just going to a dance or athletic game reveals the ways in which two or more people attune to another's motion and emotion. We join with others, attune to their states, and come to resonate as each individual influences the state of the others. Resonance reveals how the notion of a separate self is an artificial construction, a mirage of the mind, an optical delusion of consciousness. Religious rituals may draw on these mirror neuron functions to enable us to sense the internal state — the intentional stance — of another person and then enact, through shared behaviors, the symbolic meanings embedded in that particular religion's narrative about the nature of our existence. Seen from afar, many religious practices commonly give people the experience of joining as one as they explore the stories of our interconnected nature. If only those interconnections would extend beyond the boundaries of a particular house of worship, beyond the definitions of the "in-group" and the "out-group" that are evolutionary remnants likely of a hostile and aggressive past. Those individuals without such distinctions between friend or foe were killed by opponents they considered kin; those who had such distinctions went on to reproduce and tell the stories of their survival.

With the spirituality of neuroscience we see that modern studies of neuroplasticity illuminate how we can use the focus of our attention to transform the brain's connections. If we see that the neuroscience of spirituality illuminates how the top-down cortical constraints falsely define a self as separate from the rest, then we can use the focus of our attention to liberate us from such destructive and delusional prisons. We can use science and spirituality to inspire us to rewire our brains. This is both the promise and the challenge of our human legacy. The question is, are we ready to awaken ourselves to the marriage of these two great ways of knowing truth?

Part IV: The Greater Implications of Spirituality

It is clear that there is a serious deficit of compassion in today's world, so much that it is hard not to become flooded with feelings of distress and disheartened by the overwhelming amount of turmoil and suffering that exists. Numbing and denial can result, with many people avoiding topics that make them feel impotent and fearful. In an attempt to ameliorate this disillusionment, this section highlights the importance of integrating spirituality into mainstream everyday life, in the hope of creating a more loving and livable world: a life in which compassion and kindness are not only honored, but cultivated as priorities in our societies. As we discussed earlier in the chapter, we know that we have the neurobiological potential to experience the feeling of interconnectedness. We aim to describe how the interplay between spirituality, empathy, and our biology could be a catalyst for social and global change.

Compassion and Spirituality

In our efforts to define spirituality, interesting questions arose: What is the difference between compassion and spirituality? What is the difference between a compassionate act and a spiritual one? Jack Kornfield's (2008) work succinctly answers these questions using the second principle of Buddhist psychology: "Compassion is our deepest nature. It arises from our interconnection with all things" (2008: 23). In other words, spirituality (what we are defining as the awareness of interconnectedness) is the root of compassion, inspiring acts of kindness. It seems the answer to these questions is that a compassionate act is indeed a spiritual act.

Spiritual growth manifests itself as both intrapersonal and interpersonal compassion, in other words, compassion for ourselves and for one another. In essence, spirituality, the awareness of our interconnectedness, is a fundamental building block of empathy, a benevolent understanding of what another is feeling. Marco Iacoboni (2008) postulates that empathy is deeply rooted in our biological makeup as a result of our mirror neurons. These mirror neurons are cells that "re-create for us" (2008: 5) the emotions we see others experience. He explains, "our mirror neurons fire when we see others expressing their emotions, as if we were making those facial expressions ourselves" (2008: 119). In other words, this system enables us to emotionally resonate with others as well as read other people's intentions and motives. Ever wonder how fictional characters in a movie can make us cry? Just seeing celluloid images of a person undergoing a hardship can activate our mirror neurons, which then create in us a state in which we can actually feel what that person is feeling. Iacoboni argues that these mirror neurons are the foundation of empathy.

We all have this neurobiological gift, as Iacoboni calls it; an instinct to empathize. But just reading people's emotions is not necessarily benevolent. In fact, it can be used in dangerous, manipulative ways. Imagine an emotionally aware sociopath. Nothing is more frightening than someone who can detect what you are feeling and what matters to you and then use these insights into your inner world in order to harm. This is why spirituality is imperative: to serve as the link between our neurological ability to empathize and actually putting it into practice through acts of kindness and compassion. Nothing guarantees a link between empathy and action. Our focus of attention on the internal world combined with our kind intentions moves us to act compassionately. It is exciting to hypothesize that if we embraced our interconnectedness and enacted a compassionate understanding of one another, we could then cultivate and channel our empathy from indifference or malevolence into positive action for a greater good.

Spirituality as a Fundamental Component of Policy, Religion, and Science

An overwhelming amount of political conflict is rooted in tensions between various ethnicities, nationalities, religions, sexual orientations, and other human dimensions that lead to an "in-group" versus "out-group" set of distinctions. From apathetic governments who ignore vicious genocides to the gluttonous depletion of the earth's resources, the root of much political turmoil can be deconstructed as a result of this disconnection, estrangement, and apathy, if not outright animosity, toward one another.

Public policy, religion, and science are each different types of organizational constructs to which people turn for solutions, inspiration, and leadership. As international crises persist, it becomes more and more evident that these structures alone are not providing solutions, nor can they erase our self-created movement toward oblivion. Policy change alone cannot undo the prevalent perceptions that underlie prejudice, nor can it teach compassion or reveal the interconnected nature of reality. These are things we need to extract from spirituality in order to conceive, initiate, implement, and maintain a sustainable change.

As with public policy, religion also has not succeeded in correcting these injustices. Religion, although seemingly similar to spirituality, historically has had divisive qualities that spirituality — by our definition — does not. Where spirituality considers community on a macro level, seeing ourselves as part of a greater whole, religions tend to build ritualistic communities that can become insulated, separated from other groups. This is a prime example in which empathy can exist and even be encouraged very much within groups but not extended to others, as we feel "separated from the rest . . . only feeling affection for a few persons nearest to us." In this way, as discussed earlier, many religions may be at risk of perhaps even inadvertently creating an "in-group" versus "out-group" mentality, rendering their role in society as a wedge creating a greater divide between us. Yet the various religious doctrines and a secular approach to spirituality are not mutually exclusive by any means. Therefore we hope that religious and secular individuals alike can channel their connectedness to one another and "widen [their] circle of compassion to embrace all."

Science functions as yet another societal force to which some turn for solutions to modern-day struggles. Throughout history, there has been an inherent division between science and religion, leaving many clutching tightly to one view or the other. This compartmentalized approach further alienates us from realizing interdisciplinary connections and possible solutions for which our world is so badly aching. However, the world cannot rely on the extremes of either perspective, as scientific reductionism or fanatical religion alone may be unable to bridge the divide between these ways of exploring reality. Fundamental pieces are missing at the extremes of each: science does not have a foundation of morals, and religion does not have an empirical approach to discovering truth, including reevaluating what is of proven value and what is untrue and in need of revision. Spirituality may thus function as a bridge between the two. Spirituality encompasses a secular, ethical mysticism rooted in our neurobiology that can provide a "global ethic" (Kauffman 2008) inclusive of believers and nonbelievers alike.

If we can introduce the mainstream to a secular educational practice to train our mind to fight against this "optical delusion" of our cortical top-down constraints on the sense of a self and experience spirituality, compassion could become a fundamental part of our daily life. When we are living on automatic with an unawakened mind, the brain may push us to experience a distinct and singular "self," an identity separate from others. This neural propensity to shape our mental and relational experiences in this manner can have large-scale repercussions as it limits our more widely focused compassion that is rooted in our interconnectedness. Fortunately, we possess the mental tools to suspend the cortically mediated and culturally sanctioned illusion that perpetuates our disconnection. We can intentionally awaken our minds to this neural vulnerability and move the direction of cultural evolution toward compassion. Indeed, "kindness and compassion are to the brain what the breath is to life" (Siegel 2010b). Awakening the mind to our interconnected nature is good for our health and good for our relationships (Gilbert 2010). If we can harvest this perspective into an awareness of our interdependence, then hopefully acts of compassion will follow suit as we "widen our circle of compassion." Of course, as Einstein said, "Nobody is able to achieve this completely, but the striving for such an achievement is in itself a part of the liberation and a foundation for inner security" — in essence, a spiritual act itself. Spirituality does not just occur; it is an active process that needs to be taught, cultivated, and practiced in order to preserve and improve the world in which we all live.

REFERENCES

Doidge, N. 2007. *The Brain That Changes Itself: Stories of Personal Triumph from the Frontiers of Brain Science*. New York: Penguin.

Einstein, A. 1972. As cited in the *New York Times*. In J. Kabat-Zinn (1990), *Full Catastrophe Living: Using the Wisdom of Your Body and Mind to Face Stress, Pain, and Illness*. New York: Dell.

Gilbert, P. 2010. *The Compassionate Mind: A New Approach to Life's Challenges*. Oakland, CA: New Harbinger Press.

Iacoboni, M. 2008. *Mirroring People: The New Science of How We Connect with Others*. New York: Farrar, Straus & Giroux.

Kauffman, S. 2008. *Reinventing the Sacred: A New View of Science, Reason, and Religion*. New York: Basic Books.

Kornfield, J. 2008. *The Wise Heart: A Guide to the Universal Teachings of Buddhist Psychology*. New York: Bantam.

Ovtscharoff, W., Jr., and K. Braun. 2001. Maternal separation and social isolation modulate the postnatal development of synaptic composition in the infralimbic cortex of *Octodon degus*. *Neuroscience* 104: 33-40.

Searle, J. R. 2004. *Mind: A Brief Introduction*. New York: Oxford University Press.

Semendeferi, K. 2009. Neuroanatomical perspectives on the evolution of the mind. Presentation given at UCLA Center for Behavior, Evolution, and Culture, 11/09/09.

Siegel, D. J. 1999. *The Developing Mind: Toward a Neurobiology of Personal Experience*. New York: Guilford.

Siegel, D. J. 2007. *The Mindful Brain: Reflection and Attunement in the Cultivation of Well-Being*. New York: W. W. Norton.

Siegel, D. J. 2010a. *Mindsight: The New Science of Personal Transformation*. New York: Bantam.

Siegel, D. J. 2010b. *The Mindful Therapist: A Clinician's Guide to Mindsight and Neural Integration.* New York: W. W. Norton.

Thompson, E. 2007. *Mind in Life: Biology, Phenomenology, and the Sciences of Mind.* Cambridge, MA: Harvard University Press.

Tronick, E. 2007. *The Neurobehavioral and Social-Emotional Development of Infants and Children.* New York: W. W. Norton.

Wallace, B. A., and B. Hodel. 2008. *Embracing Mind: The Common Ground of Science and Spirituality.* Boston: Shambhala.

In Search of "Folk Anthropology": The Cognitive Anthropology of the Person

Emma Cohen and Justin L. Barrett

Everyday notions about personhood exhibit considerable cross-cultural variability, as documented in the vast anthropological literature on the subject. A growing corpus in developmental psychology suggests also that naturally emerging, panhuman constraints and biases inform the ways in which humans reason about persons and the social world in general. Despite the obvious potential for constructive dialogue and theory refinement across these two perspectives, there has been little such engagement to date. In this chapter, we seek to develop an ethnographically and psychologically informed understanding of personhood that bridges nativist and cultural-relativist or "blank slate" approaches. Species-specific, naturally emerging cognitive predispositions constrain the range of variability in person-related concepts cross-culturally (e.g., to do with what is intuitively recognizable as an intentional agent/action, how individual identity is construed, how people think about the relation between biological and psychological properties of the person, etc.). It does not follow, however, that no interesting variability exists. Patterns of systematic variation can be explained with reference to the interaction between specific cognitive capacities and unique features of specific cultural and historical settings. The balanced approach advanced here aims to establish a nascent comparative cognitive anthropology of the person upon an empirically and theoretically sound foundation.

In a few short decades, the cognitive sciences have made remarkable advances in our understanding of some of life's greatest and most alluring mysteries. Weighty, existential questions that were once the exclusive province of philosophical introspection have been illuminated and informed by systematic, empirical scrutiny into the content of human (and other) minds: What makes humans unique? How do newborn infants think? Do all people perceive the world similarly? Do we perceive the world accurately? What are the mechanisms of thought, inference, belief, feeling, logic, intuition, and morality? Why did they evolve and how are they formed?

Of course, there are no conclusive answers to these problems — soul has been made flesh, but precisely how flesh makes soul remains uncertain. Nevertheless, there have been illuminating and sometimes fascinating discoveries. This is perhaps particularly true for the area of the cognitive sciences that deals with how human minds understand the world of other minds and persons. In this chapter, we attempt to draw together relevant empirical developments from this area from two main domains of the cognitive sciences — developmental psychology and sociocultural anthropology. On the whole, both disciplines conduct their empirical business without much regard for each other's theories or findings. Despite these divergent trajectories, however, it is clear (at least to this anthropologist and psychologist) that there is much scope for mutually beneficial dialogue and collaboration.

To help begin our task, reflect for a brief moment on whether there are any other persons in your immediate vicinity as you read this book. For most readers, this should be a straightforward cognitive task. In a split second, you can ascertain whether you are looking at someone or something. Entities are either persons or they are not, and you are quite adept at knowing your "who" from your "what." Or are you? What about a childhood teddy bear (that may or may not be in your immediate vicinity right now), or an unborn fetus, or cremated ashes, or a beloved pet, or virtual people on the television and in cartoons, or the talking computer, or the latest Robosapien android robot?[1] Even though the boundaries of your person category might be impervious to the inclusion of all of the above entities, Robosapiens and comic book characters are likely closer to a borderline case for most of us than the telegraph pole outside the window or the chicken breast fillet in the fridge.

But where does our conceptual category of the person come from? And what aspects of it are cross-culturally recurrent? As far as familiar, everyday entities go, few are more remote from our everyday category of the person

---

1. "Robosapien is more than a mechanical companion — he's a multi-functional, thinking, feeling robot, with attitude!" WowWee Robotics (http://www.wowwee.com/en/products/toys/robots/robotics/robosapiens:robosapien). Accessed 20 October 2009.

than the prepackaged supermarket fillet in the fridge. Yet, rich ethnographic descriptions of the practices surrounding hunting and eating in cultural contexts very different from our own suggest that in this, and many other respects, the boundaries of our person concept are not universally shared. In many Amerindian cosmogonies, for example, animals hunted as prey are routinely classed as persons, having capacities to act upon the world and interact with other persons (including humans) in complex social relations. Even the dead game animal does not become food until this agentive capacity to act toward and relate to others has been removed or neutralized through shamanic treatments. Cooking completes the process that transforms these persons into objects and that allows for a distinction between the cannibalistic consumption of persons and the noncannibalistic consumption of food (e.g., Fausto 2007: 504).

The capacity to distinguish inert things from entities that can act on the world and relate with others has surely been long critical for the survival and propagation of our species. The presence of elements of this capacity across many other species and from the earliest moments of human infancy suggests that this cognitive ability is not wholly socially acquired. How, then, is there so much apparent variability in categorization of persons and things cross-culturally? If these crucial cognitive processes are in the hands of safe, consistent, evolutionarily crafted, panhuman mechanisms, why would one group of humans firmly believe that peccaries are capable of avenging the hunter who violates the hunting code of ethics (for example, by gradually transforming the hunter into one of their own species and kin; e.g., Lima 1999) while another group considers only human beings as capable of entering into mutual contracts, and yet another considers dead ancestors, whose bodies have long decayed, to be the most formidable vindicators of all?

In current mainstream sociocultural anthropology, such questions are no longer the stuff of research, but rhetoric. Cultural variability is so immense that the influence of evolved cognitive mechanisms, insofar as they are thought to exist, is assessed as negligible. The operation of such mechanisms is, therefore, considered to be of little importance for the generation of interpretive analyses of meaning construction in the variable everyday lives of different people in different cultural contexts. This culturally constructed variability is something that anthropologists endeavor to describe and understand, not something that can be satisfactorily explained in terms of something else (e.g., history, cognition, ecology, evolution, etc.) (e.g., Lambek 1989; Boddy 1989).

Recently, however, an increasing number of anthropologists and others (including us) have firmly reinstated questions linking evolution, cognition, and culture as core research foci. Since the "interpretive turn" of the discipline several decades ago, advances in the evolutionary and cognitive sciences have warranted systematic reconsideration of the causal processes guiding the acquisition, transmission, stability, and variability of culture (e.g., Sperber 1996). The beliefs, ideas, and practices reported in the pages of ethnographies are obviously variable. It is less obvious, however, that they are not constrained in important ways by species-specific cognitive mechanisms, or that these cognitive mechanisms are wholly crafted through experience and learning. By reopening such issues for systematic inquiry, these anthropologists have adopted an expressly nondualistic position that — as is the case with the dazzling variety of movements that the human body can perform, and foods the digestive system can handle — variable mental outputs are, ultimately, biologically constrained.

Developmental psychologists investigating the emergence of cognitive abilities in infants and children have conducted some of the most important scholarship of relevance to perennial themes in anthropology. The view that infants and young children indiscriminately adopt basic theories about the world around them via social learning alone has been thoroughly challenged in recent years. Novel experimental techniques have revealed that very young infants exhibit preferences, expectations, and knowledge that could not have been wholly acquired through experience or social transmission. Early-emerging theories about the world, which permit young infants and children to make consistent predictions and inferences about how the world around them works, are the foundations of later developing and adult human cognition (e.g., Yamaguchi et al. 2009).

A vast literature now exists on how infants and children understand the social world — the world of persons. The bulk of evidence strongly suggests that expectations about what kinds of things count as persons and what kinds of things do not, emerge very early in human development. These core expectations guide infants' inferences about the behavior of people and objects in their environments, and are in place long before the cognitive capacities to learn detailed cultural norms about persons and things have fully developed (e.g., see Bloom 2004; Carey 2009; Gopnik, Meltzoff, and Kuhl 1999; Siegal 2008).

In this chapter, we provide a brief review of some of this evidence, focusing in particular on cognitive mechanisms that appear to underpin cross-culturally widespread aspects of person concepts that are commonly thought to be corporeal (such as physical and biological properties) in com-

parison with aspects of the person that commonly do not directly entail cor-
poreality, though they may be closely associated with bodily function (e.g.,
agency, mentality, individual identity). This evidence suggests that there are
basic cognitive mechanisms that facilitate reasoning about person-related
phenomena. Depending on the cognitive problem at hand, different mechanisms may be activated. These cognitive mechanisms generate different
kinds of outputs, including causal inferences pertaining to different kinds of
problems that we encounter throughout daily life. Many of these problems
are effortlessly solved well beneath our conscious radar. For example, we do
not have to resort to conscious reflection in order to figure out whether our
bodies can pass through walls, or whether we, as agents, can move our own
bodies in pursuit of our goals. Mechanisms underpinning such causal reasoning emerge early in human development, and enable us to make rapid intuitive sense of our surroundings, including the behaviors of other persons.

We suggest that appreciating how these mechanisms function can potentially provide a fruitful starting point from which to identify and compare like concepts in the cross-cultural record. A better understanding of the
sets of basic expectations entailed by the physical, biological, psychological,
and other aspects of person concepts cross-culturally can facilitate comparison and explanation of the forms these aspects take, and the generation of
hypotheses concerning which aspects are likely to be cross-culturally recurrent. Finally, an illustrative survey of relevant ethnographic examples demonstrates the potential usefulness of this approach and raises a series of
questions for further research at the intersection of anthropology and psychology.

Cognitive Foundations of Persons

Persons as Objects and Mentalizing Agents

The earliest developing foundation of our "naïve anthropology" concerns
the behavior of solid objects or bodies (e.g., Spelke 1994). From early in the
first year of life, for example, infants expect solid objects to follow continuous pathways through space, to cohere or hold together, and to not merge
with other solid objects or pass through them. Infants further appreciate that
one solid object cannot influence another from a distance, but only by coming into contact with it. Agents, of course, are an important exception to this
final principle. Do young infants also understand that agents, though they

are also physical objects, can stop and start of their own accord and can influence other agents from a distance? A series of studies suggests that infants distinguish between agents and nonagents (for overviews, see Rakison and Poulin-Dubois 2001; Wynn 2008). Infants appear to suspend the contact principle in the case of agents, appreciating that agents need not first be contacted by another object for motion to be initiated. Further research suggests that the first and principal agency-cues to which infants are sensitive concern motion, particularly that it is self-generated and noninertial. The attribution of an internal causal origin, or purpose, for self-propulsion is a subsequent developmental achievement. The young toddler's appreciation that there are entities that can move around in the pursuit of goals and hold beliefs and knowledge that influence behaviors builds upon this early foundation, and, in turn, provides the foundation for complex and sophisticated reasoning about the contents of other people's minds (and how this content might differ from the contents of ego's mind) (e.g., Wellman, Cross, and Watson 2001).

Some developmental psychologists have suggested that our early emerging ability to distinguish persons from things produces an interesting cognitive by-product: mind-body dualism (e.g., Bloom 2004; Wellman and Johnson 2008). They argue that different cognitive systems underpin the set of principles that are applied to agents and the set of principles that guide expectations about objects. The different cognitive mechanisms are activated by different stimuli (e.g., different forms of motion), and yield different kinds of outputs (e.g., explanations and expectations in terms of physical causality, or in terms of psychological causality). The autonomous functioning of these systems, their exclusive focus on either physical or psychological causality, and the incommensurability of their outputs, renders psychophysical dualism cognitively natural. Although children and adults can come to appreciate the interaction and interdependence of these two domains, the default stance is to see bodily and mental phenomena as occupying separate causal domains. Indeed, notions of disembodiment (e.g., at death, during soul flight, etc.) appear to be premised on the radically dualistic position that the functioning of the mind is not only causally independent of bodily function, but it can be spatially independent also. If the intuitive dualism thesis is correct, such ideas may be only a small elaboration upon a natural cognitive stance.

Persons as Living Things

Young children recognize that bodies are more than just physical objects. Another core domain of thought in children's developing naïve anthropology concerns biological phenomena, and specifically, what makes a living thing a living thing. The bodies of agents are not just capable of certain forms of motion, or of avoiding or colliding with other physical objects; human bodies live, grow, get ill, and die. Evidence suggests that children's developing understandings of these physiological processes are framed within a "vitalistic causality" (Inagaki and Hatano 2004). Children's core causal construct in understanding life appears to hinge on an unelaborated assumption of a vital power that is fortified via the ingestion of food and water, and that serves to sustain life and health, and permit growth. The child's vitalistic theory of biological function appears to give way to physiological accounts in later childhood and adulthood (Carey 1985). Yet, there has been very little relevant cross-cultural research investigating how widespread this apparent qualitative shift is. The question of whether vitalism is universally and completely replaced, or merely dampened or veneered by later-acquired biological theories, remains largely unexplored.

As with the causal segregation of the psychological and physical domains described above, children appear to assume that biological processes are largely insulated from psychological causes. Four-year-old children distinguish biological phenomena from physical and mental phenomena, attributing different sorts of causes to events in each domain (e.g., Inagaki and Hatano 2002; Schult and Wellman 1997). They appear to encounter conceptual difficulty in reasoning about phenomena that straddle these boundaries, such as bodily reactions to psychological events. To illustrate, in a series of studies, North American children and adults were interviewed about both familiar and novel psychogenic illnesses and asked about a range of potential mental, bodily, and behavioral causes and outcomes (Notaro, Gelman, and Zimmerman 2002). In one study, participants were asked whether they thought a particular bodily ailment was due to a bodily or mental cause (e.g., in the unfamiliar case, a space alien's puffy toes being due to the ingestion of dirty water or to feeling embarrassed). Whereas older children (seven to eight years old) and adults were equally likely to choose physical and psychological responses — indicating an appreciation that psychological states can prompt bodily changes — four- to six-year-olds selected psychological causes significantly below chance, suggesting that young children segregate biological and psychological causation. Again, more research is required to investigate the nature of this developmental trajectory through to adulthood, and particularly whether tacit assumptions of autonomy between these domains persist. A recent investigation with 130 mental health professionals suggests that old divides die hard. Despite thorough training in the biological bases of pathological behaviors and despite the professed transcendence of old dualistic mind-body categories, these mental health professionals continued to employ a mind-body dichotomy when reasoning about clinical cases, readily and consistently perceiving some mental illnesses as more or less psychological and some as more or less biological. Further, compared with biological causation, psychological causation was associated with higher attributions of intentionality, controllability, responsibility, and blameworthiness on the part of the patient for illness-related behaviors (Miresco and Kirmayer 2006).[2]

Persons as Individuals

Another important aspect of folk anthropology concerns tracking the identity of individual persons. Persons are not the only targets of our capacity to distinguish and track identity — a particular desk or a particular antique, or painting, cup, or place, are perceived to have distinctive and enduring identities also — but the same strategies may not be identical when considering personal identity versus the identity of a favorite coat. After all, intentional agents such as humans can radically change their location, physical appearance, and even behavioral tendencies, both as a consequence of normal development and also intentionally. Research on identity tracking suggests that the ability to trace the identity of an individual over space and time is present from infancy (e.g., Spelke, Kestenbaum, Simons, and Wein 1995; Xu and Carey 1996). Further evidence suggests that children as young as three years represent proper names as referring to unique individuals over time and changes to location and appearance (Sorrentino 2001). A recent study with children aged between three and six showed that the children readily identi-

---

2. Developmental psychologist Carl Johnson has suggested that one early-developing set of intuitions children have concerns the existence of some kind of force that animates and energizes living things. Johnson further suggests that these intuitions are used by children to account for the difference between real and imaginary things: real things have some of this force or "spirit" (Johnson 2008). This intuition, perhaps persisting into adulthood, might help distinguish living from nonliving and also be culturally elaborated into the notion of "spirit," "Axe," or "wakonda," as sketched below.

fied perfect duplicates of their attachment item, such as a blanket or teddy bear, as in some way not the same as the original, and they preferred the original object to the exact duplicate (Hood and Bloom 2008). These findings suggest an early emerging capacity to distinguish individual entities as having unique identifying properties beyond their perceptible parts. Some developmental psychologists have suggested that Western adults and children represent individual people as having an invariant "person-essence" that confers stable identity across processes of growth and aging, and even biological death (Richert and Harris 2008).[3] Reviewing concepts from cross-cultural ethnographic accounts that closely parallel Western concepts of "mind" (having to do with mental activities) and "soul" (as our individual identity), Richert and Harris further suggest that the mind-soul distinction "is not tied to Christian or Western traditions alone but is widespread, if not universal" (2008: 115).

Cognitively Informed Comparison and Explanation

Various areas of psychological research, particularly in developmental psychology, have thus identified core cognitive mechanisms and processes underpinning thinking about persons. In addition to having corporeal properties, persons have mental, life-sustaining, and enduring, individuating properties also. The sets of cognitive mechanisms activated across the domains outlined above have different phylogenetic histories, and different ontogenetic, or developmental, schedules. For example, humans share some mechanisms, such as intuitive physics, with our close phylogenetic relatives, the chimpanzees and bonobos. Some mechanisms, such as those involved in agency detection, develop early and are operational in the first hours of the infant's life, while others, such as the ability to appreciate the basic biological principles according to which living things operate, emerge in later childhood. Further, the intuitive causal mechanisms for some of these domains are relatively well understood (e.g., physicality), while in others, plausible suggestions and hypotheses await substantiation (e.g., "person-essence").

3. Note that this need not entail that an individual has a single person-essence. Lay understandings of Dissociative Identity Disorder, for example, as well as widespread forms of spirit possession concepts, cross-culturally recurrent representations of selves as multiple or serial, and everyday ideas about moodiness (e.g., as a "Jekyll and Hyde" phenomenon) suggest that we may readily conceive of individual people as potentially accommodating more than one person-essence.

Nevertheless, current research and theory provide a useful starting point from which to identify, compare, and explain cross-culturally recurrent and variable aspects of person concepts across diverse cultural and linguistic contexts.

Insofar as these core cognitive mechanisms are panhuman, they can potentially provide a solution to the principal challenge of cross-cultural and cross-linguistic comparison; that is, the identification of like kinds. Domains of thought and practice cross-culturally can potentially be parsed and compared in terms of their common cognitive structure — that is, in terms of the cognitive mechanisms activated and the causal inferences spontaneously generated by these mechanisms (see also Cohen 2008, 2007a) — instead of in terms of superficial and arbitrarily selected features. The challenge of identifying like-kinds has not only impeded comparison across different ethnographic regions, it impedes constructive dialogue across different disciplines also. Consequently, the most valuable insights from relevant areas of research often seem to be completely lost in translation. One theorist's soul is another theorist's life force, while one scholar's agency is another scholar's reflexive consciousness. By identifying culturally elaborated representations in terms of their anchoring conceptual structures, such problems would be avoided.

A further advantage to parsing cultural forms in terms of underlying cognition is that we can generate plausible hypotheses about why certain forms are more cross-culturally recurrent than others. Cognitive mechanisms specify and govern intuitive assumptions about how the world works. Therefore, they both enable and constrain cultural expression. While some concepts come almost for free — they are the spontaneous output of the regular maturation of cognitive mechanisms — concepts that deviate from intuitive assumptions delivered by these mechanisms may be more difficult to acquire, remember, and communicate, all else being equal. Hence, these less intuitive concepts would require rehearsal, explicit instruction and indoctrination, external mnemonics, or other cultural scaffolding to assist their cultural transmission and stability. A cognitive approach therefore provides a fertile ground for the development of specific hypotheses about the generation and transmission of culture.

So, what kinds of concepts do these mechanisms readily and predictably give rise to? In the remainder of this paper, we shall focus primarily on concepts arising from mechanisms dealing with basic properties of life, agency, and identity. In comparison to ideas having to do with corporeal properties (e.g., physical, organic), these concepts appear to be more susceptible to

confusion and conflation in cross-cultural and cross-disciplinary translation. How does intuitive, early-developing knowledge about the world, delivered within these different domains, generate the recurrent features in the
catalog of person concepts we find in the cross-cultural record? In answer to
this question, we can begin by considering examples of concepts in the
ethnographic record that appear to be centrally structured around Mentality, Life, and Identity.

Recurrence in Person Concepts: An Illustrative Survey

Mentality

Among the Vezo of western Madagascar, the term *say* refers to a nonvisible
component of the person that underpins intelligence and appropriate behavior. Losing one's say or having sick say leads to odd behavior (Astuti and
Harris 2008). Similar features characterize concepts within this domain
among the Ommura of Papua New Guinea, where motives, intentions,
thoughts, feelings, emotions, sensations, and experiences are said to remain
"inside the body" (Mayer 1982: 246), or specifically "inside the belly." The
Nuer concept of *tie* was described by Evans-Pritchard as referring to the aspect of the noncorporeal person that "embraces the intellectual and moral
faculties of man, his rational soul as distinct from his mere life as a living
creature" (1956: 155). A familiar example of a Mentality concept is the Western concept of "mind," commonly conceived of as the seat of thought, judgment, and remembering (e.g., Richert and Harris 2008). Mentality is also
frequently implicated in cross-culturally widespread ideas concerning spirit
possession in which a spirit is thought to enter a person's body. When the
spirit enters the body, the agency of the host is displaced or eclipsed; "the individual is thereupon held to be the deity himself" (Herskovits 1948: 66).
The behaviors of the host are no longer attributed to the displaced agent, but
to the new agent possessing the host's body. In Mayotte (Madagascar) possession, for example, "Spirits enter the bodies of human beings and rise to
their heads, taking temporary control of all bodily and mental function. . . .
The emphasis is on the change that has occurred. Despite the fact that the
body remains the same, it is now occupied by a different person" (Lambek
1981: 40).

Life

Concepts concerning life processes stand in contrast to concepts structured by expectations of mentalistic agency, and the two are often distinguished lexically in the cross-cultural record. The notion that bodily and life processes are sustained by a life force or vital principle recurs frequently in the ethnographic literature, e.g., the Songhay of Niger ("the energy of life," Stoller 1989: 31); the Wari of the Brazilian Amazon (*jami-*, "the immaterial essence that animates human life," Conklin and Morgan 1996: 682); the Ommura of Papua New Guinea ("It is said that at death . . . the person's marauha leaves their mamanta, flesh or skin. In that it does not persist after death, marauha cannot be understood as 'soul,'" Mayer 1982: 247). The Nuer contrast *tie* (described above) with *yiegh,* translated as both "breath" and "life." Although there is some overlap in the referents of these terms, they come apart, for example, in the case of the man who "ostensibly had breath and life (yiegh), but what made him a person (ran), his soul (tie), had departed" (1956: 155). The Native American Omaha term *wakonda* refers to a "mysterious life power permeating all natural forms and forces" (Fletcher and La Flesche 1911: 597) and, in this respect, it closely parallels the concept of Axe that is fundamental to Afro-Brazilian religion (e.g., a "force or energy, fundamental to all existence," Cohen 2007b: 55). The following quotation further suggests wakonda as a potential source of mentalistic agency: "Observing the use of wakondagi, it is found that the term is applied to the first manifestation by a child of a new ability, as when it is first able to sit up, to creep, to walk, or to speak; all these actions are regarded as indications of the development within the child of an individual and independent power to act, and are spoken of as wakondagi" (Fletcher 1912: 106). Life force is frequently represented as quantifiable — it can be depleted and replenished in a variety of ways. A state of depletion is commonly accompanied by observable behavioral symptoms, such as weakness and lethargy (e.g., Evans-Pritchard 1956: 155).

Identity

References to the vital principle, or essence, of the individual are also common in the ethnographic literature. People in the West often refer to the enduring, individualizing component of the person as the "you" behind your eyes. Similarly, among the Huli of Papua New Guinea, "the dinini or soul is an invisible vapour, which, in the waking state, occupies the space just behind the eyes . . . the vital principle or vital essence of the human personality" (Glasse 1965: 30). The Wari concept of jami described above also refers to "the individuating element of the Wari personhood" (Conklin and Morgan 1996: 682). It is common for this element to be perceived as socially constructed through relational experiences. Nursing of the infant, for example, imparts social personhood. In this way, the Wari distinguish between biological and social birth — a human being may be alive but not yet a person (i.e., a *pije,* or potential person). This basic distinction parallels Nuer distinctions between tie and yiegh — the social and biological person.

The universal practice of proper naming commonly formalizes and bestows individual identity, even where the name and identity are only minimally distinguished from those of other members of one's lineage. Likewise, name changes (e.g., from Vernon Howell to David Koresh) often accompany a radical transformation or replacement of individual identity. Indeed, names often appear to function as placeholder terms that directly capture individual essence, and, in the ethnographic literature, often acquire the title "name soul." The broad absence of such an explicit concept in the West renders ethnographic translation difficult, as in the case of Tsimshian names described by Roth: "These names, to the extent that they are mere names, do not refer to individuals; they belong to individual and refer to, or rather are, immortal entities that . . . are not quite souls and not quite sentient agents but are, in fact — there is no other succinct way to put it — names" (2008: 95). The basic notion of an individuating person-essence (or "soul," viz. Richert and Harris 2008) appears to track closely on such concepts, however.

**Table 1. Noncorporeal Cognitive Components
of the Folk Concept of "Person" Summarized**

Domain	Core Causation	Examples of Cultural Elaborations
Mentality	Entities with mentalistic agency have the capacity to act upon the world in accordance with goals, beliefs, and desires.	"Mind"
Vitality	Entities with life have a vital power that sustains basic physiological processes and, perhaps, energizes them for movement. This life force requires replenishment through consuming nutrients and through rest.	"Spirit"; "Life force"; "Energy"
Identity	Individuals have unique identities beyond their perceptual parts, "personal essence."	"Soul"

We suggest that these components are typically combined in conceptualizing a person but may be differentially activated in different concepts. Likewise, as separate concepts they may be subject to variable cultural elaboration. A given culture may show little elaboration of a component notion (e.g., may lack the notion of an individual "soul") or may combine more than one component into a single concept (e.g., "mind" may include both mentalizing faculties and an individuating essence).

A Cognitive Typology

These brief examples demonstrate how one might begin to develop a cognitively informed catalog of cross-culturally recurrent and variable components of person concepts. A broader survey might consider those cultural categories that combine two or more expectation sets. There may be many such broad cultural categories, as in the example above of the Wari *jami*, referring to both life force and individual identity. Categories combining corporeal and person identity elements are highly common cross-culturally, ranging from Western folk notions of DNA to Cashinawa notions of *yuda yuxin*, or body souls, which appear to link processes having to do with life and vital force, and experiences and knowledge acquired through the body (McCallum 1999). A systematic or comprehensive survey of various configurations and combinations of person concepts and categories readily generated by relevant cognitive mechanisms is beyond the scope of this chapter. We suggest, however, that, in principle, these mechanisms and their constitutive expectation sets are individually and conjointly generative of a structured catalog of conceptual forms to do with agency, mentality, identity, biology, and physicality.

What this categorization scheme enables us to do is to parse aspects of the broad domain of what is commonly lumped together as "mind-body," or person, into causally significant categories. By focusing on the mental machinery activated in the generation and acquisition of various concepts we can identify whether concepts are underpinned by common cognitive denominators or whether they are activating different cognitive mechanisms and processes. The beauty of such an approach is that we no longer need to identify a novel concept as, for example, "roughly like the Western concept of soul" (whatever that is) but rather as entailing specific, identifiable assumptions and expectations that arise in part from panhuman cognitive function.

Another advantage of this approach is that as we increasingly understand the assumptions that are entailed by our basic cognitive mechanisms, we can potentially predict which aspects of cultural concepts are naturally entailed by the mechanisms' activation and which aspects are superfluous. For example, the intuitive expectations entailed by the activation of an agent concept, such as "ghost," will invariably entail that the ghost has the ability to act on its environment and that it will do so in accordance with goals. That it specifically causes saucepans to fly around my kitchen on Tuesday afternoons is not entailed by basic agency assumptions. Elements that are superfluous to our intuitive expectations are likely to be subject to wide variability cross-culturally as they are not tightly constrained by the cognitive expectations that are fundamental to their conceptual structure. By the same token, concepts that entail numerous elements that explicitly violate expectations that pertain to a particular domain will run counter to our naturally emerging intuitions and therefore may also exhibit distinctive transmissive dynamics. Depending on the degree to which intuitive expectations are violated, such concepts may require considerable cognitive and pedagogical resources to be faithfully communicated and remembered (following Boyer and Ramble 2001; Barrett 2008).

Further investigation could consider the contingent interactions between these cognitive tools. Some entities, such as human beings, might activate all of the expectation sets described above and more, but are all of the mechanisms active simultaneously and are their outputs commensurate with one another? Perhaps we process humans most saliently as biological entities under certain conditions (such as on the surgical operating table), physical entities under other certain conditions (such as when we collide with another human in a football match), at times as unique identities (as when we name our child), and at others times as mentalistic agents (as when we try to make someone laugh). Perhaps there are cognitively natural expectations pertaining to the links between expectation sets, and not just within them. For example, it may be that biology expectations are intuitively entailed by animacy and mentality expectations, or vice versa. Is an animate robot counterintuitive? Are bodiless spirits counterintuitive? Are spirits who are said to live in another world, but with fully functioning biological bodies that grow and reproduce intuitive or counterintuitive? Are various forms of person-body dualism — in which we posit the possibility of person identity or agency and mentality as in some way distinct and separate from the body — a natural cognitive default?

Currently, there are a number of competing hypotheses relevant to this discussion. Paul Bloom's theory of commonsense dualism suggests that we (universally) intuitively see what he refers to as the soul and the body as separate and autonomous; "we think of bodies and souls as distinct. . . . Our dualism is a natural by-product of the fact that we have two distinct cognitive systems, one for dealing with material objects, the other for social entities. These systems have incommensurable outputs. Hence dualism emerges as an evolutionary accident. . . . The notion that consciousness is separable from the body is not learned at all; it comes for free" (2007: 149). In contrast, Pascal Boyer's theory of minimal counterintuitiveness posits that disembodied-mind (e.g., ghost) concepts violate our intuitive concept of person; person entails embodiment. A person without a body is, therefore, minimally counterintuitive (Boyer 2001).

It is important that in identifying the core categories of thought in these domains that we distinguish among the several mechanisms that humans have for reasoning about the social world. If person-without-body concepts are counterintuitive, there are potentially several intuitive aspects of a person's embodiment (spanning physicality and biology) that are violated by such a concept; and, if massively counterintuitive, then, according to Boyer's account, these concepts would be difficult to remember and use, and therefore should not be widespread in cultural transmission. The ethnographic record suggests that such concepts are highly recurrent cross-culturally, however. Similarly, by conflating mentality, agency, person identity, and life force as soul on the one hand, and human biological and physical properties as body on the other, Bloom's account also potentially runs into some difficulties. How do we explain the widespread notion that body parts are not separate from the person, but that the person is in some sense contained in the very material of one's body parts? How do we explain the cross-culturally widespread notion that one can absorb something of the agency or identity of an animal or human by eating them, or by receiving their body parts in transplant surgery? Why do we have difficulty seeing corpses as merely physical objects? Can we readily detach agency and mentality from dead bodies, as Bloom's account might suggest? It appears that this account needs some qualification — that while we may readily under certain conditions divorce person identity and mentality from the body, we may also readily conceive of certain bodily properties as infused with elements of person identity and with aspects of mentality, such as memories and preferences. Specifying what these conditions and aspects are is an important next step to systematically identifying how cognition informs the ways in which people across the globe both marry and divorce core components of the person.

Conclusion

Psychological research over the past several decades has shown that humans are endowed with species-typical cognitive equipment dedicated to dealing with various kinds of person-relevant phenomena. Discovering precisely how the relevant cognitive tools are activated, and specifying the intuitive assumptions they generate, we can compare and explain, in part, cross-cultural regularities in patterns of cultural transmission. There is much to discover, however, and many more questions than answers. The necessity of cross-disciplinary engagement and collaboration between anthropologists and psychologists is apparent. Cross-cultural, psychological research is required on the basic operation and development of core cognitive mechanisms across variable cultural contexts. Ethnographic, survey, and experimental techniques are required to test cognitively informed predictions about the emergence and spread of cultural forms. Such a concerted interdisciplinary research effort will potentially generate further remarkable discoveries relevant to scholars working across the cognitive and social sciences and, ultimately, advance our scientific understanding of how children and adults construe the persons that populate their social worlds.

References

Astuti, R., and P. Harris. 2008. Understanding mortality and the life of the ancestors in rural Madagascar. *Cognitive Science* 32, no. 4: 713-40.

Barrett, J. 2008. Coding and quantifying counterintuitiveness in religious concepts: Theoretical and methodological reflections. *Method and Theory in the Study of Religion* 20: 308-38.

Bloom, P. 2004. *Descartes' Baby: How Child Development Explains What Makes Us Human.* New York: Basic Books.

Bloom, P. 2007. Religion is natural. *Developmental Science* 10: 147-51.

Boddy, J. 1989. *Wombs and Alien Spirits: Women, Men and the Zar Cult in Northern Sudan.* Madison: University of Wisconsin Press.

Boyer, P. 2001. *Religion Explained.* New York: Basic Books.

Boyer, P., and C. Ramble. 2001. Cognitive templates for religious concepts: Cross-cultural evidence for recall of counter-intuitive representations. *Cognitive Science* 25: 535-64.

Carey, S. 1985. *Conceptual Change in Childhood.* Cambridge, MA: MIT Press.

Carey, S. 2009. *The Origin of Concepts.* New York: Oxford University Press.

Cohen, E. 2008. What is spirit possession? Defining, comparing, and explaining two possession forms. *Ethnos* 73, no. 1: 101-26.

Cohen, E. 2007a. *Witchcraft and Sorcery: In Religion, Anthropology, and Cognitive Science.* Durham, NC: Carolina Academic Press.

Cohen, E. 2007b. *The Mind Possessed: The Cognition of Spirit Possession in an Afro-Brazilian Religious Tradition.* New York: Oxford University Press.

Conklin, B. A., and L. M. Morgan. 1996. Babies, bodies, and the production of personhood in North America and a Native Amazonian society. *Ethnos* 24, no. 4: 657-94. .

Evans-Pritchard, E. E. 1956. *Nuer Religion.* New York: Oxford University Press.

Fausto, C. 2007. Feasting on people: Eating animals and humans in Amazonia. *Current Anthropology* 48, no. 4: 497-530.

Fletcher, A. C., and F. La Flesche. 1911. *The Omaha Tribe.* Lincoln: University of Nebraska Press.

Fletcher, A. C. 1912. Wakondagi. *American Anthropologist* 14, no. 1: 106-8.

Glasse, R. M. 1965. "The Huli of the Southern Highlands." In *Gods, Ghosts, and Men in Melanesia,* ed. P. Lawrence and M. J. Meggitt. Melbourne: Oxford University Press.

Gopnik, A., A. Meltzoff, and P. Kuhl. 1999. *The Scientist in the Crib.* Fairfield, NJ: William Morrow.

Herskovits, M. 1948. *Man and His Works: The Science of Cultural Anthropology.* New York: Knopf.

Hood, B., and P. Bloom. 2008. Children prefer certain individuals over perfect duplicates. *Cognition* 106, 512-18.

Inagaki, K., and G. Hatano. 2002. *Young Children's Naïve Thinking about the Biological World.* New York: Psychology Press.

Inagaki, K., and G. Hatano. 2004. Vitalistic causality in young children's naïve biology. *Trends in Cognitive Sciences* 8, no. 8: 356-62.

Johnson, C. 2008. "The Spirit of Spiritual Development." In *Positive Youth Development and Spirituality: From Theory to Research,* ed. R. M. Lerner, R. W. Roeser, and E. Phelps. West Conshohocken, PA: Templeton Foundation Press.

Lambek, M. 1981. *Human Spirits: A Cultural Account of Trance in Mayotte.* New York: Cambridge University Press.

Lambek, M. 1989. "From Disease to Discourse: Remarks on the Conceptualization of Trance and Spirit Possession." In *Altered States of Consciousness and Mental Health,* ed. C. A. Ward, 36-61. Newbury Park, CA: Sage Publications.

Lima, T. S. 1999. The two and its many: Reflections on perspectivism in a Tupi cosmology. *Ethnos* 64, no. 1: 107-31.

Mayer, J. R. 1982. Body, psyche and society: Conceptions of illness in Ommura, Eastern Highlands, Papua New Guinea. *Oceania* 52, no. 3: 240-60.

McCallum, C. 1999. Consuming pity: The production of death among the Cashinahua. *Cultural Anthropology* 14, no. 4: 443-71.

Miresco, M. J., and L. J. Kirmayer. 2006. The persistence of mind-brain dualism in psychiatric reasoning about clinical scenarios. *American Journal of Psychiatry* 163, no. 5: 913-18.

Notaro, P., S. Gelman, and M. A. Zimmerman. 2002. Biases in reasoning about the consequences of psychogenic bodily reactions: Domain boundaries in cognitive development. *Merrill-Palmer Quarterly* 48, no. 4: 427-49.

Rakison, D. H., and D. Poulin-Dubois. 2001. Developmental origin of the animate-inanimate distinction. *Psychological Bulletin* 127, no. 2: 209-28.

Richert, R., and P. Harris. Dualism revisited: Body vs. mind vs. soul. *Journal of Cognition and Culture* 8: 99-115.

Roth, C. F. 2008. *Becoming Tsimshian: The Social Life of Names.* Seattle: University of Washington Press.

Schult, C. A., and H. M. Wellman. 1997. Explaining human movements and actions: Children's understanding of the limits of psychological explanation. *Cognition* 62: 291-324.

Siegal, M. 2008. *Marvellous Minds: The Discovery of What Children Know.* Oxford: Oxford University Press.

Sorrentino, C. M. 2001. Children and adults represent proper names as referring to unique individuals. *Developmental Science* 4, no. 4: 399-407.

Spelke, E. 1994. Initial knowledge: Six suggestions. *Cognition* 50: 443-47.

Spelke, E., R. Kestenbaum, D. J. Simons, and D. Wein. 1995. Spatiotemporal continuity, smoothness of motion and object identity in infancy. *British Journal of Developmental Psychology* 13, no. 2: 113-42.

Sperber, D. 1996. *Explaining Culture: A Naturalistic Approach.* Oxford: Blackwell.

Stoller, P. 1989. *Fusion of the Worlds: An Ethnography of Possession among the Songhay of Niger.* Chicago: University of Chicago Press.

Wellman, H., and C. Johnson. 2008. "Developing Dualism: From Intuitive Understanding to Transcendental Ideas." In *Psycho-Physical Dualism Today: An Interdisciplinary Approach,* ed. A. Antonietti, A. Corradini, and E. J. Lowe, 3-36. Lanham, MD: Lexington Books.

Wellman, H., D. Cross, and J. Watson. 2001. Meta-analysis of theory of mind development: The truth about false belief. *Child Development* 72: 655-84.

Wynn, K. 2008. "Some Innate Foundations of Social and Moral Cognition." In *The Innate Mind: Foundations and the Future,* ed. P. Carruthers, S. Laurence, and S. Stich, 330-47. New York: Oxford University Press.

Xu, F., and S. Carey. 1996. Infants' metaphysics: The case of numerical identity. *Cognitive Psychology* 30: 111-53.

Yamaguchi, M., V. A. Kuhlmeier, K. Wynn, and K. vanMarle. 2009. Continuity in social cognition from infancy to childhood. *Developmental Science* 12, no. 5: 746-52.

PART TWO

The Self and Multiplicity

Disunity and Disorder:
The "Problem" of Self-Fragmentation

Léon Turner

Over the final decades of the twentieth century, alongside postmodern philosophical critiques of the unified continuous self, a great many psychologists and sociologists began to embrace complex dynamic theories of the plurality of the self. The revolution has been brisk, if not always uncontroversial. Throughout the human sciences, self-multiplicity is now commonly lauded as a positive cognitive and social adaptation to the constant fluctuations, novelty, and uncertainty of human life.[1] Many Christian theologians, by contrast, have continued staunchly to defend the unity of the self. They have rejected the autonomous self-creating subject of modernity, and thereby embraced the social constructedness of personhood, but they have also challenged postmodern philosophy's fragmentation of the individual subject, and railed against the existential angst that they believe accompanies contemporary culture. In the process they have typically assumed that the loss of the sense of self-unity that characterizes contemporary psychological life represents an overtly pathological condition.

My primary intentions in this essay are to explore and explain the discrepancies between recent theological and human scientific accounts of the multiplicity of self. Self-multiplicity, I will argue, can be understood in a variety of different ways, not all of which can be considered psychopathological. Subsequently, I hope to show that the unqualified theological antipathy toward self-multiplicity, both theoretically and existentially, arises both from ethical commitments to the principle that people can and should

1. For example, see Gergen 1972; Cooper 1999; Bauman 2001.

125

experience themselves as singular and continuous beings under ideal conditions, and from the failure to acknowledge an important psychological distinction between the singularity and continuity of the self and the experiential singularity and continuity of the person. Finally, I will briefly examine some of the difficulties that arise from theologians' tendency to treat all types of self-disunity as pathological, and the broader theoretical and ethical implications of a more nuanced conception of the plural self.

Toward a Taxonomy of Multiplicity and Unity

Given that a degree of theoretical pluralism is commonly acknowledged to be inescapable in the broader study of the self, it is only to be expected that the concepts of self-multiplicity and self-unity also cannot be captured in the terms and concepts of a single theory.[2] If we are to pinpoint the source of the theoretical discrepancies between theological and secular human scientific approaches to the disunified self with any precision, then, we need first to set out the basis of a conceptual taxonomy of disunity and unity.[3] This taxonomy, distilled from a range of psychological theories and studies, is far from comprehensive, but still distinguishes between a number of very different concepts of self-multiplicity, only some of which correspond to genuinely psychopathological conditions.[4]

2. Hence, Jerrold Seigel writes in his extensive historical work *The Idea of the Self,* "Those who speak about a 'modern self' in the singular have often claimed too much for it, or blamed too much on it. . . . [It] obscures the variety of modern thinking on the topic, the motivations that have powered it, and often the real interest that contrasting meditations still retain" (Seigel 2005: 43-44). Instead, he suggests, "we should recognize a range of different solutions to the modern problematic of the self, seeking to grasp them in light of the particular purposes they have been created to serve, and to put them into an intelligible relation with each other" (43-44).

3. The imprecision with which the terms "self-unity" and "self-multiplicity" are sometimes used is, of course, reflected in the broader study of the self, where terminological confusion and conceptual opacity have blurred the boundaries between many of the field's key concepts. For detailed discussions of this problem, see Harré 1998; Levin 1992; Olson 1999; Wilkes 1999.

4. The range of psychological approaches to the multiplicity of self is very broad indeed. It has been understood, for example, by neuropsychologists in terms of the multiplicity of brain functions, by cognitive scientists in terms of multiple, independent, physiologically instantiated "modules," by cognitive psychologists in terms of multiple schematized self-concepts, and by psychoanalytic psychologists in terms of intrapsychic splitting and dissociation.

To begin, we can differentiate two different sorts of psychological theory: representational theories of self and experiential theories of self. The former are theories about the cognitive organization or structure of information about oneself. The latter are theories about the *sense* of self — about the various ways that people experience themselves at particular times and in particular contexts. In relation to each type of theory, we can distinguish between concepts of synchronic and diachronic self-unity and multiplicity.[5]

The idea that each person is capable of forming a multiplicity of self-representations, which are neither synchronically nor diachronically unified, has been clearly illustrated by Hazel Markus, Paula Nurius, and Daphna Oyserman.[6] Collectively, they have championed the idea that what has previously been described as *the* self-concept is more accurately described as a collection of interrelated self-concepts, each of which represents schematized information pertaining to personal knowledge.[7] These subsist side-by-side over time, constantly changing in response to new experiences and never merging together. Some are used more often than others, but no single one of them might be construed as *the* self, or even as the *core* self. Empirical psychological support for this idea is substantial.[8] Different representations of self can be equated from this perspective with certain patterns of self-relevant, context-dependent information that structure experience and guide behavior as the need arises.

Experiential theories of the plural self, by contrast, address questions about subjective experience. In this context, psychologists have posited the existence of multiple "subpersonalities" or "identity states," some of which might be relatively fleeting, and some of which endure throughout a person's life.[9]

---

5. Such a distinction is impossible if the self is taken to be an unchanging transcendental subject of experience. However, where the self is conceived in terms that permit for a degree of changeability over time, as is the case in the vast majority of contemporary psychology, such distinctions are extremely pertinent.

6. Markus has arguably done the most significant work in this field (see Markus 1977).

7. Many others have contributed to what is now an expansive literature. Altrocchi, for example, suggests that we might understand "self-concept differentiation" as "the degree to which one sees oneself as having different personality characteristics in different social roles" (Altrocchi 1999: 173). Others, including Wyer and Srull, suggest that multiple self-representations are constructed from and describe specific domains of self-experience (Wyer and Srull 1989).

8. See Markus 1977; Markus and Nurius 1987; Wilcox and Williams 1990; Westen 1992.

9. John Rowan has identified a large number of apparent synonyms for "subpersonalities," including "Ego states, subselves, subidentities, identity states, alter-personalities, deeper potentials and so on" (Rowan 1997: 12).

The ability to switch between different subpersonalities as the situation demands is not generally seen as either unusual or pathological.[10] As clinical psychologist Mick Cooper writes, "[I]t is by no means uncommon for individuals to describe their subjectively-felt lived experiences in fundamentally self-pluralistic terms."[11] In fact, there is now a broad consensus among psychologists both that people do experience themselves in qualitatively distinct ways over time, and that the capacity for such diachronic experiential plurality reflects the complex multidimensional structure of personality.[12]

Whatever the breadth and depth of the psychological consensus about the multiplicity of self, however, the question of how people do manage to experience themselves as singular continuous *persons* over time continues to be of critical importance. Even Ken Gergen, whose own account of the plural self has been so influential in contemporary psychology, concedes that people do experience themselves as more or less continuous beings, even if that continuity is illusory.[13] Precisely how people acquire this perception continues to be the subject of vigorous debate, but a potential solution to the problem based upon the idea of the personal narrative has become increasingly conspicuous in all areas of the human sciences, including psychology.[14] According to narrative theories of self, moments of conscious self-experience are conjoined through the stories that we tell to and about ourselves.[15] The construction of these stories, the process of narratization itself, encourages a sense of personal continuity and singularity — of having been a single continuous person through different relationships, environments, and transformations of self.[16] A personal life-story relates the histories of discrete selves to each other as if they were the characters and plots of a novel, each of which is

10. See, for example, Lifton 1973; Rosenberg and Gara 1985; Markus and Wurf 1987; Hermans and Kempen 1993; McAdams 1997; Harré 1998; Cooper 1999.

11. Cooper 1999: 53.

12. Cooper describes these senses of self as "modes of being." He argues, "[M]any — if not all — individuals, encounter their world though a variety of different 'modes.' . . . These modes of Being are not 'things' within a 'psyche,' but stances: tendencies towards particular constellations of behavioural, affective, and cognitive acts-in-the-world" (Cooper 1999: 66).

13. See Gergen 1991.

14. For example, see Sarbin 1986; Polkinghorne 1988; McAdams 1993, 1997; Crossley 2000.

15. See McAdams 1993, 1997.

16. As Schrag argues, "[T]he scripting of self retains an open texture, informed by possibilities that the self has not yet actualised, subject to a creative advance toward the future, and as such it should never be construed as simply the sedimentation of past habitual responses" (Schrag 1997: 40).

identified with a particular set of experiences, and none of which represents a single true or authentic self.

By effectively divorcing the concept of personal continuity from any notion of the singularity of self, the concept of the narrative identity provides a means of understanding how individual persons can remain continuous despite the structural plurality of self and the diversity of self-experiences over time. It also provides a neat understanding of why the sort of radical discontinuity experienced by those who suffer from severe dissociative conditions must be considered pathological, whereas the diachronic multiplicity of self-experiences might still be considered normal. As the psychologists Hardcastle, Flanagan, and Crossley have each suggested, it is the failure to successfully narratize different strands of a life-story that is truly definitive of the pathologically divided subject, not the number or variety of self-representations, or merely the commonplace disparity between different senses of self over time.[17]

Disunity and Disorder in Theological Anthropology

These distinctions between different forms of self-multiplicity are invaluable in appraising recent theological accounts of the disunified self from the perspective of the secular human sciences. The initial aim must be to establish just what forms of self-multiplicity are typically the subject of theological discourses, and how disunity has come to be identified exclusively with disorder. Those theologians who have had most to say about self-multiplicity are also those who have been most concerned with defending the continuity and particularity of relational personhood against the idea that persons are constituted simply by a series of disconnected impressions formed through passive interaction with the social environment. It is these theological accounts of the human condition, many of which are generated in explicit conversation with both sociological accounts of the modern identity crisis and psychological accounts of self-development, that are the primary focus of this essay.

As far as these theological accounts of personhood are concerned, the question of whether people are able to experience themselves, and treat others, as continuous entities has great ethical significance.[18] After all, our his-

---

17. Hardcastle and Flanagan 1999.

18. As Moreland argues, if the self "is a bundle of social roles and relations that are the

tories (and our futures) in all their gritty detail are essential to our own sense of being human. People cannot be truly unique individuals if they are not the singular products of their own histories, and they cannot have histories if they are denied a reality independent of fluctuating social currents. It is the potential or actual loss of this sense of being singular and continuous that is reflected in recent theological concern for "self-fragmentation," whether it is taken to be the product of modernity's individualism, postmodern relativism, or some individual psychological failing.[19]

Anglican theologian Vernon White, for example, suggests that individualism, with its focus upon disengaged autonomy, inspires the concept of a private self that is conceptually distinct from our social roles and relations, meaning that we have "set up an internal sense of alienation from ourselves, and mental strain is the price that is paid."[20] Matters have been made worse, according to White, by the anti-modernist critiques that have led to even deeper "pangs of personal anxiety about our existence."[21] Anthony Thiselton expresses a similar attitude when he argues, "The self of postmodernity has become *de-centred* . . . an opaque product of variable roles and performances which have been imposed upon it by the constraints of society and by its own inner drives or conflicts."[22] Both Thiselton and White are as interested in debunking postmodern relativism as they are in addressing the existential plight of the contemporary Western person, but both also share the opinion that the pervasive sense of self-fragmentation in Western culture is a result of the disparity between what people believe themselves to be and how they actually experience themselves. For White, this is the consequence of *"a particular and entirely inadequate assumption about how the individual is formed."*[23] Such disunity, for White and those other theologians to have chastised the contemporary sociocultural climate along similar lines, stands in opposition to the sense of unity enabled by a belief in the inviolable ontolog-

---

expressions of the arbitrary flux of the group . . . [it] has disastrous implications for helping people separate and individuate in any objective sense. . . . Further, on this view there is no point in owning one's pathologies, since it is always open to a patient simply to distance from an arbitrary, fleeting constructed self in which the pathology is embedded" (Moreland 2009: 13).

19. This choice of terminology is itself revealing. As Dan McAdams observes, "self-fragmentation" is a term that emphasizes the brokenness or pathology of the disunified self (McAdams 1997).

20. White 1997: 50.

21. White 1997: 6.

22. Thiselton 1995: 121.

23. White 1997: 58-59. Original italics.

ical unity of each person as relational yet particular being that is a "presupposition of Christian belief in our createdness."[24]

Although their accounts of the origins of self-fragmentation differ greatly from those with more sociological interests, similar conclusions about its overtly pathological nature have been reached by a few theologians from an explicitly psychological perspective. Lutheran Wolfhart Pannenberg, for example, suggests that egocentrism, which he takes to be an implicit denial of the *imago Dei,* manifests itself psychologically as a discontinuity between the self-experience of a given moment and the history and future of an individual's life. Such a failure of identity formation is variously described by Pannenberg as "nonidentity," "disunity," "separateness," or "self-alienation." He thus regards the tendency toward egocentrism, understood broadly in terms of St. Augustine's *amor sui,* in explicitly pathological terms as the "primary brokenness" of human nature. In a related vein, Anglican theologian Alistair McFadyen argues that there must be continuity between the various identities that a single person adopts in particular moments for interpersonal communication to remain authentic. The failure to integrate these identities corresponds to a lack of communicative consistency and the failure to conform to the authentic and dialogical openness to God and other human beings that he takes to be the ethical prescription of the *imago Dei.* For McFadyen, as for Pannenberg, the resulting fragmentation is a damaging, if not incurable, breakdown of the person's continuous identity project.

It is not just a belief in the pathological nature of self-fragmentation that is common to these various theologians' theses. They also share the same basic concept of what self-fragmentation entails — the disruption of the sense of being a singular continuous person. Significantly, in each of the above examples, self-fragmentation is understood as the experience of internal dissonance or disorder, an idea that preserves the theoretical singularity of self, even if it recognizes a multiplicity of sometimes incompatible self-investments. Indeed, this is the only sort of self-multiplicity that the vast majority of theological anthropology has been prepared to consider at all.

The closest that theologians have come to addressing other concepts of the plural self has been in those few accounts of identity formation, such as Pannenberg's and McFadyen's, that have sought to reconcile theological commitments to the particularity and relationality of individual personhood with secular social psychological thought.[25] Their concepts of self may

24. White 1997: 88.
25. Although Pannenberg's *Anthropology in Theological Perspective* and McFadyen's

be extremely different, but both Pannenberg and McFadyen distinguish between personal and subpersonal modes of psychological description, and, implicitly, between what I have referred to as the representation (or structure) of self and the sense of self. The bare bones of the conceptual taxonomy of self-multiplicity outlined above, then, appear to be in place. But both ultimately argue that persons' sense of being a singular and continuous being depends completely upon the continuity of their sense of self, which in turn depends upon the singularity and continuity of the image they have of themselves. Even McFadyen, who, to a greater extent than any other contemporary theologian, makes a point of explaining the plurality of a person's senses of self over time and in different contexts, understands the represented self to be an organized structural unity, and ties the continuity of the sense of self tightly to that unity.[26] From the perspective of much contemporary psychology, neither account does full justice to the multiplicity of self.

Since theologians typically care very little about the cognitive structure and representation of self, and since most psychological ideas about the naturalness of some forms of self-multiplicity have evaded those that do care, it is perhaps unsurprising that theologians share neither psychologists' equanimity nor their theoretical specificity regarding the pathological nature of self-disunity. Theologians simply do not make certain distinctions that enable the separation of the singularity and continuity of personhood from the singularity and continuity of either representations or experiences of self. In the absence of any other concepts of self-multiplicity, the identification of the experiential plurality of self over time — the only manifestation of self-multiplicity that theologians have been prepared to consider — with the loss of the sense of personal singularity, leads inexorably to the pathologization of self-multiplicity *per se*. This, then, is a major source of theoretical divergence between theological and secular psychological appraisals of the plural self.

Important questions remain to be asked, however, about the defensibility or adequacy of this pathologization of the sense of fragmentation spe-

---

The Call to Personhood were published in 1985 and 1990, respectively, they remain the most thorough and systematic examples of attempts to set psychology and theology in explicit conversation about the development of identity. Recent books by Browning and Cooper (2004), Beck and Demarest (2005), Dueck and Lee (2005), and Shults and Sandage (2006), all of which at times take the thesis that the self is socially constructed very seriously, make little or no mention at all of self-multiplicity as it is understood by contemporary cognitive and social psychology.

26. McFadyen eschews the language of self-representations altogether, preferring to describe the "sedimentation" of continuous identity from moments of social interaction.

cifically, and about the wider theological anthropological implications of adopting a theoretically pluralistic approach to the plurality of self. Can recent theological accounts withstand the scrutiny of the secular human sciences? Their ability to do so is of considerable importance given that so much of their understanding of what is normal and abnormal as regards people's experience of themselves is grounded in either sociological or psychological analysis, even if the ultimate reasons for such a negative portrayal of self-disunity are grounded in particular ethical and ontological commitments.

Accepting Disunity and Curing Disorder

At first sight, there appears to be a modicum of common ground between certain aspects of recent human scientific accounts of the plural self and many theologians' understanding of self-fragmentation as a transient psychopathological aberration. Everyone agrees, more or less, about the rapid and radical transformation of contemporary society, its contribution to the further pluralization of self, and the existential uncertainty that this sometimes entails. There is also some limited agreement between some theologians and at least some psychologists about the potentially unsettling nature of the experience of personal discontinuity over time. Nevertheless, there are also some significant differences between the disciplines that cannot be passed over. In conclusion, then, I want briefly to explore some of the theoretical and practical issues that, from the perspective of the pluralistic approach outlined above, must confound those theological discourses that do not distinguish between different concepts of self-multiplicity. I will focus upon two distinct but interrelated lines of criticism.

The first of these concerns the apparently profound disagreement between the disciplines over what constitutes pathological and nonpathological manifestations of experiential multiplicity over time. Given theology's explicitly ethical concerns, and the causes they variously attribute to people's experience of self-fragmentation, the stark contrast between the sense of personal continuity that they presume must inhere under ideal conditions, and the pathological sense of discontinuity that they identify with self-fragmentation and take to be a contemporary reality for so many, is comprehensible. From White and Thiselton's perspective, for example, there are no better or worse failures to understand human nature correctly in relational yet particular terms; there are only failures. From Pannenberg's and

McFadyen's psychological perspectives, there are no better or worse ways to fail to live in accordance with God's intention for human beings.

Psychologists' descriptions of intra- and interpersonal cognitive dynamics need neither challenge nor support the ethical commitments of theologians, embedded as they are in Christian metaphysics, assumptions about God's relationship to his creation, and eschatological hope. Psychology is comfortable with the possibility that modernity's individualism, postmodern relativism, or the chaos of postmodern culture might have ethically undesirable implications for the value of individual personhood. These are simply not psychological questions. And so it will concede the possibility, at least, that particular manifestations of a sense of disunity over time might be especially theologically problematic. However, psychologists are entitled to feel less comfortable with theories of identity formation and transformation that implicitly or explicitly pathologize all notions of experiential multiplicity over time. Only Alistair McFadyen of the theologians I have mentioned above leaves sufficient space in his account of personhood even for the possibility that this is not always indicative of distorted or inauthentic identity.[27] The others all imply, through their restrictive eulogistic accounts of self-unity, that any and all forms of such diachronic experiential multiplicity are overtly pathological. Unfortunately, even the most mundane examples of experiential multiplicity, such as that which accompanies the performance, diachronically, of a plurality of social roles, becomes problematic when such a sharp contrast is drawn between the unified and fragmented self. From a psychological perspective, such a strong position makes nonsense of the very concept of pathology.

It is difficult to see how the embrace of a theoretically pluralistic approach to self-multiplicity and unity could conflict with the ethical and ontological commitments to the singularity, continuity, and particularity of personhood that are shared by those theologians I have discussed in this essay. Indeed, such an approach would appear to have only benefits for a theological anthropology attempting to navigate between individuality and relationality. Recognizing the diversity of concepts of self-multiplicity, not all of which are indicative of a radical psychopathology, enables the construction of less restrictive accounts of everyday self-experience without necessarily surrendering the principle that people are more than just the products of their relations at any

---

27. Even McFadyen seeks a point of transcendent unity behind these various experiences of self to avoid the notion that people are comprised of many different autonomous subpersonalities (McFadyen 1990: 289).

given moment. Avoiding conflict with the human sciences in this context brings its own benefits. After all, if theological anthropology is to avoid theoretical isolation from the wider academic world, and maintain its relevance for current and future generations, it must listen to the finer details of a broad range of secular accounts of personhood. Certainly, where dialogue with the human sciences is an explicit aim, theologians cannot borrow only what they need and ignore all that might be potentially threatening.[28]

The second line of potential criticism concerns theologians' proposed "cures" for self-fragmentation. Sociologically, such cures typically depend upon the idea that only the self rooted in traditional Christian moral narratives — what Stanley Grenz calls "the ecclesial self" — can resist fragmentation in the modern world.[29] Consequently, the argument goes, the self might be reunified through the reestablishment of a common understanding of the good, which, it is assumed, will provide the moral and cultural stability so evidently lacking in contemporary life.[30] For White, at least, the impetus for this social transformation must begin with the recognition of our inviolable ontological unity as relational yet particular beings. In McFadyen's and Pannenberg's psychologies, the "cure" for self-fragmentation is a matter of individuals' ethical realignment of their identities in accordance with how each understands the image of God in humanity. For Pannenberg, this entails the acceptance of personhood's exocentric dimension and the identification of present with past and future manifestations of self. For McFadyen, it entails the unification of identity that accompanies the practice of authentic undistorted interpersonal communication, which itself corresponds with answering Christ's call.[31]

From the perspective of the contemporary human sciences, neither the sociological nor the psychological cures envisaged by these theologians can be satisfactory. If self-multiplicity can be understood in some sense as the

28. As David Kelsey observes in describing the secular influences upon the concept of person in the Christian tradition, such constructive dialogue with the human sciences would not be a novel development for theological anthropology: "In attempting to address anthropological questions Christian thinkers have always borrowed what they took to be the best anthropological wisdom of their host non-Christian cultures. And in borrowing the wisdom, they borrowed conceptual schemes" (Kelsey 2006: 141).

29. See Grenz 2001.

30. See Taylor 1992; Thiselton 1995; White 1997; Grenz 2001; Hauerwas 2001.

31. The renunciation of the exclusive focus upon oneself entailed by a response to the call to follow Christ represents the abandonment of a misconceived independence and the acceptance of an ex-centric self-orientation. For McFadyen, this serves to reorient the individual "properly" in all future relations.

natural product of normal psychological functioning, then "curing" society will not cure individuals' sense of self-fragmentation, or vice versa. For the human sciences, the disunity of self is not solely the result of the collapse of traditional communities, or the dissolution of shared systems of meaning, or the consequence of a theoretical misconception.[32] It can be variously conceived as all these things, but cannot be reduced to any single one of them. Nor will the successful integration of one's present experience of self into the broader context of one's life, nor consistency in the public presentation of oneself to others, succeed in banishing all the forms of self-multiplicity described by modern psychologists. These are things that might reduce the sense of internal dissonance, if it exists at all, but, as I have argued, there is more to the concept of self-multiplicity than a sense of inner disorder.

From the conceptually pluralistic perspective I have described, the very idea of a cure for most forms of self-multiplicity seems absurd. It is neither possible nor desirable. Indeed, psychologically, a person's ability to form and continuously develop a multiplicity of self-representations and relatively autonomous subpersonalities is often regarded as the source of the much-feted human capacity to adapt to social change and novel situations so efficiently.[33] Nevertheless, psychologists are not so naïve as to deny the possibility that for some people, the diversity between some of their subpersonalities and self-representations is a source of great mental strain, even if it does not always lead directly to the radical dissociation of personality that ensues the total loss of the sense of personal singularity and continuity.[34] What is usually an essential adaptive ability can at other times develop in a pathological direction. Reflection upon the ways in which this mental strain is treated psychologically suggests a possible alternative (or at least a supplementary

32. Indeed, there are good reasons to doubt that the sense of self-fragmentation is closely tied to the modern period, and to the contemporary Western world in particular. Such a thesis entails an implicit appeal to a particular transhistorical concept of undistorted unified identity. From a psychological perspective, where a degree of experiential multiplicity is conceived as the natural product of everyday cognitive life, it ought to be culturally and historically universal. Furthermore, as sociologists and philosophers have repeatedly demonstrated, self-fragmentation is an issue that has been exposed in various different forms throughout history (see Dews 1986; Hall 1992; Taylor 1992; Woodhead 1999).

33. See Gergen 1972; Boone 1995; Cooper 1999; Rappoport, Baumgardner, and Boone 1999.

34. Although no firm lines of demarcation can be drawn between pathological and adaptive manifestations of subpersonalities, some have distinguished between more or less pathological and more or less adaptive ways of structuring behavior according to distinct subpersonalities (see Turner 2008; Altrocchi 1999; Rowan 1999).

approach) to the current theological orthodoxy as regards the appropriate practical ethical response to the contemporary identity crisis.

Psychotherapy, in the form of clinical psychological intervention or counseling, for dissociative and borderline personality disorders in which the degree of disunity has progressed well beyond what is manageable, often focuses upon the acquisition of mental and behavioral tools to assist with the stresses and strains of everyday life.[35] Perhaps, then, as many psychologists would surely suggest, the sense of internal conflict that theologians have sought to resolve can also be alleviated, not by seeking to reaffirm a strong sense of self-unity, but by surrendering it, and learning instead how best to cope with our multiplicity.[36] This approach has begun to be explored by a number of theorists bringing psychoanalytic psychology into dialogue with pastoral theology, many of whom report significant success stories.[37] Unfortunately, this sort of therapeutic approach to the plural self has been largely ignored by theologians. Once more, this is to be expected given that the sense of self-fragmentation has such serious ethical (as well as existential) implications in theological accounts of personhood. But if the restoration of stable moral values in Christian community cannot be expected fully to heal the pervasive sense of self-fragmentation, then this alternative approach should not be dismissed lightly. It is beyond the scope of this essay to chart precisely how the project begun in psychoanalytic psychology might be extended into psychology more broadly, but the very possibility of such a therapeutic approach will remain inconceivable if disunity continues to be identified exclusively with disorder, and the seemingly fruitless search for a complete cure is allowed to proceed indefinitely.

REFERENCES

Altrocchi, J. 1999. "Individual Differences in Pluralism in Self-Structure." In *The Plural Self: Multiplicity in Everyday Life*, ed. J. Rowan and M. Cooper, 168-82. London: Sage Publications.

35. This is not strictly a reestablishment of self-unity, nor a healing of the sense of discontinuity (which the vast majority of people never lose), but it is plausibly a drawing together of different narrative strands of a person's life story.

36. Gergen, for example, advocates the abandonment of the idea of the particular unified self as a solution to the angst of postmodern life (Gergen 1991).

37. Several articles devoted to the topic of self-multiplicity and Christian theology published in a special issue of the journal *Pastoral Psychology* in 2008 are arguably the first to address these issues in depth. See Blevins 2008; Cataldo 2008; Lamborn 2008; Schaller 2008.

Bauman, Z. 2001. *The Individualised Society.* Cambridge: Polity Press.

Beck, J. R., and B. Demerest. 2005. *The Human Person in Theology and Psychology: A Biblical Anthropology for the Twenty-First Century.* Grand Rapids: Kregel.

Blevins, J. 2008. Different subjects: Postmodern selves in psychology and religion. *Pastoral Psychology* 57: 25-54.

Browning, D. S., and T. D. Cooper. 2004. *Religious Thought and the Modern Psychologies,* 2nd ed. Philadelphia: Fortress Press.

Cataldo, L. M. 2008. Multiple selves, multiple gods? Functional polytheism and the postmodern religious patient. *Pastoral Psychology* 57: 45-58.

Cooper, M. 1999. "If You Can't Be Jekyll Be Hyde: An Existential-Phenomenological Exploration on Lived-Plurality." In *The Plural Self: Multiplicity in Everyday Life,* ed. J. Rowan and M. Cooper, 51-71. London: Sage Publications.

Crossley, M. L. 2000. *Introducing Narrative Psychology: Self, Trauma and the Construction of Meaning.* Buckingham: Open University Press.

Dews, P. 1986. *Habermas: Autonomy and Solidarity.* London: Verso.

Dueck, A., and C. Lee. 2005. *Why Psychology Needs Theology: A Radical-Reformation Perspective.* Grand Rapids: Eerdmans.

Dunn, R. G. 1998. *Identity Crises: A Social Critique of Postmodernity.* Minneapolis: University of Minnesota Press.

Gergen, K. J. 1991. *The Saturated Self: Dilemmas of Identity in Modern Life.* New York: Basic Books.

Grenz, S. J. 2001. *The Social God and the Relational Self: A Trinitarian Theology of the Imago Dei.* London: Westminster/John Knox.

Hall, S. 1992. "The Question of Cultural Identity." In *Modernity and Its Futures,* ed. S. Hall, D. Held, and T. McGrew, 273-316. Cambridge: Polity Press.

Hardcastle, V. G., and O. Flanagan. 1999. Multiplex *vs.* multiple selves: Distinguishing dissociative disorders. *The Monist* 82, no. 4: 645-57.

Harré, R. 1998. *The Singular Self: An Introduction to the Psychology of Personhood.* London: Sage Publications.

Hauerwas, S. 2001. "Character, Narrative, and Growth." In *The Hauerwas Reader,* ed. J. Berkman and M. Cartwright, 221-54. London: Duke University Press.

Hermans, H. J. M., and G. Dimaggio, 2007. Self, identity and globalization in times of uncertainty: A dialogical analysis. *Review of General Psychology,* 11, no. 1: 31-61.

Hermans, H. J. M., and H. J. G. Kempen. 1993. *The Dialogical Self.* New York: Academic Press.

Kelsey, David H. 2006. "Personal Bodies: A Theological Anthropological Proposal." In *Personal Identity in Theological Perspective,* ed. R. Lints, M. S. Horton, and M. R. Talbot, 139-58. Grand Rapids: Eerdmans.

Lamborn, A. B. 2008. "Figuring" the self: Unity and multiplicity in clinical and theological imagination. *Pastoral Psychology* 57: 17-23.

Levin, J. D. 1992. *Theories of the Self.* London: Hemisphere Publishing Company.

Lifton, R. J. 1973. *The Protean Self.* New York: Basic Books.

McAdams, D. P. 1993. *The Stories We Live By: Personal Myths and the Making of the Self.* New York: Guilford Press.

McAdams, D. P. 1997. "The Case for Unity in the (Post)Modern Self: A Modest Proposal." In *Self and Identity: Fundamental Issues,* ed. R. D. Ashmore and L. Jussim, 46-79. New York: Oxford University Press.

McFadyen, A. I. 1990. *The Call to Personhood: A Christian Theory of the Individual in Social Relationships.* Cambridge: Cambridge University Press.

Markus, H. R. 1977. Self-schemata and processing information about the self. *Journal of Personality and Social Psychology* 35: 63-78.

Markus, H. R., and P. Nurius. 1987. "Possible Selves: The Interface between Motivation and the Self-Concept." In *Self and Identity: Psychosocial Perspectives,* ed. K. Yardley and T. Honess, 157-72. London: John Wiley.

Moreland, J. P. 2009. *The Recalcitrant Imago Dei.* Norwich, UK: SCM Press.

Olson, E. T. 1999. "There Is No Problem of the Self." In *Models of the Self,* ed. S. Gallagher and J. Shear, 49-61. Exeter: Imprint Academic.

Pannenberg, W. 1985. *Anthropology in Theological Perspective.* Translated by M. J. O'Connell. Edinburgh: T. & T. Clark.

Polkinghorne, D. E. 1988. *Narrative Knowing and the Human Sciences.* Albany: State University of New York Press.

Rosenberg, S., and M. A. Gara. 1985. "The Multiplicity of Personal Identity." In *Review of Personality and Social Psychology,* ed. P. Shaver, vol. 6, 87-113. Newbury Park, CA: Sage Publications.

Sarbin, T. R. 1986. *Narrative Psychology: The Storied Nature of Human Conduct.* New York: Praeger.

Schaller, J. E. 2008. Reconfiguring dis/ability: Multiple and narrative constructions of self. *Pastoral Psychology* 57: 89-99.

Schrag, C. O. 1997. *The Self after Postmodernity.* London: Yale University Press.

Seigel, J. 2005. *The Idea of the Self: Thought and Experience in Western Europe Since the Seventeenth Century.* Cambridge: Cambridge University Press.

Shults, F. L., and S. J. Sandage. 2006. *Transforming Spirituality: Integrating Theology and Psychology.* Grand Rapids: Baker Academic.

Strawson, G. 1999. "The Self." In *Models of the Self,* ed. S. Gallagher and J. Shear, 1-24. Exeter: Imprint Academic.

Taylor, C. 1992. *Sources of the Self.* Cambridge: Cambridge University Press.

Thiselton, A. C. 1995. *Interpreting God and the Postmodern Self: On Meaning Manipulation and Promise.* Edinburgh: T. & T. Clark.

Turner, L. 2008. *Theology, Psychology and the Plural Self.* Farnham: Ashgate.

Westen, D. 1992. The cognitive self and the psychoanalytic self: Can we put our selves together? *Psychological Inquiry* 3, no. 1: 1-13.

White, V. 1997. *Paying Attention to People: An Essay on Individualism and Christian Belief.* London: SPCK.

Wilcox, C., and L. Williams. 1990. Taking stock of schema theory. *Social Science Journal* 27, no. 4: 373-93.

Woodhead, L. 1999. Theology and the fragmentation of the self. *International Journal of Systematic Theology* 1, no. 1: 53-72.

Wyer, R. S., and T. K. Srull. 1989. *Memory and Cognition in Its Social Context.* Hillsdale, NJ: Erlbaum Associates.

Reenactors: Theological and Psychological Reflections on "Core Selves," Multiplicity, and the Sense of Cohesion

Pamela Cooper-White

The couple were resplendent in their Civil War period dress as they swept forward in the line to receive Communion at my family's church in Gettysburg, Pennsylvania — he in his Union General's dark blue with shining brass buttons, sword hanging at his side, and she in a pink dimity dress with high lace collar and billowing hoop skirt. It was Fourth of July weekend, and the town was full of Battle enthusiasts who had traveled, some from great distances, to reenact the "high water mark" of the Civil War in exacting detail, high on history, chasing a "period rush."[1] The husband and wife knelt at the Communion rail, careful to arrange sword and skirt with proper etiquette. The pastor placed the Communion bread into their gloved hands: "The body of Christ, given for you."

But who were "you"? I wondered later, as my husband and I sipped our twentieth-century lattés at The Ragged Edge, a café staffed by local college personnel. Were you well-informed tourists, attending worship in our historic church because it had served as a hospital during the days following the Battle, planks laid out across pews to receive the bodies of the wounded? Were you religiously committed Christians, lifelong Lutherans perhaps, who sought your regular weekly sustenance of faith in Word and Sacrament? Or were you here as your Civil War personae, not only reenacting the Battle, but enjoying a period rush here, too, as the General and his wife attending church in seemly fashion?

---

1. Tony Horwitz, *Confederates in the Attic: Dispatches from the Unfinished Civil War* (New York: Vintage, 1998), esp. 275-81; Jim Weeks, *Gettysburg: Memory, Market, and an American Shrine* (Princeton: Princeton University Press, 2003), esp. 209-14.

What was the "efficacy" of such a sacrament, the priest in me also wondered? *Who* was communed? To what "communion" of the baptized did they belong, and in which century? And who were they in relationship to God? Was there some essential or "core self" whom God would always recognize as a singular, distinctive person, uniquely and eternally written into the Book of Life, regardless of the era of their dress or their subjective experience of the moment?

Is There a Core Self?

Now, almost ten years later, I recognize that these questions themselves are based on a suspect foundation — namely, that there is (or should be) some essential, real, or "core" self by which each person is uniquely, irreducibly, and perhaps even eternally defined. Even after being steeped in psychoanalytic and postmodern literature about multiple subjects and subjectivities, and writing constructive theological work on the multiplicity of both persons and God, the question "Who were these people, *really?*" was irrepressible. As children of the Enlightenment, our personal anthropologies have been saturated with the notion that there is, finally, a true, core self at the heart of each person, and that this core self is the defining factor in human personality. Beneath all the various roles a person may play in his or her life in love and in work, and even in (re-)enactment, a person is finally one, singular entity — or, in more philosophical/theological language, one *soul*. This belief in the singularity of a person is no doubt heightened in the dominant culture of the United States, where the founding eighteenth-century myth of independence, combined with the Romantic era's "pioneering spirit" and "rugged individual," combine to emphasize the self-sufficiency of each human being as free citizen.

The foundation, however, is crumbling — or, perhaps, more accurately, has been *found out* to be no foundation at all, but rather a kind of façade. Our rugged individual is at best a well-functioning persona, and at worst a Potemkin house, presenting a seemingly solid front to the world, while concealing everything, anything: chaos, creativity, despair, multitudes. To twist Gertrude Stein's famous line, there *is* a "there" there — but it is not *one* "there," not one self. The façade has been pocked and chipped away over the past century by postmodern philosophy, neuroscience, psychoanalysis, postcolonial theory, feminist and queer theory, and even quantum physics, until we are able to see through cracks and fissures and larger voids into a subjectivity that is more expansive, more variegated, yet more fragile and interdependent than we were ever able to imagine.

In my writings to date,[2] I have been engaging the question of multiple selves/multiple subjects in relation to the construction of both a theological anthropology and a theology of multiplicity, drawing on the Christian doctrine of the Trinity. Following relational psychoanalytic theory, I have advocated for an expanded view of the human subject — at both conscious and unconscious levels — as a web or network of self-states. These states are not monolithic, but in themselves encompass whole worldviews, ranges of affect, systems of meaning-making, and tendencies to particular types of bodily activity. In this theory, we are not understood as a unitive, integral Self, but as a conglomerate of self-states, affect-states, and entire personalities formed in identification with objects or part-objects we have internalized from our experiences of other persons since birth. These self-states and internal personalities, further, do not function as autonomous, structured "beings," but continue to grow and change in unconscious dynamic interaction, both among themselves internally and in connection with other persons beyond the "self."

Freud's earlier metapsychology, when examined in light of unity versus multiplicity, already argued in favor of a multiple view of person and mind. From some of Freud's earliest work, notably *The Interpretation of Dreams*, his theorizing about the unconscious, and later elaboration in the form of three "institutions" of the mind — ego, id, and superego — established a way of thinking about our mental life as a fundamental disunity. The ego, in both Freud's and Jung's theories, thinks it knows more than it does. It was Freud's genius to assert in the face of the materialist-oriented scientific world of fin-de-siècle Vienna that we are not masters of our own houses, but that our actions are more often than not controlled by internal forces and dynamics be-

2. Pamela Cooper-White, *Many Voices: Pastoral Psychotherapy in Relational and Theological Perspective* (Minneapolis: Fortress Press, 2007); *Shared Wisdom: Use of the Self in Pastoral Care and Counseling* (Minneapolis: Fortress Press, 2004); "Com|plicated Woman: Multiplicity and Relationality across Gender, Race, and Culture," ch. 1 in *Women Out of Order: Risking Change and Creating Care in a Multi-Cultural World*, ed. Jeanne Stevenson Moessner and Teresa Snorton (Minneapolis: Fortress Press, 2009), 7-21; "The 'Other' Within: Multiple Selves Making a World of Difference," *Reflective Practice* 29 (2009): 23-37; "Interrogating Integration, Dissenting Dis-integration: Multiplicity as a Positive Metaphor in Therapy and Theology," along with Introduction to special issue on multiplicity, *Pastoral Psychology* 57, nos. 1-2 (Sept. 2008): 1-16; "Higher Powers and Infernal Regions: Models of Mind in Freud's Interpretation of Dreams and Contemporary Psychoanalysis, and Their Implications for Pastoral Care," *Pastoral Psychology* 50, no. 5 (2002): 319-43.

yond our conscious knowledge or control. Freud further paved the way for recognizing that we internalize others (objects) as part of the process of mental formation,[3] and that this process itself is swayed by internal forces of fantasy and desire, as well as the actual good and bad experiences coming from the environment. This attention to internal objects led to the development of "object relations theory" in the generation after Freud (including Melanie Klein, W. R. D. Fairbairn, and D. W. Winnicott). These theorists emphasized attachment to external persons ("objects") as the primary motivational force in human development. In this theory, the psyche is gradually constructed from the infant's unconscious internalization of multiple, affect-laden "objects" (an amalgam of actual people as experienced by the child, parts of people such as the mother's breast, and the child's own fantasized versions of those people and parts). Object relations theory has been expanded further by contemporary relational-psychoanalytic theory, with its concept of the normativity of multiple selves to guide both theoretical conceptualization and clinical practice.[4]

This concept of multiplicity of persons has been brought into dialogue with pastoral psychology and theology to propose a concept of God as equally and transcendentally multiple, fluid, mutable, and relational — intimately responsive to the complexity of human life and all created nature.[5] Drawing from various contemporary theologians, I have embraced a conception of the divine in terms of inherent community, relationality, and mutual desire. This expansive, multiple divinity is the "Manyone [many/one],"[6] the *Elohim* whose multiplicity is still discernible in the Book of Genesis as the "chaotic plenary source from which all being does not so much emerge, upward, as it 'unfolds,'"[7] eternally expanding in relationship as "primordial communion."[8] As a

3. Sigmund Freud, *Mourning and Melancholia*, in *Standard Edition of the Complete Works of Sigmund Freud*, ed. and trans. James Strachey, vol. 14, 243-48.

4. For an overview, see Cooper-White, *Shared Wisdom*, 47-50; see also Philip M. Bromberg, "Standing in the Spaces," *Contemporary Psychoanalysis* 32 (1996): 509-35; *Standing in the Spaces: Essays on Clinical Process, Trauma, and Dissociation* (Hillsdale, NJ: Analytic Press, 1998); and Jody Messler Davies, "Multiple Perspectives on Multiplicity," *Psychoanalytic Dialogues* 8, no. 2 (1998): 195-206.

5. Cooper-White, *Many Voices*, 77-82.

6. Catherine Keller, *Face of the Deep: A Theology of Becoming* (London and New York: Routledge, 2003), 181.

7. Gilles Deleuze, *Difference and Repetition*, trans. Paul Patton (New York: Columbia University Press, 1968), 229; see also Keller, *Face of the Deep*, 168.

8. Elizabeth Johnson, *She Who Is: The Mystery of God in Feminist Theological Discourse* (New York: Crossroad, 1994), 227.

Christian theologian, this has led me specifically to consider the Trinity as "a spacious room — even matrix/womb," a de-concretized, kenotic space for metaphorical play and imagination. I have proposed a pastoral Trinitarian metaphor of the divine as Creative Profusion, Incarnational Desire, and Living Inspiration.[9]

A conceptualization of both human persons and God as multiple still begs the question, however, whether there might be a core self — a central, defining self — amid the myriad of self-parts, self-states, and subjectivities contained within a larger multiple self.

Core Self: Some History behind the Idea

The notion of a core, nuclear, true, or essential self is ubiquitous in psychotherapy, including pastoral counseling. Each of these terms — "core," "true," and "essential" — has its own (often unacknowledged) intellectual lineage. In the psychoanalytic literature, Heinz Kohut occasionally used the term "core self" interchangeably with his concept of a "nuclear self," to refer to "the central sector of the personality."[10] As he broke with classical Freudian theory, Kohut asserted a "psychology of the self" based less on internal drives and conflict, and more on the impact of environment and parental provisions in development. For Kohut, the "core" or "nuclear self" represented an internal psychic structure undergirding "our sense of being an independent center of initiative and perception, integrated with our most central ambitions and ideals and with our experience that our body and mind form a unit in space and a continuum in time."[11] For Kohut, this nuclear self provided a sense of self-cohesion to existence. The term "core self" was used similarly around the same time in empirical studies directly observing infant behavior, to refer to babies' developing sense of self-regulation.[12] The idea of a "core self" has most recently been appropriated in the specialized treatment of childhood sexual abuse survivors, especially those diagnosed with Dissociative Identity Disorder (formerly called "Multiple Personality Disorder"). As trauma treatment was developed and refined in the 1980s, a "core self" frequently emerged among the many personality states commonly

9. Elaborated in Cooper-White, *Many Voices*, 81-94.
10. Heinz Kohut, *The Restoration of the Self* (New York: International Universities Press, 1977), 177-78.
11. Kohut, *Restoration of the Self*, 177.
12. Daniel Stern, *The Interpersonal World of the Infant* (New York: Basic Books, 1985).

identified by dissociative patients and their therapists.[13] The rediscovery of this core self had a therapeutic effect of anchoring the patient back to a sense of an original reality and identity.

The language of "core self" has increasingly migrated from these various contexts, and is now frequently used by clinicians to refer more generally to the center or most "true and authentic" source of personality and identity. It should be noted, however, that in neither Kohut's writings nor in the infant observation literature is the core self postulated as a constitutional, inherent essence. The responsiveness of the parents and other caretakers has a profound effect on the child's sense of agency and identity.

For Kohut, moreover, the nuclear self was not a single unit, but a "bipolar" schema. He posited that the child's sense of structural cohesion derived from two structural pillars, or "poles," built up gradually from the parents' provision of two crucial relational (or "selfobject") functions: mirroring (the parents' empathic responsiveness to the child's grandiosity through recognition and age-appropriate applause) and idealizing (the parents' empathic responsiveness to the child's idealization of the parents' reliability and strength). Thus, the development of the self was understood as complex, with "many shades and varieties or types," formed through a "variety of environmental factors . . . which, singly or in combination with each other, account for the specific characteristics of the nuclear self and for its firmness, weakness, or vulnerability."[14]

"True self" is a term associated with the British object relations psychoanalyst D. W. Winnicott. In "Ego Distortion in Terms of True and False Self,"[15] Winnicott described a type of patient who operates in the world out of a compliant, somewhat anesthetized "False Self." Such a person, Winnicott posited, internalized parental prohibitions and expectations so deeply that his or her spontaneity was crushed in early childhood, and the "True Self," which contained the child's spontaneity and aliveness, was effectively suppressed. The goal of therapy with such patients was to help them reconnect with this buried True Self, in order to restore their full range of affect, creativity, and zest for life.

The problem with this term is not so much in its original usage, but that, like "core self," it has leaked into common clinical parlance apart from its

---

13. E.g., David L. Fink, "The Core Self," *Dissociation* 1, no. 2 (1988): 43-47; see also http://www.coreintegrity.org/.

14. Kohut, *Restoration of the Self*, 187.

15. D. W. Winnicott, "Ego Distortion in Terms of True and False Self," in Winnicott, *The Maturational Processes and the Facilitating Environment* (London: Hogarth, 1965), 140-52.

context in Winnicott's writings. Winnicott did not intend to create a binary metaphysic in which the self is composed solely of a "true" and a "false" self. Winnicott clearly worked within a Kleinian "object relations" model of multiple internalized and fantasized objects in dynamic relation. He identified the early play of subjectivities in the psychic "transitional space" between infant and mother as the basis for all creativity, even culture and religion. Subjectivity according to Winnicott, then, is neither monolithic (supposing only the "True" self to be "real"), nor binary (with reified "True" and "False" selves in Manichean opposition). The "false self" and the "true self" in Winnicott's conception of the person do not have any reified ontological status, but rather represent two different self-states or experiences of the larger interior world of object relations.

The third term, "essential self," belongs to a strand of thought within philosophy that there is one, true, fundamental nature behind or within everything, and this true nature or "essence" is what ultimately defines it — that without which a thing could not be itself. While some psychoanalysts have traced this concept, particularly as it appears as a guiding belief about the nature of persons ("essentialism") to the influence of the Enlightenment,[16] it has its origins in the Greek philosopher Plato. Plato posited that for every phenomenon in our earthly experience, there is an Ideal, a perfect Form from which each thing derives its essential substance. We can only perceive these Forms indirectly through the senses. Earthly existence is like a cave, in which we can perceive objects outside only by their shadows.[17] The Ideal or Form of a person is the Soul, which has an eternal life independent of the body, and which flies after death back to Heaven, the pure realm of the Ideals. In the seventeenth century, Descartes' search for one irreducible foundation for the reality of the self led to the fusion of rationality ("Cogito, ergo sum") with essential selfhood, creating the autonomous, modern subject. In early twentieth-century psychology, it is most readily apparent in Jung's theory of universal Archetypes, which Jung posited as universal dynamic forces in the collective unconscious, discernible through myths and legends of many cultures across all human history.

16. E.g., Lewis Kirshner, "The Concept of the Self in Psychoanalytic Theory and Its Philosophical Foundations," *Journal of the American Psychoanalytic Association* 39, no. 1 (1991): 157-82; H. Stein, "Geometry of the 'True Self' (Winnicott): On a Psychoanalytic Leibniz Study by F. Eckstein in 1931," *Zeitschrift für klinische Psychologie, Psychopathologie und Psychotherapie* 33, no. 4 (1985): 367-76.

17. Plato, *The Republic,* trans. Robin Waterfield (Oxford: Oxford University Press, 2008), 270-75.

Feminist, postmodern, postcolonial, and queer theorists, writing from different perspectives, have mounted a multifaceted critique of essentialism as perpetuating a mind-body split that reinforces the subjugation of women, sexual minorities, and persons of color. Essentialism, as defined by the white, male, Western "self," represented an ongoing valorization of imperialist notions of the white Western self as rational and autonomous, and marked the non-Western "Other" as both exotic and inferior. Such critiques, however, often remain in academic contexts and do not trickle into popular culture. In Western culture to this day, the belief in some Ideal or defining essence continues to influence popular conceptions of mind, self, and soul, including smorgasbord-style popular spiritual movements, and implicit models of integration and what it means to be a self in counseling and psychotherapy.

Even the use of the word "self" itself to denote a concrete ontological entity "is a reification, a misuse of the reflexive pronoun."[18] Postmodern feminist psychoanalyst Jane Flax argues for the language of subjectivity and subjects rather than "self" and "selves":

Language to discuss multiple subjectivity requires terms with less bounded or solid connotations than "self." Subjectivity . . . is a dynamic, constantly rewoven web of processes . . . [whose] meanings are shifting and often reconstituted. The term subjectivity also captures the multiple positions of subjects as agent and object, as neither purely determined nor determining.[19]

The terms "core self," "True Self," "essential self," "soul," and even "self" itself, then, have often been used interchangeably to mean the real person as who she or he "really is" — both as the subjective sense of having an authentic identity, and as a character or set of character traits (including native virtues and besetting sins) that can be defined externally as his or her "personality" or way of being a person in the world. In psychotherapy, heavily influenced by twentieth-century humanism and existentialism, "finding oneself" is held explicitly or implicitly as a kind of ideal state to be reached through a therapeutic process of integration,[20] or "self-actualization."[21]

18. Stephen Mitchell, "Contemporary Perspectives on Self," *Psychoanalytic Dialogues* 1, no. 2 (1991): 124, citing Gilbert Ryle and Ludwig Wittgenstein.

19. Jane Flax, "Taking Multiplicity Seriously," *Contemporary Psychoanalysis* 32, no. 4 (1996): 577-93.

20. Cooper-White, "Interrogating Integration, Dissenting Dis-integration."

21. E.g., Abraham Maslow, *Toward a Psychology of Being*, 3rd ed. (New York: Wiley, 1998).

As an ideal, this also bears a slippery relation to morality in the form of "character," with the implication that a healing of "character pathology" (the earlier twentieth-century ego psychology term for the DSM[22] "personality disorders") should result in a higher capacity for moral judgment. As Philip Rieff so trenchantly pointed out, psychology does not operate with the pure scientific neutrality Freud so vigorously (and defensively) asserted.[23] Just as the term "character" has been equated with virtue in twentieth-century social and educational movements[24] and in academic philosophy ("virtue ethics"[25]), its diagnostic meaning in psychology retains the color of social mores. Character can be characterized as weak or strong, bad or good; and clinical labels such as "borderline," "dependent," "depressive," or "narcissistic" — especially when patients are perceived as difficult — can function judgmentally as reinscriptions of familiar "deadly sins" (anger, sloth, acedia, pride) or classic humors (choleric, phlegmatic, melancholic, sanguine).

Problematizing the Core Self

This idea(l), then, of a central, true, core, or essential self, together with its moral overtones, permeates our Western understanding of what it means to be a human being. But, like all idea(l)s, the "core self" is a social construc-

22. *Diagnostic and Statistical Manual of Mental Disorders DSM-IV-TR, 4th rev. ed. with Text Revision* (Washington, DC: American Psychiatric Publishing, 2000).

23. Phillip Rieff, *Freud: The Mind of a Moralist,* 3rd ed. (Chicago: University of Chicago Press, 1979).

24. Alexis de Tocqueville, *Democracy in America* (New York: Penguin Classics, 2003), 336; Robert Bellah et al., *Habits of the Heart: Individualism and Commitment in American Life,* 3rd ed. (Berkeley: University of California Press, 2007). Taking an opposite position valorizing individualism, William J. Bennett advocates for the cultivation of individual virtues in *The Book of Virtues* (New York: Simon & Schuster, 1996). See also The Virtues Project at www.virtuesproject.com.

25. The relationship between virtue and character can be traced to Aristotle — see Nancy Sherman, *The Fabric of Character: Aristotle's Theory of Virtue* (Oxford: Oxford University Press, 1991). See also Philippa Foot, *Virtues and Vices* (Oxford: Blackwell, 1978) and *Natural Goodness* (Oxford: Clarendon Press, 2001); Alasdair MacIntyre, *After Virtue* (London: Duckworth), 3rd ed. (Notre Dame: University of Notre Dame Press, 2007); Owen Flanagan and Amelie Oksenberg Rorty, eds., *Identity, Character and Morality* (Cambridge, MA: MIT Press, 1990); "Virtue Ethics," in Stanford Encyclopedia of Philosophy, available online at http://plato.stanford.edu/entries/ethics-virtue/#2; Gilbert Harman, "Virtue Ethics without Character Traits," online at http://www.princeton.edu/~harman/Papers/Thomson.html.

tion, and as such, can be interrogated as to its cultural, political, and social purposes. The problematic aspect of a "core" or essential self is not so much what it contains, but what it excludes, i.e., the inherent relationality and interdependence of persons. The notion of a core self reinforces individualism, and the belief that somewhere, "deep down"[26] inside a person, there is finally an insoluble unity. As long as there is a core, no matter how much multiplicity, variation, inconsistency, and even chaos there may be in the outer layers of the personality, there is finally a place deep within the person that is an unconflicted, unalloyed, defining One. This may be of comfort, particularly to those who have experienced only violation, rupture, and traumatic fragmentation. Paradoxically, the more fragmented I am (as opposed to a healthy, fluid dissociability), the more I am likely to feel trapped in whatever state I am currently in as my only self (however painful or frightening that state may be), because I cannot flow readily among my many self-states, and cannot imagine ever feeling any different.[27] Relational analysts have distinguished between multiplicity (as normative fluidity, mutability, and diversity of the self) and fragmentation (a pathological sense of being in pieces without any reliable cohesiveness or going-on-being),[28] or at least conceptualize them as opposite ends of a spectrum.[29] All of us probably need some subjective sense of a floor to stand on, or an anchor in the storm.

Lisa Cataldo, a relational analyst, has argued brilliantly for retaining *both* multiplicity *and* a sense of self-cohesion, as mutually dependent, illusory constructs, operating in a kind of dialectical tension:

> Without a sense of cohesive, continuous self, we have nowhere to stand. Or rather we might ask, "who is standing in the spaces?" Bromberg does not say, but I cannot help but think of Winnicott's image of the child who has not had good enough holding in infancy; this is the child (and later, adult) who experiences him or herself as "falling forever," a terrifying way to exist. . . . As much as I have experienced and affirmed my own multiplicity, I keep coming back to the question, "if we are only standing in the spaces, what keeps us from falling forever?"
>
> I think we need to expand Bromberg's idea that the creative space is

26. Cooper-White, "Higher Powers and Infernal Regions," and *Many Voices,* 51-63.

27. Bromberg, "Standing in the Spaces," 516-17.

28. Bromberg, "Standing in the Spaces"; Jane Flax, "Multiples: On the Contemporary Politics of Subjectivity," in *Disputed Subjects: Essays on Psychoanalysis, Politics, and Philosophy* (London and New York: Routledge, 1993), 92-110.

29. Davies, "Multiple Perspectives on Multiplicity."

in the spaces between selves. The creative space is not between selves only, but in the space between a sense of self as multiple and a sense of self as unified and continuous. They are mutually dependent illusions. It is moving between these illusions that gives us a sense of "real" — the more we are able to be both multiple and singular, the more we are able to play in the real world of our experience. And the more we are able to play with multiplicity and unity as possible images of God.[30]

However, as long as the "floor" or the "anchor" is conceived as existing only within ourselves, we remain isolated — literally (if impossibly) *self-contained*. Winnicott critiqued the notion of isolated selves in his well-known statement, "There is no such thing as an infant . . . [and] whenever one finds an infant, one finds maternal care."[31] Both the floor and the anchor in Winnicott's conception do not exist initially within the self, but in the arms and on the breast of the nursing mother. When the mother is "good enough," and the infant feels reliably held and responded to, it gradually internalizes the holding function into itself. This is a developmental achievement[32] always occurring (with more or less success) in and through relationship — even if such relationality is unrecognized or denied.

Furthermore, the One, the isolate, the individual and individual*istic* "I," has negative social and political ramifications. A solitary construct of what it means to be human participates in an exaggerated heroic narrative, which cannot be disentangled from the myths of conquest that undergird both imperialism and colonialism. Dominance maintained through violence is recast as heroism, and the "I" asserts its individuality while standing on the invisible-ized bodies of the conquered. Such individuality is a self-serving illusion, won/one at the unacknowledged price of others' lives. There is no such actual oneness, only the *illusion* of oneness, maintained by excluding and even forbidding knowledge about and relationship with the subjugated other. Devotion to oneness benefits the "One" who masquerades as the universal, whereas multiplicity makes space for the marginalized, those constructed as "Other" in the binary dualism of One versus Many.

Insistence upon such isolated oneness is reinscribed in theologies that

---

30. Lisa Cataldo, "Multiple Selves, Multiple Gods? Functional Polytheism and the Postmodern Religious Patient," *Pastoral Psychology* 57, nos. 1-2 (2008): 45-58.

31. D. W. Winnicott, "The Theory of the Parent-Infant Relationship," in *Maturational Processes and the Facilitating Environment* (London: Hogarth, 1965), p. 39 n. 1.

32. Philip M. Bromberg, "'Speak! That I May See You': Some Reflections on Dissociation, Reality, and Psychoanalytic Listening," *Psychoanalytic Dialogues* 4, no. 4 (1994): 517-48.

emphasize a single, monolithic, imperial God. As theologian Laurel Schneider has written:

> Oneness, as a basic claim about God, simply does not make sense. The world in its tenacious natality, mutability, and flesh has always exceeded and undermined oneness and totality, whether in Akhenaten's Egypt, Josiah's Israel, Constantine's Rome, or Luther's Germany. It repeatedly puts the lie to the One God's attempts at closure and control. For multiplicity, it turns out, is not just the flesh behind the mask of the One, it is the mask and masquerade of totality as well, popping the seams of the One's oneness in every instance. Multiplicity, which is not a synonym for "many," is a preliminary gesture, an experiment in naming a logic that is supple, adaptive, and rhizomatic rather than fixed, or merely predictive. Multiplicity turns out the story of the One, in the paradoxical sense of rejecting the One's totality and in the sense of producing it. This can be no either/or reduction. When the flow of multiplicity disrupts the pretensions of the One, we discover that God, so often a synonym for the One, is more and less than one, after all.[33]

The genius of Trinitarian theology, and the Cappadocians' beautiful imagery of *perichoresis,* is that it holds divine oneness and multiplicity in a never-ending creative tension. The image of the three "persons," Anselm's three Unimaginables (*nescio quids*[34]), holds relationality as a primary attribute of divinity, and at the same time invites humanity *into* the divine relation by incorporating the embodied human Jesus as one of the (at least) Three-in-One.

"Core Self" as Part, not Center

If we reject the binary division between "core self" and "multiple self" as definitive of what it means to be a person, does this mean that the sense of a "core self" is illusory, and multiplicity is what is real? As Cataldo has noted,[35] *both* concepts are illusory, in the Winnicottian sense that reality can only be known through the mediation of illusion, play, and imagination, in the tran-

---

33. Laurel Schneider, *Beyond Monotheism* (London and New York: Routledge, 2008), ix-x.

34. Anselm, *Monologion,* cited in Johnson, *She Who Is,* 203.

35. Cataldo, "Multiple Selves, Multiple Gods?" 49.

sitional spaces among and between internal objects and external relationships. Or, we might say, both concepts are equally "real" or "true," in the way that all constructs function to create the reality they purport to define. If singularity and multiplicity are ontological assertions, however, they must remain mutually exclusive. Only if both constitute subjectivities can they be mutually compatible. As constructs representing different experiences of one's own solidity or complexity, they can be represented as "existing" not in binary opposition, but on a continuum of experience.[36]

To return to the question, then, whether there might still be a "core self" amid the myriad of self-parts, self-states, and subjectivities contained within a larger multiple self — I would answer "yes," but *only* if understood as an *aspect* of all one's subjectivities, and not as an actual, definitive, or central locus of identity, agency, and purpose. I think there is no question that some people (I would not say all) experience their mental and emotional well-being as "grounded" in a unified, coherent sense of "I," or organizing fantasy or "self-concept,"[37] which has an enduring set of character traits, desires, and agentic capacity, and even an overarching sense of purpose or "calling." I would also agree that an unremitting sense of fragmentation and absence of going-on-being, or a sense of "falling forever" without any ground to stand on (mother's arms to catch you) can be a terrifying and anguished mode of existence. However, I do not believe that the felt *sense* of having a "core self" or "ground of being" (and I use this term deliberately for both its psychological and theological connotations) is the same thing as there *actually being one.*

This leads me, therefore, to see multiplicity as the overarching paradigm,[38] within which the concept of the One is admissible, but only as one illusory part. It is a subjective feeling of "having arrived," being grounded in an essential truth, yet it is not necessarily as "true" as it feels, because it excludes the knowledge of itself as a contingent part of a larger whole. Its confidence depends on a denial of multiplicity. There is still no singular "truth" or "essence" defining the whole.

Nor does the "core self" have an identifiable, fixed location within the self. Two metaphors from Gilles Deleuze offer helpful alternatives: the *rhizome,*[39] a more spatial, associative model of consciousness and uncon-

---

36. Davies, "Multiple Perspectives on Multiplicity."

37. William I. Grossman, "The Self as Fantasy: Fantasy as Theory," *Journal of the American Psychoanalytic Association* 30 (1982): 919-38.

38. Contra Frank M. Lachmann, "How Many Selves Make a Person?" *Contemporary Psychoanalysis* 32, no. 4 (1996): 595-614.

39. Cooper-White, *Many Voices,* 57-61 et passim.

sciousness; and the *fold*,[40] a more organic, mutable, and unpredictable model of mental life. There are origins but no single point of origin; depths and shadows, but no single locatable, penetrable "depth." There is a shape — in the way an iris corm or a fall of silk drapery has a shape — but it is fluid and ever-changing — formed, contingent, and permeable to forces beyond itself.

Moving beyond dualisms or fixed geometrical structures for metaphors of self and mind, the "core" is meaningless as a structural reality.[41] The subjective perception that "I" am being "true to myself," "keeping it all together," "grounded," or "centered," can arise along various nodal points of my experience from moment to moment, or in a more enduring way, even as the "ground" shifts and crumbles imperceptibly "under my feet" — making way for my hungry, expanding, foraging roots. But that "I" — including my sense of "core self" — will change and grow, even as relationships and circumstances impinge and mold me intersubjectively, at both conscious and unconscious levels.

This, too, has ethical resonances. Mutability of the self makes way for new relations. Willingness to surrender a particular subjective experience of "core self" in favor of other selves, or even a revised sense of what is "core," is necessary for true mutuality to occur in relations with others. To quote Korean feminist scholar Wonhee Anne Joh:

> I find the notion of the "annihilation of the self" a meaningful part of my spirituality of resistance and transformation — individual and social — when I understand it as a call to practice emptying out of self so that I might better let a multiplicity of selves into my being in the world. Such emptying out and letting in gives birth to a "co-arising" of many selves in relation with, to, and for one another. The annihilation of self then is a call to practice a kind of way of being in the world whose arch is bent toward the other. To use Gayatri Spivak's term, such a way of being in the world, bent and directed toward the other, is a kind of love that seeks to slowly make possible a "non-coercive rearrangement of desire."[42]

---

40. Cooper-White, "Com|plicated Woman."

41. I disagree here with Bromberg's distinction between "dissociative process" and "dissociative structure." Any notion of "psychic structure" must remain metaphorical, to avoid being reinscribed as an ontological attribute of intrapsychic experience.

42. Wonhee Anne Joh, "Authoring a Multiplicity of Selves and No-Self," *Journal of Feminist Studies in Religion* 24, no. 2 (2008): 171.

As I have argued previously,[43] I believe that the concept of multiple selves/subjects is a powerful bridge to empathy, especially toward others we perceive to be different. A genuine openness to difference, one that can move beyond social inequalities and the dominating power, "requires more than a liberal 'tolerance,' or even a sincere but naïve form of curiosity about the 'Other.'" To experience genuine empathy for other persons outside ourselves calls us to engage and even befriend the parts of our multiple selves that we have most denied or wished to disavow. Being willing to explore our alien self-parts, and to recognize that the very fact of alien-ness is built into the fabric of our own character, is the beginning of empathic understanding of other persons, with all of their own complexity and alien-ness. In the words of Julia Kristeva, "How could one tolerate a foreigner if one did not know one was a stranger to oneself?"[44]

Such openness requires courage, because it invites a level of annihilation of any certainty we may have clung to for our sense of identity, security, even "reality." Being thus "undone," in order to be capable of reaching out toward the Other, requires a sense of having a self to undo in the first place (and, presumably, to do again). But this *sense* of having a self, whether experienced as being one-self at the core, or being a cohesive amalgam of multiple selves, does not need to be conceived as primary, central, or foundational — except in the most metaphorical sense. Paradoxically, the capacity to feel secure enough to tolerate and use one's own multiplicity is related to the infantile experience of being held, and this always requires the actual experience of holding by a "good enough," reliable enough (m)Other outside one-self.

So what holds each of us together as healthy "multiples"? If we are not, as we once imagined, bound by the gravity of an inner core, what keeps us from flying to pieces? And what allows us to perceive ourselves (at least most days) to be the same person from day to day and year to year? What constitutes our going-on-being?

The Feeling of Being Oneself: Braided Selves

To return to the metaphor of the fold, I have proposed that there is a thread, or threads, holding together the fabric of our mental lives, at least as we ex-

---

43. Cooper-White, "The 'Other' Within: Multiple Selves Making a World of Difference."

44. Julia Kristeva, *Strangers to Ourselves*, trans. Leon Roudiez (New York: Columbia University Press, 1991), cited in Donald Capps, *Freud and the Freudians on Religion* (New Haven: Yale University Press, 2001), 328.

perience our selves from moment to moment. Rather than identifying this thread as a singular conscious identity formation, however, I have proposed a metaphor for the multiple self as *braid*, whose strength derives precisely from the interweaving of its disparate conscious and unconscious threads.[45] I have provisionally identified four strands that "hold" a sense of self together without erasing or undoing our multiplicity: (1) our bodies; (2) our relationships; (3) our spirituality; and (4) our embodied ethical practices.[46] This braid is best conceptualized not as a single straight line, but as itself a network or weaving. Such a web of threads, taken together, constitutes a "whole" — but a whole whose very coherence and binding power is made up of our multiple subjective experiences and states of being in relation.

Like all theories of what constitutes a healthy self, there are certainly value judgments embedded in this conceptualization — quite explicitly so. They draw on a Judeo-Christian ethic of love and justice, from the particularity of my own context as a Christian theologian. The concept of the multiplicity of selves, then, as a pastoral theological anthropology, valorizes both increasing knowledge and harmonious relations among the parts of a person, and the arch of empathy in interpersonal relations.

Life in the Body

The most obvious unifying factor in our experience of ourselves is that we live in one body. We are contained by the primal boundary of our skin, and as infants it is primarily through the skin that we first experience the boundary between ourselves and the rest of the world.[47] While there is some convincing evidence that our bodies react quite differently in relation to our many different self-states,[48] even persons suffering with Dissociative Iden-

---

45. Cooper-White, "Com|plicated Woman."

46. Cf. Cooper-White, "Com|plicated Woman." This article represents a slight revision from that article, where I separated relationality as an overarching theme.

47. E.g., Esther Bick, "The Experience of Skin in Early Object Relations," *International Journal of Psycho-Analysis* 49 (1968): 484-86; Thomas Ogden, *The Primitive Edge of Experience* (Northvale, NJ: Aronson, 1992), 31.

48. Graham Bass, "Sweet Are the Uses of Adversity: Psychic Integration through Body-Centered Work," in *Bodies in Treatment: The Unspoken Dimension*, ed. Frances Sommer Anderson (New York: Analytic Press, 2007), 151-68; Richard Stolorow and George Atwood, "The Mind and the Body," *Psychoanalytic Dialogues* 1, no. 2 (1991): 181-95; Mary Gail Frawley and Jodie Messler Davies, *Treating the Adult Survivor of Childhood Sexual Abuse* (New York:

tity Disorder do not have multiple bodies. Our various affective states and selves must share a physical being — blood, bones, organs, nerves, flesh, hair, and all. Our bodily experiences become a part of the shared history of our many selves. The arrowhead-shaped scar on my elbow, the wrinkles and freckles kissed and seared into my skin by the sun, the fracture line on my kneecap — these are permanent reminders of the fifty-three years "I" in all my subjective states have dwelled in this particular, irreproducible "temple" that is my body. Although my body may respond very differently to different conscious and unconscious states of being, especially emotional states, and may do the bidding of different self-parts as I move through my days (curled up, stretched out, taut with anger, soft with compassion, laboring dutifully, running bravely toward, shrinking back, lounging heedlessly, arcing sensually), I am able in some sense to know myself through all these variations as one person because I am located in this living, pulsing, breathing animal-being of skin and bones.

Life in Relationship

Being held by others in infancy in a state of utter dependency, as Winnicott understood, is the beginning of a lifelong sense of security or insecurity.[49] We also come cognitively to know who we are because our relationships locate us both temporally and spatially, and in particular, give us a name. The power of naming is well recognized, as in the Book of Genesis. Naming is a form of stewardship in this Judeo-Christian creation story. As human beings, we are called to care for one another as stewards, because we also have the power to name and define one another. The power of naming can be used or abused. When we are limited and confined by myths that maintain dominance and subordination, naming becomes a strategy for subjugation of the "Other." On the other hand, naming is a powerful force for encouragement and nurture by "good enough" parents, siblings, friends, and intimate partners. None of us can escape the mirrors that others hold up to us, mirrors that can tell us truths about our diverse selves, tell us lies, and show us pictures of what we might or might not be in the future. Our sense of iden-

Basic Books, 1994), 68-72; Bessel van der Kolk, "The Body Keeps the Score: Memory and the Evolving Psychobiology of Posttraumatic Stress," *Harvard Review of Psychiatry* 1, no. 5 (1994): 253-65.

49. Analogous to Erik Erikson's first developmental stage, "basic trust vs. basic mistrust," *Childhood and Society* (New York: W. W. Norton, 1963), 247.

tity and ongoingness of being oneself depend, for good or for ill, on this naming and mirroring by others.

Spirituality

I have specified spirituality as an element that shapes our sense of identity because it evokes those qualities of experience, often previously assigned to an essential or "core" self, that appear to shape our sense of purpose or "calling," and represent our most cherished values and ideals. These aspects of subjectivity are akin to what James Fowler identified as "faith": "our way of finding coherence in and giving meaning to the multiple forces and relationships that make up our lives . . . a person's way of seeing him- or herself in relation to others against a background of shared meaning and purpose."[50]

While I have argued against the notion that such shaping values reside inherently in some essential, central part of our being, our "soul" or "character," I do not dispute the presence of such values and ideals as a part of the self-experience — and, in keeping with multiplicity of the self in general, these values and ideals are both multiple and intersubjectively constructed in relationships. They are both conscious and unconscious, and so may be diverse, even conflicting. There may be a "majority view" that directs our lives more or less coherently, but we all contain worlds within us, some of which are repressed or habitually disavowed. The more we can bring these differing values into consciousness and honest dialogue, the better we may be able to understand what function the various "faiths" perform in our inner life. The better we are able to mediate among them toward a more harmonious, collaborative feeling of purpose and meaning (akin to Carl Rogers's idea of "congruence"[51]), the more reliable we may also be able to be in our relations with others. But the meaning-making in which we engage is not a simple process of consciously deciding to be a certain kind of person, or plumbing the depths to discover our one "true" character, or soul. Healthy multiplicity is a lifelong negotiation, not a model of finality, certainty, or perfection.

Within Christian traditions of spirituality, again, there are resources to enhance this sense of inner collaboration, rather than collapsing back into a vision of undifferentiated oneness. Bonhoeffer's well-known poem "Who

---

50. James Fowler, *Stages of Faith: The Psychology of Human Development,* 2nd ed. (New York: HarperOne, 1995), 4.

51. Carl Rogers, *On Becoming a Person* (Boston: Houghton Mifflin, 1961).

Am I?" resolves an anguishing sense of contradictions and multiple subjectivities by resting in the faith statement that "Whoever I am, Thou knowest, O God, I am Thine!"[52] Just as our God-images reflect our infantile state of utter dependency, and cannot be separated entirely from our earliest experiences of our seemingly omniscient and omnipotent parents, the function of maternal holding that we internalize for our sense of personal security in the world is also reflected in this description of divine holding. We are held by God, as surely or even more surely than by any earthly parent. In Julian's words: "when we fall, quickly [God] raises us up with his loving embrace and his gracious touch. And when we are strengthened by his sweet working, then we willingly choose him by grace, that we shall be his servants and his lovers, constantly and forever."[53]

Embodied Ethical Practices

Finally, we also experience a sense of identity as it grows and is formed over time by our actual behaviors and actions in the world. Our bodies not only experience, but act. Our agency, and sense of agency, are intertwined with our actual history, involving our bodies, our relationships, and our spirituality — our sense of values, meaning, and purpose — and the ways in which we have acted in the world. To quote Elaine Graham, theological "truth" itself, because of "the contingency and situatedness of human existence and knowledge, and the provisionality of our apprehension of the divine," would be understood as realized within and through human practices and material transformation.[54]

Our actions are not identical with our *memories* of actions or events. Memory is multiple, mutable, and always subject to interpretation and reinterpretation. It is neither fixed nor factual.[55] It also cannot be reduced only to narrative,[56] although what is narrated about and to us deeply influences

---

52. Dietrich Bonhoeffer, "Who Am I?" *Christianity and Crisis,* March 4, 1946. Online at http://www.religion-online.org/showarticle.asp?title=385.

53. Julian of Norwich, *Showings* (New York: Paulist Press, 1977), 300.

54. Graham, *Making the Difference,* 227; also citing Seyla Benhabib, *Situating the Self* (Cambridge: Polity, 1992), and Don Browning, *A Fundamental Practical Theology: Descriptive and Strategic Proposals* (Minneapolis: Fortress Press, 1991), 2-10. See also Graham, *Transforming Practice* (London: Mowbray, 1996).

55. Cooper-White, *Shared Wisdom,* 50-52.

56. For a careful review of narrative social psychology in relation to theological anthro-

and shapes our sense of identity and our actions. Our concrete practices amid other living beings, while subject to selective and fluid interpretation by others, leave a mark in our communities and on the earth. We have impact, both for good and for ill, and the tracings we leave behind are maps by which others may come to know something about us, quite apart from our own subjective sense of identity and purpose. As these maps are read back to us by others, we may confirm old directions or discern new pathways. The history we have written on the world, to be read intersubjectively by ourselves and others, gives us a further sense of going-on-being, but always with the possibility of change and new creation.

Conclusion: Implications for Theological Anthropology

In my book *Many Voices,* I argued for a construction of theological anthropology as prior to the positing of a doctrine of God, because all conceptions of God are necessarily incomplete, partial, and filtered through the lenses of a human perspective. All concepts are projections of our internalized personal, familial, and cultural inheritances, and in spite of its transcendent subject matter, theology does not escape the trap of conceptualization (the hermeneutical circle). In Christian theology, the biblical assertion that we are made in the "image and likeness of God" provides a hinge, however, that both offers and demands a symmetry in our conceptions of both God and humankind. Multiplicity, then, as a metaphor for theological anthropology, must have descriptive power in relation to our experiences of both ourselves and the divine. Even as the Trinity provides one such specific imagery for the multiplicity and intrinsic relationality of God, the image of a threefold braid provides a Trinitarian metaphor for multiple selves in a state of well-being. We are "like God" in our capacity for multiplicity, fluidity, creativity, and loving relationality, just as we experience God through our multiply constituted subjectivity as being "like us" — unimaginably, transcendently yet immanently, multiple, fluid, creative, and lovingly related.

Such doctrinal musings, however, do not necessarily lead us to anything new, unless they also are lived into, through our practices. Finally, a theology

---

pology, see Léon Turner, "First Person Plural: Self-unity and Self-multiplicity in Theology's Dialogue with Psychology," *Zygon* 42, no. 1 (2007): 7-24. Cf. Zygmunt Bauman, *The Individualised Society* (Cambridge: Polity, 2001), and Kenneth Gergen, *The Saturated Self: Dilemmas of Identity in Modern Life* (New York: Basic Books, 1991).

and theological anthropology of multiplicity must be situated as ortho*praxis,* not merely ortho*doxy.* If our sense of cohesion is drawn from life lived in the body and its relationships, with both God (spirituality) and other human beings (practices of love and justice), then we cannot *not* find ourselves in the realm of ethics. In Schneider's words:

> Love is a synonym, therefore, for incarnation just as both are a synonym for divine multiplicity. To follow a God who becomes flesh is to make room for more than One. It is a posture of openness to the world as it comes to us, of loving the discordant, plenipotential worlds more than the desire to overcome, to colonize, or even to "save" them.
>
> Love, the only ethics imaginable in a theology of divine multiplicity, is a promise, not a threat. It is the presence/s of the divine, available for encounter if we leave the scripts aside, if we are prepared to have our hearts broken by beauty, awe, and the redemption of responsibility.[57]

Most especially, we will inhabit our lives through the choices and relations of every ordinary day — what Ada María Isasi-Díaz calls *lo cotidiano* (the daily).[58] As we engage our own alien-ness, with courage and compassion, we are better able to open the door of compassion toward the "alien" beyond ourselves. As multiple subjects, we are able to engage difference with a greater degree of flexibility, creativity, and empathy for their competing desires and truth claims.

We are *all* "reenactors," that is, daily reinhabiting the subjectivities that act in and through the flux of the world, never quite the same way twice,[59] but guided by braided threads of body, relationship, spirituality, and ethical practices of both recommitment, and responsiveness to new demands for love and justice. Like the ancient Greek philosopher, we are able to say "Nothing human is alien to me,"[60] thereby daily (re-)exercising an embodied intuition for the "Other" that extends more deeply into the margins of our

---

57. Schneider, *Beyond Monotheism,* 207.

58. Ada María Isasi-Díaz, *Mujerista Theology: A Theology for the Twenty-First Century* (Maryknoll, NY: Orbis Books, 1996), 63-73 et passim.

59. Cf. Deleuze, *Difference and Repetition.* John Milbank uses the term "nonidentical repetition," to refer both to the plenitude of God's creative gift (*The Word Made Strange: Theology, Language, Culture* [Oxford: Blackwell, 1997], 55-83) and to the pattern of Jesus' life as it may be repeated uniquely in each new context and person ("Postmodern Critical Augustinianism," 276).

60. Terence, *Heautontimorumenos (The Self-Tormenter)* (New York: Rutgers University Press, 1974), I.i.25.

own contexts. We are more able to envision new horizons of meaning, because our vision is expanded beyond encapsulated identities that can only reinscribe singular positions and commitments. Such expanded vision is necessary to move beyond our reified oppositions, which perpetuate patterns of dominance, conflict, hatred, and anomie.

Epilogue

So what of the Civil War reenactors described at the beginning of this essay? "Who" were they? I would argue that they were in some sense *all* of the persons they presented as they walked forward to receive the sacrament that summer Sunday — including the identities given to them by others at birth, their selves-in-relation as they engaged in community, their subjective selves in a state of worship, their nineteenth-century "impressions"[61] whom they inhabited for intense periods of time as reenactors. The entire conscious and unconscious multiplicity of their embodied selves can only be known fully and finally by God. We only came to "know" them by their particular acts among us that one day, but they are continually being known in their various communities and contexts, and continually formed in their multiple selfhood, by the quality of the sum total of their embodied ethical engagements with others in the world. They are "their own persons," but also much more — in all their complexity, conscious and unconscious, they are *ours*. We are all reenactors, moving through our particular times and places, leaving and reworking our distinctive tracings on the earth. Beyond this, our knowledge dissolves again into mystery and faith: that in all our fathomless complexity we are known and loved by God — more valuable than two sparrows, always attended when falling, every self counted.[62]

61. The term used by reenactors for the person or type of person on whom they pattern their reenactment persona. Horwitz, *Confederates in the Attic,* 127; Weeks, *Gettysburg,* 214.
62. A play on Matthew 10:29-30.

The Existential Self in a Culture of Multiplicity: Hubert Hermans's Theory of the Dialogical Self

Hetty Zock

"This Is the Real Me": The Existential Sense of Self

Once, during a course on psychological identity theory for religious studies students some years ago, we discussed contemporary views of self and identity. The self, I explained, is nowadays no longer seen as an unalterable essence, something which is really there. The self is plural and dynamic, I went on, changing in time and according to circumstances; it is a process that is socially constructed by language, culture, and power relations, rather than an innate essence. Suddenly Harmen, a tall 22-year-old student, stood up and said: "Sorry, I have to leave the classroom. I'm feeling dizzy; I'm afraid I'm going to faint." Later, after he had recovered, he told me: "I really cannot cope with the idea that there is no *real* self somewhere inside me. Don't you need a sound basis, an anchorage for living?"

Harmen, who grew up as the son of a farmer on a very small island on the north coast of the Netherlands, demonstrated what Erik H. Erikson, the "founder" of psychological identity theory, has called "existential anxiety": the awareness of the finiteness and relativity of human existence, and of the plain fact that "nonbeing" is possible. This is indeed a dizzying and paralyzing feeling. According to Erikson, existential anxiety is, paradoxically, fundamental to people's sense of identity: facing the possibility of nonbeing, we have to develop a well-delineated psychosocial identity, finitely anchored in a particular sociocultural space and time. In order to gain agency of our lives, we need "a sense of continuity and sameness," that is, a sense of being the same person, both diachronically (i.e., in all the different episodes of our life history) and synchronically (i.e., in all the different roles, contexts, and activities we are part of at a particular time in our lives) (Erikson 1963: 235). It is during adolescence that this process of identity formation comes to the fore, during the search for what Erikson, quoting William James, calls "the real me" (1968: 19). Discovering who one really is, was, and wants to become also leads to the feeling "it is me who is in charge." Thus, the sense of identity and the sense of agency in the face of infiniteness (which cannot be controlled) go together. Erikson calls this sense of self "existential identity," as it is defined by "the relation of each soul to its mere existence" (1958: 177). Erikson, in this respect also inspired by James, links the existential identity with the capacity to say "I," "I am." The "I" is "the center of awareness and volition," the center of the self as a conscious and responsible subject. As such, it is "an inner 'agency' safeguarding our coherent existence" (1968: 135, 218). It keeps together and synthesizes our various selves. As such, it is the foundation of all psychosocial identity (Zock 2004), and the center of what I call "the existential sense of self."

This existential sense of self — the self as an experiential and coherent agent — is not only crucial for all psychosocial identity development, but is also the basis of all human meaning-making, and of moral and religious development in particular. The capacity to say "I" is at the center of spiritual and religious practices (Zock 2004: 100-103). Let me emphasize first of all that this absolutely does not imply an individualistic view of self and religion. On the contrary, together with Erikson and all contemporary identity theorists I am deeply convinced that identity processes have an inherently social and relational character. Yet, I will argue that the existential sense of self, which includes the view of the self as a conscious, responsible, and coherent agent, is crucial for meaning-making in our time.[1]

However, it is precisely this existential sense of self that is being contested in the postmodern cultural context of multiplicity, fragmentation, and continual change. Léon Turner fittingly speaks about "the conceptual dethroning of the unified essential subject" in this context (2008: 2). The key question of this chapter, then, is:

How is the existential sense of self constituted in a plural, globalized, postmodern context, where countless cultural options are available and

---

1. In an earlier article Hans Alma and I addressed the issue of the tension between the self as a social construct and as a unique center of experience, by way of a discussion of Herbert Mead's and Donald Winnicott's views on the "I." See Alma and Zock 2002.

the subject is under the pressure of decentering forces? How can people take an existential stance when they experience themselves as multiple yet "one-and-the-same"?

This issue is highly relevant not only for the psychological study of existential and religious processes of meaning-making, but also for psychotherapists and pastoral caregivers. These practitioners all start from and focus on the "I" as "the core of human self-awareness, the capacity which, after all, makes self-analysis possible" (Erikson 1968).

I will address the issue of the existential sense of self in a culture of multiplicity by critically discussing the theory of the dialogical self developed by the Dutch psychologist Hubert Hermans. In order to be able to situate this theory, which sees the self as radically social and multiple, I will first sketch the contours of the contemporary discussions on identity and self.

Contemporary Theorizing on Self and Identity

The Turn toward the Subject . . .

The philosopher Charles Taylor has given an impressive account of the development of the modern notion of self as caused by the loss of the natural, cosmic order of meaning from the eighteenth century onward. The self has become "disengaged" from the cosmic order, and the subject has now to turn inwards, to inner life, to find moral and spiritual sources for a meaningful life (Taylor 1989). Authentic individual experience has become a prerequisite for establishing a meaningful personal identity, and hence for all religious and spiritual development. Thus, the "I" (the core of the subject as a conscious and reflexive agent) has acquired an important function in constructing a meaningful life. As Anthony Giddens argues, self-reflexive capacities have become central to meaning-making and identity construction (1991).

The turn toward the subject explains the current dominance of the narrative paradigm in identity theories. Narrative psychologists emphasize that it is by way of stories that the self acquires shape. Dan P. McAdams, currently the most influential theorist in the field,[2] emphasizes the narrative character

---

2. Dan McAdams initiated the "Narrative Study of Lives" project of the APA (American Psychological Association), together with Ruthellen Josselson and Amia Lieblich.

of the "I": "The I emerges, many developmental psychologists suggest, in the second year of life as a narrating autobiographical self — a nascent sense that one is a narrator of one's own experience" (McAdams, Josselson, and Lieblich 2006: 3). McAdams further argues that in the present cultural context the "grand narratives" of cultural traditions no longer speak for themselves, but have to be applied to personal life in order to become meaningful. Meaning is to be found in the personal life history as constructed by the subject. The turn toward the self is also clearly visible in the field of pastoral care, where the focus currently is on the subjects and their faith as it is lived (Luther 1992; Gräb 1998), and where the narrative paradigm has also become dominant (Gerkin 1984).

. . . and the Decentering of the Self

At the same time, however, a countermovement can be seen. Social-constructionist thinkers emphasize that the self is socially constructed and call into question the self as a coherent, unified subject that would be in charge of its own life. It is argued that meaning and self are social products, dependent on the contexts individuals are in. Postmodern theorists prefer to speak not only about multiplicity, but also about fragmentation and decentering of selves. Kenneth Gergen phrased this as "multiphrenia": the "splitting of the individual into a multiplicity of self-investments" (Gergen 1991: 74). In radical social-constructionist thinking, the self threatens to be dissolved in social contexts and lose its agency (Alma and Zock 2002).

To summarize, in our time the seminal importance of the self as the unified core of meaning-making is simultaneously emphasized and contested. Contemporary theorists of self and identity are wrestling with the question of how multiplicity and unity, discontinuity and continuity of the self go together.[3] Let us now turn to Hermans, and consider what light his theory of the dialogical self may shed on this issue.

3. See Léon Turner's excellent analysis of the debates about the multiplicity/unity of the self in psychological and theological thinking (Turner 2008 and his contribution in this volume). In the following discussion of Hermans I have greatly benefited from Turner's clarifying distinctions between representational and experiential theories of the self, and between the synchronic and diachronic level of unity/multiplicity.

Hubert Hermans: The Dialogical Self

Hubert Hermans is an emeritus professor in personality and clinical psychology at the Radboud University in Nijmegen and is still very active in the field.[4] He developed the theory of the dialogical self in the early 1990s and has continually elaborated on it since then. After a short summary of the inspirational ideas behind the theory, I will present its main features. Next, I will investigate the unity/multiplicity issue and the role Hermans assigns to the self as an existential experiential agent. Finally, I will discuss the danger of artificial unity and the role Hermans attributes to religion in this respect.

Foundational Ideas: William James and Mikhail Bakhtin

Hermans developed the idea of the dialogical self together with the cultural psychologists Harry Kempen and Rens van Loon (cf. Hermans, Kempen, and van Loon 1992; Hermans and Kempen 1993). The theory is founded on William James's distinction between "I" and "me" (the self-as-knower and the self-as-known) on the one hand, and the literature theorist Mikhail Bakhtin's ideas on the polyphonic novel on the other. Although James acknowledged the multiplicity of the self in the notion of self-as-known (which has a social character, also encompassing, among other things, one's relations), he safeguarded the distinctness and continuity of the self in the notion of self-as-knower.

Hermans, however, sees the relation between unity and multiplicity of the self as still more complex, using Mikhail Bakhtin's insights. In his analysis of Dostoevsky's novels as "polyphonic," Bakhtin showed that there is no single author-thinker. Dostoevsky's characters are independent thinkers, who, as Hermans phrases it, present "a plurality of consciousness and worlds instead of a multitude of characters and fates within a unified objective world, organized by Dostoevsky's individual consciousness" (Hermans 2001c: 245). It is from Bakhtin that Hermans takes the key notions of dialogue, multivoicedness, and the intertwining of internal and external dialogical relationships. The metaphor of the polyphonic novel "allows for a multiplicity of positions [in the self] among which dialogical relationships may emerge" (Hermans 2002: 147). The "I" can take various positions, depending on particular social contexts. Thus, it was Bakhtin who, even more

---

4. See http://www.huberthermans.com/.

than James did, led Hermans to challenge the notion of the unity of the self and the distinction between self and other (Hermans 2001c: 244-48). The "I," Hermans points out, is plural, too, and the "other" is an integral part of the self.

The Theory of the Dialogical Self — an Outline

In their 1993 book Hermans and Kempen set out the background and the basic features of the theory of the dialogical self. Hermans was later to implement the theory in clinical practice and in psychological research.[5] His dense definition of the dialogical self is: "a dynamic multiplicity of 'I positions' in the landscape of the mind, intertwined as this mind is with the minds of other people" (Hermans and Dimaggio 2007: 36). The concept of "I," taken from James as we have seen, is linked to what I call the "existential sense of self." It refers to the *self-reflexive* and *evaluating* capacities of a person: to a symbolic point in the self where experience is evaluated and identity is constructed. The "I," the self-as-subject, is not an objective observer, but makes "valuations": value judgments, affect-laden meaningful interpretations of experiences. Thus, the "I" is the center of moral development.[6]

The self is *dynamic* in the sense that it consists in a process of taking different positions. Just like a character in the polyphonic novel or an actor on the stage, the "I" tells a different story about itself, dependent on the *I-position* that is taken.[7] Hermans speaks about "voicing the self" (Hermans 1996). From each I-position, the subject speaks with a different voice, which is value-laden: a particular situation may be judged in different ways, and depending on the I-position taken, different behavioral repertoires may be triggered. Here we see the basic narrative character of Hermans's theory: it is

5. The Valuation Theory and the related Self-Confrontation Method have been applied in clinical practice (see Hermans and Hermans-Jansen 1995), and the Personal Position Repertoire is used especially in psychological research. See Hermans 2001b and 2008.

6. Peter Raggatt emphasizes that all positioning has a moral edge: "taking positions" is taking sides. Stimulating the "I" leads to personal positioning, in a moral framework: moral and political formation of the self takes place by way of social positioning (one is governed by what is expected from the outside) and personal positioning (a conscious "I" is dominant). "Personal positioning . . . is generated from internal dialogues, in which the person grapples with the problem of 'the good' and their 'orientation in moral space.'" Raggatt 2006.

7. Hermans speaks about both "positions" and "I-positions." Positions in the self may be more or less conscious, and are called "I-positions" when they are in the sphere of I-consciousness.

by way of meaningful language that the self is constituted, acquires shape. The "I" continually moves among positions, which is how change and development in the self are possible.

The dialogical self has a *social and cultural* character. "The other" — other persons and cultural groups — are part of the self, in the sense that they manifest themselves as voices speaking in the self. Hermans speaks about *external I-positions* to indicate others speaking in the self. These may be the individual voices of people we are related to, either friendly or hostile (e.g., "my husband," "my mother," "my friend X," "my hated colleague Y"), but also the collective voices of the groups we are part of (e.g., "the Dutch people," "the Protestant church"). Apart from external positions, Hermans distinguishes *internal I-positions*. These may have a more personal character (e.g., "I as jealous," "I as perfectionist," "I as sensitive") or a more social character related to the I as a member of social and cultural groups (e.g., "I as a Dutch woman," "I as a Christian," "I as a scholar"). Yet all the voices that sound in the self are colored at the same time by one's personal character and life history, and by the cultural groups one is part of or is in touch with. For instance, when I take the I-position "I as a woman" I speak as a member of a specific group; but this voice is also colored by my personal experience, life history, and ambitions. External I-positions, such as "the Dutch people," are personal reconstructions of collective voices. Personal I-positions, on the other hand, are always colored by one's social and cultural background (e.g., "I as aggressive" is influenced by a particular cultural view on aggression and how it may be expressed). So, the dialogical self is inherently cultural because each particular I-position is always tied to a specific location and time (Hermans 2001c: 249), and accordingly culture and self, identity and society, self and other, are conceived as mutually inclusive (Hermans 2004b: 297). There is no essential difference between "the positions a person takes as part of the self and the positions people take as members of a heterogeneous society" (Hermans 2002: 147). Hence, global societal changes — the increasing plurality, the fragmentation and hybridization of identities, the postmodern condition of living in the contact zone of cultures (Hermans and Dimaggio 2007; König 2009) — have an enormous impact on self-development.

The dialogical self is substantially characterized by *conflict, tension, and power*. Not all voices in the self have the same value, and they are not all accepted by the self in the same way and to the same extent. Voices may be in conflict with each other, voices may be repressed, and voices, internal or external, may be a threat to the self (e.g., the voice of Richard Dawkins who views Christians as "backward," which resounds in the space of my self).

Hermans speaks about "dominance relations" between the voices, which are, among other things, influenced by "social dominance" in the respective contexts. External power relations and cultural conflicts play an important role in the self.

The dynamic nature of the self is further clarified by the central notion of *dialogue*. In Hermans's view, the self is a dialogical process between voices via which external and internal dialogues are closely interrelated. For instance, the current public debate between the liberal Protestant minority I belong to and the orthodox Protestant groups in the Netherlands does influence my internal dialogue between "I as a Christian" and "I as a liberal intellectual." Internal dialogues may be stimulated by external dialogues with a counselor who helps to explore hidden, suppressed, or marginal I-positions, or to engage in a dialogue between two contradictory positions that may develop into a new, so-called "third position,"[8] via which new valuations and behavioral repertoires are introduced into the personal meaning system.[9]

Although Hermans describes the self as a predominantly narrative process, he does not belong to the social constructionists who consider psychic life and meaning-making a purely discursive phenomenon. The *spatial* language in the theory of the dialogical self — taking positions — is not (or at least not only) metaphorical. Hermans emphasizes the *embodiedness* of the dialogical self, its rootedness in bodily development and neurobiological structures. He points for instance to the rudimentary bodily forms of intrapersonal activity of the infant (double-touch stimulation, and the give-and-take of the process of feeding; Hermans 2001c: 259-61) and to the dialogical nature of brain functioning.[10] The narrative, dialogical self is not

---

8. "[W]hen there is a conflict between two positions in the self, this can be reconciled by the creation of a third position that has the potential of unifying the two original ones without denying or removing their differences (unity-in-multiplicity)." Hermans and Hermans-Konopka 2009. See also Hermans 2006a.

9. Internal dialogues can also be stimulated by a researcher. The Personal Position Repertoire consists of asking people to tell stories about the self, and to identify internal and external positions and their mutual relations and affective value. These kinds of external "promoters" of dialogue may cause the rise of what Hermans calls a "promoter position," that is, a central, unifying, and synthesizing I-position that allows for a repertoire of I-positions, and guards the continuity of the self while at the same time keeping space for discontinuity. See Hermans 2004a and 2006a: 46-47.

10. See Hermans 2001c: 44-46, and Lewis 2002. Lewis explains that I-positions are the neurological substrate of the relationships with significant others early in life. Relational schemata — social I-positions: I-in-relation, with X, Y, or Z — are highly influential in dialogues. There are many similarities between this line of thinking in the theory of the

something that only arose in the postmodern era, but has a universal bodily, neurobiological basis; yet, dialogical capacities are increasingly called upon in the pluralistic, fragmented, globalized world.

We may conclude, first of all, that the dialogical self is radically plural, *multiple,* in the sense that there is not one single, unified I-experience, but rather many different I-experiences, dependent on the I-position taken. Hermans speaks about "a decentralized multiplicity of I-positions as authors of a variety of stories" (Hermans 2001c: 252). Second, the dialogical self is seen as a social process constituted by language and cultural meanings, and in which social-dominance relations play an important role. Therefore, the cultural plurality and postmodern fragmentation is found back in the self. However, the dialogical self also has a physical substrate in the body and the brain. Hermans does not adopt a radical social-constructionism, in which "meaning is just a matter of linguistics and social negotiation," in which "the inner mental space is replaced by social relationships" (Salgado and Hermans 2005: 6). He wants to avoid "social solipsism" (which he considers the social-constructionist counterpart of the individual solipsism of computational science) and to safeguard subjectivity and agency: an internal subjective space, the center of conscious experience.

Thus, the theory of the dialogical self clearly belongs to what Léon Turner calls experiential theories of self: theories that "attempt to answer existential questions about the *sense* of self."[11] Hermans focuses on the experience of "I" as the center of self processes that are radically dynamic, sociocultural, and most of all: multiple. This raises the following questions: Is someone in charge here? Who or what is taking positions and is involved in dialogues? If there is "nothing there," I can completely understand

---

dialogical self, and in established psychodynamic, object-relational theories; see Bromberg 2004. In a later article, Hermans and Dimaggio present a theory of emotions that starts from the idea that dominant I-positions — especially those linked with early relationships — have a neurological substrate in the brain. They emphasize that this is not a return to an essentializing and physiological view of emotions, but that emotions are intrinsically social and societal (2007: 46). Emotions are always position-bound: the position one takes determines which emotions can come to the fore, and how they acquire shape. Think, for instance, of emotions of grief, which will be different for the I-positions as I-as-a-daughter, I-as-scholar, I-as-dependent, and I-as-competent; the expression of grieving and coping strategies are highly determined by one's early relationships and by the cultural and religious context.

11. Besides experiential theories of the self, Turner distinguishes representational theories that focus on the self as it is represented and structured in the psyche (e.g., self-representations, self-concepts, self-schemata). See Turner 2008: 76-78.

Harmen's anguish. What about the unity, the sense of continuity and coherence of this multiple "I"?

Unity in the Multiple Dialogical Self

Possibly because of his clinical background, Hermans is very much concerned about the unity and continuity of self-experience, while at the same time emphasizing its radically multiple character. He speaks about "multiplicity-in-unity" and "Unitas multiplex" (Hermans 2008: 189, 248). I will summarize Hermans's argument on this point, showing that this goes for both the diachronic and synchronic levels of self-experience, and will also point to similarities and dissimilarities with Léon Turner in this respect.

Both Hermans and Turner state that multiplicity is a "normal" (i.e., nonpathological) feature of the self, and refer to the importance of narrative capacities to explain the experience of self-unity: narrative coherence consists in telling one's life-story, the same subject being the narrator and protagonist. Hermans undergirds this further by referring to the dynamic ability of the "I" to move across a variety of positions (Hermans 2008: 189) and, in particular, to its dialogical character. "[D]ialogism has the potential to surpass the dichotomy unity-multiplicity and to create a perspective about selfhood processes that equally values those two poles of human experience" (Salgado and Hermans 2005: 4). "Self" becomes a complex narrative process, in which the story of the self is told from the perspective of various I-positions, "each one functioning as interacting characters in a story" (Salgado and Hermans 2005: 9). "The difference between a multivoiced self and dissociative phenomena," Hermans states, "must be found not so much in the parts of the self but in their organization. In the dissociated self, the I is unable to move flexibly from one part of the self to another and the dialogue between the different parts is impeded" (Hermans 2008: 189).

In a similar vein Turner argues that, despite the multiplicity of the self, persons can experience themselves as "singular," as the same persons speaking about various aspects of themselves, both in the present and over time (Turner 2008: 90). There is a difference between Turner and Hermans, however, in their view on the possibility to experience synchronic multiplicity. According to Turner, synchronic multiplicity does not exist on the experiential level (except in pathological cases), because "people experience themselves in different ways at different times, and . . . although each person has the potential to experience him or herself in a number of ways at any given moment, *whichever sense of self inheres at any particular time is necessarily unified*" (Turner 2008: 119; italics mine). Hermans, on the other hand, assumes that it is possible to experience oneself as multiple at a particular moment. His arguments on this point are related to two features of the theory of the dialogical self: the presence of the "other" in the self, and the view of the self as spatial and embodied.

The first argument for experiential synchronic multiplicity relies on *the spatial character* of the dialogical self. At first sight, the spatial view of the self as taking positions may seem to support Turner's idea that experiential synchronic multiplicity is impossible: literally, you can only take one position at a time. However, in Hermans's view, the notion of space has simultaneous properties: the different positions, voices, and valuations are bound together in one space. In a dialogical narrative (such as the polyphonic novel), temporal associations are translated into spatial relations: "temporally dispersed events are contracted into spatial oppositions that are *simultaneously* present" (Hermans 2001c: 246; italics mine). "The *I* moves in an imaginal space (which is intimately intertwined with physical space) from the one to the other position" (Hermans 2001c: 252).

The second argument concerns *the presence of the other in the self*. As we have seen, Hermans radicalizes James's view of the extension of the self. Others — even hostile others — all belong to one's experiential world in the form of external I-positions. Hermans claims that the boundaries between self and other are diffuse and fluid. He quotes the phenomenologist Erwin Straus, who states: "In sensory experience I always experience myself and the world at the same time, not myself directly and the Other by inference, not myself before the Other, nor without the Other, nor the Other without myself" (Hermans 2006a: 101). Because the other is part of the self and because other and self cannot strictly be separated, there is always an experience of "otherness" — and hence of multiplicity — in the self (Salgado and Hermans 2005). Although Turner does concede that there might be an experiential hunch of the other (Turner 2008: 93-95), and hence a touch of a synchronic experience of multiplicity, Hermans goes much farther. According to him, all self-experience implies the experience of an "other," and this is what explains the experience of synchronic multiplicity. Moreover, the self is multivoiced, not only because of the "simultaneous existence of different individual voices" (which includes others) but also because of "the simultaneous existence of the voice of an individual and the voice of a group" (Hermans 1996: 46). Notwithstanding this multiplicity, there is continuity in the experience of one's external positions — the others in the self — as "mine," belonging to the sphere of "me"; the "others" are experienced as extensions of the same self (Hermans 2001a: 47-48). So, Hermans combines the notion of a radical decentralized self in which unity and continuity are contested, with the notion of the continuity of the self in the line of James's self-as-knower.

Until now we have seen that according to Hermans, several I-positions may be active (and thus experienced) at the same time and place, and that each I-position may be experienced as multiple in itself because the "other" is part of the self. This suggests that a person hears and speaks with different voices at the same time — which again raises the question of agency. Who is having the conversation? Who is moderating the dialogue? Who is directing the actors/protagonists in the life-story? Does not Hermans here presuppose a unified, "essential" self, an overarching "I" that is in charge?

The True Self — a Spiritual Anchor

Hermans acknowledges the deep human need of and search for "an inner core," *a true self* that is central to shaping one's own life in an authentic, personal way. This self, he points out, is often credited with a spiritual meaning (2006a: 38); he deems this search for a "deep, true self" necessary to counter the postmodern experience of discontinuity and fragmentation, and the superficial, material focus dominant in postmodernity. Here we find echoes from Taylor's exposé on the modern subject and his or her search for moral and spiritual meaning — for "depth." In Hermans's view, the experience of such a true self is not at all at odds with experiencing the self as multiple and characterized by diversity, conflicts, and oppositions. His clinical work demonstrates the possibility of taking up two contrasting positions at the same time, which are both simultaneously experienced as "true" and active, for instance, in the case of biculturality. Further, there is the possibility of a coalition of contrasting positions, which can be experienced together as the true self (2001b: 354). So, the true self may contribute to the unity and continuity of the self, when it functions as a "special position" (2006a: 39-40). Taking this position manifests itself in the feeling of "being near to oneself" at the same time as "near to the other" (self and other being closely connected parts of the self, as we have seen).

Hermans links the idea of the true self with the notion of *meta-position*, a reflexive I-position from which the subject may observe and examine the other I-positions (2001b: 354). It is the distance from other positions that enables the subject to have an overarching view (which, however, is always relative; 2006a: 213) and hence to evaluate other positions and their coalitions. Taking a meta-position not only supports the process of self-development, but also accounts for the experience of being a multiple yet coherent whole. In Hermans's view, "the meta-position contributes, more than most other positions, to the integration and the unity of the repertoire" (2001b: 354).

The experience of coherence and continuity that may result from taking a meta-position goes together with what I have called an "existential sense of self": "this is exactly me as I am," "this is really me." We have to keep in mind, however, that this experience of a core-self changes over time, as it is connected to the dynamic constellation of I-positions in a changing social context. Taking a meta-position may lead to the combining of multiple positions into a new configuration that is experienced as the true self. There definitely is a spiritual edge for Hermans here: it is at this point that the existential sense of self is anchored, and it is the point of departure for the search for moral and spiritual meaning.

To summarize: the experience of unity is itself dynamic — it changes over time, and it is the result of the narrative, dialogical, and spatial features of the self. The experience of the self as "true" consists of an existential experience of oneself as multiple yet unified, continually moving between positions in internal and external dialogues. It is clear that for Hermans, just as for Taylor, spiritual meaning can only be found in a personal process of constructing meaning.

The Danger of Artificial Unity: Cultural Multiplicity and the Reduction of Dialogues

Would it not be great if a person were a multiple and dynamic whole, engaged in a continual dialogue with a pluralistic context, experiencing him- or herself as a meaningful and coherent center of experience, exclaiming: "This is the real me"? This view of the self definitely has an optimistic, ideological edge, derived as it is from humanism, one of the intellectual traditions Hermans is rooted in (see Hermans 2006b). In this tradition, human meaning-making is a deeply personal, dynamic, and interactive process of self-realization.

However, although viewing the self as open, multiple, and dialogical by nature, Hermans also discerns tendencies in it that reduce dialogue and diversity. These tendencies are reinforced by the pluralistic, fast-changing, multicultural globalized context with its increasing amount of contradicting collective voices, which makes both external dialogues between individuals and groups and internal dialogues (and hence self-development) more complex. In their 2007 article Dimaggio and Hermans emphasize the huge influence of deep emotional needs for safety, stability, and certainty, which may lead to "monological closure" of the self and the restriction of dialogues (see also Hermans and Hermans-Konopka 2009). Here we have a correction of the view of the self as multiple — open to growth, diversity, and constructive dialogues with "others." Although "[t]he experience of uncertainty (in the neutral sense of the term)" is seen as "an intrinsic feature of a dialogical self," the biological emotional need for certainty and stability risks restricting the dialogical self (Hermans and Dimaggio 2007: 34-35).

The heterogeneity, ambiguity, complexity, and unpredictability of postmodern culture and society make it impossible to understand and control everything. This leads, Hermans argues, to the counter-reaction of *defensive localizations:* the cherishing of a local identity (ethnic, national, cultural, or religious) that aggressively excludes others — thus reducing dialogues. Such stereotypical collective voices, creating an artificial unity by reducing complexity and closing the self, are a reaction to the increasing uncertainty that is part of globalization. Too much uncertainty and feelings of insecurity lead to monological closure of the self, and the construction of collective identities that are artificially unified.[12] This is dangerous, because of the stereotyping, excluding, and "othering"[13] mechanisms at work here. A sense of secure self and identity is built on a dichotomy between "us" who are superior, and "them," the inferior "others." In this case, external dialogues are no longer open and symmetric, but asymmetric, and a negative identity is imposed on "other" groups. As we know, this is the basis of much violent social conflict.[14]

12. The multivoiced dialogical self "is conceived of as open to an ambiguous other and is in flux toward a future that is largely unknown . . . this uncertainty challenges our potential for innovation and creativity to the utmost, and at the same time, it entails the risks of a defensive and monological closure of the self and the unjustified dominance of some voices over others." Hermans and Dimaggio 2007: 35.

13. In a similar line of reasoning, Gerd Baumann and Andre Gingrich speak about the mechanisms of "selfing" and "othering." See Baumann and Gingrich 2004.

14. Catherine Kinnvall uses psychoanalytic theories, in particular the work of Julia Kristeva, to make her argument (2004). Similar insights are found in other psychoanalytic theories. See, for instance, Erik H. Erikson's view on "pseudospeciation" and Ernst Schachtel's distinction between the longing for security and protection on the one hand (the *principle of embeddedness*), and the longing for discovering the unknown, for freedom (the *principle of transcendence*) on the other.

Religion now figures in Hermans's work first of all as an important source of defensive localizations. Following Catherine Kinnvall (2004) he notes: "Particularly (institutionalized) religion and nationalism are identity markers in times of rapid change and uncertain futures" (Hermans and Dimaggio 2007: 40).[15] In this case, there may be an experience of unity and coherence of the self, but it is established at the cost of the multiplicity that is present both inside and outside the self.

The question must be asked here if religion always needs to have such a defensive, localizing function. Many authors point to the globalizing, binding functions of religion; for instance, Islam and Christianity have proved capable of binding together people with various cultural, social, and ethnic backgrounds.[16] Without denying the defensive functions of religion, it can also be argued on the basis of Hermans's theory that religious voices, when anchored in a special I-position that is experienced as "the true self," can promote dialogue. God may function as such an "I-position."[17]

In my view, Hermans's theory of the dialogical self is highly relevant for pastoral care and counseling in a secularized and pluralistic cultural context, where religion is to a high degree deinstitutionalized. Pastoral counselors should focus on the "I" as the experiential and reflexive center of the person as the starting point for the search for moral and spiritual meaning. Hermans's work offers insights into how to activate this center of consciousness, and into how to analyze the function of religious voices, personal and collective, in internal and external dialogues.

Concluding Remarks

Hermans's theory of the dialogical self demonstrates all the characteristics deemed typical of contemporary, postmodern psychological and sociologi-

---

15. This is in line with theologians and social theorists who have given religion the function of coping with contingency.

16. Erik Erikson, for instance, has argued that religion can manifest itself in both ways: as a defensive form of countering the threat of loss of collective identity, and as an open form of binding together; as a force with both destructive and constructive potentials. Erikson 1969; Zock 2004: 166-71.

17. Cf. the case of Sylvia, a Dutch woman married to an Algerian, who felt a conflict between those two national-cultural positions. In her position repertoire, the God position had an integrating function as it was linked to both her own family members and her in-laws. Hermans 2001b: 355-58.

cal thinking about the self (cf. Turner 2008). The self is considered a multiple, dynamic process rather than a unified essence. It is seen as an inherently interpersonal, cultural, and narrative phenomenon, consisting and expressed in meaningful language. Moreover, Hermans uses insights from neuroscience and biopsychology to show the embodied nature of the self.

Hermans addresses in particular the tension between unity and multiplicity of the self against the background of the current pluralized and globalized, diffuse cultural context. In his view, self processes are radically multiple. By focusing on I-consciousness as a dynamic, spatial, sociocultural, and dialogical phenomenon, he explains the unifying tendency of the self, both diachronically (in constructing and telling one's life-story) and synchronically. By focusing on the subject as a conscious agent in charge of his or her life, and in particular on the I as the center of existential experience and meaning-making, he clarifies how meaning is constructed in the relativistic postmodern context.

The strong points of Hermans's theory I consider to be, first, that it throws light on the radically multiple and social nature of the self, which is heightened even more in a globalized cultural context. He pays attention to the power dynamics that play a role in both society and the self; combines psychological, sociological, and cultural insights in his explanation of the perpetual, often conflict-laden cultural interactions; and discusses the contested role religion plays in this context.

Further, Hermans offers insight into the way in which people construct moral and spiritual meaning. His theory throws light on the experiential self that is at the heart of contemporary meaning-making. It is relevant for both clinical and pastoral professionals who assist people in coping with sociocultural plurality, and in keeping in touch with oneself as an existential, conscious center of experience in a complex and confusing time. The theory of the dialogical self is a useful tool by which to further intercultural and interreligious dialogues (Zock, in press), but it also explains how easily religious traditions and collective identities may be used to restrict dialogical capacities.

The theory is fluid and versatile, and has already proved a powerful bridging concept in interdisciplinary research.[18] It has been applied in many disciplines, from developmental child psychology to postmodern cultural

18. In 2002 the International Society for Dialogical Science (http://web.lemoyne.edu/~hevern/ISDS/) was founded. It organizes international conferences and since 2006 has published the *Journal of Dialogical Science*.

theory, and is used by social scientists, scholars from the humanities, and clinical and pastoral practitioners alike (Hermans 2008: 185-86). It has definitely promoted interdisciplinary research on the postmodern self and on actual and important social problems such as fundamentalist violence and stereotypical behavior. Although it is to a certain extent a translation to another, agile frame of insights (psychoanalytic, developmental, biological, etc.) long known, this does not mean it is less usable. Hermans's theory is not only about dialogue; it is dialogical itself.

References

Alma, H., and H. Zock. 2002. I and me: The spiritual dimension of identity formation. *Journal of Education and Religion* 3, no. 1: 1-15.

Baumann, G., and A. Gingrich, eds. 2004. *Grammars of Identity/Alterity: A Structural Approach.* New York and Oxford: Berghahn Books.

Bromberg, P. M. 2004. "Standing in Spaces: The Multiplicity of Self and the Psychoanalytic Relationship." In *The Dialogical Self in Psychotherapy,* ed. H. J. M. Hermans and G. Dimaggio, 138-49. New York: Brunner-Routledge.

Erikson, E. H. 1958. *Young Man Luther: A Study in Psychoanalysis and History.* New York: W. W. Norton.

Erikson, E. H. 1963. *Childhood and Society.* New York: Norton, 1950; 2nd, enlarged ed.: New York: W. W. Norton.

Erikson, E. H. 1968. *Identity: Youth and Crisis.* New York: W. W. Norton.

Erikson, E. H. 1969. *Gandhi's Truth: On the Origins of Militant Nonviolence.* New York: W. W. Norton.

Gergen, K. J. 1991. *The Saturated Self: Dilemmas of Identity in Contemporary Life.* New York: Basic Books.

Gerkin, C. V. 1984. *The Living Human Document: Re-visioning Pastoral Counseling in a Hermeneutical Mode.* Nashville: Abingdon.

Giddens, A. 1991. *Modernity and Self-identity: Self and Society in the Late Modern Age.* Cambridge: Polity Press.

Gräb, W. 1998. *Lebensgeschichten, Lebensentwürfe, Sinndeutunge: Eine praktische Theologie gelebter Religion* [Life-stories, Life-designs, Interpretations of Meaning: A Practical Theology of Lived Religion]. Gütersloh: Kaiser/Gütersloher Verlagshaus.

Hermans, H. J. M. 1996. Voicing the self: From information processing to dialogical interchange. *Psychological Bulletin* 119, no. 1: 31-50.

Hermans, H. J. M. 2001a. Conceptions of self and identity: Toward a dialogical view. *International Journal of Education and Religion* 2, no. 1: 43-62.

Hermans, H. J. M. 2001b. The construction of a personal position repertoire: Method and practice. *Culture & Psychology* 7: 323-66.

Hermans, H. J. M. 2001c. The dialogical self: Toward a theory of personal and cultural positioning. *Culture & Psychology* 7: 243-81.

Hermans, H. J. M. 2002. The dialogical self as a society of mind. *Theory & Psychology* 12: 147-60.

Hermans, H. J. M. 2004a. "The Dialogical Self in Movement: State of the Art." Keynote address at the Third Conference on the Dialogical Self, Warschau, August 26-29.

Hermans, H. J. M. 2004b. Introduction: The dialogical self in a global and digital age. *Identity: An International Journal of Theory and Research* 4, no. 4: 297-320.

Hermans, H. J. M. 2006a. *Dialoog en misverstand: Leven met de toenemende bevolking van onze innerlijke ruimte* [Dialogue and misunderstanding: Living with the increasing population of our inner space]. Soest: Nelissen.

Hermans, H. J. M. 2006b. Moving through three paradigms, yet remaining the same thinker. *Counselling Psychology Quarterly* 19, no. 1: 5-25.

Hermans, H. J. M. 2008. How to perform research on the basis of dialogical self theory? Introduction to the special issue. *Journal of Constructivist Psychology* 21, no. 3: 185-99.

Hermans, H. J. M., and A. Hermans-Konopka. 2009. *The Dialogical Self: Positioning and Counter-positioning in a Globalizing World*. Cambridge: Cambridge University Press.

Hermans, H. J. M., and E. Hermans-Jansen. 1995. *Self-Narratives: The Construction of Meaning in Psychotherapy*. New York: Guilford Press.

Hermans, H. J. M., and G. Dimaggio, eds. 2004. *The Dialogical Self in Psychotherapy: An Introduction*. New York: Brunner-Routledge.

Hermans, H. J. M., and G. Dimaggio. 2007. Self, identity, and globalization in times of uncertainty: A dialogical analysis. *Review of General Psychology* 11, no. 1: 31-61.

Hermans, H. J. M., and H. J. G. Kempen. 1993. *The Dialogical Self: Meaning as Movement*. San Diego: Academic Press.

Hermans, H. J. M., H. J. G. Kempen, and R. J. P. van Loon. 1992. The dialogical self: Beyond individualism and rationalism. *American Psychologist* 47: 23-33.

Kinnvall, C. 2004. Globalization and religious nationalism: Self, identity, and the search for ontological security. *Political Psychology* 25: 741-67.

König, J. 2009. Moving experience: Dialogues between personal cultural positions. *Culture & Psychology* 15, no. 1: 97-119.

Lewis, M. D. 2002. The dialogical brain: Contributions of emotional neurobiology to understanding the dialogical self. *Theory & Psychology* 12: 175-90.

Luther, H. 1992. *Religion und Alltag. Bausteine zu einer Praktischen Theologie des Subjekts* [Religion and Daily Life: Building Stones for a Practical Theology of the Subject]. Stuttgart: Radius Verlag.

McAdams, D. P., R. Josselson, and A. Lieblich. 2008. *Identity and Story: Creating Self in Narrative*. Washington, DC: American Psychological Association, 2006.

Pastoral Psychology 57. Special Issue on the Theme of Multiplicity.

Raggatt, P. T. F. 2006. "Multiplicity and Conflict in the Dialogical Self: A Life-Narrative Approach." In *Identity and Story: Creating Self in Narrative*, ed. D. P. McAdams, R. Josselson, and A. Lieblich, 15-35. Washington, DC: APA Books.

Salgado, J., and H. J. M. Hermans. 2005. The return of subjectivity: From a multiplicity of selves to the dialogical self. *E-journal of Applied Psychology: Clinical Section* 1, no. 1: 3-13.

Taylor, C. 1989. *Sources of the Self: The Making of the Modern Identity.* Cambridge, MA: Harvard University Press.

Turner, L. 2008. *Theology, Psychology and the Plural Self.* Farnham, UK, and Burlington, VT: Ashgate.

Zock, H. 2004. *A Psychology of Ultimate Concern: Erik H. Erikson's Contribution to the Psychology of Religion.* Amsterdam and New York: Rodopi.

Zock, H. 2010. "Voicing the Self in Postsecular Society: A Psychological Perspective on Meaning-making and Collective Identities." In *Exploring the Postsecular: The Religious, the Political, the Urban*, ed. J. Beaumont, C. Jedan, and A. L. Molendijk. Leiden: Brill.

The Multiple Self

Helene Tallon Russell and Marjorie Hewitt Suchocki

This article examines the self with special attention to its structure and form. The Western philosophical and theological tradition has constructed the self as ideally a hierarchical unity of internal parts, singular in form. We argue that this formulation is inadequate to a contemporary understanding of personhood because it does not adequately account for the multiple forms of relationality that are essential for the becoming of human selfhood. We suggest a vision of personhood in which the person is comprised of multiple internal and external relations, with changing forms of relating these relations to self and others. This, in turn, argues against settled notions of personhood in favor of continual openness to the richness of relation.

Since the era of Plato, Western notions of the self have tended to follow his tripartite scheme of reason, emotion, and the appetites, with these optimally organized in a hierarchy ruled by reason. At times "will" took the place of "appetites," with the will, like the appetites, to be brought within the control of reason. In Plato's *Republic,* he further elaborates his schematism of the soul by relating different virtues to each element of the soul: wisdom to reason, courage to emotions, and temperance to appetites, with the harmony of the three elements of the soul producing the fourth virtue, justice. This tripartite theory of the soul was a mirror of Plato's understanding of society as a whole.

St. Augustine contributes to this view of the self through an explicitly theological view of the tripartite structure of the soul. He understands the human soul as an analogy of the divine Trinity. Whereas God is conceived as a trinity of the lover, the beloved, and the love that unites them, the human soul is an analogous trinity of the mind, the mind knowing itself, and the mind's love of itself. Augustine uses three other triads to understand the self: memory, understanding, and love; the vision (ideal), the expression (word), and the execution (will); and contemplative mind, practical mind, and will. The highest form is contemplative mind, contemplating God and communicating consequent visions to the practical mind, which in turn communicates forms of implementation to the will, which is responsible for carrying out the directives. The defect caused by sin is found in the will's division against itself, not in any lack in the mind's knowledge. Thus Augustine's notion of the soul trapped in sin, which knows the good but does not do it. The unity of the self is disrupted by disobedience to the hierarchical order.

With the advent of psychology as a field, the triadic self was reorganized as ego, superego, and id. The superego represented not only individual conscience, but the cumulative mores of the culture impinging upon the individual, whereas the id represented the repressed and sometimes dark urges of personality toward self-fulfillment. Ego was the seat of consciousness, negotiating the rational demands of the superego, and the urgent strivings of the id.

Throughout these tripartite notions of the self, the body is almost irrelevant, reduced to a tool through which the self works. And apart from Augustine's relation of the contemplative mind to God, the tripartite structure of the soul (or self) is self-referential: external relations are in no way determinative of the self. With regard to the body, theorists such as theologian James Nelson and feminist and gay theologians/theorists began to integrate the self's embodiment into theories of personhood, and feminist and process theologians/philosophers expanded upon the importance of external relations to the conception of the self. Throughout these developments, there is an assumption that the self is a unified being: multiplicity yields unity, so that the self emerges as unified from its multiplicity. Our present article takes these insights further, arguing that multiplicity and unity are not hierarchical, with unity trumping multiplicity. Rather, multiplicity and unity are continuously negotiated realities within the complex relationality of the self. Further, without irreducible diversity, there would be nothing with which to relate.[1] The self as relational is necessarily multiple.

We utilize two philosophers to push a view of the multiple self — per-

---

1. This logic is seen in Marjorie Suchocki's *Divinity and Diversity* when she addresses the unity of God, which she says "is created in and through irreducible diversity." *Divinity and Diversity* (Nashville: Abingdon Press, 2003), 66.

haps an unlikely pair, but appropriately so, since we are arguing for an essential multiplicity to the self. From Søren Kierkegaard we work with a multi-sphered dialectic of the self that is both internally and externally related, and from Alfred North Whitehead we critique his notion of selfhood as a "regnant series of actual occasions" within the brain by arguing that multiple series and shifting unities are essential for establishing a relational self. The relational self is the multiple self.

Kierkegaard and the Relational Self

Kierkegaard is a significant thinker in the Western tradition who offers an intriguing alternative understanding of the self. His view is characterized by inner relationships within the self and being before God, with the structure of the self as relational, multiple, and composite, comprised of multiple parts or spheres. These parts/spheres are interrelated to each other dialectically. Further, the relation of these parts is a reflexive relation that is related not only to itself, but also to another, which is outside itself.

In *The Sickness unto Death,* we find his most direct treatment of the self. Here he asserts his view of the self as consisting in a dialectical relationship of three sets of polar factors. He states:

> A human being is spirit. But what is spirit? Spirit is the self. But what is the self? The self is a relation that relates itself to itself, or is the relation's relation itself to itself in the relation; the self is not the relation but is the relation's relating itself to itself. A human being is a synthesis of the infinite and the finite, of the temporal and the eternal, of freedom and necessity, in short, a synthesis. A synthesis is a relation between two. Considered this way, a human being is still not a self.[2]

In other words, the structure of selfhood consists in a process of reflexive relating between pairs of conflicting elements. A person holds together in tension that which is eternal about the self with that which is temporal, the inner element and the transcendent element, that which is necessary about the self with that which is free. At any given moment in any given person, these factors are held together in various stages of balance. For instance, I know that I am free to make choices in many situations, but there are also con-

2. Kierkegaard, *The Sickness unto Death,* trans. and ed. Howard V. Hong and Edna H. Hong (Princeton: Princeton University Press, 1980), 13.

straints limiting what I can choose and necessary conditions that must be met. I have to eat to continue to survive, yet I can choose between Juanita's burrito and leftover pesto. The task of balancing these two types of factors is the first step in the human task of willing to become oneself. The second step is a positive, conscious reflexive relating of the relationship of these conflicting elements. It is through this process that the self emerges as it relates the relation of these disparate parts to itself in a dynamic and dialectical way. The Kierkegaardian dialectic is the form of the relationship of these contradictory elements as they are brought into dialogue with each other. This reflexive relating constitutes an individual. In Walter Lowrie's older translation, Kierkegaard writes that it is a "dialectical fact that the self is a synthesis [of two factors], one of which is constantly the opposite of the other."[3] Thus the individual is constituted by the dialectic relationality of the dualities of elemental realities: finitude and infinity, etc.

However, Kierkegaard is not done, for this self is such that this synthesis is "established by another."[4] The becoming of oneself is willing to become oneself in relation to one's disparate parts, as this relation relates to itself dynamically *and* in relation to God and God's power. Thus, the "self is the conscious synthesis of infinitude and finitude that relates itself to itself, whose task is to become itself, which can be done only through the relationship to God."[5] The self then is comprised of internal relationships upon relationships *and* the external power that established it, God.

Kierkegaard views the self as spirit, and spirit as the relation of disparate parts of the self.

Since spirit is an inherently relational category that must hold together several pairs of ontological elements, then Spirit must embrace multiplicity. This human spirit must ground itself on a foundation outside of itself. "Did you make yourself?" the psalmist says. In this formulation Kierkegaard declares that we are established by that which is beyond our immediate conscious sense of ourselves, in terms of other entities outside ourselves as well as our own interior otherness. The self is essentially and inherently relational because it is established by a power outside itself. Kierkegaard dwells upon this assertion and argues that it is the foundational truth of human existence.

---

3. Søren Kierkegaard, *The Sickness unto Death,* trans. Walter Lowrie (Princeton: Princeton University Press, 1970), 163. See also Kierkegaard, *The Sickness unto Death* (trans. Hong), 30.

4. Kierkegaard, *The Sickness unto Death* (trans. Hong), 13.

5. Kierkegaard, *The Sickness unto Death* (trans. Hong), 29-30.

In his theory of the spheres of existence, the self is understood as moving in and through three stages or spheres of existence: aesthetic, ethical, and religious. These three stages or spheres of existence reflect different modes and models of living, suggesting in their respective ways forms of how to live and how to be related to the facts and processes of one's existence. Kierkegaard exemplifies each sphere through his pseudonymous works.

Two of these three spheres also contain two subspheres, or poles. The aesthetic sphere consists of the immediate pole and the reflective pole.[6] In the religious sphere, the relationship of religiousness A and religiousness B creates a mini-dialectic within the religious sphere. The polarity within these spheres, the structure and the content of each of the three spheres, and the dialectical interaction between the spheres indicate one aspect of the complexity inherent in Kierkegaard's view of human selfhood.

The aesthetic realm is characterized by its emphasis on the immediate and whatever is the closest external object of immediate stimulation, such as gratification, satisfaction, pleasure, and even sorrow. There is no self-examination, or self-reflection, and thus no self-knowledge or any true decisions. Its form is like a stream that wanders this way and that, reacting to the resistance of the rocks and earth without any intentional direction. The one living in the aesthetic sphere is completely determined by external stimuli. It simply flows as the wind blows.

The ethical sphere is about careful and reflected decisions. One in the ethical realm wills to be conformed to the universal ethical norms. He or she acts to maintain relationships with and among other persons that are consistent with objective and reasonable ethical principles. Here duty reigns, and it demands decisions that are made according to objective logical and universal principles. The ethical sphere is about thoughtful reflection, reflective self-awareness, committed actions, and careful judgments. Here one is self-made by consistent decisions that lead into a consistent, logically defensible, and unified self.

The religious sphere is the most recondite, for it contains elements of both of the other spheres, such as the aesthetic's emphasis on the needs of the particular individual, and the careful self-reflection of the ethical. It is primarily concerned with one's relationships to God, to oneself, and to one's decisions. While the ethical sphere is concerned *that* ethical decisions are

6. See Mark C. Taylor, *Kierkegaard's Pseudonymous Authorship* (Princeton: Princeton University Press, 1975), 76-77.

made, the religious sphere is concerned about *how one relates to the decisions that are made*. The religious sphere asks for infinite passionate commitment for what one decides.

These spheres are dialectically related to each other within the single individual person. A self in the religious sphere is constantly in the process of balancing elements and modes from the other spheres. The highest and most developed sphere, then, includes elements of the first two and is structured in part by the dialectical tension between them. It seems paradoxical because it brings together these two conflicting ways of living and transcends them as well in the absolute relation to the absolute.

Thus, Kierkegaard suggests that the self consists of polar elements of existence that are brought together and held in balanced dialectical tension. This structure of the relation of the ontological elements is applicable to the spheres as well. The first two spheres are dialectically related, with the conscious attention moving back and forth between the spheres. This dialectical structure of the self is the underlying form of the religious sphere and the structure of Christian existence. Thus interrelationality governs the dialectical movement between and within the spheres of existence internal to the individual moving toward becoming oneself before God. This multivalent integration of the self is only possible because, "in relating itself to itself and in willing to be itself, the self rests transparently in the power which established it."[7]

The self according to Kierkegaard is a fluid, self-reflexive, internally multivalent, externally constituted, never-ending task of becoming in relation to God. The human self is a task, not a thing. Accomplishing this task entails consciously relating to oneself and to the external power that made one. There are two points of foundation: the self dimension and the Other dimension. The self side itself includes three aspects: the complex, multisphered, multidimensional modes of relating to the outside world in the theory of spheres; the dialectic of paired ontological elements, such as infinite and finite; and the fluid conscious and self-reflective relation of this dialectic to itself. In other words, becoming oneself requires that the polar elements be in the process of relating together in an equilibrium and that this equilibrium relate itself dynamically to itself consciously and reflectively.

The second side of this formula for selfhood is the relation to the other. The self is constituted by that which is beyond itself. I was not consulted in coming into being. Kierkegaard calls this power that establishes the self as

7. Taylor, *Kierkegaard's Pseudonymous Authorship*, 131.

God. God is one of the integral points of the self. And the interior portion of the task of becoming oneself cannot be accomplished without radical relation with God.

Whitehead and the Relational Self

Whitehead goes further than Kierkegaard in that external relations constituting every subject are not reducible to God, but include the subject's whole past actual universe. The move from "self" to "subject" at this point is intentional, for Whitehead's primary emphasis is not an analysis of human personhood, but of the dynamics that constitute the most fundamental reality of the quantum world, the actual entity. And each entity is a subject. In many ways, process thinkers easily make the transition from analysis of the actual entity to analysis of selfhood, following Whitehead's speculations that personhood is created through a dominant series of actual occasions. This section of the article critiques that view, arguing that process metaphysics requires a nonhierarchical view of many strands of influence yielding a complex, multiple understanding of human personhood.

At first glance, Whitehead's metaphysics provide a tripartite notion of self, albeit in a way radically different from the tradition. Its analysis of the primary subject, the actual entity, draws on three modes of creativity: that of the past, which elicits the becoming of a new subject,[8] that of the future,[9] which calls the new subject to a particular mode of responding to the past, and that of the individual, which creatively adapts and integrates past and future as it comes into being. Unlike the tradition, which defines the self totally within the confines of the individual, a Whiteheadian model is necessarily relational. No subject can be understood in and through itself alone; rather, every subject whatsoever is what it is in and through its relation to that which is in its past, in and through its relation to the possibilities before it, and in and through its own integration of that which it has received in the becoming of itself. The model of the actual entity, with its tripartite modes of creativity, is taken also as a model for the self, even though the actual entity

8. There is disagreement among Whiteheadians concerning whether the past has power. One interpretation has it that the past no longer has power; it is stubborn fact, simply "there." Along with Nancy Frankenberry, I argue that the creativity of an occasion is not exhausted in its becoming, but that the appetition within an occasion radiates beyond itself as superjectivity, evoking its future into becoming.

9. For Whitehead, God as the ground of all possibilities is the power of the future.

is atomic, and a person is far more complex, being a composition of countless actual entities. Because of the composite nature of a person, then, the model of the individual actual entity must be qualified when applied to a discussion of the human experience of the self. This section of our article first examines the relationality inherent in the actual entity as subject, and then works out the consequent complexities in the relationality of the human self.

In our understanding of a process metaphysics, an entity becomes with a twofold sense of what Whitehead calls "appetition." This is always a feeling for what the nascent entity can become, but also includes some sense of how its own becoming can influence future becomings. Thus appetition has a double reference: that which it might become, and that which it might affect because of its becoming. Whitehead also refers to this latter aspect of appetition as the "superjective" nature of an actual entity. An entity's feelings of appetition beyond itself form part of the creative nexus that evokes the becoming of its successors.

These successors, each in its own way from its own standpoint, originate from their feelings of otherness. This otherness is itself manifold, both past and future. There is the otherness of the preceding entities, whose appetition pushes their own becoming, but there is also the otherness of God, whose appetition for the becoming subjects suggests ways in which the appetitions from the past might be successfully integrated in the becoming present.[10]

A fascinating aspect of Whitehead's system is that one cannot presuppose a subject who then has feelings of otherness. Rather, the feelings of otherness evoke a subject into becoming. Relation precedes, evokes, and creates subjectivity. This means that the feelings of otherness — relatedness — are quintessential for the process of becoming a subject; there is no becoming whatsoever apart from relation. Relationality to that which is beyond the self is internal to one's becoming, even while that to which one relates is more than the self. Thus there is a sense in which every subject is itself and more than itself.

In the process of becoming, then, a subject emerges with integral feelings of otherness, called "prehensions" by Whitehead. That which begins as

---

10. There are "naturalistic" Whiteheadians who argue that Whitehead unnecessarily includes God in his system. For the purposes of this article I am assuming rather than arguing that Whitehead rightly introduces the notion of God as the necessary source of all possibilities. God's creative power, in Whitehead's system, operates as an enabling power of that which is possible. God is the power of the future.

the appetition of others "there" becomes the prehended subjective experience of others "here," creatively adapted into coherence. Whitehead refers to the becoming of a subject as a process of "concrescence" through which all the disparate feelings of otherness are compared, contrasted, rejected, accepted, or otherwise adapted into the new configuration that is the becoming subject. The feelings from the appetition of God serve as a tentative guide toward a particular way of integrating the past, but this appetition from God (Whitehead's "initial aim") is suggestive, not determinative. All feelings, whether from God or the world, are finally integrated through the decisions of the subject. This process of integration entails adaptation of God's initial aim into the subject's "subjective aim," with its appetitions for its own becoming and for its effects beyond itself.

The actual entity, then, is essentially relational, not optionally relational. That an entity is internally related to that which is not itself is a given; how an entity internally relates to that which is not itself finally rests with the creativity of the becoming entity. Thus a subject arises through an admixture of freedom and determinism: the parameters of what an entity becomes are determined by its standpoint relative to its past, but how it actualizes itself within those parameters rests with the freedom of the present. Determinism and freedom yield indeterminism as the way of things in a thoroughly relational universe.

Using this relational model of the actual entity — the becoming subject — two process philosophers have particularly applied it to an understanding of the self. John B. Cobb Jr., in *The Structure of Christian Existence*,[11] analyzes the cultural evolution of the self through human history, arguing that the self within Christianity develops an emphasis on the capacity of a self to transcend its own interests through empathy with another. In *From a Broken Web*,[12] Catherine Keller integrates process philosophy with feminist analysis and discerns two primary modes of selfhood in the world: the primarily male "separative self" and the primarily female "soluble self." In corrective response to both, she concludes that "[t]here is always the world, coming in: its immanence. We make something of it, flowing out: our transcendence. . . . We arise from the matrix; we redesign its elements; we are woven back into the matrix."[13] If the separative self overemphasizes transcendence

11. John B. Cobb Jr., *The Structure of Christian Existence* (Philadelphia: Westminster, 1969).

12. Catherine Keller, *From a Broken Web: Separation, Sexism, and Self* (Boston: Beacon Press, 1986).

13. Keller, *From a Broken Web*, 248.

to the neglect of immanence, and the soluble self overemphasizes immanence to the neglect of transcendence, then clearly the guidelines for selfhood must take account of both — for both are in reality the way of things, and we neglect one or the other to the detriment of our fullness. Whether the self is separative or soluble, Keller recognizes that multiple others are taken into the concrescing self, reduced time and again to unity through the latest dominant occasion in the successive series of occasions that constitute the self.[14]

In both Cobb and Keller, we see the direct application of Whitehead's analysis of the actual entity applied to the understanding of what constitutes human selfhood, and both are certainly illuminative for the human condition.[15] But since the human self in Whitehead is not simply an actual entity, but a society of actual entities, this added complexity introduces a dimension of selfhood that is lost if only the dynamics of an entity are taken into account. That is, it is not sufficient simply to argue that, as in a single actual entity, the relationships that begin the self are integrated into the self and then affect others beyond the self, and that identity must take into account both of these elements, or what Keller calls immanence and transcendence. In the complexity of selfhood, there are many, many strands of actual entities, each of which experiences this receptive and transitional form of creativity, and all of which together contribute to what human selfhood is. Whitehead speaks of a "dominant actual occasion" within the self, rather whimsically described as wandering within the interstices of the brain and coordinating the activities of all the substrands of actual entities. But even this does not sufficiently explore the multiplicity that is necessarily involved in human personhood. It reduces that multiplicity to unity too quickly, as if it did not contribute materially to the complexity of human selfhood. If we take that multiplicity seriously, we must explore the possibility that selfhood is not so easily reduced to the unitary sense of self — and that the unitary sense of experience may be in some sense illusory.

Whitehead spent far more time considering the dynamics of the individual actual entity than he did on the implications of these dynamics for so-

---

14. Keller, *From a Broken Web*, 247: "[W]e may acknowledge two intertwining dimensions of multiplicity: my many selves as the fabric of other persons, plants, places — all the actual entities that have become part of me — and my many selves as the necklace of experiences that make up my personal history from birth to now."

15. In a sense, just as Plato applied his description of the self to the description of the state, even so both Cobb and Keller apply the description of a single actual entity to a description of the far more complex condition of human selfhood.

cieties of entities, so our own development requires imagination as well as attention to the strictures of the metaphysics. But it is clear that a Whiteheadian structure of the self must take note of the way in which animals depend upon all the complexities of a body, with its muscular, skeletal, and visceral networks of many strands of societies. Each of these strands has its own system of receiving, integrating, and transmitting the successive becomings in its series, as well as coordinating data affecting it from other serial strands within the body. Many separate strands are required for each system within the body, be it a heart, a bone, or an ear; and perhaps all strands are felt by strands within the brain, with its own coordinating strands of societies that enable it to create a system of consciousness. Consciousness depends upon a vast multiplicity of events, most of which must be suppressed even while they are essential to the maintenance of consciousness.

At this point I break from the attempt to apply a more complex Whiteheadian analysis of the self to speak about the unity and multiplicity of the self in experience. Some years ago I broke my knee. Prior to breaking my knee (while running along a beach in the Bahamas), I loved to dance: dancing was a smooth rhythmic engagement of my whole self in interaction with music and with a partner. I experienced the deep unity of my whole self in the process of dancing. But when I broke my knee, this sense of unity was disrupted: my knee felt like a seceding state in the union that had been my body. In addition to following all medical advice, I used to talk to my knee, because I experienced it as "other" to myself, and wanted it to integrate itself back into the rest of me. Was my knee really "other"? The answer must be yes and no, of course. Its integral union with the rest of me was disrupted, and to that degree it was separate, other. But of course any medical person would have thought me quite confused if I had mentioned that my knee was no longer a part of myself in its old integrative way, since it was clearly still attached to me. And my healed knee still "remembers" that brokenness of long ago, since it can no longer bear the twisting and turning involved in dancing. So myself as dancer is myself as past — is it still "me"? And what about an amputated portion of the self? Is that still "me"? Is "otherness" a matter of degrees? It is probably the case that to be a person is to be many "othernesses" within a relatively fragile unity we call self. Illness, brokenness, or amputation highlights the fragility of that union, perhaps disclosing the fact that the union is to some degree illusory.

When we see 35mm films, we see many, many different frames. But our eyes cannot process the multiplicity as multiplicity; hence they — or our retinas, or our brains — impose a unity on that multiplicity so that we can perceive it as a smooth unity. What if the same obtains with what we call our selfhood, not with a single strand, as in a film, but with multiple strands happening with a degree of simultaneity? Given the complexity of multiple strands of experience that make up a body at all, the integrative unity of that body is perhaps tough and fragile at the same time, with its unity imposed upon as well as emergent from the body as a whole.

But the complexity of selfhood — and its inherent multiplicity — is external to the body as well as internal to the body. The sensa of the body are structured to receive sensa from that which is beyond as well as within the body; we could not exist apart from these external-become-internal relations. The very need of our bodies for the energy that comes from other bodies through the act of eating is certainly witness to this essential dependence of bodies on that which is other to themselves. In addition to the physical energy we require from others, there is also the emotional energy required. Sadly, it is well established that infants who do not receive loving and sustained care from birth are slow to develop physically as well as emotionally, and if they grow to adulthood, they are usually plagued with psychological disorders. We depend upon positive relations to others beyond ourselves, integrating this positive energy into our own becoming, and giving emotional energy in return.

If we take the emotional energy of others into our becoming, then our relations to those others are both external and internal: in a partial sense, they become part of our selfhood — not in the subjectivity that originated them, but in our adaptation within our own subjectivity of that which we receive from the other's subjectivity. In our objectification and adaptation of the other's subjectivity we make it part of our own. There are then, in addition to multiple strands of bodily influences feeding into who we are, multiple strands of other persons feeding into who we are. I suppose we could also take this analysis into consideration of the strands of DNA and RNA that we each receive from our parents, but perhaps we have achieved a sufficient basis for the multiplicity that goes into selfhood simply from this brief consideration of the multiplicity that makes up our bodies, and the multiplicity of relationships beyond our embodied self that also enter into who we are. These others are not simply those close to us, but the religious, ethnic, political, and national cultures in which we are embedded. Selfhood is derived from an essential multiplicity seeking unity.

Whitehead's notion of a single dominant strand of actual occasions roaming the brain in order to account for the experience of unified personality may, then, be too simple given the complex multiplicity of strands of influence flowing into our being. Instead, that which we call consciousness is more likely to be composed of a multiplicity of strands, none of which has claim to a particular dominance. What we experience as focused consciousness is likely a dynamic and continuous shifting among many experiential strands according to shifting contexts. In ordinary experience, this shifting acquires a sense of unity not unlike that unity superimposed upon separate frames in a 35mm film. In what we call pathological experience, the ability to superimpose unity upon the multiplicity within is disrupted, and what we call "multiple personality disorder" may occur. Oddly enough, such disorder is more primal than the superimposed unity, reflecting the actuality of the multiplicity essential to our being.

Kierkegaard and Whitehead

Kierkegaard and Whitehead can themselves form a dialectic not too dissimilar from the dialectic proposed by Kierkegaard, both together strengthening our thesis that the self is multiple as well as one, and one as well as multiple, with each as important to the other.

Kierkegaard's formulation offers three significant aspects that Whitehead's lacks. First is the mutuality of the dialectical relationship between the essential elements of selfhood, which are foundational to what it means to be a self. In the above discussion of Whitehead, we moved away from Whitehead's suggestion that the sense of self derives from a single strand of occasions within the brain — the "regnant dominant occasion" — to the notion of multiple strands that together provide a basis for unity. That basis may well be like Kierkegaard's dialectic, of self-reflexive relating to the relations. For Kierkegaard, the dialectic was between aesthetic and ethical spheres, and between the pairs of ontological elements (infinite and finite; temporal and eternal; freedom and necessity). For Whitehead the dialectic would be between the multiple strands of influence from both within and beyond the body. But the dialectic becomes the mode whereby shifting forms of unity emerge to create the self that is multiple and one simultaneously. The unity is not through a single dominant strand, but through shifting dominances among many strands.

Second, Kierkegaard's Christian ethics argues that the relationship to other persons is theologically rather than metaphysically based. For Whitehead, the relation to others is neither optional nor accidental; it necessarily follows from a relational metaphysics. For Kierkegaard, the relation to others is created by God's commandment to love the neighbor as ourselves, and it could be argued that this affords a deeper relationship or connectedness between persons, allowing conscious and intentional relatedness characterized by love. Process theology argues that the self is essentially related to other entities by metaphysical fact. The basis for relating is natural rather than supernatural, and most relationships occur at nonconscious levels of existence. The analogue to Kierkegaard would be through the initial aim of God, which presumably guides each individual occasion (rather than the person as a whole) toward optimum ways of dealing with a multiplicity of relationships. In a sense, this could easily parallel Kierkegaard's "command of God" as a basis for relationships of love and mutual edification, but in a more contextual way. For Kierkegaard, the command is evidently generic, universal: in Whitehead, it is an influence within the context of every moment, relating to the issues and individuals within that moment. Again, Kierkegaard's system is oriented fundamentally to human existence alone, whereas Whitehead's system begins with analysis of the basic nature of relational existence, whether organic or inorganic. Kierkegaard's universal command becomes Whitehead's particularized call.

A third contrast is the way each thinker understands the relationship of the self to itself and its own otherness as being. Kierkegaard views this personal self-reflexive relation as unique to human selves. In a Whiteheadian way of understanding the human self's relationship with otherness, the multiplicity of the self originates from external and internal strands of experience. Each relational influence stems from its own serial strand of actual entities, with the latest entity in the series cumulatively summing up and responding to earlier entities within the strand, and exerting its influence on its immediate successors. Those successors go beyond those that continue the strand, however, given the multiple influences of any actual entity. Other entities from other strands also pick up those influences. It is a multiple world.

Kierkegaard's theory also makes a space for otherness, multiplicity, and relationality within the person, albeit this originates within the person rather than from external sources (other than God). The self is constituted in and by the self, and by God. It is a dual constitution. The self is grounded upon God, an external power that constitutes it as well its own internal relational network. While there is a place for relationships with the external otherness of the world found in Kierkegaard's view of the command to love one's neighbor as oneself, the other from outside is not in the constitutional dimension of selfhood, but in its culmination. The self is driven toward care of and for the neighbor, but one's relationship with oneself is unique in the foundation and constitution of the self. This formulation enables us to account for the uniqueness of the way the individual can relate to him- or herself. Further, the implication of this claim yields a view in which the multiplicity of the self is internal to the self itself.

The fruitfulness of Kierkegaard relative to developing a Whiteheadian sense of the self as multiple rests with the internal dialectic that establishes the Kierkegaardian self. That is, if the self is multiple because a multiplicity of strands simultaneously creates the grounds for selfhood and consciousness, Kierkegaard's dialectic may answer the implicit question as to how these multiple strands account for the sense of a unified consciousness. Consciousness is not as unified as it appears; the unity is imposed. How is this unity imposed, if we are not to suppose a single "regnant actual occasion" doing the imposing? Kierkegaard's dialectic of "reflexive relationality" is suggestive. If we imagine the multiplicity of ongoing strands within the brain, each affecting its own ongoingness as well as its immediate and extensive environment, then we have an organic basis for Kierkegaardian "reflexive relationality." Kierkegaard's "opposites within" are paired elements within each self that pull in opposite directions, and yet do so in keen sensitivity to that from which they pull. Each reflects its opposite as contrast, and in this mutual reflecting, continuously oscillates into unity. The multiplicity is not only preserved, but is the basis of the relatedness that functions as unity. Applied to Whitehead, the multiple strands that compose the most intimate aspect of what we call one's identity, one's selfhood, continuously feel the otherness of the other strands as well as the seriality of one's own unique strand. The oscillation that results in and through this reflexive relationality within the brain provides the basis for the sense of unity within the resultant consciousness.

The Multiple Self

Using Søren Kierkegaard and Alfred North Whitehead, we have argued that the self is composite, not singular; it is constituted in and through multiple relationships. This multiplicity is essential to the self, and is also, through dialectic, the basis for the common experience of the self as a unity. Whereas much of the Western tradition has understood the human self to be a hierarchy of parts — reason, will, emotions — our Kierkegaardian/Whiteheadian construction of the self bypasses these familiar distinctions, speaking instead of internal and external multiplicities. For Kierkegaard, these are the multiplicities of spheres and polar structures internally related through dialectic, and externally related and grounded in God, through whom the command to love expands external relations to others. For Whitehead, the multiplicities are bodily and environmental strands of influence from God and the world that jointly constitute the becoming person.

We suggested that acknowledgment of the multiple nature of the self could lead to a deeper richness of human experience. The underlying assumption here is that the hierarchical dominance of the One so prevalent in human self-understanding easily extends to behavior that seeks to replicate such dominance in social, cultural, and political spheres. Privileging multiplicity, with dialectic rather than dominance being the means of a sense of unity, could lead to very different social, cultural, and political behaviors. If multiplicity is valued rather than conquered, could we not more easily live with a multiple society as well as a multiple self?

On the Elusive Nature of the Human Self: Divining the Ontological Dynamics of Animate Being

Maxine Sheets-Johnstone

Introduction

Notable methodological and experiential similarities exist between Husserl's phenomenology and vipassana (Buddhist) meditation[1] that have sizable import in themselves and sizable import for divining the nature of the self, divining not in the sense of prophesying or conjecturing — or of endowing with a divine spirit — but in the sense of experiencing outside the natural attitude, hence in the methodologically nuanced sense of following along lines of the "supernatural." Divining rods are thus in this instance empirically proven rods, i.e., bona fide methodologies. Methodological and experiential

---

1. Vipassana (insight) is the oldest form of Theravāda Buddhism, "the Buddhist heart of the Theravāda meditational discipline" (Winston L. King, *Theravada Meditation: The Buddhist Transformation of Yoga* [Delhi: Motilal Banarsidass Publishers, 1992], 82).

Bhikkhu Bodhi points out in his introduction to *The Middle Length Discourses of the Buddha* that "[i]n the Buddha's system of mental training the role of serenity [samatha] is subordinated to that of insight because the latter is the crucial instrument needed to uproot the ignorance at the bottom of saṃsāric bondage" (Bhikkhu Bodhi, "Introduction," in *The Middle Length Discourses of the Buddha*, trans. Bhikkhu Ñāṇamoli and Bhikkhu Bodhi [Boston: Wisdom Publications, 1995], 38). King echoes this placement of vipassana when he observes that "it is implied in sacred scripture that vipassanā alone *could* be a discipline sufficient for salvation." He suggests further that "a kind of consensus exists that the modern age and modern people are best suited to vipassanā as an independent spiritual technique for achieving enlightenment, largely bypassing jhānic-style practice" (King, *Theravada Meditation*, 116), i.e., bypassing yogic practices, and cultivating "bare insight" alone.

similarities between a Western philosophy and an Eastern practice indeed provide mutually validating evidence of a consciousness beyond the natural attitude — a "supernatural" consciousness. The mutually validating evidence might well intensify present-day interests of scientists in phenomenology and correlatively motivate them to study meditational practices to the point they approach the study of these areas of experience with the same vigor and zeal they study deficits such as blindsight, for example, and conditioned "motor" responses such as eye-blinking. The mutually validating evidence would in fact ordinarily count as experimental replication, cross-cultural replication at that, of a scientifically arrived-at ontological truth about humans, a fact testifying to the importance of understanding consciousness or mind from what we might call the cultivated end of the cognitional spectrum. Such understanding ultimately involves not merely an acknowledgment but an illumination of "the subjective." With that illumination comes the possibility of insight into the nature of "the self." The self is not equated to consciousness but is understood in the context of the lived and living temporal dynamics of consciousness.

I begin with a general comparison of phenomenological and Buddhist understandings of mind and proceed from there to examine four features relative to phenomenological and vipassana practice: the reduction, the attentive onlooker, content, and the stream of experience. The general comparison and the ensuing exposition of features are of course interrelated; they are considered separately only at an analytical level and for analytical purposes. Once the foundational reduction is achieved, each feature is in fact a methodological and experiential stage or stratum contingent on the previous one. The inherent interrelationships will become evident in the course of analysis and summary conclusion.

General Comparison: Everything Comes from the Mind

In the beginning verse of *The Dhammapada*, the Buddha says, "All phenomena are preceded by the mind, issue forth from the mind, and consist of the mind."[2] He says something similar, but with a teleo-epistemological rather than ontological emphasis, in the *Ratnameghasutra*: "All phenomena are preceded by the mind. When the mind is comprehended, all phenomena are

2. Alan B. Wallace, "The Buddhist Tradition of Samatha: Methods for Refining and Examining Consciousness," *Journal of Consciousness Studies* 6, nos. 2-3 (1999): 175-87, 176 n. 1.

comprehended."[3] While subjective idealism might be read into the Buddha's sayings, it is rather a question of the active nature of the mind. In other words, the sayings are not statements of philosophical positions taken by the Buddha, but conclusions drawn from and about meditative experience. In meditating, we can experience the nature of the mind and how it works by cultivating mindfulness, which means being mindful of bodily sensations; feelings of pleasantness, unpleasantness, or neutrality; thoughts — as when we plan, judge, or remember, for example; and emotions — as when we feel joyful, fearful, or bored, for example; and of the continually changing nature of sensations, feelings, thoughts, and emotions. These "mental factors," as they are called, flow from the mind. They are phenomena that arise in the form of expectations, desires, aversions, memories, smells, sounds, preferences, pains, and so on. Through diligent meditational practice we come to experience the nature of the mind, and in and through this experience to understand how the mind shapes and colors experience, and in habitual ways. In brief, the nature of the mind is revealed and so also is the way in which habits of mind — reactive patterns, repeated thoughts, recurrent aversive feelings, and so on — determine experience, motivating us to certain preferences, acts, and so on.

The meditational journey thus has both epistemological and ontological dimensions. By practicing meditation, one develops and cultivates a capacity for mindfulness and gains insight into the ways in which one conditions one's own experiences. Practice is challenging precisely because the mind is by nature active; sensations, feelings, thoughts, emotions arise by themselves in an ongoing, ever-changing stream. Jack Kornfield, a Buddhist monk and teacher trained and ordained in Asia and a psychotherapist as well, captures the challenge of practice when he likens the mind to a puppy:

> [M]editation is very much like training a puppy. You put the puppy down and say, "Stay." Does the puppy listen? It gets up and it runs away. You sit the puppy back down again. "Stay." And the puppy runs away over and over again. Sometimes the puppy jumps up, runs over, and pees in the corner or makes some other mess. Our minds are much the same as the

3. Wallace, "The Buddhist Tradition of Samatha," 176. Multiple statements of the Buddha underscore the same observation: "Consciousness leads, rules, makes all modes of mind. . . . By mind the world is led, by mind is drawn" (Bhadantacariya Buddhaghosa, *The Expositor: Buddhaghosa's Commentary on the Dhammasangani*, vols. 1, 2, trans. Pe Maung Tin, ed. and rev. Mrs. Rhys Davids [Pali Text Society/London: Routledge & Kegan Paul, 1976], 91).

puppy, only they create even bigger messes. In training the mind, or the puppy, we have to start over and over again.[4]

As progress comes in meditation, the nature of the mind and of every-day habits of mind become epistemologically revealing: "[W]e are able to go from the level of 'My back hurts,' which is a concept, to the level of what is really happening, which are certain sensations, arising and passing."[5] In this way, meditators "awaken" to the way things really are.[6]

"Mind" is a rarely used term in phenomenology where, if anything, it has a psycho-ontological rather than epistemological meaning.[7] The comparable or correlative term in phenomenology is "consciousness," in some instances, "psyche" or "subjectivity," and in a special sense, "transcendental ego" or "transcendental subjectivity." To facilitate comparison, but also in light of the close resemblance in meaning between the phenomenological term(s) and the term "mind" as used in Buddhist texts, "mind" will be used in what follows.

In *The Crisis of European Sciences*, Husserl makes several statements that underscore the fact that everything comes from the mind. He remarks, for example, that "during the consistently carried-out epochē, it [the world] is under our gaze purely as the correlate of the subjectivity which gives it ontic meaning, through whose validities the world 'is' at all."[8] In *Cartesian Meditations*, he states that "this world, with all its Objects, . . . derives its whole sense

---

4. Jack Kornfield, *A Path with Heart* (New York: Bantam Books, 1993), 59; see also Joseph Goldstein and Jack Kornfield, *Seeking the Heart of Wisdom: The Path of Insight Meditation* (Boston: Shambhala, 1987), 48.

It should be noted that far from being popularized Western versions of Vipassana Buddhism, Western sources used in this essay are the work of Westerners trained and ordained as monks in Asia. Of the writings of Goldstein and Kornfield, the Dalai Lama wrote, "It is encouraging to find Westerners who have sufficiently assimilated traditions of the East to be able to share them with others" (in Goldstein and Kornfield, *Seeking the Heart of Wisdom*, unpaginated). He wrote a similarly praising foreword to Mark Epstein's first book, calling attention to his "twenty years' experience in both Western psychotherapy and Buddhist meditation" (in Mark Epstein, *Thoughts without a Thinker* [New York: Basic Books, 1995], x).

5. Goldstein and Kornfield, *Seeking the Heart of Wisdom*, 18.

6. To awaken to the way things really are is to follow the experiential path of the Buddha, whose name means "one who is awake."

7. Edmund Husserl, *Ideas Pertaining to a Pure Phenomenology and to a Phenomenological Philosophy (Ideas III)*, trans. Ted E. Klein and William E. Pohl (The Hague: Martinus Nijhoff, 1980), 22.

8. Husserl, *The Crisis of European Sciences and Transcendental Phenomenology*, trans. David Carr (Evanston, IL: Northwestern University Press, 1970), 152.

and its existential status, which it has for me, from me myself, *from me as the transcendental Ego.*"[9] "Mind" is not named as such, but it is clearly at the core of the phenomenological theme of constitution. There is furthermore in *Cartesian Meditations* a remarkable passage that repeats in phenomenological terms the initial statement made by the Buddha in the two passages quoted above, namely, that everything not only comes from the mind but that "[a]ll phenomena are preceded by the mind." The passage occurs in the context of Husserl's explaining the nature of bracketing and its effect, that is, the "'putting out of play' of all positions taken toward the already-given Objective world" and the consequent revelation of the ego alone as source of all meanings and validities.[10] Husserl writes, "Thus the being of the pure ego and his *cogitationes*, as a being that is prior in itself, is antecedent to the natural being of the world — the world of which I always speak, the one of which I *can* speak."[11] Husserl's "prior," like the Buddha's "preceding," is not a temporal-ontological priority but a logical-existential priority.[12]

The phenomenological journey is an epistemological one through and through. For example, in the context of explicating "the total transformation of attitude" of the phenomenologist, Husserl speaks of how horizons are in "constant motion," surrounding our everyday actions in the world and feeding into our constitution of the world:

> [T]he particular object of our active consciousness, and correlatively the active, conscious having of it, being directed toward it, and dealing with it — all this is forever surrounded by an atmosphere of mute, concealed, but cofunctioning validities, a *vital horizon* into which the active ego can also

9. Edmund Husserl, *Cartesian Meditations,* trans. Dorion Cairns (The Hague: Martinus Nijhoff, 1973), 26.

10. Husserl, *Cartesian Meditations,* 20-21.

11. Husserl, *Cartesian Meditations,* 21.

12. A temporal, ontological priority might perhaps not be altogether excluded insofar as the transcendental ego is a universal form or "absolute" (see, e.g., Edmund Husserl, *Ideas Pertaining to a Pure Phenomenology and to a Phenomenological Philosophy [Ideas II],* trans. Richard Rojcewicz and André Schuwer [Dordrecht: Kluwer Academic, 1989], 420-21). Something similar might be said for Nibbāna (Sanskrit, Nirvāna), which at various places the Buddha links with that which is not born and does not become or die. Bhikkhu Bodhi makes brief but pointed references to these passages when he discusses Nibbāna — e.g., "there is an unborn, unbecome, unmade, unconditioned, the existence of which makes possible 'escape from the born, become, made, and conditioned,'" or again, "[Nibbāna is] the unborn, unageing, unailing, deathless, sorrowless, undefiled supreme security from bondage" (Bodhi, "Introduction," 31-32).

direct itself voluntarily, reactivating old acquisitions, consciously grasping new apperceptive ideas, transforming them into intuitions. Because of this constantly flowing *horizonal character*, then, straightforwardly performed validity in natural world-life always presupposes validities extending back, immediately or mediately, into a necessary subsoil of obscure but occasionally available reactivatable validities, all of which together, including the present acts, make up a single indivisible interrelated complex of life.[13]

The phenomenologist's task is to uncover what is horizontally hidden as well as what has been taken for granted or assumed in "natural, normal life,"[14] i.e., everyday experience. Uncovering sedimentations of meaning and validities leads back to *origins,* thus to elucidations of the way in which meaning and value are constituted. Through the practice of phenomenology, an *"inner structure of meaning"* is revealed,[15] and with it, "subjective origins,"[16] i.e., understandings of consciousness and object, intending and sense, or, in other words, understandings of "mind." As we will see in progressively greater detail over the following four sections, the meditator's concern with *what* — what is actually present — is corollary to the phenomenologist's concern with *how* — how what is actually present comes to have the meaning and value it has.

The Reduction

The aim of reduction is different in phenomenology and vipassana meditational practice, but the act of reducing is comparable and the consequence of reduction is similar: quite simply, reduction reduces the everyday living world, allowing us to investigate it at bare minimum. In phenomenology, the reduction literally reduces our customary attitude toward the world by suspending everyday beliefs and judgments (in strict phenomenological terms, by performing the *epoché*): we now take everything as a "mere phenomenon."[17] In vipassana, the reduction reduces our customary bodily atti-

---

13. Husserl, *The Crisis of the European Sciences,* 149.
14. Husserl, *The Crisis of the European Sciences,* 149.
15. Edmund Husserl, "The Origin of Geometry," in *The Crisis of European Sciences,* 353-78, 371.
16. Husserl, *Cartesian Meditations,* 49.
17. Husserl, *Cartesian Meditations,* 20.

tude toward the world: we sit still, we close our eyes. In notably different ways, but in both instances equally, *the reduction takes the individual out of the natural attitude*. The world is still present, but the meditator and the phenomenologist suspend or withdraw from their everyday ways of being in it: everyday ways of engaging it, everyday involvements with it, and most important, everyday ways of being present to it and knowing it. In each case, the initial act of reduction makes the familiar strange. The quest, in turn, is to make the strange familiar, i.e., to come to know the bare truths of experience.

In phenomenology, the act of reduction is effected by "bracketing": "[E]verything transcendent that is involved must be bracketed, or be assigned the index of indifference, of epistemological nullity, an index which indicates: the existence of all these transcendencies, whether I believe in them or not, is not here my concern; this is not the place to make judgments about them; they are entirely irrelevant."[18]

Though there is no mention of "bracketing" in vipassana, the practice institutes a comparable "index of indifference." It is effected by what Buddhist monk Achaan Chah describes as "taking the one seat," an act by which "[w]e create the compassionate space that allows for the arising of all things."[19] Quoting Achaan Chah (his teacher), Kornfield writes, "'You will see it all arise and pass, and out of this, wisdom and understanding will come.'"[20] By taking the one seat, as by bracketing, we come to see everything that we add to experience. Through meditative practice, we see what is actually present — how things really are[21] — and how we embellish what is actually present with concepts, habits of thought and feeling, judgments, and so on, in a way similar to the way in which, through phenomenological practice, we come to understand how the object *as meant* goes beyond the sensuously present object. In each instance, the reduction leads to deepened understandings of both what is actually present and how we go beyond what is actually present.

---

18. Edmund Husserl, *The Idea of Phenomenology*, trans. William P. Alston and George Nakhnikian (The Hague: Martinus Nijhoff, 1973), 31.

19. Kornfield, *A Path with Heart*, 31.

20. Kornfield, *A Path with Heart*, 31.

21. In his Introduction to *The Middle Length Discourses of the Buddha*, Bhikkhu Bodhi writes, "The task of insight meditation is to sever our attachments by enabling us to pierce through [the] net of conceptual projections in order to see things as they really are" (Bodhi, "Introduction," 40). The purpose of the task set by vipassana meditation — "to see things as they really are" — will surface thematically in many ways in the course of this essay.

The Attentive Onlooker

Noticing is at the core of vipassana meditational practice. Mindfulness is cultivated through the practice of attention. A description by Buddhaghosa, a monk who lived nearly a thousand years after the Buddha's death (c. 500 BC), vividly captures the rigor demanded by mindful attention:

> Now suppose a cowherd wanted to tame a wild calf that had been reared on a wild cow's milk, he would take it away from the cow and tie it up apart with a rope to a stout post dug into the ground. . . . [S]o too, when a bhikkhu [a monk] wants to tame his own mind which has long been spoilt by being reared on visible data, etc., as object . . . he should take it away from visible data, etc., . . . and bring it into the forest or to the root of a tree or to an empty place and tie it there to the post of in-breaths and out-breaths with the rope of mindfulness.[22]

A beginning meditator is instructed to concentrate on breathing, and in concentrating, to notice movement of the abdomen rising and falling, or the sensation of breath in and out at the nostrils, and to notice as well thoughts, feelings, a sense of pleasantness or unpleasantness, and so on, as these experiences arise in the course of concentrating on the breath. The meditator may be surprised to find that neither concentration nor noticing comes easily. Concentration on breathing, a singular object, wavers and may disappear altogether many times in the course of a sitting; similarly, mindfulness of the flow of consciousness — the stream of sensations, thoughts, feelings, and so on — lapses: there are gaps in noticing all that arises and passes away. Some teachers of vipassana liken the disappearance of concentration and lapses in mindfulness to riding on a train. One boards a train; one notices where one gets on and the first changes in scenery; but then some time later, one finds oneself in totally different scenic surrounds and with not the slightest idea of how one arrived there or what one missed along the way. Not only has concentration of one's attention vanished but one has no idea at what point noticing disappeared. Thus Goldstein and Kornfield remark of beginning meditators: "At first in meditation our moments of awareness are far apart and we may only notice thoughts in the middle or even at their end, after many cars of the train have passed and we've taken a long ride."[23] In short,

22. Bhadantacariya Buddhaghosa, *The Path of Purification*, trans. Bhikkhu Ñyānamoli (Colombo, Ceylon: A. Semage, 1964), 288-89 (VIII.153).
23. Goldstein and Kornfield, *Seeking the Heart of Wisdom*, 55.

the mind wanders quite on its own, which is why it can be likened to a puppy that will not stay put.

There is no phenomenological equivalent to training the puppy, though there is certainly an apprenticeship necessary to dedicated phenomenological practice. The lack of an equivalent is due not to divergent conceptions of everyday mind (consciousness) in phenomenology and vipassana, but to the fact that the practice of phenomenology and the practice of vipassana meditation utilize different though not unrelated methodologies, and correlatively, have different though not unrelated ends. To put the point concisely, *turning toward* and *turning inward* are fundamentally different epistemological orientations and pursuits, but both entail a radical attitudinal shift that is not altogether unique in its results. A transcendental attention characterizes phenomenological methodology; bare attention characterizes vipassana methodology. We will consider each in turn.

Phenomenological methodology involves what Husserl at one point terms "the splitting of the ego":[24]

> If the Ego, as naturally immersed in the world, experiencingly and otherwise, is called *"interested" in the world,* then the phenomenologically altered — and, as so altered, continually maintained — attitude consists in a *splitting of the Ego*: in that the phenomenological Ego establishes himself as *"disinterested onlooker,"* above the naively interested Ego. That this takes place is then itself accessible by means of a new reflection, which, as transcendental, likewise demands the very same attitude of looking on "disinterestedly" — the Ego's sole remaining interest being to see and to describe adequately what he sees, purely as seen, as what is seen and seen in such and such a manner.[25]

The "disinterested onlooker" is the "nonparticipating" reflective ego,[26] the phenomenological ego who takes what is seen, for example, "purely as seen." Because in the phenomenological attitude, the ego abstains from predicating, valuing, believing, and so on, phenomenological reflection is attentively, and in turn, substantively different from natural reflection:

> In the *"natural reflection"* of everyday life . . . we stand on the footing of the world already given as existing — as when, in everyday life, we assert:

24. Husserl, *Cartesian Meditations*, 35.
25. Husserl, *Cartesian Meditations*, 35.
26. Husserl, *Cartesian Meditations*, 34-35.

"I see a house there" or "I remember having heard this melody." In *transcendental-phenomenological reflection* we deliver ourselves from this footing, by universal epoché with respect to the being or nonbeing of the world. The experience as thus modified, the *transcendental experience,* consists then, we can say, in our *looking at* and describing the particular transcendentally reduced *cogito,* but without participating, as reflective subjects, in the natural existence positing that the originally straightforward perception . . . contains or that the Ego, as immersing himself straightforwardly in the world, actually executed.[27]

Reflection in both the natural and transcendental attitude makes possible "an experiential knowing,"[28] but a knowing that, as is evident, is radically different in the two instances. Transcendental reflection discloses ongoing cognitional processes undergirding a subject's natural experiential knowing of the world, and indeed, his or her experiential having of such a world in the first place. In effect, the transcendental *epoché* opens up *constitutional* dimensions of natural experience: horizons of meaning, unifications, sedimentations, and syntheses that are the formative backbone of everyday experience. As Husserl remarks, "[a]s an Ego in the natural attitude, I am likewise and at all times a transcendental Ego, but . . . I know about this only by executing phenomenological reduction."[29] The transcendental ego is thus not a new arrival on the scene, but a discovered dimension of consciousness made possible by a radical shift in attitude. With the shift in attitude an attentive onlooker comes to the fore in a particular mode of reflection: the attentive onlooker looks at natural everyday experience through the prism of transcendental subjectivity: *constituting consciousness.*

Now in phenomenology, the attentive onlooker is consistently described as *above* the flow of everyday experience:[30] "[D]uring the consistently carried-out epoché, it [the world] is *under* our gaze purely as the correlate of the subjectivity which gives it ontic meaning";[31] "[T]hrough the epoché a new way of experiencing, of thinking, of theorizing, is opened to the philosopher; here, situated *above* his own natural being and *above* the natural world, he loses nothing of their being and their objective truths and

27. Husserl, *Cartesian Meditations,* 34.
28. Husserl, *Cartesian Meditations,* 34.
29. Husserl, *Cartesian Meditations,* 37.
30. A *transcendental* shift is, etymologically, a shift that basically involves *climbing* (from Latin *transcendere, trans,* "across, over," *scandere,* "to climb").
31. Husserl, *The Crisis of the European Sciences,* 152; italics added).

likewise nothing at all of the spiritual acquisitions of his world-life or those of the historical communal life";[32] "Our epochē . . . denied us all natural world-life and its worldly interests. It gave us a position *above* these";[33] "This is not a 'view,' an 'interpretation' bestowed upon the world. Every view about . . . , every opinion about 'the' world has its ground in the pregiven world. It is from this very ground that I have freed myself through the epochē. I stand *above* the world, which has now become for me, in a quite peculiar sense, a *phenomenon.*"[34]

In contrast to the phenomenologist's position as *above* the flow of everyday consciousness, the attentive meditative onlooker notices — one might even aptly say *listens to* — the flow of experience just as it happens, taking it all in just as it is, without interfering with it. The attentive meditative onlooker is in this sense *alongside* experience rather than looking on it from above. This *alongside presence* specifies a capacity to be with what is scary, for instance, and to be attentively present to the experience, however long it might last, as Kornfield's experience attests:

> When I was a young monk I traveled with my teacher Achaan Chah to a branch monastery on the Cambodian border eighty miles away from our main temple. We were offered a ride in a rickety old Toyota with doors that didn't close fully. Our village driver was really speeding that day, recklessly passing water buffalo, buses, bicycles, and cars alike around blind curves on a mountainous dirt road. As this continued I felt sure I would die that day, so for the whole time I gripped the seat-back and silently prepared myself. I followed my breath and recited my monks' prayers. At one point I looked over and saw my teacher's hands were also white from gripping the seat. This reassured me somehow, even though I also believed him to be quite unafraid of dying. When we finally arrived safely, he laughed and said simply, "Scary, wasn't it?" In that moment he named the demon and helped me make friends with it.

Other passages in vipassana texts are similarly instructive. Consider the following meditational instructions, for example:

> Pain is a good object of meditation. When there's a strong pain in the body, the concentration becomes strong. The mind stays on it easily, with-

---

32. Husserl, *The Crisis of the European Sciences,* 152; italics in original.
33. Husserl, *The Crisis of the European Sciences,* 175; italics added.
34. Husserl, *The Crisis of the European Sciences,* 152; italics in original.

out wandering very much. Whenever sensations in the body are predominant make them objects of meditation. When they are no longer predominant, return to the breath. The awareness should be rhythmic, not jumping or clutching at objects, just watching "rising-falling," "pain," "itching," "heat," "cold," "rising-falling." When you find yourself tensing because of pain, carefully examine the quality of unpleasantness, the quality of painfulness. Become mindful of that feeling.[35]

The term "bare attention" — a Burmese phrase used to describe the practice of noticing "the arrival and departure of all self-activities from the grossest physical motion to the most subtle emotional nuance or half-thought"[36] — captures the alongside attitude of the attentive onlooker:

> Bare Attention is a clear and single-minded awareness of what actually happens *to* us and *in* us, at the successive moments of perception. It is called "bare," because it attends just to the bare facts of a perception.... [It is] a bare registering of the facts, without reacting to them by deed, speech, or by mental comment which may be one of self-reference (like, dislike, etc.), judgment or reflection.[37]

> Bare attention means observing things as they are, without choosing, without comparing, without evaluating, without laying our projections and expectations onto what is happening; cultivating instead a choiceless and non-interfering awareness.[38]

In sum, the attentive onlooker in vipassana focuses on what is present, examining it closely, monitoring its changes, watching it heighten or fade, and finally vanish. What comes with this practice is an "opening of what is closed," a "balancing of what is reactive," and an "exploration of what is hidden."[39] By hewing to direct experience, by staying present to what is present and only what is present, one discovers flowing subjective processes — sensations, cravings, aversions, judgings, restlessness, contentment, and so on. Staying present requires being mindful, and cultivating mindfulness requires an attentive onlooker who is at the same time both inside and alongside experiences of everyday life, who is thereby attentive to his or her own

---

35. Joseph Goldstein, *The Experience of Insight* (Boston: Shambhala, 1976), 18.
36. King, *Theravada Meditation*, 72.
37. Thera, *The Heart of Buddhist Meditation*, 30.
38. Goldstein, *The Experience of Insight*, 20.
39. Goldstein and Kornfield, *Seeking the Heart of Wisdom*, 15-24.

subjective processes as they unfold in the course of experience, and who is thus able to open to pain, for example, and to examine it instead of immediately or simply reacting to it. In just this sense, the attentive onlooker in vipassana observes *alongside* rather than looks down from above. We see this attitude from an intensified inward perspective in a description of meditation on "the dynamic body-self," the end phrase of which was quoted above:

[T]he meditative center of attention proceeds ever more inward until the feeler and thinker contemplates his own feeling and thinking processes, catching them on the wing, as it were. The general picture of the meditator in this type of meditation is that of a person sitting slightly aside from "himself" in all his activities, physical and mental, and coolly, detachedly watching them go on, as though completely outside himself in another person. Sometimes with respect to breaths, the illustration used is that of a city watchman who counts the carts, cattle, chariots, and people of all sorts going in and out of the city gate. The same observational attitude can be extended to thoughts and emotions as well as breaths. Thus, with the detachment of a watchman, the meditator just registers the arrival and departure of all self-activities from the grossest physical motion to the most subtle emotional nuance or half-thought.[40]

The positional difference between the attentive onlooker in phenomenology and in vipassana meditation corresponds to a difference in methodologies. What is accomplished by an active suspension of beliefs and judgments in phenomenology is accomplished in vipassana by an active attention to the bare facts of experience. The attentive onlooker's aim, however, is in each case fundamentally the same: *to be true to the truths of experience*. Through bare attention, the meditator comes to know what is present as it is and for as long as it is. Attention may come and go in the process of meditating, but what is being cultivated is the ability "to see things as they truly are."[41] Husserl's call "to the things themselves" echoes this aim. Husserl would indeed have no quarrel with "Bare Attention":

After the practice of Bare Attention has resulted in a certain width and depth of experience in its dealings with mental events, it will become an

40. King, *Theravada Meditation*, 71.
41. King, *Theravada Meditation*, 92.

immediate certainty to the meditator that *mind is nothing beyond its cognizing function.*[42]

Content

However different their positional attitudes and methodologies, both phenomenologist and vipassana meditator are disinterested spectators of experience and are thus uninvolved in the actual content of experience — what will henceforth be designated *content as such.* In seeing a house, for example, the phenomenologist is not concerned with whether its address is visible, whether it has a good foundation, or whether its color has faded. The phenomenologist's concern is only with the perception of the house, how this particular thing seen — this object of visual perception — is recognized as a house, with all the judgments, memories, and values that recognition entails. In effect, to elucidate the intentional structure of "seeing a house" is to be uninvolved with the house in any everyday sense — as something to buy, something to admire, or something that one regularly passes on the way home. The phenomenologist's attention is directed toward *constitution* — toward the "how" of experience, as in *how* we come to see a house.

In vipassana meditation, there is equally a lack of concern with content *as such* and an attention instead to the processes of mind ongoing in experience. The meditator's attention is directed not toward understanding how things come to have the meaning and value they do, but toward something closely related: how things "truly are," and by contrast, how we embellish experience with habitual judgments, reactive feelings, future plans, and so on. The content of experience — being anxious about being caught in a traffic jam, for example — becomes grist for the meditator's mill: the meditator notices simply what is there, without getting caught up in the feelings, thoughts,

---

42. Thera, *The Heart of Buddhist Meditation,* 38. In this passage on Bare Attention, Thera is actually concerned with showing that no "I" is to be found in experience. The quoted passage continues as follows: "Nowhere, behind or within that [cognizing] function, can any individual agent or abiding entity be detected. By way of one's own direct experience, one will thus have arrived at the great truth of No-soul or Impersonality. . . , showing that all existence is void of an abiding personality (self, soul, over-self, etc.) or an abiding substance of any description" (38). This culminating truth of Vipassana Buddhism — the realization of no-self — is different from, but not incompatible with, Husserl's phenomenological understandings of transcendental consciousness, even as seemingly personified in and by a transcendental Ego.

and situation *as such,* that is, without allowing the feelings, thoughts, and situation to spill over and, in effect, take over the experience of what is actually present. Thus, the meditator may simply feel sensations of heat and a tightness in the chest, for example, to name two among many possible bodily sensations he or she might feel. In noticing only what is present, the meditator may softly label or name it — for example, with respect to sensations, heat, "heat"; tightness, "tightness"; with respect to thoughts, trapped, "trapped"; hours, "hours"; with respect to feelings, anxious, "anxious"; worry, "worry"; with respect to perceptions, cars, "cars"; noise, "noise"; and so on, following the mind wherever it goes, or until, as Goldstein suggests with respect to mindfulness of pain, "the mind . . . naturally come[s] to a state of balance."[43] In effect, the meditator notices an unfolding process of sensations, thoughts, and feelings as they come and go, arise and disappear. Goldstein and Kornfield at one point briefly characterize nonattention to content *as such* as an uninvolvement with *story.* They remark, "You can actually observe the thought process with mindfulness, noticing the arising of thought without getting lost in each story. It is a powerful and freeing realization to see that you are not your thoughts, to observe the stream of inner thought and be aware of it without being identified and caught up in it."[44]

One might say that, rather than being carried along by the content of experience, one follows *the form* of experience in both vipassana meditation and phenomenology. Formal tethering is most clearly exemplified in phenomenology by Husserl's elucidation of the constitutive structures of meaning, the formal elements giving rise to experience and making experience possible. Foremost among these formal structures are internal time consciousness with its protentions (experienced as expectations) and retentions (experienced as recollections), unifying syntheses that draw on both passive synthesis and sedimentations of past experience, and horizons or surrounding spheres of meaning that enter experience as complex synchronic and diachronic fields of awareness. All of these formal structures of mind contribute to and condition habitual modes of cognition. "[T]endencies of consciousness" that translate into "doxic" habits are present in habitual modes of feeling and moving as well;[45] "unnoticed, 'hidden' motivations, which are to be found in habit, in the events of the stream of consciousness,"[46] are part

---

43. Goldstein, *The Experience of Insight,* 18.
44. Goldstein and Kornfield, *Seeking the Heart of Wisdom,* 58.
45. Husserl, *Ideas II,* 268-69.
46. Husserl, *Ideas II,* 235-36.

and parcel of all facets of experience. In the practice of phenomenology, the *form* of experience takes precedence over the content *as such,* content that would otherwise impel one to do certain things, for example, or to react in certain ways. In the practice of phenomenology too, one is caught up not in *a story* — whether a story told by thoughts, judgments, feelings, memories, or whatever — but in the process of "meaning-bestowing," of constitution.

A similar formal concern structures vipassana meditation but to a different end. The aim here is not to elucidate *how* experience is constituted, but to awaken to the elemental realities of everyday experience. When we experience things as they really are, we awaken to what is actually present but, as noted, we also awaken to the many ways in which we embellish the present with plans, memories, worries, and desires. In this sense, we might say that we catch ourselves in acts of meaning-bestowing, "meaning-bestowings" we see through because we have left content *as such* behind. But in this sense, we might also say that we experience content at *its* level, i.e., simply as a *phenomenon.* Kornfield exemplifies the phenomenal character of content in his instructions on noticing the breath, though he does not label the experience in this way:

> [A]wareness of breathing does not come right away. At first we must sit quietly, letting our body be relaxed and alert, and simply practice finding the breath in the body. Where do we actually feel it — as a coolness in the nose, a tingling in the back of the throat, as a movement in the chest, as a rise and fall of the belly? . . . As we feel each breath we can sense how it moves in our body. Do not try to control the breath, only notice its natural movement, as a gatekeeper notices what passes by. What are its rhythms? Is it shallow or long and deep? Does it become fast or slow? Is there a temperature to the breath?[47]

Kornfield's questions about the breath and the earlier example of seeing a house demonstrate a restricted attention; the intent in each instance is to grasp the object purely as a phenomenon. One might thus say that attention is directed to a particular object without its usual baggage. But, as we have seen, one may also say that both phenomenologist and meditator are in different ways attentive to the particular object precisely *with* its baggage, baggage in the phenomenal sense of disclosing the subject. In other words, in their restricted or concentrated attention, phenomenologist and meditator become aware both of the phenomenal object and of what they are bringing to experi-

---

47. Kornfield, *A Path with Heart,* 60-61.

ence over and above the phenomenal object, what they are importing conceptually, imagistically, and linguistically; what they are presuming or taking for
granted; and so on. Phenomenologists penetrate to the core structures of
sense-making; meditators penetrate to the core nature of the mind. In each
instance, it is a question of holding fast to experience, examining and awakening to what is there. From this perspective, both practices may be characterized as a *turning inward* to elucidate the subject of experience.

The Stream of Lived Experiences

The passing nature of all experience, of things in the world, and of life itself
is a fundamental insight of Buddhist meditation and basically structures
Buddhist thought. In this sense, ontology rather than epistemology might be
thought to be at the core of Buddhist meditational practices and systems of
thought. But in fact the fundamental ontological truth — the bare experiential fact of impermanence — is rooted epistemologically, and as so rooted,
has psychological implications. Brief consideration of these implications
will bring basic experiential and theoretical aspects of vipassana meditation
to light.

Impermanence causes suffering, or *dukkha:* "From the fact of the impermanence of the world, it follows that all things are unsatisfactory. . . . The
word *dukkha* is rendered variously as 'ill,' 'suffering,' 'pain,' and so on, . . .
[b]ut in other contexts, . . . the term is used in the wider sense of 'unsatisfactory.'"[48] Buddhist scholar David Kalupahana explains the reason "the impermanence of the world" causes suffering: "The nature of man is such that he
craves for eternal or permanent happiness. But the things from which he
hopes to derive such happiness are themselves impermanent. . . . Hence his
suffering. The things from which he tries to derive satisfaction may therefore, in the ultimate analysis, be *unsatisfactory*."[49] The fact that things come
and go, arise and pass away, are born and die is a fact of life; experience demonstrates and bears out impermanence. In the practice of vipassana meditation, impermanence is experienced directly in the very character of mind or
consciousness itself. Goldstein gives a concise experiential account of impermanence when he says that in turning attention inward, we at first find

48. David J. Kalupahana, *Buddhist Philosophy* (Honolulu: University of Hawaii Press,
1976), 37.
49. Kalupahana, *Buddhist Philosophy*, 37.

only "self" or "I," but that "slowly this self is revealed as a mass of changing elements, thoughts, feelings, emotions, and images, all illuminated simply by listening, by paying attention."[50] In another text, he and Kornfield ask, "What do we see when we look at the mind?" They answer, "Constant change. . . . It is like a flywheel of spinning thoughts, emotions, images, stories, likes, dislikes, and so forth. There is ceaseless movement, filled with plans, ideas, and memories. Seeing this previously unconscious stream of inner dialogue is for many people the first insight into practice."[51]

Nyanaponika Thera, a Ceylonese monk, presents a more everyday account of impermanence when he writes that "Bare Attention brings order into the untidy corners of the mind. It shows up the numerous vague and fragmentary perceptions, unfinished lines of thought, confused ideas, stifled emotions, etc., which are daily passing through the mind."[52] Mark Epstein, a practicing Western psychiatrist who trained as a monk in Asia, presents a similarly familiar account of "constant change" when he writes of meditation vis-à-vis the "everyday mind":

> Meditation is ruthless in the way it reveals the stark reality of our day-to-day mind. We are constantly murmuring, muttering, scheming, or wondering to ourselves under our breath: comforting ourselves, in a perverse fashion, with our own silent voices. Much of our interior life is characterized by this kind of primary process, almost infantile, way of thinking: "I like this. I don't like that. She hurt me. How can I get that? More of this, no more of that."[53]

The meditator's attention is tethered to the experienced fact that sensations, thoughts, and so on, arise and perish. She does not become caught up in their "story," but is attentive only to the sensations and thoughts as phenomenal objects. In this way, the meditator comes to know only "whatever arises, as it arises, when it arises, in the bare fact of its arising" — and when it vanishes.[54] Meditative attention to the breath is of central moment in this regard. The breath is a mirror of the mind that meditators seek to comprehend. However much one's breath may be interrupted by thinking, wishing, liking, and so on, when one returns consistently to the breath, one finds

50. Goldstein, *The Experience of Insight*, 22-23.
51. Goldstein and Kornfield, *Seeking the Heart of Wisdom*, 47.
52. Thera, *The Heart of Buddhist Meditation*, 41.
53. Epstein, *Thoughts without a Thinker*, 109.
54. King, *Theravada Meditation*, 144.

there the paradigm of impermanence: in-breath, out-breath, pause; in-breath, out-breath, pause — each phase and the sequence as a whole arising and passing away. The phenomenon of breathing makes self-evident the basic truth of impermanence; it demonstrates experientially the fact that impermanence is literally built into our lives. With the practice of bare attention on the breath, "the moment-to-moment nature of mind and self" is experienced, and with this experience "comes a shift from a spatially based experience of self to a temporal one."[55]

How is a meditator's changing field of sensations, thoughts, and emotions related to phenomenology, or more concretely, how is impermanence — a specifically temporal awareness — related to Husserl's investigations and analyses of time-consciousness? The relationship lies in a joint recognition of and attention to the ongoing stream of experience. What a meditator discovers and follows diligently is the transitoriness of experience, the vagaries of the mind that arise and pass away within the stream, to the end that the nature of the stream itself — the mind — is comprehended. What a phenomenologist discovers and follows diligently are the undercurrents constituting temporal objects within the stream — e.g., perceptions, images, memories — and the temporal nature of the stream itself — transcendental subjectivity in the form of internal time consciousness. The stream of experiences in meditating is a streaming present in the same way that the stream of experiences in phenomenologizing is a streaming present: for meditator and for phenomenologist alike, it is an ongoing, ever-changing now. The stream is in fact the same stream experienced and examined from a different perspective. To crystallize the underlying similarity requires a closer look at Husserl's internal time consciousness.

Husserl characterizes the initial moment of any experience as a primal impression that is constantly changing: "This consciousness is engaged in continuous alteration. The actual tonal now [Husserl is using a melody as an example] is constantly changed into something that has been; constantly, an ever fresh tonal now, which passes over into modification, peels off."[56] In the internal consciousness of time, primal impressions recede; they flow into the past, and in so doing, are altered: "The now-phases of perception constantly undergo a modification. They are not preserved simply as they are."[57]

55. Epstein, *Thoughts without a Thinker,* 142.

56. Edmund Husserl, *The Phenomenology of Internal Time Consciousness,* ed. Martin Heidegger, trans. James S. Churchill (Bloomington: Indiana University Press, 1966), 50.

57. Husserl, *The Phenomenology of Internal Time Consciousness,* 88.

Husserl goes on to show specifically how retentions and protentions — intentionalities with respect to past and future — are modes of internal time consciousness. Though not characterized as such, the experience of impermanence is clearly "the transcendental clue"[58] for phenomenological understandings of temporal constitution. In other words, how we hold onto sounds in such a way as to hear a melody, for example, or how we hold onto various perceptions of a flower or perspectives on a statue in such a way as to grasp a unitary object are questions whose point of departure is the experience of impermanence: the sounds die away; the flower blossoms and withers;[59] the view of the statue changes as I approach it from the front. The central question Husserl seeks to answer — "how temporal Objectivity . . . can be constituted in subjective time-consciousness"[60] — is clearly tied to the experience of impermanence. Taken purely at a descriptive level, primal impression and recession testify over and over to impermanence: what is present continually passes away, recedes, or as Husserl also says, "sinks back, withdraws."[61] Constitution is thus indeed an accomplishment: without the "open and implicit intentionalities [of constitution]," Husserl writes, "objects . . . would not be there for us"; they are "subjective *accomplishments.*"[62] From this perspective, temporal constitution is a subjective victory over impermanence. What Husserl terms "continuous flux" is obviously, even if not explicitly, characterized by continuous change — impermanence.

It is of interest to note, too, that Husserl qualifies the word "flux" as metaphorical, and indeed says with respect to "the primal source-point and a continuity of moments of reverberation," that "[f]or all this, names are lacking."[63] The Buddha says something similar about Nibbāna (Nirvana) when he describes it as "profound, hard to see and hard to understand, . . . unattainable by mere reasoning."[64] Bhikkhu Bodhi in fact writes that "[N]o con-

58. See, for example, Husserl, *Cartesian Meditations.*

59. This example is given in order to indicate Husserl's concern with memory as well as with retention and his specific differentiation of the two in his analysis of internal time consciousness.

60. Husserl, *The Phenomenology of Internal Time Consciousness,* 22.

61. Husserl, *The Phenomenology of Internal Time Consciousness,* e.g., 94.

62. Husserl, *The Crisis of the European Sciences,* 160.

63. Husserl, *The Phenomenology of Internal Time Consciousness,* 100.

64. Bodhi, "Introduction," 31. The complete statement in *The Middle Length Discourses of the Buddha* is as follows: "This Dhamma that I have attained is profound, hard to see and hard to understand, peaceful and sublime, unattainable by mere reasoning, subtle, to be experienced by the wise. But this generation delights in worldliness, takes delight in worldliness, rejoices in worldliness. It is hard for such a generation to see this truth, namely, specific

ception in the Buddha's teaching has proved so refractory to conceptual pinning down as this one."[65] Yet however refractory or lacking in names, the flux of internal time consciousness and Nibbāna are experiential realities. We can thus *not* depend wholly on language but must consult experience, in particular, consult experience within the transcendental *epochē* or within vipassana meditational practice for verification. The appeal to experience and the limits of language aside, the essential core of the epistemological relationship between constitution and impermanence becomes apparent in just this context. A "continuity of moments of reverberation" adumbrates how, from a temporal perspective, constitution is the reverse of impermanence: constitution is a matter of *putting together — unifying, making continuous — what is impermanent*. The "continuity of moments of reverberation" refers to the temporal structures of sense-making with their retentional and protentional modes. Temporal constitution is thus the phenomenological-epistemological corollary of impermanence; it unifies what arises and passes away into a singular object *as meant*.

In sum, what Husserl consistently describes in *The Phenomenology of Internal Time-Consciousness* as a "continua of running-off phenomena"[66] and elsewhere as a "streaming psychic life,"[67] "lived experience streaming away,"[68] "subjective time . . . existing in the mode of 'streaming,' existing as lived experience in the streaming,"[69] is in essence a description of impermanence, but impermanence transcended through the unifying structures of internal time consciousness. We might thus justly conclude that "[t]he marvelous time-structure of the streaming transformation"[70] is indeed the phenomenological equivalent of "the movement of mind."[71] Both attest to the impermanent temporal structure of the mind. Thus, in strictly theoretical terms, *how* we constitute is the phenomenological equivalent of *what* we constitute, and *what* we constitute is the Buddhist equivalent of *how* we con-

---

conditionality, dependent origination. And it is hard to see this truth, namely, the stilling of all formations, the relinquishing of all attachments, the destruction of craving, dispassion, cessation, Nibbana" (260; Sutta 26.19).

65. Bodhi, "Introduction," 31.

66. Husserl, *The Phenomenology of Internal Time Consciousness*, 48.

67. Edmund Husserl, *Phenomenological Psychology*, trans. John Scanlon (The Hague: Martinus Nijhoff, 1977), 107.

68. Husserl, *Phenomenological Psychology*, 108.

69. Husserl, *Phenomenological Psychology*, 130.

70. Husserl, *Phenomenological Psychology*, 107.

71. Goldstein and Kornfield, *Seeking the Heart of Wisdom*, 54.

stitute. Buddhism validates phenomenological findings regarding constitution, and phenomenology validates Buddhist findings regarding impermanence.

Conclusion

The empirically sound methodological divining rods offered by vipassana meditation and phenomenology tell us why the nature of the self is elusive: the self is nowhere to be found in experience. What is found in experience are cognitive-affective-kinetic habitualities that are experientially evident in preferences, dispositions, styles of movement, ways of feelings, and patterns of thinking. The self is, in short, a construct. The construct is based on animate realities, but has no reality in and of itself. The construct is obviously fortified by language: by "myself," "oneself," "yourself," "ourselves," and so on, all of which reify a "self." What the empirically sound methodological divining rods essentially reveal and illuminate is the living temporal dynamics of being: the impermanent nature of all that is. The "self" is no exception. It is no more than the sum of habitualities evident in what Husserl describes at one point as "personal character"[72] and that vipassana monks describe as "habits of mind."

72. Husserl, *Cartesian Meditations,* 67.

PART THREE

The Self and Identity

The Quest for Self-Identity

Calvin O. Schrag

It was in ancient Greece that the Athenian Socrates issued the challenge "Know thyself" to all seekers of wisdom. Throughout the ages philosophers of various stripes have struggled to respond to this challenge by addressing the travails of self-knowledge and self-constitution. What resources are available for becoming a self and attaining knowledge of what and who we are? This quest for self-identity in the annals of Western thought encountered a formidable roadblock in Nietzsche's summation of the state of affairs having to do with self-knowledge. The opening lines of his provocative *Genealogy of Morals* presage the difficulties in responding to the Socratic challenge. We knowers who indeed know much about many things remain for the most part unknown to ourselves. This was Nietzsche's brief assessment of matters pertaining to self-identity.

The vocabularies of selfhood and personhood have become increasingly problematized in recent times, and within these vocabularies the concepts of "transcendental" and "ego" in particular have become issues of less-than-friendly scrutiny. Michel Foucault's assault on Kant's transcendental/empirical doublet as the matrix for understanding the roots of selfhood and personhood has been enthusiastically supported by certain partisans of postmodernity. And more generally, current philosophers addressing the structure and dynamics of human behavior shy away from any classical concepts of the human soul and any classifications of an essence or nature of the self, as well as from the more modern grammars of "mind" and "consciousness." All of this leaves us somewhat at sea on what one might be able to make of the notions of self and personal identity.

Our current project acknowledges the contributions in the assorted current critiques of both the classical and modern vocabularies designed to delineate the chief marks of human reality. Nonetheless we choose as our point of departure a critical revisiting of the vocabularies of transcendental and ego relating to matters of the human self as we proceed to the landscape of a wider cultural contextualization of the dynamics of selfhood and personhood. In what follows we begin with a hermeneutical read on Kant's transcendental unity of apperception, inviting Kant to travel with us in tracking the descent of the transcendental ego into the density of a concretely experienced lifeworld. We then move on to an examination of certain implications of this descent for achieving knowledge of self-identity in our historicized sociopolitical existence. It is thus that our quest for self-identity takes shape as an inquiry into the experiential sources of the transcendental ego, attending to the consequences of hermeneutical inquiries, and addressing certain implications for the sociopolitical status of selfhood that augur in the direction of a postnational self-identity.

The Experiential Sources of the Transcendental Ego

Revisiting the Transcendental Unity of Apperception

Aware that none of our conversations and reflections begin at the beginning, we need nonetheless to begin somewhere. We shall begin with Kant and what may well have been his greatest epistemological achievement — the discovery of the dynamics at work in the transcendental unity of apperception. Kant's account of this dynamics unfolds as a tripartite synthesis of apprehension in perception, synthesis of reproduction and production in the imagination, and synthesis of recognition in conception.

In his detailing of the tripartite syntheses comprising the unity of apperception, time and space as the forms of perception, the schemata of the imagination, and the categories of the understanding play their decisive roles. The forms of time and space filter the data of the sensory manifold and order them in their succession and simultaneity, their contiguity and separateness. The schemata of the imagination contextualize the contents of perception into constellations of remembered and revisioned images. The categories make possible the determination of rules for cognition by the understanding.

Now plainly enough for knowledge to be possible, the demonstration of which is the singular project of Kant's first *Critique,* the economy of these three syntheses of apprehension in perception, reproduction and production via the imagination, and recognition in conception needs to have a common epistemic origin in a unified self. Clearly it is one and the same self that does the perceiving, the imagining, and the conceiving. Herein resides the status and function of the transcendental ego, itself neither an object of perception nor an object of conception but the indispensable condition for there being perception and conception at all, underwriting the claim that percepts without concepts are blind and concepts without percepts are empty. A transcendental semantics provides the mark of the ego as never directly experienced but nonetheless required as a necessary epistemic prerequisite for there being knowable contents of experience.

Experience is the pivot and the point of departure for Kant, as it was also for the British empiricists who were the first to lay the ground for a consistent and consecutive philosophy of experience. However, according to Kant the British empiricists came up lame because the conceptual foundations for a viable philosophy of experience were lacking. British empiricism was long on percepts but short on concepts. Hence, what is required according to Kant is a move to the transcendental so as to secure the epistemic foundations for knowledge claims. Granted, all of our knowledge *begins* with experience. However, from this it does not follow that all of our knowledge *arises* out of experience. Such is made abundantly clear on the very first page of Kant's first *Critique.* To provide for an account of the origins of knowledge we need a supplement — a specification of the conditions that make knowledge possible. And it is this that comprises Kant's transcendental turn.

In maneuvering this turn, however, we need to be careful so as not to fall back into a metaphysical constructionism in which we become lost in concepts that are empty of empirical content. It is at this juncture that we need to be reminded that Kant's philosophy is at once transcendental *and* critical. Its transcendental thrust provides a corrective to the empiricists' floundering in percepts without conceptual determinants; its critical thrust is aimed at classical rationalist metaphysics with its scaffolding of concepts that are experientially empty. Thus in Kant's consummate philosophical program the limitations of empiricism are overcome as the extravagances of rationalistic metaphysics are undermined.

In this transcendental and critical epistemological project clearly the transcendental ego plays a decisive role, providing the origin and source of knowledge claims. And knowledge claims, we are quick to learn, require the constructs of an *Urteilstheorie,* a theory of judgment, that is able to sort out that which passes for apriori and aposteriori claims. The presence of an ego as knower in this epistemological scheme of things would indeed appear to be undeniable. The "I think" accompanies its multiple representations of knowledge. Yet, one might be disposed to inquire if perchance the constructionist designs of a theory of judgment might be set in brackets so as to open a path for a regressive move to a pre-epistemological understanding of self, in advance of theoretical constructs, that is found to be at work in the communicative praxis of everyday life. This would involve a probing of the underbelly of the transcendental ego in search of an economy of practical affairs of discourse and action that at once gives life and limb to the self as abstract knower. Such a regressive procedure would enable a descent of the transcendental ego into the lived experience of our quotidian existence and offer suggestions of how we as knowers, who indeed know much about this and that, can also become knowers of ourselves.

We begin this search for self-knowledge by soliciting as much help from Kant as possible, seeking traces for a vibrant self-identity within the economy of his transcendental unity of apperception with its networking of perception, imagination, and conception. Sticking with experience, as Kant would have us do, we probe the vibrations and vectors of experience to find within them a time and space that marks out horizons of experience in its lived concreteness. Prior to the formalization of time and space as abstracted formal transcendental conditions *for* perceptual experience, time and space are sought *within* perceptual experience. Time and space are set forth as moving horizons in which perception works with that which is earlier and later, at hand and at a distance. At issue here are the notions of *lived* time and *lived* space, the qualitative coloring of time and space as variable dimensions that are concretely *lived-through,* as orientations within experience vitalizing perception in advance of its epistemological formalization and chronometric mapping.

As is well known, the notions of lived time and lived space have received widespread attention in twentieth-century continental philosophy in the works of Martin Heidegger, Jean-Paul Sartre, and Maurice Merleau-Ponty. Heidegger's analytic of Dasein places the lived time of human existence very much at the center of his monumental work, *Being and Time.* Merleau-Ponty's *Phenomenology of Perception* still stands as the classic treatment of lived space as it comes to expression in the embodiment of the perceiving subject orienting its existence in the value-laden dimensions of here and there, above and below, front and back — all of which mark out concrete horizons for objects to be perceived and tasks to be done. In revisiting Kant's theory of perception, transcendentally grounded in a priori forms of time and space, one does well to pick up the conversations with the likes of Heidegger and Merleau-Ponty in pursuing a critical dialogue that comes to terms with the contributions of each.

Such a dialogue is required not only with Kant on his theory of the unity of apperception as a synthesis of apprehension in perception by dint of the forms of time and space, expanding their significance so as to set forth their traces within the density of lived experience, but it is also important to bring in the role of the workings of the imagination and the relevance of the schemata in which time and space continue to be very much in play. Such would seem to be the case particularly with regard to time, acknowledged by Kant himself when he defines the schemata as nothing more than transcendental determinations of time. It is thus that the imagination is seen to be profoundly temporalized in its functioning, which involves the twin moments of receptivity/reproduction and activity/production.

The structure of the imagination is one of a complementarity of reproducing past perceptions and producing or creating horizons for the entertainment of concepts as categorical determinants of the understanding. Such is the task of schematizing that enables the mediation of percepts and concepts within the apperceptive unity. On the one hand the imagination exhibits an orientation backwards, highlighting the role of remembrance in the quest for knowledge, maintaining a liaison with the past; on the other hand it exhibits an orientation forwards, anticipating concepts in the service of categorial understanding. The orientation backwards, however, is never that of a simple recall of isolated sensory contents; it is rather that of a reminiscence within a schematic horizon that opens a space for an application of the categories and hence is a reminiscence that remains open to a creative revisioning of possibilities for understanding. It is in this manner that the unity in the transcendental apperception is realized, bringing percepts into concert with concepts against the background and foreground horizons supplied by the schemata as transcendental determinations of time, entwining past and future within the economy of cognition.

The Hermeneutical Turn

In tracking the apperceptive unity that binds perception, imagination, and conception in the workings of a transcendental ego we continue our project of thinking with Kant while thinking against him, offering suggestions for a transition beyond what his epistemological frame of inquiry enabled him to say. This move beyond epistemology opens the path to a hermeneutics that guides the descent of the ego into the lived experience of everyday concerns and preoccupations. We propose that the transcendental analytic of category-based concepts in the quest of a trustworthy theory of judgment needs to be viewed as working hand in glove with a hermeneutical structure of experience in which percepts, images, and concepts are already taken as carriers of sense. It is in this manner that the understanding operative in conceptualization becomes linked with interpretive understanding. Understanding has both categorial and pre-categorial, predicative and pre-predicative, theoretical and pre-theoretical dimensions. Within the wider economy of thought and action, understanding and interpretation are brought into a fruitful alliance.

A chief feature of the consequence of hermeneutics is the highlighting of a holism, requiring attention to background and foreground horizons in which the elemental percepts, images, and concepts move about and gather into changing whole/part configurations. Understanding is seen to function within a holistic web of pre-theoretical and pre-predicative percepts, feelings, desires, emotions, and thoughts that are already meaning laden and disclose truths about the human condition. Hermeneutical holism binds categorial and pre-categorial understanding within wider parameters of interpretation. Herein reside the fruits of the hermeneutical turn. It forges a path *beyond* epistemology as a foundational discipline caught up in the conceptual incoherence of providing a knowledge of knowledge, a *logos* of an *episteme,* designed to be the arbiter of all sense and reference. An analytic of knowledge indeed retains its legitimacy, but it is now contextualized within a broader framework of considerations.

Within the holistic configuration of the workings of perception, imagination, and conception, amalgamating the pre-cognitive and the cognitive into patterns of interwoven pre-theoretical and theoretical horizons of interpretive understanding, the role and function of the ego is portrayed in a new and expanded posture. Its transcendental epistemic function is now coupled with a life-experiencing self that is compelled to define itself no longer simply as an abstracted thinking subject, a disembodied *res cogitans,* but as a subject that undergoes a spate of emotive, volitional, and cognitive functions in responding to other subjects within the proximate lived space of the neighborhood as well as those situated in a wider public arena. This ego or self as subject having descended from its epistemic transcendental status into the thick of lived-through experiences refigures and revisions the economy of transcendence in such a wise as to incorporate time and space into the projects of the subject in its perpetual process of becoming itself. No longer are time and space simply abstracted forms of perception, and no longer are the schema of the imagination simply epistemologically required determinations of time; time and space already ingress into the projects of self-knowledge and self-constitution.

Time and space are as much *in* the lived experience of the ego as they are transcendental conditions *for* experience. They are not simply abstracted forms *of* perception; they are forming operations *within* perception. This requires an expansion of the meaning of "transcendence." Ingressing into lived experience, enabling one to speak of *transcendental experience,* transcendence takes on the dynamics of a projection from a present state of dissatisfaction to a future realization of aims and goals yet to be achieved. In the situation of a self in despair, the hope for a deliverance from its distressing condition in the future transcends the confining space of a trammeled present, opening new avenues for self-evaluation. The transcendental ego in its epistemological function takes on the experiential and existential sense of transcendence as a self-transcending dynamics within the dimensions of a lived time and a lived space. It is in such a wise that the transcendental ego descends into the concrete lifeworld and becomes incarnate in historical existence.

Hermeneutical Self-Implicature

It is within the density of the everyday experienced lifeworld, unfolding as a tapestry of amalgamated discourse and action in the economy of communicative praxis, that the phenomenon of hermeneutical self-implicature eventuates. This is an event of implicature as a praxis-oriented intentionality, riding the crest of interpretive understanding that is able to bring forth and disclose traces of a who of discourse and a who of action engaged in processes of saying something about something to others and responding to prior action upon it. This is not, at least not yet, the epistemic valued implication and predicative intentionality that does service in the construction of a theory of judgment. The speaking and agentive subject that is at issue here, as the who of discourse and the who of action, makes its presence known as engaged speaker and actor understanding him- or herself in conversing with interlocutors and in executing the tasks at hand. This praxis-oriented and life-experiencing self announces its presence on the landscape of the multiple communicative involvements more like an event than like an object for inspection, an event of speaking that does not originate language but always speaks *from* a language, and an event of action that is always a response to prior action upon it.

At stake in the phenomenon of hermeneutical self-implicature are issues that are key for coming to grips with the longstanding problem of self-identity and self-consciousness. Knowledge of self has a pre-categorial and pre-theoretical dimension. It is not delivered via a theory-based intentionality bent upon the achievement of self-knowledge as a knowing *what*, a species of categorial determination. More like a knowing *how* than a knowing *what*, it is a type of comprehension that makes an end run around the aporia of the traditional self-reference model of self-consciousness that is unable to avoid circularity because of its search for a strictly conceptual knowledge of the self. Any such conceptual knowledge needs to remain attuned to the pre-reflective imputation of self via the implicature of speaker and actor in the act of speaking and doing.

Another issue at stake in this pre-reflective turn of self-implicature is the provision of a sheet anchor against the foundationalism that has been a recurring troublesome dogma in the history of philosophy from the very beginning, and particularly since the advent of modern epistemology and metaphysics with its search for foundationalist epistemic principles and irreducible traits of mind, of either a mentalist or materialist sort. The hermeneutical play of perspectives and the open texture of interpretive understanding problematize all ventures of securing unimpeachable foundational facts and concepts, and the self that is implicated in its discourse and action appears on the scene of experience as an *emergent* from the history of communicative praxis rather than an impermeable *foundation* for it.[1]

The Embodied Ego

In the descent of the transcendental ego into the communicative lifeworld with its manifold skills and social practices, further defining the descent of the ego as an avatar into lived time and space, another feature of its constitution as a life-experiencing subject becomes apparent. It undergoes an incar-

---

1. For an extended discussion of the phenomenon of hermeneutical self-implicature, see Calvin O. Schrag, *Communicative Praxis and the Space of Subjectivity* (West Lafayette, IN: Purdue University Press, 2003), 115-38.

nation into a lived body that coordinates its lived space with its lived time and bridges the chasm between mind and matter, culture and nature. Embodiment is at once an event of spatialization and temporalization. Plainly enough, the spatiality at issue here is not that of an objectivized space within a measurable extensive continuum. Anisotropic rather than isotropic, it is the lived space of the embodied ego marking off the locality where the world is to be perceived, where the other is to be encountered, and where a task is to be done. It is what Merleau-Ponty has felicitously named "the spatiality of situation" as contrasted with the "spatiality of position" conceptualized as a serialization and juxtaposition of abstracted geometrical points. We are here dealing with existentially experienced space rather than with abstracted and measured space. And what is at issue is the phenomenon of the body-as-lived *(le corp vécu)*, which needs to be more appropriately described as *inhabiting* a spatiality of situation rather than as an inert physical substance *occupying* a geometrically defined spatiality of position.[2]

William James had already put us on the path to a comprehension of the body-as-lived in his *Essays on Radical Empiricism* when he noted: "The world experienced comes at all times with our body as its centre, centre of vision, centre of action, centre of interest."[3] This description/redescription of the human body in terms of its concrete perceiving and acting requires a critical revisiting of traditional theories of the so-called "mind/body problem" that have bedeviled philosophical inquiry from the ancients up through the moderns. Descartes is usually cited as the principal contributor to this problem, mainly because his accentuated dualism of mind and body as separable substances provides such a readily available target, eliciting Gilbert Ryle's well-known assault on the Cartesian doctrine as speculation on the mind as a "ghost in a machine." This concept of mind as an elusive apparition in a machine, according to Ryle, requires a deconstruction so as to deliver us from the category mistake of representing mental events as belonging to one logical type when in fact they belong to another.[4]

Clearly, Professor Ryle may well have a point in his requirement for a deconstruction of the theory of mind as a physically nondependent mental substance able to somehow function on its own and known by way of a rig-

---

2. See Maurice Merleau-Ponty, *Phenomenology of Perception*, Part I, chapter 3: "The Spatiality of One's Own Body and Motility," trans. Colin Smith (New York: Humanities Press, 1962).

3. William James, *Essays in Radical Empiricism* (New York: Longmans, Green, 1942), 170n.

4. Gilbert Ryle, *The Concept of Mind* (New York: Barnes & Noble, 1949), 11-13.

orous introspection. However, his claim that Descartes ascribed to such a boldfaced separation of mind and body may well come up for discussion. But the point at issue has to do with Ryle's continuing purchases on an understanding of the human body as a machine. Apparently Descartes was wrong in conceiving of the mind as a ghost; however, according to Ryle he was correct in his notion of the human body as explained via a physiological mechanics. But herein resides the "problem" of the mind/body problem. The tacit presumption is that the body is indeed a machine. The rules of mechanics are the laws of nature and govern the movements of the human body as an instance of finite extended substance in general. So runs Descartes' argument. The human body is a machine — admittedly a "soft" machine, but a machine nonetheless, subject to the laws of mechanics. On this Ryle apparently remains in agreement as he sets out to devise a species of behaviorism so as to expunge Descartes' ethereal specter from the body.

But let us suppose that what the situation requires is a *dual* deconstruction — a deconstruction of the Cartesian concept of the human body as a machine in conjunct with a deconstruction of the mind as a ghost that dwells in a mechanistic arrangement of external parts. In the aftermath of such a dual deconstruction we discover a new perspective on both body and mind, requiring explications of the self as a consciousness always already embodied, calling for experimentations with appropriate vocabularies so as to elucidate the entwinement of mind and body in the existential projects of the embodied ego. Terms such as "embodied existence" and "incarnate consciousness" are more apt indicators of what is at issue in the mind/body relationship than is the grammar of mental and physical entities inviting an externalization and objectivization of the body as a thing among other things, an entity that the mind somehow possesses in its claim to *have* a body. More a relationship of being than having, more an event than an entity, embodied existence or incarnate consciousness is an event as a locus of perception and motility, action and reaction, from which the world is seen and from which projects are launched. The dominant question then becomes not a *what* question, probing the essential and accidental properties of abstracted and objectified entities, but rather a *who* question, inviting inquiries into the *who* that is implicated in the perception, imagination, conception, and action of the embodied event.[5]

---

5. A more detailed analysis of the phenomenon of the body-as-lived and its relevance for addressing the longstanding mind/body problem can be found in Calvin O. Schrag, *Experience and Being: Prolegomena to a Future Ontology*, Part II, chapter 4, "The Embodied Experiencer" (Evanston, IL: Northwestern University Press, 1969), 125-55.

In probing the incarnation of the ego as embodied event one comes upon a new perspective on the old subject/object dichotomy that has perplexed epistemological theorists from the ancients to the present and particularly since the time of Descartes. With the recognition of a pre-theoretical functioning intentionality in the motility of the body as lived, the theoretical construct of a subject at a distance from the body as object is undercut. The body as event is older than the body as either subject or object of representational knowledge. Embodiment is a quasi-transcendental condition for objectification and subjectification alike. Embodiment makes possible the encounter of entities that stand over against it, whereby the entity in question is properly defined as *ob-ject* or *Gegen-stand*. The functioning intentionality within the motility of the body makes objectification possible. Such is the case also with the constitution of the subject as an underlying substrate of consciousness, a metaphysical basement of mental properties. There is a pre-reflectively experiencing "who" that comes before the subject and returns after the deconstruction of the subject as a metaphysical residuum or indeed a ghost in a machine.

The origin of the epistemologically constructed subject/object dichotomy can be tracked in the pre-reflective life of the embodied ego. In the sensory experience of the hand touching other parts of the body, the incarnated consciousness of embodiment is at once as it were subject *and* object, an event of a coupled activity and passivity, a doing of the touching and a being touched. In the throes of a painful injury the embodied self experiences its being in pain as a phenomenon of conjoined experiencing and being experienced. Self and body are inseparable in the pain experience, calling forth a poignant self-identity — I *am* my body in the circumstance of being in pain. The various types and intensities of feelings and moods in the affective life of the self, such as the discomfort of pain sensations, the disquietude of moods of boredom and melancholy, and the suffering that can bring the self to the brink of despair, all provide testimony of the embedding of consciousness in its embodiment. The affective states in their varied configurations offer their own pre-cognitive disclosure of who the self is. Mood functions as a disclosure of the embodied self in advance of the conceptualization of it within an enframed subject-versus-object dichotomy. The separation of myself from my body, whereby my body becomes something that I *have* rather than someone that I am, is the consequence of the insinuation of an abstract matrix in which the self as subject is set over against the self as object.

Reassessing the Markers of Unity and Identity

The path that we have traveled in revisiting Kant's transcendental unity of apperception, effecting the hermeneutical turn, garnering the phenomenon of hermeneutical self-implicature, and sketching a portrait of the ego as embodied, opens up the requirement for new notions of unity and identity in addressing matters of *self*-identity. The design of the transcendental unity of apperception needs to be broadened so as to accommodate pre-categorial dimensions of self-understanding and self-constitution. In conjunct with the expansion of the transcendental to incorporate the transcending of the experiencing subject in its lived time of coming from a past and moving into a future, a broadening of the notion of unity is required. Such a broadening notion of unity would transgress the epistemic-theoretic binding of the moments of perception, imagination, and conception into a transcendental foundation for a trustworthy theory of cognitive judgment upon which to erect necessary and universal truths. This new sense of unity would be that of a pre-epistemological and pre-metaphysical pliant and adaptable unifying enabled by a holistic involvement with an experienced lifeworld of changing circumstances in which the rigid and inflexible criteriological markers of necessity and universality with the accompanying metaphysical dichotomies of mental and physical, mind and matter, culture and nature, have not yet taken up residence.

Within this holistically defined unity, always in processes of moving from part to whole and whole to part, difference and multiplicity are very much in play. This adds a further challenge to our quest for self-identity. Shifting the focus from the ego as epistemological pole or anchor unifying percepts and concepts to the ego as world-experiencing embodied subject, addressing the impingement of difference and multiplicity becomes unavoidable. It soon becomes evident that difference plays a decisive role in the constitution of self-identity. The relevance of the issues pertaining to sameness and difference, unity and multiplicity, needs to play itself out in clarifying the wider context of achieving knowledge of who each of us singularly is. Clearly the identity at work in self-identity cannot be that of a monarchical self-sameness insulated from the temporality of becoming. And the unity at issue will need to be of an open-texture sort so as to accommodate multiple profiles of the existing ego in its changing horizons. This requires a shift of focus to matters of the historical inherence of an embodied ego in the temporality and spatiality of a wider cultural and sociopolitical existence.

The Historical Chronotope of Selfhood

The Historical Turn

Our quest for self-identity has put us on a path of numerous twists and turns. We have followed Kant in his account of the transcendental ego and its pivotal role in his maneuvering of the epistemological turn; we have addressed the consequences of interpretation and the self-implicature of a speaking, acting, and embodied subject that makes its appearance in the hermeneutical turn; and it is now our task to explore the landscape of the historical turn as it relates to self-knowledge and self-constitution against a horizon that we have come to call the historical chronotope.

Plainly enough, in our use of the grammar of "chronotope" we are engaging in a conversation with the inventor of the term, a kindred probing inquirer about self-identity, the Russian literary theorist and philosopher Mikhail Mikhailovich Bakhtin. With his concept of the chronotope Bakhtin was able to elucidate a vital interconnection of time and space that antedates the abstract a priori forms of perception detailed by Kant. Time and space are set forth by Bakhtin as a concretely assimilated complex within the domicile of the life of discourse and action as dramaturgically emplotted in the structure of the novel. The pivotal and suggestive concept that is brought to our attention here is that of a lived historical time and space that comes to a decisive expression in narration. Bakhtin succinctly summarizes matters on the issue at hand regarding the relevance of the lived coordinate of time and space for historical understanding when he writes: "Time, as it were, thickens, takes on flesh, becomes artistically visible; likewise, space becomes charged and responsive to the movements of time, plot, and history."[6] The self within this assimilated time and space achieves self-identity through the hard struggle of self-knowledge and self-constitution in the travails of its historical existence.

It is thus that the Bakhtinian chronotope of historically infused time and space provides an appropriate background and context for addressing the relevance of narration and history in the challenges en route to an entwined self-knowledge and self-constitution. The chronotope marks out an expanding horizon with additional profiles for a comprehension of the human self as the who of narratival inherence and historical involvement. As

---

6. Mikhail M. Bakhtin, *The Dialogic Imagination,* trans. Caryl Emerson and Michael Holquist (Austin: University of Texas Press, 1951), 84.

we address the consequences of the historical turn in our search for self-identity it is important to underscore that the concept of history in question is not that of the Enlightenment doctrine of historicism with its peculiar stance on the three dimensions of time. The past within the historicist perspective of the Enlightenment is portrayed as an arena for objective historiological research wherewith to garner pure facts sans interpretation; the view of the future is one of an accentuated optimism promising a resolution of all social problems made possible by the unlimited resources of science and technology; and the attitude toward the present is that of a theoretically detached and untroublesome relativism in which there are no obliging moral claims for historical action. This Enlightenment historicism of the eighteenth and nineteenth centuries, as critically assessed by Nietzsche in particular, was destined for an abrupt metaphysical disappointment. It placed an unwarranted faith in the rational resources of the modern epistemological subject to design a portrait of the perfect society and a correspondingly inordinate trust in a controlling historical subject to bring it to fruition.[7]

In the wake of the bankruptcy of the Enlightenment ideal of an excessively technologized controlling subject we are presented with the charge to sketch a new portrait of historical agency in its role of shaping self-identity. The task becomes that of developing a critique of the naïve rationalism of modern historicism with its doctrines of the perfectibility of human nature and unlimited resources for social engineering. The requirement of the time is that of a disciplined interrogation along the lines of a critique of historical reason and historical action to supplement Kant's critiques of pure and practical reason as backdrop for fleshing out the narrative of self-identity within the lived-through travails of historical discourse and action. Such a project will need to reclaim certain voices of the tradition so hurriedly discarded by the Enlightenment, but not at the expense of a critical posture wherewith to evaluate the delivered contents of the tradition. The who of historical understanding and action always stands in a tradition while avoiding being imprisoned by it.

The self emerges in the throes of a historically contextualized lifeworld as at once a speaking/narrating and a deliberating/acting subject, at once a

---

7. Friedrich Nietzsche, *The Use and Abuse of History*, trans. Adrian Collins (New York: Liberal Arts Press, 1949). For a more general discussion of some of the misdirections of Enlightenment historicism, see Carl. L. Becker, *The Heavenly City of the Eighteenth Century Philosophers* (New Haven: Yale University Press, 1932).

homo narrans and a *homo faber,* a teller of stories and a maker of commodities and creator of institutions. The self achieves its self-identity through the telling and hearing of stories and in the production of goods and contriving social organizations through collaborative deliberations, decisions, and action. Narrativity and agency come together in the event of the historical turn. The insertion of such into the density of a historical becoming requires a redefinition of the identity that is in play in the phenomenon of *self* or *personal* identity. Self-identity takes on a peculiar coloring and characteristic, like that of a character in a novel or a *dramatis persona* in a theatrical performance. It is not the identity of strict numerical identity nor that of the more open-textured notion of identity ascribed to physical objects as a sameness and unity undisturbed by temporality. Such notions of identity have as their touchstone a rigid immutability and unbroken continuity that is immune to the ravages of time. They signify a permanence *outside* of time. As is well known, this objectivating concept of identity, proceeding from an analytic of relations of number and quantity, found a convenient but troublesome abode in Western metaphysics in its search for an abiding substratum, a *hypokeimenon,* quite unaffected by its changing attributes.[8]

This concept of transtemporal identity may have its utility, however tenuous, in defining relations of number and quantity, but it encounters profound limitations in coming to terms with the qualitative and value-laden identity that is at issue in the historical becoming of the self. Self or personal identity is an identity *within* time. More specifically, it is a *temporalized identity.* Temporality is veritably constitutive of self-identity. We are not dealing with a perduring substance above and beyond time but rather with a being that is temporalized from bottom up. And such is the state of affairs because in the first case what is at issue is not an inert object among other inert objects but rather a being that first defines itself as a negation of inert objects; and in the second case we are dealing not with quantitative and objectively measured time as a series of abstracted now-points but rather with a lived temporality in which the being of the self is constituted by and achieves its identity within a historical becoming of a creative appropriation of the past,

---

8. For help in sorting out the difference between the concept of identity in its application to relations of number and quantity from that having to do with self or personal identity, see Paul Ricoeur's use of the distinction between *idem* and *ipse* identity in an effort to arrive at a more precise semantics for addressing the issue. See his work, *Oneself as Another,* trans. Kathleen Blamey (Chicago: University of Chicago Press, 1992). In this connection, see also Calvin O. Schrag, *The Self After Postmodernity* (New Haven: Yale University Press, 1997), particularly 45-58.

projection into the future, and continuing process of deciding within the opportune present.

The Co-Constitution of Self with Other

The shift of analysis to the historical chronotope as horizon for self-knowledge and self-constitution opens another important profile on self-identity — a profile that renders explicit the societal sources of self-identity. Within this profile the self is understood as being constituted with other selves through shared language, kindred memories, and common social practices. The historical turn yields a vision of selfhood as an entwinement of narration and action, depicting a who that is at once storyteller and history-making agent in concert with other storytellers and other history-making agents. The stories that are told and the actions that are performed testify of a complementarity of personal identity and social solidarity. Self-knowledge and self-constitution find their source in the shared communicative practices of the discourse and action within a given community.

In shifting attention from the more restricted focus on personal and individual being to a being-with-others, we command a move from the phenomenon of the "I-experience" to that of the "we-experience," phenomena which at their root are inseparable. The self takes on the Socratic charge "Know thyself" by tracking the consequences that the attitudes, beliefs, and actions of other selves have for its coming to terms with who it is. In the main we see ourselves as others see us, taking on their attitudes toward us as we progressively redefine that which makes us who we are, at times simply appropriating the perspectives issuing from the other and at times defining ourselves in opposition to the perspective that the other has of us. Herein resides the economy of the societal sources of self-knowledge. In its quest for self-identity the self knows itself by responding to the stories that other selves tell and constitutes itself by involving itself in the shared social practices of the community.

The phenomenon of the we-experience issuing from the co-constitution of self with other selves forces one to attend, and quite directly, to an increasingly important social fact of our present age, namely, the fact of multiculturalism. This ever-present reality of our postmodernity introduces new challenges to our view of the world and our entwined personal and social existence. In the present age the society in which the self defines itself is a society composed of multiple sociocultural demarcations. Racial, ethnic, religious, and political differences play themselves out across a landscape that is made up of a mosaic of patterns of thought and micro-practices. The social fabric falls out as a multiplicity of features and designs. Insofar as the self understands and constitutes itself only against the backdrop of this social fabric it takes on a multiplicity of profiles over time. This occasions a redefinition of the unity that underlies self-identity. Self-identity morphs into a *collective* self-identity. No longer can one speak of a unified, monarchical, wholly self-governing selfhood. The who of discourse and action is a multidimensional self that bears the signature of multiplicity.

The multiplicity that informs the multidimensional mosaic of selfhood unfolds along a number of different directions and avenues and congeals into a variety of profiles. There are the more specific bio/gender profiles of racial distinctions and sexual orientations. There are family-constitutive profiles of marital, parental, sibling, proximate, and distant relative stereotypes and roles. There are the profiles of more institutionalized social and vocational roles depicting relations of doctor and patient, pastor and parishioner, teacher and student, governor and governed, citizen and alien. This multiplicity of profiles is very much in play in any determination of the historical dimension of selfhood. The journeying self finds itself in any number and combination of these bio/social/vocational roles. It defines itself in response to the attitudes, attributes, and functions that are displayed in these sundry roles. Some of these attitudes, attributes, and functions are consciously chosen; others are bequeathed to it as situational givens, requiring of the self that it work out its own destiny in a struggle of freedom with facticity.

Globalization and Postnational Self-Identity

A consequence of the globalization in the current situation of our time, with its spawning of multicultural voices and transnational networks of communication made possible by new technology, challenges us to address some urgent questions for the present age: "How does it stand with self-identity within the mix of transnational networks of information dissemination and increasing international cultural exchanges? As a multidimensional phenomenon how does self-identity accommodate the multicultural voices and associated practices without taking recourse to one of these voices and practices as pivotal and ultimately normative?" These questions become particularly sticky when dealing with the citizen/alien profile within the narrative on selfhood.

The modern nation-state ideology that provides the underbelly for managing international relations and which has been with us since the Treaty of Westphalia carries with it the invitation to consolidate the multicultural voices and variegated social roles in such a wise as to place nationalism at the center, subordinating the different voices and roles to a common allegiance to the symbols of territorial sovereignty. In answering the question "Who am I?" the nationalist finds the most decisive mark of self-identity to reside in a celebration of a national solidarity that transcends racial, gender, and ethnic differences. Whether male or female, black or white, straight or gay, theist or atheist, Jew or Gentile, each of us in our situated co-constitution with the other are members of a particular nation-state with its distinctive administrative, legislative, and juridical policies and demarcated geographical borders that separate our nation-state from foreign or alien nation-states. Plainly enough, in determining who each of us singularly is we note straightaway a heavy investment in being a member of a distinct political configuration with its territorial boundaries calling for unbroken loyalty to its established form of government. Self-identity becomes closely tied to, if indeed not simply defined by, citizenship classification. The bottom-line marker of who I am is found on the photo and the number on my passport. Such is the voice of nationalism.

It is becoming increasingly apparent that this voice of nationalism presents its own perils in our postmodern world of transnational globalization, with its multicultural conversations and multiple agencies operating across geographical borders. A nationalism that locates its principal criterion for self-identity and social solidarity in a fidelity to a particular nation-state opens the floodgates to a species of political idolatry that confers upon the ideals and principles of a particular form of government a status of infallibility and universality, absolutizing a historically relative construct of human contrivance. The consequences of absolutizing the relative in such a political state of affairs are far-reaching and profoundly distressing, setting conditions for the emergence of the mindset of genocide.

The major threat of genocide resides in an accentuated nationalistic mindset in which an alien society with its interwoven ethnic, racial, religious, and political beliefs and practices is deemed to be so corrupt that it needs to be indiscriminately annihilated, shoring up nationalistic aspirations with talk about evil empires and Satanic nation-states. Given such a standpoint in which the targeted nation-state is considered to be evil by virtue of its otherness, the stage is set for a diminution of the resources of diplomacy and a hurried taking of recourse to the technology of the war-machine to eradicate that which is deemed to be intrinsically evil.

It was the divisive consequences of nationalism, with the unsettling possibility of unleashing the mindset of genocide, that prompted the historic assessment by Albert Einstein: "Nationalism is an infantile disease, the measles of mankind." Against the backdrop of the coupling of conflicting nation-state ideologies with the accelerated race for nuclear armaments, Einstein proposed the establishment of a world federation to override the designs of independent sovereign nation-states. "The only salvation for civilization and the human race lies in the creation of world government. As long as sovereign states continue to have armaments and armaments secrets, new world wars will be inevitable."[9]

This call for a transnational world federation by Einstein has found a similar and more recent voice in Jürgen Habermas's proposal for a postnational matrix of global politics in his challenging work, *The Postnational Constellation*.[10] The charge that these proposals by Einstein and Habermas relating to the reorganization of world politics lay before us is indeed quite tremendous, but it is a charge that requires a fitting response. The charge places the modern nation-state ideology into question in a projected move toward a postnational set of conditions enabling a global solidarity and world citizenship. Within such a postnational constellation the quest for self-identity in the adventure of its co-constitution of self with others within the historical chronotope takes on a new direction. It needs to take into account the consequences, good and bad, of historical trends auguring toward a wider and more expansive planetary world society. Global narratives designed to integrate a multiplicity of cultural predicates take the place of divisive nation-state narratives. Postnational self-identity and cosmopolitan citizenry become twin-halves of an august event of the postmodern world.

Summary Afterword

Every extended portion of discourse requires an afterword, a brief epilogue, wherewith to summarize the terrain that has been traversed. Our journey has taken us along the paths of a transcendental, a hermeneutical, and a historical turn. In maneuvering these turns an effort has been made to illustrate

---

9. Walter Isaacson, *Einstein: His Life and Universe* (New York: Simon & Schuster, 2007), 386.

10. Jürgen Habermas, *The Postnational Constellation: Political Essays*, trans. and ed. Max Pensky (Cambridge, MA: MIT Press, 2001).

how our central question regarding the problem of self-identity becomes an issue in each of these turns in a progressive movement of continuing to clarify the dynamics of self-knowledge and self-constitution.

Our exploration of the transcendental turn required revisiting Kant's doctrine of the transcendental ego as unitary epistemological foundation. We learned that the transcendental ego is the source for the unity of apperception whereby the forms of perception, the schemata of the imagination, and the categories of understanding are synthesized, yielding a determination of the contents of experience as objects of knowledge. It was in this manner that the transcendental turn was able to secure the epistemic self-identity of a knowing self that accompanies its several representations.

The hermeneutical turn yielded the self-implicature of a praxis-oriented self in its concretely embodied functioning intentionality of everyday concerns and preoccupations. Stated in its most general terms, the hermeneutical turn is a turn from the primacy of theory to the primacy of praxis, from the conditions of the self as reflective cogito to the self as existential project in process of constituting itself in its discourse and action.

The historical turn broadens the horizon of self-identity in which the search for the conditions of self-knowledge and self-constitution moves in the direction of a constitution of self with other selves and opens a wider multicultural vista in which the sociopolitical features of selfhood become explicit, auguring toward a postnational self-identity in a new world order of cosmopolitan citizenry.

Posthuman Selves:
Bodies, Cognitive Processes, and Technologies

Jennifer Thweatt-Bates

In narrating "how we became posthuman," N. Katherine Hayles begins with a "roboticist's dream" that struck her "as a nightmare . . . a fantasy scenario in which a robot surgeon purees the human brain in a kind of cranial liposuction, reading the information in each molecular layer as it is stripped away and transferring the information into a computer. At the end of the operation, the cranial cavity is empty, and the patient, now inhabiting the metallic body of the computer, wakens to find his consciousness exactly the same as it was before." The self, which once inhabited a biological human body, now inhabits a computer, but is essentially unchanged. Hayles's reaction is incredulous: "How could anyone think consciousness in an entirely different medium would remain unchanged, as if it had no connection with embodiment?"[1]

The "Human" in the Posthuman

Thus Hayles begins her tale "of how a historically specific construction called *the human is giving way to a different construction called the posthuman.*"[2] This "historically specific construction" of the human Hayles

---

1. N. K. Hayles, *How We Became Posthuman: Virtual Bodies in Cybernetics, Literature, and Informatics* (Chicago: University of Chicago Press, 1999). Hayles is referring to Hans Moravec, *Mind Children: The Future of Robot and Human Intelligence* (Cambridge, MA: Harvard University Press, 1988).

2. Hayles, *How We Became Posthuman*, 2; italics original.

dubs the "liberal humanist subject," the passing of which she herself does not mourn, implicated as it is "with projects of domination and oppression," but which, she argues, the original architects of the posthuman did not intend to supplant.[3] Hayles writes of Norbert Wiener's pioneering work in cybernetics: "The revolutionary implications of this [cybernetic] paradigm notwithstanding, Wiener did not intend to dismantle the liberal humanist subject. He was less interested in seeing humans as machines than he was in fashioning human and machine alike in the image of an autonomous, self-directed individual. . . . For Wiener, cybernetics was a means to extend liberal humanism, not subvert it."[4]

Similarly, the scientists who coined the term "cyborg" in 1960 intended to describe a "a human agent with some additional, machine-controlled, layers of automatic (homeostatic) functioning"[5] that would allow for survival in alien or inhospitable environments. These cyborgs would simply be human beings provided with "an organizational system in which such robot-like problems were taken care of automatically, leaving man [sic] free to explore, to create, to think and to feel."[6] The addition of technology to the human body would not change human nature; it would, in fact, provide human beings with more opportunity to engage in the expression of those characteristic activities that demonstrate our unique humanness — freeing the conscious mind to explore, create, think, and feel, without the distraction and burden of having to attend to bodily needs.

Further, the perceived bodilessness of the information processes that define the cybernetic posthuman implies that "embodiment is not essential to human being. Embodiment has been systematically downplayed or erased in the cybernetic construction of the posthuman in ways that have not occurred in other critiques of the liberal humanist subject, especially in feminist and postcolonial theories."[7] Hayles argues that erasure of embodiment is a feature of the liberal humanist subject continued, indeed strengthened, in the cybernetic posthuman: "Although in many ways the posthuman deconstructs the liberal humanist subject, it thus shares with its predecessor an emphasis on cognition rather than embodiment. . . . To the extent that the

---

3. Hayles, *How We Became Posthuman*, 5.

4. Hayles, *How We Became Posthuman*, 7.

5. Andy Clark, *Natural-Born Cyborgs: Minds, Technologies, and the Future of Human Intelligence* (Oxford: Oxford University Press, 2003), 32.

6. Manfred Clynes and Nathan Kline, "Cyborgs and Space," *Astronautics* (1960).

7. Hayles, *How We Became Posthuman*, 4.

posthuman constructs embodiment as the instantiation of thought/information, it continues the liberal tradition rather than disrupts it."[8]

At the same time, however, Hayles sees the cybernetic posthuman, at least potentially, as "the deconstruction of the liberal humanist subject."[9] The unbounded flow of information between the subject and the environment is the key aspect of the cybernetic posthuman that challenges the assumptions of self crucial to the liberal humanist subject. Quoting C. B. Macpherson, Hayles reminds us that the essence of the liberal humanist subject is autonomy; yet the posthuman subject, a "material-informational entity," is enmeshed with its environment in ways that are negotiable and unfixed. Hayles writes, "We have only to recall how Robocop's memory flashes interfere with his programmed directives to understand how the distributed cognition of the posthuman complicates individual agency. If 'human essence is freedom from the wills of others,' the posthuman is 'post' not because it is necessarily unfree but because there is no *a priori* way to identify a self-will that can be distinguished from an other-will."[10] Hayles therefore perceives the flexible and porous boundaries of the posthuman self as a challenge to the fixity and stability of the autonomous, self-directing liberal humanist subject.

The tension between the continuities and discontinuities of the liberal humanist subject and the posthuman are well illustrated in what Stephen Garner calls "narratives of apprehension."[11] Elaine Graham's analysis of *Star Trek: The Next Generation*'s storyline surrounding Captain Picard's transformation into the posthuman Locutus of Borg demonstrates the instinctive technophobia of the liberal humanist subject. Picard, the "everyman," loses his personal identity, autonomy, and freedom, that is, his selfhood, and therefore his humanity, as the result of invasive technology. In this narrative of apprehension, the posthuman is dehumanizing; it must be resisted if the self is to be preserved (the ultimate threat, of course, being that "resistance is futile").

---

8. Hayles, *How We Became Posthuman*, 5. Hayles's perception of the continuity between the liberal humanist subject and the transhumanist self is verified in the transhumanists' characterization of their movement as a direct philosophical heir to Enlightenment humanism. See, for example, James Hughes, *Citizen Cyborg: Why Democratic Societies Must Respond to the Redesigned Human of the Future* (Boulder, CO: Westview Press, 2004).

9. Hayles, *How We Became Posthuman*, 2.

10. Hayles, *How We Became Posthuman*, 4.

11. Stephen Garner, "Transhumanism and the *Imago Dei*: Narratives of Apprehension and Hope" (Ph.D. dissertation, University of Auckland, 2006).

Narratives of apprehension, however, are countered with equally fervent narratives of hope. One such narrative is the "upload scenario" described in the opening paragraph, championed by some in the small but growing international movement known as transhumanism (H+). Uploading is "the process of transferring an intellect from a biological brain to a computer," and several hypothetical scenarios exist for potential brain-mapping procedures.[12] Nick Bostrom lists the anticipated advantages of uploading, according to its H+ adherents: uploads would not be subject to biological senescence; backup copies of uploads could be created regularly, making one's lifespan potentially as long as the universe's; one could potentially live much more economically, without need of physical food, housing, transportation, etc.; running on a fast computer, one would think faster than in a biological implementation, and thus get to experience more subjective time, and live more, during any given day; one could travel at the speed of light as an information pattern, which could be convenient in a future age of large-scale space settlements; radical cognitive enhancements would likely be easier to implement in an upload than in an organic brain.[13] Uploaders, like Wiener, Clynes, and Kline, thus see the posthuman as a liberated liberal humanist self, in which the definitive aspects of the human — rationality, freedom, autonomy — are freed from biological limitations, and are therefore augmented, not subverted, through the merging of humanity and technology.

A sharply contrasting narrative of hope, however, comes from Donna Haraway's appropriation of the cyborg as a feminist icon in a self-consciously ironic move. Haraway is well aware of Clynes and Kline's original vision of the cyborg as the self-sufficient space explorer liberated from bodily needs, or, in her words, "the awful apocalyptic *telos* of the 'West's' escalating dominations of abstract individuation, an ultimate self untied at last from all dependency, a man in space."[14] Haraway's desire is to subvert this dominant narrative of the self. She argues that the cyborg, despite its advent as the definitive "man in space," may be constructed differently: "The cyborg is a kind of disassembled and reassembled, postmodern collective and personal self. This is the self feminists must code."[15]

12. Nick Bostrom, "The Transhumanist F.A.Q.: A General Introduction" (2003), http://transhumanism.org/index.php/WTA/faq/.

13. Bostrom, "The Transhumanist F.A.Q."

14. Donna J. Haraway, "A Cyborg Manifesto: Science, Technology and Socialist-Feminism in the Late Twentieth Century," in *Simians, Cyborgs and Women: The Reinvention of Nature* (New York: Routledge, 1991), 151.

15. Haraway, "A Cyborg Manifesto," 163.

The posthuman challenge to the stability and fixity of the boundaries of the liberal humanist subject perceived by Hayles is exactly the disassembled, reassembled, collective, and personal self that Haraway celebrates as the cyborg.[16] And, not coincidentally, it is these characteristics that Hayles identifies as the challenges the posthuman represents to the specific historical construction of the human she tags as "the liberal humanist subject." The transgression of natural boundaries, and the fluidity of the boundary between self and other, means that this subversive posthuman self is not defined as a single, autonomous "thinking mind," but is embedded within constant, if constantly shifting, social and physical relationships.

This anthropology of hyper-relationality is one in which the posthuman subject is embedded in multiple, overlapping, shifting relationships, with both human and nonhuman partners. N. Katherine Hayles writes, "The posthuman subject is an amalgam, a collection of heterogeneous components, a material-informational entity whose boundaries undergo continuous construction and reconstruction."[17] Thus, significantly, the cyborg also signals a shift away from what Hayles calls "the liberal humanist subject," with its definition of person as an autonomous, rational, and free unified consciousness: "the presumption that there is an agency, desire or will belonging to the self and clearly distinguished from 'the wills of others' is undercut in the posthuman, for the posthuman's collective heterogeneous quality implies a distributed cognition located in disparate parts that may be in only tenuous communication with one another."[18] As Hayles notes, while that presumption prevails, humans must define their machines in ways that preserve conscious agency as the exclusive characteristic of human beings alone, denying the role that machines and other nonhuman components actually play in human decision-making.[19] "As long as the human subject is envisioned as an autonomous subject with unambiguous boundaries, the human-computer interface can only be parsed as a division between the solidity of real life on one side and the illusion of virtual reality on the other. . . . This view of the self authorizes the fear that if the boundaries are breached at all, there will be nothing to stop the self's complete dissolution."[20]

16. Haraway, "A Cyborg Manifesto," 164ff.

17. Hayles, *How We Became Posthuman*, 3. See also N. K. Hayles, "Refiguring the Posthuman," *Comparative Literature Studies* 41, no. 3 (2004).

18. Hayles, *How We Became Posthuman*, 3-4.

19. Hayles, *How We Became Posthuman*, 287-91. Hayles's discussion of and contrast of Joseph Weizenbaum and Edwin Hutchins's notion of distributed cognition is particularly rich in demonstrating this point.

20. Hayles, *How We Became Posthuman*, 290.

This explains the narratives of apprehension surrounding the posthuman, for, as Hayles notes, "When the self is envisioned as grounded in presence, identified with originary guarantees and teleological trajectories, associated with solid foundations and logical coherence, the posthuman is likely to be seen as antihuman because it envisions the conscious mind as a small subsystem running its program of self-construction and self-assurance while remaining ignorant of the actual dynamics of complex systems."[21] However, the posthuman, in Hayles's view, is only "antihuman" in the extremely limited and narrow sense that it signals the end of "a certain conception of the human, a conception that may have applied, at best, to that fraction of humanity who had the wealth, power, and leisure to conceptualize themselves as autonomous beings exercising their will through individual agency and choice."[22]

If, however, such a conception of the human distorts rather than describes what it means to be human, then "the prospect of humans working in partnership with intelligent machines is not so much a usurpation of human right and responsibility as it is a further development in the construction of distributed cognition environments, a construction that has been going on for thousands of years."[23] Further, "[W]hen the human is seen as part of a distributed system, the full expression of human capability can be seen precisely to *depend* on the splice rather than being imperiled by it."[24]

The Extended Self

In "The Extended Mind," Andy Clark and David Chalmers describe the process of human cognition as just such a collaboration between mind and environment. Clark and Chalmers describe "the general tendency of human reasoners to lean heavily on environmental supports" and suggest that epistemic actions deserve epistemic credit. The use of pen and paper for multiplication, the rearrangement of Scrabble tiles, the use of a slide rule, and the visual rotation of shapes in the game of Tetris with the use of a rotation button constitute "epistemic actions": actions that alter the world so as to aid and augment cognitive processes. "If, as we confront some task, a part

21. Hayles, *How We Became Posthuman*, 286.
22. Hayles, *How We Became Posthuman*, 286.
23. Hayles, *How We Became Posthuman*, 289-90. See also Clark, *Natural-Born Cyborgs*.
24. Hayles, *How We Became Posthuman*, 290.

of the world functions as a process which, *were it done in the head,* we would have no hesitation in recognizing as a part of the cognitive process, then that part of the world *is* (so we claim) part of the cognitive process."[25]

The cases of Inga and Otto are offered as an illustration of Clark and Chalmers's contention that not only cognitive processes but also states of mind, such as beliefs, can be constituted partly by features of the environment. Inga represents a "normal case of belief embedded in memory": she decides to go to an exhibition at the Museum of Modern Art, thinks for a moment, and recalls that the MoMA is on 53rd Street. Otto, however, has Alzheimer's; when Otto decides to go to the MoMA exhibition, he consults the notebook that he carries with him wherever he goes to write down information, which tells him that MoMA is on 53rd Street. Both Otto and Inga believe that MoMA is on 53rd Street — only the location of the content of this belief, and (perhaps) the way in which the content is accessed, differs. Clark and Chalmers suggest, "in relevant respects, the cases are entirely analogous: the notebook plays for Otto the same role that memory plays for Inga. The information in the notebook functions just like the information constituting an ordinary non-occurrent belief; it just happens that this information lies beyond the skin." Or, as Clark puts it elsewhere, "It *just doesn't matter* whether the data are stored somewhere inside the biological organism or stored in the external world. What matters is how the information is poised for retrieval and for immediate use as and when required."[26]

Clark and Chalmers conclude by asking, "What, finally, of the self? Does the extended mind imply an extended self?" Their answer is yes: "Most of us already accept that the self outstrips the boundaries of consciousness; my dispositional beliefs, for example, constitute in some deep sense part of who I am. If so, then these boundaries may also fall beyond the skin. The information in Otto's notebook, for example, is a central part of his identity as a cognitive agent. What this comes to is that Otto *himself* is best regarded as an extended system, a coupling of biological organism and external resources."[27]

In *Natural-Born Cyborgs,* Clark pursues this insight, arguing that the tendency to "off load" cognitive processes onto the environment is precisely

25. David Chalmers and Andy Clark, "The Extended Mind," *Analysis* 58, no. 1 (1998).

26. Clark, *Natural-Born Cyborgs,* 69.

27. Chalmers and Clark, "The Extended Mind," 19. The first clause lays down an important condition for the plausibility of the extended mind thesis, namely, that "the self outstrips the boundaries of consciousness"; and, as the opening clause suggests, "most," but not "all," accept this proposition.

what makes human beings unique, and that the term "posthuman" is a mis-nomer; rather, "my goal is not to guess at what we might soon become but to better appreciate what we already are: *creatures whose minds are special precisely because they are tailor-made for multiple mergers and coalitions.*"[28] New waves of technology, Clark believes, will bring this age-old process to a cli-max, as our minds and selves become ever more enmeshed within the nonbiological matrix of our technologies, but this is continuous rather than discontinuous with our evolutionary past and our current existence. The difference is that our emerging technologies "actively, automatically and continually tailor themselves to us just as we do to them . . . the line between tool and user becomes flimsy indeed. Such technologies will be less like tools and more like part of the mental apparatus of the person."[29]

Thus, Clark argues, "There is *no self*, if by self we mean some central cognitive essence that makes me who and what I am. In its place there is just the 'soft self': a rough-and-tumble, control-sharing coalition of processes — some neural, some bodily, some technological — and an ongoing drive to tell a story, to paint a picture in which 'I' am the central player."[30] Further, "My sense of myself as the protagonist in my own ongoing story is condi-tioned by my understanding of my own capacities and potentials — an un-derstanding which must be impacted, in deep and abiding ways, by the tech-nological cocoons in which my projects are conceived, incubated, and matured."[31]

This posthuman, or as Clark prefers, "soft self," is an embodied self, in

---

28. Clark, *Natural-Born Cyborgs*, 7.

29. Clark, *Natural-Born Cyborgs*, 7. It is worth noting that Clark's version of "extended mind" is contestable; Mark Rowlands argues, for instance, that the extended mind hypothe-sis is distinct from "embeddedness," whereas Clark seems to view the extended mind as the logical consequences of embeddedness. See Mark Rowlands, "Extended Cognition and the Mark of the Cognitive," *Philosophical Psychology* 22, no. 1 (2009), and "The Extended Mind," *Zygon* 44, no. 3 (2009). Lynne Rudder Baker disagrees with a more fundamental point when she argues that "there is no tool use without a user," and therefore that "persons cannot have extended minds in the sense of EM; shifting and transitory hybrids can hardly be persons"; Baker's "modest proposal" is that "persons can have partly (or perhaps wholly) inorganic, bionic bodies, and some persons currently do have bodies with bionic parts that play essen-tial roles in cognitive and motor activity" (656). Central to Baker's disagreement with Clark is an insistence on the importance of maintaining a sense of permanence, and therefore boundary, between bodies and transient cognitive aids in the environment. Lynne Rudder Baker, "Persons and the Extended-Mind Thesis," *Zygon* 44, no. 3 (2009).

30. Clark, *Natural-Born Cyborgs*, 138.

31. Clark, *Natural-Born Cyborgs*, 142.

which the body is definitive, but plastic, incorporative, flexible, and not necessarily or essentially biological. As Hayles and Haraway argue, technologies — even virtual and information technologies — are not about "leaving the body behind," but "extending bodily awareness in highly specific, local, and material ways that would be impossible without electronic prostheses."[32] Thus the significance of emerging technologies is not how they allow the *mind* to extend or instantiate itself in novel ways, but the way in which technologies extend and reconfigure the *body*.[33] The reconfiguration of the posthuman self, therefore, is a consequence of the reconfiguration of human bodies, rather than an "extension" of the "mind." For this reason, the term "distributed cognition," favored by Hayles, seems more apt than Clark and Chalmers's original term, "extended mind."[34]

The Posthuman Self and Theological Anthropology

Precisely how do such cyborg subjectivities transversally connect with theological notions of the human articulated as *imago Dei*? Elaine Graham asks the question this way: "If 'critical posthumanism' is asking the question, 'What does it mean to be human in an age of technologies?' where is it to look for an answer? If *homo sapiens* are to be succeeded by *techno sapiens*, what happens to our accounts of human subjectivity, and in particular the basis on which we might ascribe it a moral status?"[35] Ted Peters asserts that "Christian theologians think in terms of a centered self, the unifier of all that is disparate in a person's experience and relationships," but what happens when the very notion of "centered self" is itself undermined in the posthuman self?[36]

A relational anthropology that identifies the *imago Dei* as constituted in the divinely initiated relationship of God with humans is a first step;[37] but

32. Hayles, *How We Became Posthuman*, 291.

33. Haraway, "A Cyborg Manifesto," 164.

34. Mark Rowlands quips, "It is arguable that the only things wrong with [the label] the extended mind are the words *extended* and *mind*." Rowlands, "The Extended Mind," 628-29.

35. Elaine Graham, "In Whose Image? Representations of Technology and the 'Ends' of Humanity," *Ecotheology* 11, no. 2 (2006): 166.

36. Ted Peters, *Anticipating Omega: Science, Faith and Our Ultimate Future* (Göttingen: Vandenhoeck & Ruprecht, 2006), 135.

37. F. LeRon Shults's thesis of a "turn to relationality" suggests a growing consensus regarding relational anthropologies both philosophically and theologically. See F. LeRon

the concept of relationality itself must be somewhat refigured in light of the posthuman, as there are no longer stable, autonomous, and well-bounded selves to do the relating.[38] Such a concept of the human is already being challenged within the Christian tradition; Roberto S. Goizueta's anthropology of accompaniment, for example, is constructed as a deliberate alternative to the liberal humanist subject: "For modern liberal individualism, then, the individual (or 'socially unsituated self') exists prior to his or her relationships with others," but Goizueta defines the self as "always *intrinsically* relational."[39]

Goizueta's relationality, however, is described in problematic terms: "an *organic* worldview, which would presuppose an essential, intrinsic, or 'organic' relationship between the particular and the universal."[40] From a posthuman point of view, neither relationships, ontologies, nor particularities of embodiment can be regarded as organic givens; thus, while Goizueta's relational anthropology provides a theological starting point that recognizes the necessity of relationship, the importance of embodiment, and the significance of particularity, a posthuman anthropological perspective offers a corrective to its metaphors of organicism, wholeness, givenness, and ontological uniqueness.

Rather, in a cyborg anthropology, "emergence replaces teleology; reflexive epistemology replaces objectivism; distributed cognition replaces autonomous will; embodiment replaces a body seen as a support system for the

Shults, *Reforming Theological Anthropology: After the Philosophical Turn to Relationality* (Grand Rapids: Eerdmans, 2003), and *Christology and Science* (Grand Rapids: Eerdmans, 2008).

38. Posthuman subjectivity dismantles not only the anthropology of the liberal humanist subject but also the theology of the God to whom that subject was in relation. Shults writes, "[W]e may still ask whether the Bible describes a God whose highest goal is glorifying himself as a single self-conscious Subject." Shults argues that a lack of attention to the Trinitarian personal relations of the three persons of God "led to a picture of an infinitely intelligent and powerful Subject who is intent on self-glorification" — a description eerily reminiscent of Haraway's description of the (im)modest witness of the gentleman scholar in the narratives of the scientific revolution. (God is not just an old man in the sky; he is a man in a lab coat in the sky, and scientific objectivity is a god-trick.) Shults's observation is salutary: if that single self-conscious subject is not who we are, it's not who God is, either. Shults, *Reforming Theological Anthropology,* 240. Donna J. Haraway, "Modest_Witness@Second_Millennium," in *Modest_Witness@Second_Millennium.Femaleman_Meets_Oncomouse: Feminism and Technoscience* (New York: Routledge, 1997), 23-33.

39. Roberto S. Goizueta, *Caminemos Con Jesús: Toward a Hispanic/Latino Theology of Accompaniment* (Maryknoll, NY: Orbis Books, 1995), 50.

40. Goizueta, *Caminemos Con Jesús,* 65.

mind; and a dynamic partnership between humans and intelligent machines replaces the liberal humanist subject's manifest destiny to dominate and control nature."[41] There is much here that echoes Goizueta: the importance of material reality, the affirmation of the particular, the repudiation of a notion of autonomous individuality, the concept of a constitutive relationship in "dynamic partnership." The introduction of the dimension of the technological, however, implicit in the figure of the cyborg, emphasizes the necessity and the responsibility of (post)human agency in the construction and maintenance of constitutive relationships. Goizueta writes, "My identity is given me," but the cyborg's identity is not given, it is manufactured.[42]

The displacement of the liberal human subject, as Calvin Schrag notes, "does not entail a dissolution of the subject and consciousness in every manner conceivable . . . one still has to end with the subject, duly decentered and refigured . . . without loss of either the speaking or the acting subject."[43] Cyborg subjectivity is not loss of subjectivity or agency; indeed, for Haraway, the cyborg is a means of reclaiming agency and relationship, not losing them to technological determinism.[44] But it is an agency whose boundaries are incorporative, not fortified; an agency that invites collaboration rather than insisting on autonomy. This is true on multiple levels: material, ontological, epistemological, social, and political; I believe we may fairly add, as well, theological. As we desire, seek out, and perfect the relationship with God that defines the *imago Dei*, we invite the collaboration of divine agency to intertwine with our own.[45]

Not My Will, but Thine: The Prayer of the Cyborg Christ

While we must be careful not to anachronistically project a modernist anthropology of the liberal humanist subject onto the philosophical and anthropological framework of the early Christian tradition, there is a similar presumption of the unity of the subject that should be noted. Thus, just as

41. Hayles, *How We Became Posthuman*, 288.
42. Goizueta, *Caminemos Con Jesús*, 50. As Hayles puts it, "[W]ho cyborgs will be is the question." Hayles, *How We Became Posthuman*, 5.
43. Calvin Schrag, *The Resources of Rationality: A Response to the Postmodern Challenge* (Bloomington: Indiana University Press, 1992), 151.
44. Haraway, "A Cyborg Manifesto," 165.
45. This might offer a new and interesting way of articulating a doctrine of divinization.

the posthuman subverts the unity of the liberal humanist subject, it subverts the unity of the subject taken for granted, for instance, in the classic Christological definition of Chalcedon. The gain for theology in this posthuman subversion is the way in which it simplifies one of the most vexing questions of Christian belief: that Jesus is both fully divine and fully human. In a philosophical framework in which selves are complete, single, unified, and bounded entities, it is impossible to construct an understanding of the selfhood of Jesus that does justice to the claim of Chalcedon; either the humanity or the divinity is compromised, perhaps obliterated, or Jesus is essentially two selves.

The substantive framework of the Logos-*sarx* Christology of Alexandria, in conjunction with the presumption of the unity of Christ's subjectivity, for example, led inevitably to the historical heresy of Apollinarianism; if Christ were the Logos enfleshed, then "the mind of Christ" was, simply, the Logos, and there was no room for a purely human mind, the coexistence of which would, in Richard Norris's words, "render Jesus in effect schizophrenic."[46] Here, it is not simply the Logos-*sarx* construction that forces the heretical conclusion, for this is, after all, the construction that emerges as orthodox. It is rather the combination of the presumed unity of subjectivity and the Logos-*sarx* construction that forces Apollinarian logic to its consistent and heretical conclusion that Christ could have no human mind.

In contrast, Theodore of Mopsuestia's Christological construction defines the relationship between God and humanity in the incarnation in terms of will rather than in terms of substance.[47] For Theodore, the unity of Christ's person resulted as the unity of the divine and human wills; this not only preserves a full humanity in Christ, in deliberate contrast to the Apollinarian heresy, but also creates a picture of Jesus maturing into this unity that does not threaten human identity and agency. Further, Theodore's language of "indwelling" is inherently relational, and, while Jesus' relationship to God may indeed have been ontologically unique, other human beings, too, are invited into this relational possibility of the indwelling of the Spirit of God.

Thus, as we revisit Chalcedon as posthumans, Theodore's Antiochene Christology may be reconstructed as an expression of the distributed cognition of a human being specially indwelt by God, embodying the possibility

---

46. Richard A. Norris, ed., *The Christological Controversy*, Sources of Early Christian Thought (Philadelphia: Fortress Press, 1980), 22.

47. Norris, *The Christological Controversy*, 25.

of joining with the divine in a posthuman hybridity that includes a component of divine indwelling in our daily lives. In moving away from the constraints of substance categories and the corresponding necessity of the unity of subjectivity assumed at Chalcedon, and toward a posthuman subjectivity characterized by the collective, heterogeneous distributed cognition described by Hayles and others, it becomes entirely possible to conceive of Christ's human subjectivity in a way that includes a divine component that neither usurps nor threatens Christ's human identity. To rephrase Hayles above, when Christ is seen as part of a distributed system, the full expression of Christ's humanity and divinity can be seen precisely to depend on the splice, rather than being imperiled by it. This is, one might say, a "cyborg Christ," in ontological relation to the divine.

Finally, this opens the possibility for understanding Jesus' prayer in the Garden of Gethsemane, "not my will, but thine," as well as the prayer offered to us as the template for human communication with God, "thy will be done," in a way that is empowering, active, present, material, and incorporative. This does not signify the obliteration of our free will by a stronger, more compelling divine will, but a negotiation of the boundaries that define these wills. The very act of prayer is one in which the boundary between our wills and God's will is renegotiated, so that we may desire what God desires — without loss of personal subjectivity, agency, or identity, but rather, in the transformation through relationship from the self-defined human into a posthuman indwelt with the spirit of God.

The Erotic Self and the Image of God

Jan-Olav Henriksen

Eros and desire are intimately linked. This link manifests itself not only in the realm of sexuality, which is where eros and desire are most commonly depicted in current culture. We also find this link expressed in a child's longing for its mother's love, as well as in our desire to be recognized and as a result feel that we are valuable and lovable. On the other hand, people also have the desire to love somebody, and one could say without much exaggeration that love and our love stories are part of what defines us as human — in good respects as well as bad: our lost as well as our fulfilled love is, as part of the relational web with others that eventually defines us, part and parcel of who we turn out to be. Hence love — *eros* — is central to the development of the self and self-perception. Love is what is desired, and love also expresses itself (or rather: oneself!) in desire. The self is shaped by the erotic — and by our struggle and desire for eros.[1] The experience of how these struggles for love and for becoming a self permeate our lives and are connected requires a theological interpretation.

This essay will, accordingly, develop an understanding of how eros and desire may be interpreted in a theological framework that takes into account the understanding of the development/constitution of the self as relational, in a manner that interprets desire and the erotic dimension of human life in

---

1. As will become apparent in the following, I find a sharp distinction between *eros* and *agape* futile in the content of the present argument. For a more developed phenomenological argument that problematizes such a sharp distinction, cf., e.g., Jean-Luc Marion, *The Erotic Phenomenon* (Chicago: University of Chicago Press, 2007), 221.

light of what it means to be created in the image of God. As an exploration into philosophical theology, it will develop an understanding of how basic phenomena of human life may be seen as integral to what shapes the content of important theological constructions like *imago Dei*.

Desire and Love: The Erotic Struggle to Become a Self

In a profound sense, as humans we desire to be loved, and to love. This desire for love is present even before we can talk of an "I," before the self is constituted. The desire for the love of the other is part of what makes me into who I am — it is part of what makes me a self. If we see the self as an instance that is able to have a perception of oneself as distinguishable from others, and who slowly also becomes able to thematize this distinction in terms of language, and refer what happens or takes place back to oneself in a way that is able to distinguish more clearly between self and other, it becomes apparent that the self is only slowly becoming what it is. To become aware of oneself is to become aware of present desires as *mine*. Hence, there are many ways of becoming a self (and to be able to recognize such desire) as well as many obstacles on the path toward becoming a full, integrated self (e.g., when desires are not sanctioned, not recognized by others, negated, etc.). All this notwithstanding (and not entering further into the psychological dimensions of becoming a self), the desire to love and be loved, the quest for the other, is among the first and most important ways in which we become aware of ourselves. We can also put it differently: present in my desire is the struggle toward becoming a self, and present in my desire for the other is my desire for being recognized by the other as a self. Present here also are some of my chances to develop into a more fully integrated, mature self who is aware of and understands the desire I am harboring in my engagements with the world and others.

Hence, the desire for love that all humans harbor is at the very core of what it means to become a self. It is in this quest for love that we struggle to become the ones we want to be, and this is why love (eros) plays such a great part in people's lives: love is from the outset the very thing by which we define ourselves, and it is what helps us define ourselves as humans. Hence, the human desire for self and for other constitutes the interplay between the becoming self, the relation to others, and love. My main point here is simply to state that love from the outset proves to be the most important factor in the shaping of the self — and for harboring desires for others and the world in a way that opens us up to the world in creative and constructive modes. It is no accident, then, when the New Testament speaks of God as love (1 John 4:8): God may be seen as the source of that which makes us become who we are, makes us become selves, namely, love. In this sense, a phenomenology that further clarifies the relationship between self, love, and God is called for.

In phenomenology, there are important strands of interpretation that help us deepen the understanding of this interplay without ending up in a psychological or biological interpretation of what constitutes the self. This phenomenological approach also helps us understand the desire that is present from the outset in what I have here called the erotic struggle for becoming a self, as something prior to subjectivity (the reflective self-awareness by means of symbolically mediated self-relation).

According to Maurice Merleau-Ponty, desire is not adequately understood if seen only as a primitive biological notion. Desire is neither the result of an involuntary biological impulse, nor a phenomenon apparent for a lucid mind. Desire is neither the result of biology nor calculation, and hence, humans cannot produce their own desire. Desire is prior to the self. I cannot and do not say that "I want to desire X" and by these words force desire to appear. Desire exists in another type of structure. Desire is a way of relating to the world, expressing a type of intentionality that *conditions* human existence[2] and the wills and wants that we articulate. Desire is an integral element in my embodied direction toward the world and toward myself — a moment in my being-in-the world. Desire emerges spontaneously in my experience of the world as the other, and out of the pre-thematic emotional being in the world. Desire is thus not primarily an element in consciousness that can be appropriated intellectually, but exists in the world as the world is given through my body and its perception. This is the reason why we say that it is the other who stirs my desire. Hence, it is not only the case that I desire; desire is also what *happens* to me. Desire has its origin not in me, nor in the Other as such, but in the relation. We need to see desire as a *relational* phenomenon, and as something that is part of what in turn constitutes the relational self.

Merleau-Ponty sees desire as a motivating force for my choice of experiences. Thus, desire opens up to a dimension of value in my being-in-the world. I prefer some actions and experiences over others. These preferences

---

2. The following builds especially on Maurice Merleau-Ponty, *Phenomenology of Perception* (New York: Humanities Press, 1962), Part I, ch. 5 (178ff.).

are given through desire, and thus, desire *directs*. Desire directs me toward what I see as valuable, what is desirable, and thereby becomes a constitutive part of my action. Desire is thus not only of importance in the instances of the erotic, but is poured out into the whole of my existence. Only thus can it also be said to define my being-in-the-world. Desire is, accordingly, not only to be defined as sexual desire in a narrow sense, but as something that shapes my directedness toward the Other, or to others, in a variety of different ways.

Desire as experienced is nevertheless always *mine,* and something related not only to the object, but to my embodied self. Desire exists in a dialectical structure, in the movement, or the oscillation, between my relation to the Other and my relation to myself. This happens even before desire becomes conscious as *my* desire and is appropriated as mine in my subjectivity. Hence, it is of crucial importance for my relationship to the other — and is no less important because of the opportunities that desire gives me so that I may perceive myself in new and different ways. Desire demands that I live in the given situation in a specific manner — and acquire a specific mode of being-in-the-world. Thus, it defines my subjectivity, and shapes the concrete situation by virtue of relating me to what is exterior to my immediate self. Against this background, it becomes important to understand desire as a pre-subjective phenomenon, prior to the subjectivity that emerges out of the intersubjectivity that allows me to become a subject.

Let us reflect for a moment on some of the most important implications of Merleau-Ponty's descriptions of how love (eros) is part of becoming a self. Saying that love is part of becoming a self means that love is a given condition (be it in terms of being experienced as present or absent) for becoming a self: the desire for love, or the love that may emerge in a desiring relationship with the Other, must in some sense be met in order for the desiring individual to not be totally preoccupied with herself, and instead become open to the other. Presence or absence of love is reflected in the mode in which desire is shaped, expressed, and articulated. At the basis of everything is love (present or absent). It is when love is absent that other desires may take over, compensate, turn the situation into something else, and turn the mode of being in the world into something preoccupied with a self that only relates to its own desires, and not to the other in/of desire.

To repress and ignore desire has severe consequences. From a specific point of view, to ignore desire for the other (whatever it may be) implies more than losing a specific mode of possibility for self-transcendence (because you then lose the other who presents herself to you as the other, the one who can open your world). You also lose a specific chance for self-relation, for relating to yourself in the modus of desire, i.e., as someone who directs you outside yourself. The crucial consequence of this is that you end up in a situation (or a lack of situation, really) that we may describe as a way of absolutizing finitude: i.e., here we are left facing a finite (or *finited,* to use an odd expression) mode of existence in which the other that is present in desire is not really playing any role in who you are able to become. Desire is not allowed to function as an opportunity for self-transcendence, for other-relatedness. The severity of this is, however, not only expressed in the fact that one may lose the relation to the other that is constituted by desire; in the repression of, e.g., erotic desire, or the desire for creativity, you may lose the relationship to *yourself as a body,* or as a spontaneous agent. This fact points to the centrality of embodiedness for becoming and being a self — a theme that I am not able to develop fully in the present context.

Sexual erotic desire among adults illustrates this possible opportunity and loss well: one can take the situation that this desire constitutes seriously, and realize that the desire in question requires an expression, its own fulfill-ment in an erotic situation, where we not only focus on our desire as such, but also hand ourselves over to the Other. In this "handing ourselves over to" is implied a moment of lack of control, an openness to the radical otherness of the situation, an openness to another situation than the one previously ex-isting. This is not a finite mode of being-in-the-world. But the opposite may also happen: if we ignore the desire emerging in this situation, we lose the chance for the expression of desire, but also the chance for being open in a manner that may give us a possibility for truly experiencing the other. Hence, *to recognize desire is to recognize oneself as a being who is open to what lies beyond the immediate presence of the situation and one's own clearly de-fined projects.* This *openness* in desire is, I will argue, structurally linked to the openness that is implied in a trusting religious belief in God.

In what may become an erotic situation, one has to express desire in or-der for the situation to become exactly that. If I do not express my desire for the other to her, she will not know of me and of the openness that I invite her to participate in. A desire without any expression is closed, captured, cannot breathe, says Merleau-Ponty. When desire constitutes the presence of the other, it is thus only in the expression that the situation can be realized as what it is — as erotic. Erotic desire is thus to be seen as a chance for love to realize itself — and thus a chance for what lies at the foundation of the self to come to a full and relational expression.

At this point it seems apt to take a step further and consider a point in

Hegel's analysis of desire in chapter 4 of *Phänomenologie des Geistes*. There are features in his analysis that suggest that desire be understood as what *negates* the desired, by integrating it into the horizon of the active subject. However, this understanding of desire appears as one-sided and not very nuanced in the light of the above. As we have seen, embodied desire not only is the function of a curious mind — eager to know and to integrate the other into the "sameness" of rationality — but also may serve to open up the self in ways that are emotionally, perceptively, and rationally unpredictable. The ethical thrust of this openness, which is brilliantly developed in Levinas's understanding of what he calls metaphysical desire (especially in *Totality and Infinity*), safeguards the Other from being negated; instead, it allows for the other to break in, to crack open the self-encumbered, finite, or absolutized self.

At this point we face a possible positive function of enjoying desire itself, and not only its gratification. When we are able to recognize unfulfilled desire as a constituent in human life that cannot be fully overcome, but which nevertheless relates the subject to a reality where its own finitude is affirmed and appreciated as part of what it is to be a human being open to the Other, desire takes on a *reminding* function with regard to my finitude. As we shall see below, this is not without relevance for the understanding of the human being as *imago Dei* — as the finite image of the infinite God. Desire for love and desire emerging from love disclose me, make me appear, as being more than the self-sufficient self. Desire is thus — for ethical, phenomenological, and positive theological reasons — that which *disrupts* a self-sufficient subjectivity without leaving it behind; that which transcends what is conceived in the rational subject's already given understanding of the world. It reminds us of how our self has its origin in the Other who gives content to our world; in that which creates fissures and disturbances in our complacencies by stirring our desires. Or, to say it with Alexandre Kojève, desire is not only negating and negative, it does not necessarily destroy the other, but makes something new appear. What appears is the reality of self-consciousness and subjectivity,[3] where, I would like to add, the Other may appear as a constitutive part, and *where I am called to appropriate desire in the way I want to lead my life.* Hence, desire is not only pre-subjective; it also has important bearings for how I constitute my own subjectivity.

Judith Butler points out how contemporary interpreters of Hegel's no-

---

3. Cf. Alexandre Kojève, *Hegel. Kommentar zur Phänomenologie des Geistes* (Frankfurt: Suhrkamp, 1975), 54-58.

tion of desire have developed an understanding that sees this notion as something that increasingly signifies the impossibility of a coherent subject, against other interpretations that operate with harmony models of the relationship between reason and desire. One main reason for preferring the latter interpretation is that desire as an instantiation of the Other in consciousness is what enables the subject to grow, develop, and reflect.[4] The otherness of desire thus suggests that reason is not alone in constituting the subject. This interpretation implies that the subject of desire has a project with *itself* in order to develop a subjectivity that comprises both reason and desire so that it may attain a sufficient stability. The theologically fruitful result of this development (and of the growing insight into the Hegelian project) is that reason alone, and the self-conscious subject, can no longer be seen as *the* principles that establish human identity. Human identity is due to elements exterior to the subject (as in Levinas), elements that operate within and beyond (as well as behind) desire, but are never possible to overtake or fully integrate into rationality.[5]

Paul Ricoeur's analysis of desire seems to go even further in the same direction. He situates desire in the "between"; between opening and closing, between vision of the world and point of view.[6] In Ricoeur, the emphasis is not primarily on the possibility of the self to become aware of itself, of subjectivity, but on how desire places the subject *outside* of itself, in the world. His description here is accordingly not very different from the one given by Merleau-Ponty:

> Desire does not show me my way of being affected, nor does it shut me up within my desiring self. It does not speak to me at first of myself because it is not at first a way of being aware of myself, even less an "internal sensa-

4. Cf. Judith Butler, *Subjects of Desire: Hegelian Reflections in Twentieth-Century France* (New York: Columbia University Press, 1999), 33: "[W]e learn that human desire is distinguished from animal desire in virtue of its reflexivity, its tacit philosophical project, and its rhetorical possibilities. At this point, however, we are equipped only with the insights that Force and Explanation have provided us; we understand *movement* as the play of Forces, and Explanation as the necessary *alterity* of consciousness itself. Predictably enough, the experience of desire initially appears as a synthesis of movement and alterity."

5. In Wolfhart Pannenberg's theological anthropology, this testifies not only to the hubris of a philosophy of mind but also, more positively, to how the divine providence guides the processes that establish human identity in a manner that is still open to the future, and never self-enclosed. Cf. *Anthropology in Theological Perspective* (Philadelphia: Westminster Press, 1985).

6. Paul Ricoeur, *Fallible Man*, rev. ed. (New York: Fordham University Press, 1986), 53 (hereafter abbreviated as FM).

tion." It is an experienced lack of . . . an impulse oriented toward. . . . In desire I am outside myself; I am with the desirable in the world. In short, in desire I am open to all the affective tones of things that attract or repel me. It is this attraction, grasped on the thing itself, over there, elsewhere, or nowhere, which makes desire an openness onto . . . and not a presence to the self closed on itself. (FM 53)

This is as far as Ricoeur follows Merleau-Ponty, however. In the next steps of his analysis, he views the functions of desire in relation to the self and the body in a manner that underscores the *mediating* role of the self between the body and the world. "[T]he body, the flesh of desire, does not manifest itself as a closed figure but as a practical mediation, in other words as a *projecting body* in the same sense that we were able to speak of the *perceiving body*" (FM 53; italics in original). The parallel he here suggests between desire and perception is noteworthy, because it suggests that both perception and desire, although intertwined as bodily conditioned functions of the self, are not only similarly anchored in finitude, but are also what allow us to transgress finitude: "My flesh of desire is wholly anticipation, that is, a prefigured grasp or hold, over there, elsewhere, nowhere, outside myself. The desiring body steals away in advance, proffering the *élan* of its flesh to the projecting self" (FM 53). Again, we see how the self is constituted as relational from the outset, and how desire is part of the mode in which this relationality expresses itself.

As I have hinted toward, to understand desire as an integral part of the self's being-in-the-world sheds important light on the role of *finitude* in relation to desire. In the same manner as the *perspective* makes the content of the perceiving body finite, there is an affective equivalent in desire that may obscure its content. Desire may have a certain type of clarity, but this obscuring function of the affections may darken it. As a result, desire is linked to the emotional confusion that it may give rise to (FM 53). Ricoeur's intention in pointing this out is related to his understanding of the relationship between intentionality and desire. In intentionality, the "clarity of desire" is to be found. Without intentionality, desire may lead us into darkness. Ricoeur here speaks, however, of an intentionality that — in spite of being fully anchored in the perceptive and desiring body — allows for us to relate the object to the anticipated states of self given in our hermeneutically constituted understanding of the world:

Desire is a lack of . . . a drive toward. . . . The "of" and the "toward" indicate the oriented and elective character of desire. This specific aspect of

desire, taken as desire of "this" or of "that," is susceptible of being elucidated — in the precise sense of the word — by the light of its representation. Human desire illuminates its aim through the representation of the
absent thing, of how it may be reached, and the obstacles which block its
attainment. These imaging forms direct desire upon the world; I take
pleasure in them; in them I am out of myself. The image is even more; not
only does it anticipate the perceptual outlines of gestural behavior, but it
also anticipates pleasure and pain, the joy and sadness of being joined to
or separated from the desired object. This imaging affectivity, held in
pledge by the affective effigy or by the representative or analogue of future
pleasure, ends by bringing me in imagination to the goal of desire. Here
the image is nothing other than desire. The image informs desire, lays it
open, and illuminates it. (FM 53-54)

Hence, one can say that the desired is "worked over" by means of
intentionality in order to overcome the immediate character of the desired
object. But this also indicates that it is I, who *by constituting the image of desire,* open up to desire as that which enters into my field of motivation. My
motivation is not given with the desired object alone, but with its relation to
me as myself. This is why desire has to be appropriated in my subjectivity.
Consequently, desire can achieve clarity only from *my intentions.* These intentions are shaped by my values and preferences. "From the standpoint of
value, desire may be compared to other motives and thereby sacrificed or
privileged, approved or reproved" (FM 54). It is in this manner, then, that we
can say that in a qualified sense, desire relates us to the good, to goodness.
Without the clarity established by intentionality, this is not necessarily so.
Again, I see some valuable points here that may contribute to a more positive and nuanced understanding of desire in a Christian context: desire is
not given up, but refined in terms of its moral contribution given with its relation to the good.

The theme of goodness suggested here indicates that when we go from
Ricoeur to Levinas, they have something in common with regard to this
topic. Goodness can only prevail if desire is constituted as metaphysical, i.e.,
as a desire for something that is more than an object to possess. We see the
ethical thrust of this in Levinas's analysis, when he describes how desire
opens up totality to infinity:

> The infinite in the finite, the more in the less, which is accomplished by
> the idea of Infinity, is produced as Desire — not a Desire that the posses-

sion of the Desirable slakes, but the Desire for the Infinite which the desirable arouses rather than satisfies. A Desire perfectly disinterested — goodness. But Desire and goodness concretely presuppose a relationship in which the Desirable arrests the "negativity" of the I that holds sway in the Same — puts an end to power and emprise. This is positively produced as the possession of a world I can bestow as a gift on the Other — that is, as a presence before a face.[7]

Here Levinas also anticipates an important element in more recent phenomenology, not least as developed in Derrida and Marion, namely, the *gift*. The gift is undetermined by a symmetrical relation; it is, in their understanding, beyond economy, beyond calculation.[8] As gift I offer myself to the other in a way that puts my power to rest. This is — in a specific and profound way — an expression of my desire for the Other — not as a possible holding in my possession, but for her as an Other, not determined or controlled by me. This desire is thus the opposite of the desire for control. Instead, this is a desire where I am not in control, because this desire is in no way determined by the content of the I — the same. Paradoxically, this also implies that in offering myself and my world as a gift to the Other, I myself am also in a position where I am able to receive a gift — something that was not there before, something undetermined by me, but still enriching me, and expanding my world. I will develop this as a fruitful way of understanding the notion of *imago Dei* in the next section of this paper. It is as a result of this desire that the face of the Other manifests a surplus compared to everything preexisting in my ideas of her, and thus destroys my totality:

> For the presence before a face, my orientation toward the Other, can lose the avidity proper to the gaze only by turning into generosity, incapable of approaching the other with empty hands. This relationship established over the things henceforth possibly common, that is, susceptible of being said, is the relationship of conversation. The way in which the other presents himself, exceeding the idea of the other in me, we here name face. This mode does not consist in figuring as a theme under my gaze, in spreading itself forth as a set of qualities forming an image. The face of the

---

7. Emmanuel Levinas, *Totality and Infinity: An Essay on Exteriority* (Pittsburgh: Duquesne University Press, 1969), 50.

8. For an extensive analysis of this understanding of gift, cf. Jan-Olaf Henriksen, *Desire, Gift, and Recognition: Christology and Postmodern Philosophy* (Grand Rapids: Eerdmans, 2009).

Other at each moment destroys and overflows the plastic image it leaves me, the idea existing to my own measure and to the measure of its *ideatum* — the adequate idea. It does not manifest itself by these qualities, but *kath'auto.* It *expresses itself.*[9]

The presence of the other does thus not open up an abstract possibility for the expansion of my world, but for me to show my generosity. When I am only in me, in my totality, gifts and giving are not an issue. However, as soon as the Other appears and presents me with the opportunity to desire metaphysically, to desire goodness in a way that is not extinguished in a certain number of acts, we can say that the infinity contained in this metaphysical desire concretely shapes my concrete subjectivity and overflows it. In my gifting, I transgress the borders of my self, I engage with the Other — for the sake of the Other, and not only for the sake of my self (although of course also for the sake of my self: for the sake of no longer being self-enclosed, but open, desiring, participating in goodness, and thus becoming a richer, more generous self). It is this positive relation to goodness, opened by desire, which is the possible way to approach desire fruitfully in Christian theology.

The Self as Emerging out of Love: An Interpretation of *Imago Dei*

Another way of describing the relational constitution of the self along the lines I have done in the previous section is by addressing the *decentered* character of this constitution. This approach implies several things. First of all, there is no given and privileged or taken-for-granted stance on which we can describe the human being. The description has to take place from a lot of different perspectives — and none of these offer a coordinating and harmonizing center that brings everything together in a synthesis. In the above, we have seen how being and becoming, gift and otherness, desire for love and love in desire are all such elements that allow for different ways of description of the same field of "self."

A center stabilizes, and creates the impression that there is a given stance on which we can build and make sure that we grasp the identity of the human being. But, I will argue, the Christian doctrine of human being precludes exactly such a centered understanding. This is intimately linked to an understanding of God as love and as the ultimate source of self. Most people

---

9. Levinas, *Totality and Infinity,* 50-51.

may think that this is a likely approach because the human being cannot be understood from itself, but only from its relation to God. That is correct, but it is not everything there is to say about it. It is true that the very notion of a human being created by God decenters the human, and makes us what we are only in our relation to God. But what exactly are we, then? To this, as well, there is no final answer. There are several answers, a *plurality* of answers, all contained in the historically established bulk of Christian doctrine, and they all contribute to underlining the provisional character of human self and identity, and thus every attempt to have a final understanding of what it means to be human. Let me spell this out more concretely.

According to the doctrine of creation, God creates the human being in his own image. This gives the human being a distinct qualification. We are willed by God, recognized by God, loved by God. We emerge out of the love of God. This very relation to God gives us our dignity, human dignity. It also makes us persons, in the sense that God calls forth a distinctive awareness of our selves as being something more and other than what we actually are and do. To be a person is to transcend the perceptible positivity of our actions and capabilities — it is to have a distinct identity that is grounded in something not positively given, but yet present — in desire. To say it in a simple way: being a person is the opposite of being a *thing*. Human beings can thus not only experience themselves and others to be more than things; we also realize that if we conceive of ourselves or others as things, we are degraded as humans — and that there is something lacking, even degrading, in such an approach to humans.

To be created as a person by God thus also implies that we are called to goodness, to witness and to realize the good of the loving God who created us. God made us capable of doing good, leading good lives — and of desiring goodness. Created life is good and God-willed, and our destiny as humans is, from the point of view of the doctrine of creation, that we live according to the desire for goodness that emerges out of the fact that we are created in the image of God. That is to say that we live in such a way that God's goodness and love are made manifest in the world, thus expressing his glory.[10] Hence, *our love and our desire for goodness are related intrinsically to being created in the image of God.*

In this way, the Christian doctrine of human beings as created in the image of God not only relates God and humans to each other, but also allows us

---

10. Cf. C. Gestrich, *Die Wiederkehr des Glänzens in der Welt* (Tübingen: Mohr, 1996), passim.

to see how the goodness of God and the desire for love and for goodness in human life are closely related. Simultaneously, the destiny of the human being as created in the image of God not only lends the human his or her dignity, but it also offers us the task set for our lives: to be mirrors of the God who created us.

Can this then be a center, a way of creating and even stabilizing human identity in spite of the fragility and vulnerability that we are exposed to when being thrust into the desire for others' love? Does the logic inherent in this way of speaking about the human create a pattern in which everything that is possible to say about us and about human experience fits in and is made meaningful? This is exactly *not* the case, and Christian theology has always made it clear that this perspective of the human being as created is insufficient — even false — when taken to be the sole and only description of what it means to be human. We all know the reason behind this: it is sin. Consequently, to say that the human being is created in the image of God is not the last or only word theology has to say about being human.

Whereas the doctrine of creation spells out humanity's relation to God and how our desire for love and loving desire are what orient us and may shape our being in the world, the doctrine of sin spells out how the human being separates itself from God in ways that alter this fundamental situation. Whereas the doctrine of creation affirms the goodness of the human being and its origin in the love of God, the doctrine of sin articulates how the will of the human being is not shaped by love and by desire for the other as one who may open up my world. Instead, here my desire is lacking the true eros, which is exchanged for a desire for what is already present in me and my perception of how the world should be, a perception not shaped by interaction with or openness toward others. This closing off to others, or absolutizing of finitude, as we called it above, is the reason why Augustine and others locate sin in the will — as the faculty that is shaped and oriented by desire, be it for good or for bad. Whereas the understanding of the human being as created in God's image makes it possible to understand the human as being dependent upon God's loving and creative powers — and expressing these in the witness that is given in life and deed — the doctrine of sin opens up an understanding of humanity that not only describes our attempts to be self-sufficient and independent of God, but also our actual attempts to construct our own reality without openness to God and without being shaped by love. Thereby, we not only attempt to construct our reality and our selves in a way that neglects the given qualities of God's creation, but we are also ourselves — tacitly at least — trying to establish ourselves as

God, i.e., as the center of reality and with the power to uphold and control it. Hence, as sinners we not only oppose God — we negate God by our very lives by excluding love from what constitutes our selves.

On this basis, it makes no sense to say that the description of what makes humanity human is something that implies that we *add* an understanding of the human as sinner to the understanding of the human as created. The understanding of the human as sinner opposes the very description of the human being as created from the loving desire for otherness in God, while at the same time it presupposes it. There is a contradiction here that cannot be sublated (in the Hegelian sense), but which also does not lead to the denial of the validity of either of the alternative perspectives. Therefore neither perspective can be taken for granted, but each is put to the question by the other. As different approaches, these descriptions offer alternative types of logic of the constitution of the self (with or without love as the content of desire), so that what is implied in one type of description allows a coherent explication of the basis given for it — but without any chance of being reconciled with other approaches.

The uneasiness created by this lack of closure is not overcome when we add the third possible perspective on humanity that is offered by theological anthropology, which is that of the human being as being offered the grace and salvation of God.[11] Surely, this perspective presupposes insights gained by the two previous ones, but it in no way implies that those perspectives are overcome as relevant descriptions of humanity. There is no talk of sublation

---

11. I think this is well expressed in Miroslav Volf, *Exclusion and Embrace: A Theological Exploration of Identity, Otherness, and Reconciliation* (Nashville: Abingdon, 1996). Volf states that the new identity of the self in Christ implies both a decentering and a recentering of the self. However, the following description offered by Volf does not rule out the necessity of maintaining and expressing the human being in terms of the two other perspectives I have elaborated here. Writes Volf: "By being 'crucified with Christ' the self has received a new center, — the Christ who lives in it and with whom it lives. Notice that the new center of the self is not a timeless 'essence,' hidden deep within a human being, underneath the sediments of culture and history and untouched by 'time and change,' an essence that waits only to be discovered, unearthed, set free. Neither is the center an inner narrative that the reverberating echo of the community's 'final vocabulary' and 'master story' has scripted in the book of the self and whose integrity must be guarded from editorial intrusions by rival 'vocabularies' and competing 'stories.' The center of the self — a center that is both inside and outside — is the story of Jesus Christ, which has become the story of the self. More precisely, the center is Jesus Christ crucified and resurrected who has become part and parcel of the very structure of the self" (70). This story and this center is open; it cannot be seen as a closure of the quest for the human being's identity.

into a third and higher, more all-encompassing perspective here: by being restored, humanity becomes more and something other than what it has been as created and as sinner. That the recapitulation of humanity is more than the restoration of creation is an insight that theology has affirmed since Irenaeus.[12] Just as speech about the human being as sinner is related to speaking about us as created, so too is speech about the human being as being saved by the grace of God related to, but not reduced to, what is said by or within the two previous perspectives expressed in the doctrines of creation and sin.

From this we can draw the conclusion that the desire that comes from goodness, and which expresses itself in every part of human activity and desire, is to be seen as emerging out of our relationship to God. It is an expression of how we are, from the outset, determined by God's love in the innermost core of our being. It is when we separate ourselves from the love of God, and stop loving God, that our desire goes astray, and we no longer express to a full extent our calling to be the image of God, and bear witness to God's love and God's desire for goodness and justice. But when we do, our *eros* may be seen as the presence and manifestation of divine creativity, and as something that opens us and others up to the world of God.

To be the image of God implies three important things:

- To be the image of God means recognizing that we are ourselves not God (God is the Other), but that we are nevertheless related to God in love and in our desire for goodness.
- To be such an image of God means that my identity or my self is something not yet fulfilled, and that it contains an element of futurity that I am directed toward in my desire. Hence, my final identity is not yet realized, but something I am directed toward in my desire to become a self. To become a mature self is to be able to recognize oneself as an unfinished project, and as someone that is related to others in order to be able to grow further toward this destiny.
- In relation to other humans, I am called to represent and manifest God's goodness and love for them, and at the same time to let them be carriers of God's gifts to me. Thus, to recognize the image of God in myself and in others is a way of realizing my destiny as a human being. I am to *represent* God in the world. The full theological understanding of love and desire's place in human life is given within this framework.

12. Cf. e.g., Irenaeus, *Adversus Haereses* III.18.7.

Paradoxically, it seems that when the human being is seeking him- or herself in a not-yet-fulfilled destiny, realizing that this destiny cannot be wholly appropriated or fulfilled at the present safeguards the possibility of living here and now in a way that recognizes the vulnerability of both others and oneself. We are not perfect, and to realize this is to be confronted with the vulnerability that is given with the fact that we are dependent upon others, and live exposed to the power of others. This is one of the reasons why love, and the safeguarding function that love has, is so important in human life.

To be aware of the fact that neither God nor my own self is something that I can acquire and make present myself, or fully appropriate by means of striving to fulfill my desires, is also to realize that these "instances" or the relationships I have to these are not controllable and that they cannot be reduced to something I know or can handle. This awareness is liberating to the extent that it lets me give up the search for constituting my own self, and live in trust and faith in God.

The presence of the Other in desire may thus open up a new entry to our own lives, and to new ways of relating to oneself. Thus, the presence of the Other in love and desire gives rise to new possibilities of experience. However, it is only possible to realize these when the individual is able to transcend his or her present or closed self and be open in his or her desire — and thereby appropriate the resources or gifts present in relation to, or made available by, the Other.

In connection to this, we should also note the importance of the other person. He or she is, as an image of God, *God's representative,* and can help me realize and come to grips with my present situation. God, as the present-absent third party in this situation, can become represented by an Other, and the Other can make what God wants to give appear — as a gift of life, experience, and identity — to a human being. This is why love (eros) is so important in what takes place in the meeting with another person, and why it has implications for our understanding of what it means to function as an image of God — as a true self. The Other in this respect contributes to the clarification and transparency of who I am and what I am to become, and thus to my understanding of the given relationships in which I am challenged to live my life.

Theological anthropology should help us to see ourselves in our distinct otherness — from different centers and perspectives. It should help us interpret our experience of what it means to be human, harboring love, desire, and the struggle to become a self and find our own identity. Who we are is based not only on what we already have in our possession, but also on what we still are to become and what we relate to in our desire. To neglect the role of desire in theological anthropology is equal to neglecting the very embodied manifestation of God's future in us. To recognize desire and the erotic as ways in which the Divine is present as creativity in our lives is, on the other hand, a way of making theology come alive in human life.

Human Pharmakon:
The Anthropology of Technological Lives

João Biehl

This essay discusses the pharmaceuticalization of mental healthcare in Brazil and charts the social and subjective side-effects that come with the unregulated encroachment of new medical technologies in urban poor settings. I focus on how an abandoned young woman named Catarina talks about psychopharmaceuticals — the drug constellations that she was brought into — and how she tries to find, mainly through writing, an alternative to the deadly experiment she literally became. Her "ex-family," she claims, thinks of her as a failed medication regimen. The family was dependent on this explanation to excuse itself from her abandonment. In her words: "To want my body as a medication, my body." Catarina's life thus tells a larger story about shifting value systems and the fate of social bonds in today's dominant mode of subjectification at the service of global science and capitalism. But language and desire continue, and Catarina integrates her drug experience into a new self-perception and literary work. Her "minor literature" grounds an ethnographic ethics and gives us a sense of becoming that dominant health models would render impossible.

Without a known origin and increasingly paralyzed, a young woman named Catarina spent her days in Vita, an asylum in southern Brazil, assembling words in what she called "my dictionary" (Biehl 2005). Her handwriting was uneven and conveyed minimal literacy. "I write so that I don't forget the words," she told me in January 2000, three years after I first met her in this institution of last resort. "I write all the illness I have now and the illnesses I had as a child."

Vita was initially conceived as a Pentecostal treatment center for drug addicts, but since the mid-1990s it has been run by a philanthropic association headed by a local politician and a police chief. Over time, it became a dumpsite for people who, like Catarina, had been cut off from social life and formal institutions. Caregivers referred to Catarina as "mad" and haphazardly treated her — and the more than one hundred surplus bodies who were also *waiting with death* in Vita — with all kinds of psychiatric drugs (donations that were by and large expired).

The dictionary was a sea of words. Blended with allusions to spasm, menstruation, paralysis, rheumatism, paranoia, and the listing of all possible diseases from measles to ulcers to AIDS were names such as Ademir, Nilson, Armando, Anderson, Alessandra, Ana. Catarina writes to remain alive, I told myself. These are the words that form her from within. She is fighting for connections. Yes, a human form of life that is not worth living is not just bare (as philosopher Giorgio Agamben would have it in *Homo Sacer* [1998]). Language and desire continue. As Catarina wrote: *"Recovery of my lost movements. A cure that finds the soul. The needy moon guards me. With L I write love. With R I write remembrance."*

Why, I asked her, do you think families, neighbors, and hospitals send people to Vita?

"They say that it is better to place us here so that we don't have to be left alone at home, in solitude . . . that there are more people like us here. And all of us together, we form a society, *a society of bodies."* And she added: "Maybe my family still remembers me, but they don't miss me."

Catarina had condensed the social reasoning of which she was the human leftover. I wondered about her chronology and about how she had been cut off from family life and placed into Vita. How had she become the object of a logic and sociality in which people were no longer worthy of affection and accountability, though they were remembered? And how was I to make sense of these intimate dynamics if not by trusting her and working through her language and experience?

I picked up the dictionary and read aloud some of her free-associative inscriptions: *"Documents, reality, truth, voracious, consumer, saving, economics, Catarina, pills, marriage, cancer, Catholic church, separation of bodies, division of the estate, the couple's children."* The words indexed the ground of Catarina's existence; her body had been separated from those exchanges and made part of a new society.

What do you mean by the "separation of bodies"?

"My ex-husband kept the children."

When did you separate?

"Many years ago."

What happened?

"He had another woman."

She shifted back to her pain: "I have these spasms, and my legs feel so heavy."

When did you begin feeling this?

"After I had Alessandra, my second child, I already had difficulty walking. . . . My ex-husband sent me to the psychiatric hospital. They gave me so many injections. I don't want to go back to his house, he rules the city of Novo Hamburgo."

Did the doctors ever tell you what you had?

"No, they said nothing." She suggested that something physiological had preceded or was related to her exclusion as mentally ill, and that her condition worsened in medical exchanges. "I am allergic to doctors. Doctors know how to be knowledgeable, but they don't know what suffering is. They only medicate." Catarina knew what had made her an abject figure in family life, in medicine, in Brazil — "I know because I passed through it."

"When my thoughts agreed with my ex-husband and his family, everything was fine," Catarina recalled, as we continued the conversation later that day. "But when I disagreed with them, I was mad. It was like a side of me had to be forgotten. The side of wisdom. They wouldn't dialogue, and the science of the illness was forgotten. My legs weren't working well. . . . My sister-in-law went to the health post to get the medication for me."

According to Catarina, her physiological deterioration and expulsion from reality had been mediated by a shift in the meaning of words, in the light of novel family dynamics, economic pressures, and her own pharmaceutical treatment. "For some time I lived with my brothers. . . . But I didn't want to take medication when I was there. I asked: why is it only me who has to be medicated? My brothers want to see production, progress. They said that I would feel better in the midst of other people like me."

You seem to be suggesting that your family, the doctors, and the medications played an active role in making you "mad," I said.

"I behaved like a woman. Since I was a housewife, I did all my duties, like any other woman. . . . My ex-husband and his family got suspicious of me because sometimes I left the house to attend to other callings. He thought that I had a nightmare in my head. He wanted to take that out of me, to make me a normal person. I escaped so as not to go to the hospital. I hid myself; I went far. But the police and my ex-husband found me. They took my children. . . . I felt suffocated. I also felt my legs burning, a pain, a pain in the knees, and under the feet." Catarina added that "[h]e first placed me in the Caridade Hospital, then in the São Paulo — seven times in all. When I returned home, he was amazed that I recalled what a plate was. He thought that I would be unconscious to plates, plans, and things and conscious only of medications. But I knew how to use the objects."

Through her increasing disability, all the social roles Catarina had forcefully learned to play — sister, wife, mother, worker, patient — were being annulled, along with the precarious stability they had afforded her. To some degree, these cultural practices remained with her as the values that motivated her memory and her sharp critique of the marriage and the extended family who had amputated her as if she had only a pharmaceutical consciousness. But she resisted this closure, and, in ways that I could not fully grasp at first, Catarina voiced an intricate ontology in which inner and outer states were laced together, along with the wish to untie it all: "Science is our consciousness, heavy at times, burdened by a knot that you cannot untie. If we don't study it, the illness in the body worsens. . . . Science . . . If you have a guilty conscience, you will not be able to discern things."

"After my ex-husband left me," she continued, "he came back to the house and told me he needed me. He threw me onto the bed saying, 'I will eat you now.' I told him that that was the last time. . . . I did not feel pleasure though. I only felt desire. Desire to be talked to, to be gently talked to."

In abandonment, Catarina recalled sex. There was no love, simply a male body enjoying itself. No more social links, no more speaking beings. Out of the world of the living, her desire was for language, *the desire to be talked to.*

Technological Lives, *Terrae Incognitae*

In this essay, I explore Catarina's ties to pharmakons and chart the interpersonal and medical crossroads in which her life chances took form. *"Not slave, but housewife. Wife of the bed. Wife of the room. Wife of the bank. Of the pharmacy. Of the laboratory. . . . The abandoned is part of life."* Her "ex-family," she claims, thinks of her as a failed medication regimen. The family is dependent on this explanation as it excuses itself from her abandonment. In her words: *"To want my body as a medication, my body."* Catarina fights the disconnections that psychiatric drugs introduced in her life — between body and spirit, between her and the people she knew, in common sense —

and works through the many layers of (mis)treatment that now compose her existence. While integrating drug experience into a new self-perception (the drug AKINETON, which is used to control the side-effects of antipsychotic medication, is literally part of the new name Catarina gives herself in her notebooks: CATKINE), she keeps seeking camaraderie and another chance at life.

By working with Catarina I came to see that subjectivity is neither reducible to a person's sense of herself nor necessarily a confrontation with the powers that be. It is rather the material and means of a continual process of experimentation — inner, familial, medical, and political. Always social, subjectivity encompasses all the identifications that can be formed by, discovered in, or attributed to the person. Although identity-making mechanisms are quite difficult to detect, this process of subjective experimentation is the very fabric of moral economies and personal trajectories that are all too often doomed not to be analyzed. I am thinking here of a diffused form of control that occurs through the remaking of moral landscapes as well as the inner transformations of the human subject (Biehl, Good, and Kleinman 2007).

Subjectivities have quickly become "raucous *terrae incognitae*" for anthropological inquiry, writes Michael M. J. Fischer: "landscapes of explosions, noise, alienating silences, disconnects and dissociations, fears, terror machineries, pleasure principles, illusions, fantasies, displacements, and secondary revisions, mixed with reason, rationalizations, and paralogics — all of which have powerful sociopolitical dimensions and effects" (2007: 442). According to Fischer, subjectivity continually forms and returns in the complex play of bodily, linguistic, political, and psychological dimensions of human experience, within and against new infrastructures and the afflictions and injustices of the present (see also DelVecchio Good, Hyde, Pinto, and Good 2008). To grasp the wider impact of how technologies are becoming interwoven in the very fabric of symptoms and notions of well-being, we must account ethnographically and comparatively for the ways such life forms are fundamentally altering domestic economies and value systems in both affluent and resource-poor contexts (Reynolds Whyte 2009; Fassin and Rechtman 2009; Garcia 2008; Pinto 2008; Rofel 2007; Tsing 2004).

In many ways, Catarina was caught in a period of political, economic, and cultural transition. Since the mid-1990s, Brazilian politicians have deftly reformed the state, combining a respect for financial markets and innovative and targeted social programs. Many individuals and families have benefited from pharmaceutical assistance and income-distribution programs, for example. An actual redistribution of resources, powers, and responsibility is taking place locally as part of these large-scale changes, and for larger segments of the population, one could argue, citizenship is increasingly articulated in the sphere of consumer culture (Biehl 2007; Caldeira 2000; Edmonds 2007). Yet, without adequate investments in infrastructural reforms, many families and individuals are newly overburdened as they are suffused with the materials, patterns, and paradoxes of these various processes and programs, which they are, by and large, left to negotiate alone.

I am particularly interested in how psychiatric drugs become part of domestic economies — the ways they open up and relimit family complexes and human values — and the agency that solitary and chemically submerged subjects such as Catarina/CATKINE express and live by. Catarina's life thus tells a larger story about the fate of social bonds and the limits of human imagination in today's dominant mode of subjectification at the service of capitalism. Throughout the essay, I probe the significance of some of Jacques Lacan's insights on the pervasiveness of the "discourse of the capitalist." In a 1972 lecture, Lacan said that capitalism was now the new discourse of the master and as such it overdetermined social bonds. Lacan spoke of the effects of an absolutization of the market: subjects do not necessarily address each other in order to be recognized but experience themselves in the market's truths and things. While these subjects have access to the products of science and technology, those countless objects are made to never completely satiate their desires (Biehl 2001; Declercq 2006; Lacan 1989; Zizek 2006).

A few years earlier, Lacan had stated that "[t]he consumer society has meaning when the 'element' that we qualify as human is given the homogenous equivalent of any other surplus enjoyment that is a product of our industry, a fake surplus enjoyment" (1991: 92). As Catarina suggests, these days one can conveniently become a medico-scientific thing and *ex-human* for others. In the contemporary version of the astute capitalistic discourse we seem to be all proletariat patient-consumers, hyperindividualized psychobiologies doomed to consume diagnostics and treatments (for ourselves and surrounding others) and to fast success or self-consumption and absolute lack of empathy. Or, can we fall for science and technology in different and livelier and more caring ways?

By staying as close as I could, for as long as I could, to Catarina's struggles to articulate desire, pain, and knowledge, I also came to see the specificity and pathos of subjectivity and the possibilities it carries. While her sense of herself and of the world was perceived as lacking reality, Catarina found in thinking and writing a way of living with what would otherwise be unendurable. Thus, subjectivity also contains creativity, the possibility of subject adopting a distinctive symbolic relation to the world to understand lived experience. By way of speech, the unconscious, and the many knowledges and powers whose histories she embodies, there is a subjective *plasticity* at the heart of Catarina's existence.

The currents of medical isolation and technological self-care that shape Catarina's existence represent actual global trends (Good et al. 2007; Ecks 2005; Lakoff 2006; Luhrman 2000; Martin 2007; Petryna, Lakoff, and Kleinman 2006). Technoscience enables novel types of experiments and interventions and allows people to imagine and articulate different desires and possibilities for themselves and others (Boellstorff 2008; Dumit 2004; Farmer 2008; Inhorn 2003; Petryna 2009; Rajan 2006; Rapp 1999; Whitmarsh 2008). Science and medicine are more than tools of control or even personified inanimate objects, but rather represent one actor in a process that always involves at least two sides acting on each other (Biehl and Moran-Thomas 2009; Turkle 2008).

"I need to change my blood with a tonic. Medication from the pharmacy costs money. To live is expensive." Catarina embodies a condition that is more than her own. People are increasingly grappling with the healing and destructive potentials of technology at the level of their very self-conceptions. While painfully wrestling with symptoms and drug side-effects, kinship ties are recast, patterns of consumption are redefined, and possibilities for alternate futures are opened from within sick roles. Technology thus becomes a complex intersubjective actor, with transformative potential that must be negotiated with and even cared for in order to actualize its fragile chance for a new beginning. As medical technology becomes a potential way to explore the new people we might be or the relationships we might imagine, Sherry Turkle notes: "Inner history shows technology to be as much an architect of our intimacies as our solitudes" (2008: 29).

Drug-Sets: Vital/Deadly Experimentation

"Clearly no one knows what to do with drugs, not even the users. But no one knows how to talk about them either," wrote Gilles Deleuze in a 1978 article titled "Two Questions on Drugs" (2006: 151). The use of illegal substances was then on the rise and, according to Deleuze, those who knew of the problem, users and doctors alike, had given up a deeper understanding of the phenomenon. Some spoke of the "pleasure" of drug use, something quite difficult to describe and which actually presupposes the chemical. Others evoked extrinsic factors (sociological considerations such as communication and incommunicability and the overall situation of the youth). For Deleuze, such drug-talk was of little help, and addiction therapeutics remained *terrae incognitae*. The philosopher posed two questions: (1) Do drugs have a specific causality and how can we explore this track? (2) How do we account for a turning point in drugs, when all control is lost and dependence begins?

Deleuze's answers were tentative. Yet, he sketched a few ideas and concepts that I find useful for my own inquiry into the widespread and largely unregulated use of legal substances — psychiatric drugs — among the urban poor in Brazil today. Data from the government's database for health resource use between the years 1995 and 2005 show that the country's psychiatric reform was accompanied by a significant fall in the percentage of resources dedicated to psychiatric care (Andreoli, Almeida-Filho, Martin, et al. 2007). In 1995, for example, psychiatric hospital admissions accounted for 95.5 percent of the mental health budget, down to 49.3 percent in 2005. Meanwhile, there has been a dramatic increase in resource allocation for community services and for pharmaceutical drugs. Drug provision rose from 0.1 percent in 1995 to 15.5 percent in 2005 — a 155-fold increase in the national budget. Second-generation antipsychotic drugs were responsible for 75 percent of the expenses with drugs in this period. Interestingly, the rise in drug allocation was followed by a relative decrease in the number of psychiatrists hired — psychologists and social workers have been hired at three times and twice the rates of psychiatrists from 1995 to 2005. Catarina's travails are entry points into the anthropological communities and ways of being in the world that have emerged in the wake of this pharmaceuticalization of mental health in the service of a diffused form of governance and of market expansion.

Back to Deleuze, for a moment, to the time when psychiatric markets had not yet further confounded the drug scene. I have no grand philosophical aspirations and do not wish to reduce Deleuze's enormously complicated venture into a theoretical system or set of practices to be applied normatively to anthropology. Deleuze's insights on drugs elicit broader concerns on the relationships between power/knowledge, desire, and sublimation, which I share and want to explore in this essay. In emphasizing the powers and potentials of desire (both creative and destructive), the ways in which social fields ceaselessly leak and transform (power and knowledge notwithstanding), and the in-between, plastic, and ever-unfinished nature of *a* life, Deleuze lends himself to a richer interpretation of technological lives — how to chart and account for, at once as it were, the *determinants and dynamism* of the everyday and the *literality and singularity* of human becomings. In other words, Deleuze's cartographic approach makes space for possibility, *what could be* as a crucial dimension of what is or was. It brings crossroads — places where other choices might be made, other paths taken — out of the shadow of deterministic analytics (Biehl and Locke 2010).

For Deleuze, the question about whether drugs have a "specific causality" does not imply exclusively a scientific (i.e., chemical) cause on which everything else would depend. Likewise, Deleuze makes clear that he was not after a metaphysical causality or trying to identify transcendental organizational planes that would determine popular drug use. After all, Deleuze did not share Michel Foucault's confidence concerning power arrangements. In a 1976 article called "Desire and Pleasure," Deleuze reviewed Foucault's then recently published *The History of Sexuality* (1976). In that book, Foucault took a new step with regard to his earlier work in *Discipline and Punish* (1975): now power arrangements were no longer simply normalizing; they were constituents of sexuality. But "I emphasize the primacy of desire over power," wrote Deleuze. "Desire comes first and seems to be the element of a micro-analysis. . . . Desire is one with a determined assemblage, a co-function" (2006: 126).

Attentive to historical preconditions *and* singular efforts of becoming, Deleuze said that he pursued "lines of flight." For him "all organizations, all the systems Michel calls biopower, in effect reterritorialize the body" (2006: 131). But a social field, first and foremost, "leaks out on all sides" (2006: 127). In an interview with Paul Rabinow in the mid-1980s, Deleuze once again emphasized that he and Foucault did not have the same conception of society. "For me," he said, "society is something that is constantly escaping in every direction. . . . It flows monetarily, it flows ideologically. It is really made of lines of flight. So much so that the problem for a society is how to stop it from flowing. For me, the powers come later" (2006: 280).

The analytics of biopolitics and of normalization cannot fully account for the drug phenomenon, nor can the Freudian unconscious. The failure of psychoanalysis in the face of drug phenomena, Deleuze argues, "is enough to show that drugs have an entirely different causality" than sexuality or the oedipal theory. The libido follows world-historical trajectories, be they customary or exceptional. And real and imaginary voyages compose an interstitching of routes that must be read like a map. These internalized trajectories are inseparable from becomings (Deleuze 1997: 61-67). Deleuze thus distinguishes his cartographic conception of the unconscious from the archeological conception of psychoanalysis. "From one map to the next, it is not a matter of searching for an origin, but of evaluating displacements" (1997: 63). Every map is a redistribution of impasses, breakthroughs, thresholds, and enclosures on the ground. "It is no longer an unconscious of commemoration but one of mobilization" (1997: 63). Unconscious materials, lapses, and symptoms are not just to be interpreted, but rather it is a question of identifying their trajectories to see if they can serve as indicators of a new universe of reference, "capable of acquiring consistency sufficient for turning a situation around." Maps should not only be understood in terms of extension, of spaces constituted by trajectories, adds Deleuze: "There are also maps of intensity, of density, that are concerned with what fills the space, what subtends the trajectory" (64).

Thus, when it comes to studying the domain of drugs, Deleuze brings desire into view as part and parcel of drug assemblages. He speaks of specific "drug-sets" engendered by the flows of drugs and people and of the need to map their territory or contours. "On the one hand, this set would have an internal relationship to various types of drugs and, on the other to more general causalities" (2006: 151). Deleuze is particularly concerned with "how desire directly invests the system of perception" of both drug users and nonusers (families and experts, for example) and how systems of perception (especially space-time perception) are connected to more general external causalities (contemporary social systems, chemical research, and therapeutics). This project would require, it seems, a distinctive ethnographic sensibility and new analytical tools. This sensibility and the tools would address the ways drug consumption/dependence is at once a chemical, intimate, social, and economic matter, and how historical changes and technopolitical apparatuses coalesce around drugs in the emergence of new kinds of subjectivities and social pathways as well as new kinds of expertise and authority.

Deleuze is also concerned with the extent to which "microperceptions are covered in advance" and whether there is variation in dependence built into drugs (2006: 153). "The drug user creates active lines of flight. But these lines roll up, start to turn into black holes, with each drug user in a hole, as a group or individually, like a periwinkle. Dug in instead of spaced out" (153). For Deleuze, two things must be distinguished: *the domain of vital experimentation* and *the domain of deadly experimentation*. "Vital experimentation begins when any trial grabs you, takes control of you, establishing more and more connections, and opens you to connections" (153). This kind of experimentation can blend with other flows, drugs, and dangers. "The suicidal occurs when everything is reduced to this flow alone: 'my' hit, 'my' trip, 'my' glass. It is the contrary of connection; it is organized disconnection" (153).

In what follows, I revisit my ethnographic data and Catarina's writing. I further explore (1) the treatment constellation (or "drug-set" in Deleuze's words) in which Catarina became the woman who no longer exists — "My ex did everything to get medication"; "I am a sedative" — and the knowledge she produced as an abandoned psychopharmaceutical subject; (2) how Catarina redirected her clinical and familial abandonment and invented a new name and an alternative existential stage for herself with whatever means she had available, particularly writing — "The pen between my fingers is my work. I am convicted to death" — writing as a therapeutic means, as a possibility of life: "To be well with all, but mainly with the pen."

Ethnography can indeed help to chart the set of symptoms the world is and how the world merges with women, men, and children. It can also account for the ways people activate their creative capacities in order to become physicians of themselves and of their immediate worlds, as Deleuze would put it — that delicate and incomplete health that stems from efforts to carve out life chances from things too big, strong, and suffocating (see Corin 2007; Doane 2003; Scheper-Hughes 2008). These efforts, in Deleuze's words, give people "the becomings that a dominant and substantial health would render impossible" (1997: 3).

The Body as Medication

People's everyday struggles and interpersonal dynamics exceed experimental and statistical approaches and demand in-depth listening and long-term engagement. From 2000 to 2003, I took numerous trips to southern Brazil to work with Catarina, sometimes for weeks, sometimes for months. Catarina's puzzling language required intense listening. And I have chosen to listen to her on a literary rather than on a clinical register. Since the beginning, I have thought of her not in terms of mental illness but as an abandoned person who, against all odds, was claiming experience on her own terms. She knew what had made her a void in the social sphere — "I am like this because of life" — and she organized this knowledge for herself and for her anthropologist, thus bringing the public into Vita. "I learned the truth and I try to divulge what reality is."

Catarina's free and elusive verse slowly began to shape the terms of my own inquiry and cognition. *"João Biehl, Reality, CATKINE."* I studied all the twenty-one volumes of the dictionary Catarina was composing and discussed the words and associations with her. Her knowledge revealed complicated realities. In her recollections and writing, I found clues to the people, sites, and interactions that constituted her life. As an anthropologist, I was challenged to reconstruct the worldliness, the literality of her words. With Catarina's consent, I retrieved her records from psychiatric hospitals and local branches of the universal healthcare system. I was also able to locate her "ex-family" members in the nearby city of Novo Hamburgo. On a detective-like journey, I discovered the threads of her life. Everything she had told me about the familial and medical pathways that led her into Vita matched with the information I found in the archives and in the field. As I juxtaposed her words with medical records, family versions, and other considerations, I was able to identify those noninstitutionalized operations that ensured Catarina's exclusion and that are, in my view, the missing contexts and verbs to her disconnected words. The verb *to kill* was being conjugated and she knew it: *"Dead alive, dead outside, alive inside."*

Catarina was born in 1966, and grew up in a very poor place, in the western region of the state of Rio Grande do Sul. After finishing fourth grade, she was taken out of school and became the housekeeper as her youngest siblings aided their mother in agricultural work. The father had abandoned the family. In the mid-1980s, two of her brothers migrated and found jobs in the booming shoe industry in Novo Hamburgo. At the age of eighteen, Catarina married Nilson Moraes, and a year later she gave birth to her first child. Shady deals, persistent bad harvests, and indebtedness to local vendors forced Nilson and Catarina to sell the land they inherited to take care of Catarina's ailing mother, and in the mid-1980s the young couple decided to migrate and join her brothers in the shoe industry. In the coming years, she had two more children. As her illness progressed and her marriage disintegrated, her eldest two children went to her husband's family, and her youngest daughter was given up for adoption.

Catarina was first hospitalized at Porto Alegre's Caridade Hospital on April 27, 1988. The psychiatrist who admitted her recalled what he heard from the neighbor who brought her in: "Patient experienced behavioral changes in the past weeks, and they worsened two weeks ago. Patient doesn't sleep well, speaks of mystical/religious matters, and doesn't take care of herself and the house. She says that God gives signs to her when people mock or doubt her, and that she has received a gift of transmitting her thoughts to people." The doctor reported that she "had no clinical ailments and no psychiatric history." Catarina was placed in a unit for chronic schizophrenic patients. The doctor prescribed Haldol, Neozine, Mogadon, and Akineton. At discharge, her diagnosis was "Acute paranoid reaction."

In multiple admissions at the Caridade and São Paulo hospitals between 1988 and 1995, the diagnosis given to Catarina varied from "schizophrenia" to "post-partum psychosis" to "unspecified psychosis" to "mood disorder" to "anorexia and anemia." In tracing Catarina's passage through these psychiatric institutions, I saw her not as an exception but as a patterned entity. Caught in struggles for deinstitutionalization, lack of public funding, and the proliferation of new classifications and treatments, the local psychiatry didn't account for her particularity or social condition. Thus, she was subjected to the typically uncertain and dangerous mental health treatment reserved for the urban working poor. Clinicians applied medical technologies blindly, with little calibration to her distinct condition. Like many patients, Catarina was assumed to be aggressive and thus was overly sedated so that the institution could continue to function without providing adequate care.

Although Catarina's diagnosis has softened over the years (mimicking psychiatric trends), she continued to be overmedicated with powerful antipsychotics and all kinds of drugs (such as Akineton) to treat neurological side-effects. On several occasions, nurses reported hypotension, a clear indicator of drug overdose. Consider this entry from March 9, 1992: "Patient is feeling better, dizzy at times. She keeps saying that she needs to sign her divorce. She says that she is no longer hearing God talking to her. As patient walks, she stumbles and leans against the walls. Patient complains of strong pains in her legs." For Catarina, as for others, treatment began with a drug surplus and was then scaled down, or not, through trial and error. As I read her medical records, I could not separate the symptoms of the psychiatric illness from the effects of the medication, and I was struck by the fact that doctors actually did not bother to differentiate between the two in Catarina.

To say that this is "just malpractice," as a local psychiatrist puts it, misses the productive quality of this unregulated medical automatism and experimentalism: *pharmaceuticals are literally the body that is being treated.* And the process of overmedicating Catarina caused many of the symptoms that she called "rheumatism." As doctors remained fixated on her "hallucinations," the etiology of her walking difficulties, which nurses actually reported, remained medically unaddressed. The medical records also showed that her husband and family were difficult to contact, that they left wrong telephone numbers and addresses, and that, on several occasions, they left Catarina in the hospital beyond her designated stay.

I visited the Novo Hamburgo psychosocial service where Catarina was serviced in between hospitalizations. I found the following record by a nurse, written on December 12, 1994: "I drove Catarina home. But as she now lives alone, I left her at the house of her mother-in-law, called Ondina. Catarina was badly received. The mother-in-law said that Catarina should die, because she was stubborn and aggressive, didn't obey anyone, and didn't take her medication."

"We have at least five hundred Catarinas in here right now," said Simone Laux, the coordinator of the service, after I told her about Catarina and my work with her. By "five hundred Catarinas," she meant most of the female clientele of the service, which was treating around 1500 people a month. About half of the clients got free psychiatric medication at the city's community pharmacy.

"When the service began in the late 1980s, it was meant to deal mainly with schizophrenia and psychosis," reported psychologist Wilson Souza, "but this has changed a lot, both diagnostically and numerically. There is an immense growth of mood disorders." Souza cited "unemployment, harsh struggle to survive, no opportunities for social mobility, urban violence" as contributing to this "epidemic of mental suffering." And he suggested that the service had become the vanishing social world, the welfare state, and the social medicine that was no more: "Many factories are closed, people don't have jobs or health plans or family support. . . . They need some form of recognition and help, and they demand it from SUS [the universal healthcare system]. Nothing is isolated."

"We have three women's groups here," continued Laux. "Most of them are not psychotic. But at some points in their lives, they had a crisis or were at risk of committing suicide. All of them have a story that resembles Catarina's." Daniela Justus, the service's psychiatrist, replied: "Catarina is not searching for a diagnostics, but for life." Catarina's story shows that the patterning of the mass patient and her dying at the crux between abandonment and overmedication are both public and domestic affairs, I noted. "Indeed," replied psychologist Luisa Ruckert, "families organize themselves so that they are no longer part of the treatment and care." The major exception is when cash is involved, stated Andreia Miranda, the service's occupational therapist. "Families keep their mentally ill relatives as long as they can manage their disability income."

Dr. Justus then expanded on the family's role in fostering illness: "When patients improved — and we saw this quite often at the Caridade — families discontinued treatment, and the person had to be hospitalized again." Crisis situations were constantly induced. The relation between the family and mental illness, I was told, is made explicit in the culture of psycho-pharmaceuticals: "In our group sessions, we can see that the fragility of a minimal social integration is revealed in everyone's relation to the medica-tion, the fight over its discontinuation, the lack of money to buy it, or the problems with forgetting to take it." Families, in fact, come into the service demanding medication: "When I ask them to tell their story," said Ruckert, "many times they say, 'No, I came here to get a medication for her.' They want to leave with a prescription."

In sum, the family crystallizes its way of being in the ways it deals with psychiatric drugs. "Bottom line, the type of ethics the family installs," said Ruckert, "serves to guarantee its own physical existence." The decision to make persons and things work or to let them die is at the center of family life. And science, in the form of medication, brings a certain neutrality to this decision-making process. "In the meetings," added Ruckert, "the patient quite often realizes that, given the continuing process of exclusion, she has already structured her own perception and codification of reality." *Rather than psychosis, out of all these processes a para-ontology comes into view — a Being beside itself and standing for the destiny of others.* The "irreversible" condition of the mentally afflicted gives consistency to an altered common sense (Geertz 2000). "She died socially," said Laux, pushing the conversation back to Catarina. "That is the pain that aches in us . . . when we realize this: she cannot opt to live."

Biological Complex

In 2003, I was able to get the genetics service of the Hospital das Clínicas, one of the ten best in the country, to see Catarina. Fourteen years after enter-ing the maddening psychiatric world, molecular testing revealed that she suffered from a genetic disorder called Machado-Joseph Disease, which causes degeneration of the central nervous system (Jardim et al. 2001). Her brothers had the same diagnostics. I was happy to hear the geneticists who saw Catarina say that "she knew of her condition, past and present, and pre-sented no pathology." Dr. Laura Jardim was adamant that "there is no mental illness, psychosis, or dementia linked to this genetic disorder. In Machado-Joseph your intelligence will be preserved, clean, and crystalline." Of course, biopsychiatrists could argue that Catarina may have been affected by two concomitant biological processes, but for me the discovery of Machado-Joseph was a landmark in the overwhelming disqualification of her as mad, and shed light on how her condition had evolved over time.

While reviewing the records of the one hundred families that are cared for by Dr. Jardim's team, I found that spousal abandonment and an early onset of the disease were quite common among women, just as it had happened with Catarina, her mother, her younger aunt, and a cousin. Affective, relational, and economic arrangements are plotted and realized around the visible carriers of the disease, and these gendered practices ultimately impact the course of dying. I also learned that after the onset, Machado-Joseph patients survive on average from fifteen to twenty years, most dying from pneumonia in wheelchairs or bedridden. Scientists have firmly established that the graver the gene mutation, the more it anticipates disease. And while the gravity of the gene mutation can account for 60 percent of the probability of earlier onset, the unknown 40 percent remains. Among siblings, Dr. Jardim told me, "the age of onset is almost always the same." How then to explain Catarina's early onset, in the late teens, and her brothers' onset in their mid to late 20s?

The various sociocultural and medical processes in which Catarina's biology was embedded, I thought, pointed to the materiality and morality of this "unknown 40 percent" — in other words: *the social science of the biological mutation.* To this Dr. Jardim responded: "At the peak of her suffering, they were dismembering her . . . this dying flesh is all that remained." Rather than being the residue of obscure and undeveloped times, Catarina's condition was part of a regularity, forged in all those public spaces and hazy interactions where a rapidly changing country, family, and medicine met.

In ancient Greece, every year two men — "true scum and refuse" — were chosen to be cast out of cities, as part of the festival of the Thargelia (Harrison 1921: 97). Initially, they were seen as the remedy for a city suffering from famine or pestilence; later, they became the means through which cities prevented mischief (Girard 1996). These men were called *pharmakoi,* and, for them, there was no return to the city. Historians disagree over the ways in which they were chosen for this scapegoat role and whether they were actively killed or simply allowed to die (Harrison 1921: 104, 105; Derrida 1981: 132).

Catarina is, in a literal sense, a modern-day *pharmakos.* The handling of her defective body was at the heart of the various scenarios people empirically forged and in which they saw themselves with her through institutions such as medicine, city government, and law. Consider the words of her ex-husband: "After we married, they told me the problems the family had. My mother's cousin said 'Poor Nilson, he doesn't know what he has got his hands in.' I didn't believe it until I saw it. *Deus me livre* [May God free me from this]. . . . I got to know her relatives. An aunt of hers died of this problem, and so did some of her cousins. . . . *I told myself, 'Ah, that's how it is . . . they will see.'*

These were revenge-laden words — as if through Catarina the man had taught them all a lesson. In retrospect, Catarina has meaning not as a person but as a representative of a collective and its pathology. Her growing social irrelevance took form around this medical unknown and its physical expressions, allowing Nilson now to read family ties as a retaliatory exchange.

And what are your plans? I asked Nilson.

"To make my life. To progress. I am content with my family now. This woman doesn't give me the problems I had before. A person must help herself. As I said, the doctor gave Catarina treatment so the illness would not come back. It was just a matter of taking the medication, but she didn't help herself. . . . What has passed is over. One must put a stone over it."

Catarina is physically cast out, a stone set over her in life. As her naturalized destiny reveals, medical science has become a tool of common sense, foreclosing various possibilities of empathy and experience. Pharmaceutical commerce and politics have become intimate to lifeworlds, and it is the drug — the embodiment of these processes — that mediates Catarina's exclusion as a *pharmakos*. Both the empirical reality through which living became practically impossible for Catarina and the possibility of critique have been sealed up. As Catarina repeatedly told me: "They all wouldn't dialogue and the science of the illness was forgotten. I didn't want to take the medication. . . . Science is our conscience, heavy at times, burdened by a knot that you cannot untie. If we don't study it, the illness in the body worsens."

In *Plato's Pharmacy,* Jacques Derrida follows the term *pharmakon* as it is stands for writing in Platonic philosophy. Acting like a *pharmakon,* both as remedy and as poison, writing is the artificial counterpart to the truth of things that speech allegedly can apprehend directly. According to Plato, argues Derrida, writing is considered "a consolation, a compensation, a remedy for sickly speech" — "writing is the miserable son" (1981: 115, 143). While living speech is conformity with the law, writing is a force wandering outside the domain of life, incapable of engendering anything or of regenerating itself: "a living-dead, a weakened speech, a deferred life, a semblance of breath. . . . It is like all ghosts, errant" (143). For Derrida, however, writing qua *pharmakon* is an independent order of signification. Operating as *différance* — "the disappearance of any originary presence" — writing is at once "the condition of possibility and the condition of impossibility of truth" (168).

The term *pharmakon* that Plato used has been overdetermined by Greek culture, Derrida points out: "All these significations nonetheless appear. . . . Only the chain is concealed, and to an inappreciable extent, concealed from the author himself, if any such thing exists" (1981: 129). The contemporary philosopher sees as a concealed connection between *pharmakon* as writing and *pharmakos,* the human figure excluded from the political body. Derrida thus brings to light the scapegoat figure of the *pharmakos,* which, interestingly, is absent from Platonic philosophical reflection. "The city body proper thus reconstitutes its unity, closes around the security of its inner courts, gives back to itself the word that links it with itself within the confines of the *agora,* by violently excluding from its territory the representative of an external threat or aggression. That representative represents the otherness of the evil that comes to affect or infect the inside by unpredictably breaking into it" (Derrida 1981: 133).

The figure of the *pharmakos* in philosophical thought is quite pertinent, but the place kept by the death of the Other in city governance also remains a key problem to be addressed. In speaking of Catarina as a modern-day *human pharmakon,* I argue that her life and story are paradigmatic of a contemporary familial/medical/political structure that operates like the law and that is close to home. Pharmaceutically addressed, she was now the evil cast out, both subjectively and biologically. In the end, Catarina was a failed medication that, paradoxically, allowed the life, sentiments, and values of some to continue in other terms.

The ethnography of Vita and Catarina also makes it painfully clear that there are places today, even in a state founded on the premise of guaranteeing human rights, where these rights no longer exist — where the living subjects of marginal institutions are constituted as something other, between life and death. Such places demonstrate how notions of universal human rights are socially and materially conditioned by medical and economic imperatives. Vita also confirms that public death remains at the center of various social structures, animating and legitimating charity, political actors, and economic strategies.

The being of the people in Vita is fundamentally ambiguous. This ambiguity gives the anthropologist the opportunity to develop a human, not philosophical, critique of the machine of social death in which these people are caught (see Rancière 2004). This entails: (1) making explicit that Vita and zones of social abandonment elsewhere, in both poor and rich contexts, are not spheres of exceptionality but rather extensions of what is becoming of family, state, medicine — they are the negative nature, so to speak, of common sense in this moment of capitalism; (2) illuminating the paradoxes and dynamism involved in letting the other die; (3) repopulating the political stage with ex-humans; (4) bringing into view the insights, ambiguities, and desires (alternative human capacities) they also embody and inquiring into how they can be part and parcel of the much-needed efforts to redirect care.

The Work of Sublimation

Catarina's vision was to be absolutely real. But while trying to speak she was overwhelmed by the chemical alterations of drugs, layers and layers of chemical compounds that other people used to work on her, and drug side-effects that were her body and identity now. To speak the unspeakable, she resorted to metaphors and to writing. In the following dictionary entry, for example, she tries to break open the reader's blindness and brings a Greek tragic figure and her three brothers and three children together with her re-named self and the always lacking clinical register:

> *Look at Catarina without blindness, pray, prayer, Jocasta, there is no tonic for CATKINE, there is no doctor for any one, Altamir, Ademar, Armando, Anderson, Alessandra, Ana.*

Medical science is part and parcel of Catarina's existence — the truths, half-truths, and misunderstandings that brought her to die in Vita and upon which she subsisted. *"Pharmacy, laboratory, marriage, identity, army, rheumatism, complication of labor, loss of physical equilibrium, total loss of control, govern, goalkeeper, evil eye, spasm, nerves." "In the United States, not here in Brazil, there is a cure, for half of the disease."*

Catarina's dictionary is filled with references to deficient movement, to pain in the arms and legs, to muscular contractions. In writing, as in speech, she refers to her condition, by and large, as "rheumatism." I followed the word *rheumatism* as it appeared throughout the dictionary, paying close attention to the words and expressions clustered around it.

At times, Catarina's writings relate her growing paralysis to a kind of biological and familial marker, alluding to a certain *"blood type becoming a physical deficiency,*" "*a cerebral forgetfulness,*" and an "*expired brain and aged cranium*" that "*impede change.*" Most of the time, however, Catarina conveys the human-made character of her bodily afflictions. In the following inscription, for example, she depicts rheumatism as a mangling of the threads people tinker with:

> People think that they have the right to put their hands in the mangled threads and to mess with it. Rheumatism. They use my name for good and for evil. They use it because of the rheumatism.

Her rheumatism ties various life-threads together. It is an untidy knot, a real matter that makes social exchange possible. It gives the body its stature and it is the conduit of a morality. Catarina's bodily affection, not her name, is exchanged in that world: "*What I was in the past does not matter.*" Catarina disappears and a religious image stands in her place: "*Rheumatism, Spasm, Crucified Jesus.*" In another fragment, she writes: "*Acute spasm, secret spasm. Rheumatic woman. The word of the rheumatic is of no value.*"

Catarina knows that there is a rationality and a bureaucracy to symptom management: "*Chronic spasm, rheumatism, must be stamped, registered.*" All of this happens in a democratic context, "*vote by vote.*" We must consider side by side the acute pain Catarina described and the authoritative story she became in medicine and in common sense — as being mad and ultimately of no value. The antipsychotic drugs Haldol and Neozine are also words in Catarina's dictionary. In a fragment, she defiantly writes that her pain reveals the experimental ways science is embodied: "*The dance of science. Pain broadcasts sick science, the sick study. Brain, illness. Buscopan, Haldol, Neozine. Invoked spirit.*"

An individual history of science is being written here. Catarina's lived experience and ailments are the *pathos* of a certain science, a science that is itself sick. There has been a breakdown in the pursuit of wisdom, and there is commerce. The goods of psychiatric science, such as Haldol and Neozine, have become as ordinary as Buscopan (hyoscine, an over-the-counter antispasmodic medication) and have become a part of familial practices. As Catarina's experience shows, the use of such drugs produces mental and physical effects apart from those related to her illness. These pharmaceutical goods — working, at times, like rituals — realize an imaginary spirit rather than the material truth they supposedly stand for: *medical commodities are then supposed subjects.* There is a science to Catarina's affects, a money-making science. As transmitters of this science, her signs and symptoms are of a typical kind.

In Catarina's thinking and writing, global pharmaceuticals are not simply taken as new material for old patterns of self-fashioning. These universally disseminated goods are entangled in and act as vectors for new mechanisms of sociomedical and subjective control that have a deadly force. Seen from the perspective of Vita, the illnesses Catarina experienced were the outcome of events and practices that altered the person she had learned to become. Words such as "Haldol" and "Neozine" are literally her. As I mentioned earlier, the drug name Akineton (biperiden) is reflected in the new name Catarina gave herself: "*I am not the daughter of Adam and Eve. I am the Little Doctor. CATKINE.*"

Abandoned in Vita to die, Catarina has ties to pharmakons. Her desire, she writes, is now a pharmaceutical thing with no human exchange value:

> *Catarina cries and wants to leave. Desire, watered, prayed, wept. Tearful feeling, fearful, diabolic, betrayed. My desire is of no value. Desire is pharmaceutical. It is not good for the circus.*

I asked her, why did you invent this name?

"I will be called Catkine now. For I don't want to be a tool for men to use, for men to cut. A tool is innocent. You dig, you cut, you do whatever you want with it. . . . It doesn't know if it hurts or doesn't. But the man who uses it to cut the other knows what he is doing."

She continued with the most forceful words: "I don't want to be a tool. Because Catarina is not the name of a person . . . truly not. It is the name of a tool, of an object. A person is an Other."

I find Gilles Deleuze's insights on "Literature and Life" (1997) quite helpful in this inquiry into Catarina's work with language. Deleuze says that writing is "a question of becoming, always incomplete, always in the midst of being formed, and goes beyond the matter of any livable or lived experience" (1997: 1). He thinks of language as a gate through which limits of all kinds are crossed and the energy of the "delirium" unleashed. "Delirium" suggests alternative visions of existence and of a future that clinical definitions tend to foreclose. To become is not to attain a form through imitation, identification, or mimesis, but rather to find a zone of proximity where one can no longer be distinguished from a man, a woman, or an animal — "neither imprecise, nor general, but unforeseen and nonpreexistent, singularized out of a population rather than determined in a form" (1997: 1). One can institute such zone of indifferentiation with anything "on the condition that one creates the literary means for doing so" (1997: 2).

For Deleuze, the real and the imaginary are always coexisting, always complementary. They are like two juxtaposable or superimposable parts of a single trajectory, two faces that ceaselessly interchange with one another, a mobile mirror "bearing witness until the end to a new vision whose passage it remained open to" (1997: 63). In Catarina's words, real and imaginary voyages compose a set of intertwined routes. *"I am a free woman, to fly, bionic woman, separated." "When men throw me into the air, I am already far away."* These trajectories are inseparable from her efforts of becoming. *"Die death, medication is no more." "I will leave the door of the cage open. You can fly wherever you want to." "I, who am where I go, am who am so." "To follow desire in solitude."*

Coda

As fieldwork came to a close, Oscar, one of Vita's volunteers on whom I depended for insights and care, particularly in regard to Catarina, told me that things like this research happen "so that the pieces of the machine finally get put together." Catarina did not simply fall through the cracks of various domestic and public systems. Her abandonment was dramatized and realized in the novel interactions and juxtapositions of several contexts. Scientific assessments of reality (in the form of biological knowledge and psychiatric diagnostics and treatments) were deeply embedded in changing households and institutions, informing colloquial thoughts and actions that led to her terminal exclusion. The subjects in Vita are literally composed by morbid scientific-commercial-political changes. Following Catarina's words and plot was a way to delineate this powerful, *noninstitutionalized ethnographic space* in which the family gets rid of its undesirable members. The social production of deaths such as Catarina's cannot ultimately be assigned to any single intention. As ambiguous as its causes are, her dying in Vita is nonetheless traceable to specific constellations of forces.

Once caught in this space, one is part of a machine, suggested Oscar. But the elements of this machine connect only if one goes the extra step, I told him. "For if one doesn't," he replied, "the pieces stay lost for the rest of life. They then rust, and the rust terminates with them." Neither free from nor totally determined by this machinery, Catarina dwelt in the luminous lost edges of human imagination that she expanded through writing.

Catarina remarked that other people might be curious about her words, but she added that their meaning was ultimately part of her living: "There is so much that comes with time . . . the words . . . and the signification, you will not find in the book. It is only in my memory that I have the signification. . . . And this is for me to untie." Catarina refused to be an object of understanding for others. "Nobody will decipher the words for me. With the pen, only I can do it . . . in the ink, I decipher."

We might face Catarina's writing in the same way we face poetry. She introduces us to a world that is other than our own, yet close to home; and with it, we have the chance to read social life and the human condition via pharmakons differently. To engage with her life and writing is also to work upon oneself. "I am writing for myself to understand, but, of course, if you all understand I will be very content."

Catarina refused to be consigned to the impossible, and she anticipated an exit from Vita. It was as difficult as it was important to sustain this anticipation: to find ways to support Catarina's search for ties to people and the world and her demand for continuity, or at least its possibility. Out of this intricate ethnographic tension emerges a sense of the present as embattled and unfinished, on both sides of the conversation and of the text.

REFERENCES

Agamben, G. 1998. *Homo Sacer: Sovereign Power and Bare Life*. Stanford, CA: Stanford University Press.
Andreoli, S. B., N. Almeida-Filho, D. Martin, M. D. Mateus, and J. de J. Mari. 2007. Is psychiatric reform a strategy for reducing the mental health budget? The case of Brazil. *Revista Brasileira de Psiquiatria* 29, no. 1: 43-46.
Biehl, J. (with D. Coutinho and A. L. Outeiro). 2001. Technology and affect: HIV/ AIDS testing in Brazil. *Culture, Medicine and Psychiatry* 25, no. 1: 87-129.
Biehl, J. 2005. *Vita: Life in a Zone of Social Abandonment*. Berkeley: University of California Press.
Biehl, J. 2007. *Will to Live: AIDS Therapies and the Politics of Survival*. Princeton: Princeton University Press.
Biehl, J., B. Good, and A. Kleinman, eds. 2007. *Subjectivity: Ethnographic Investigations*. Berkeley: University of California Press.
Biehl, J., and A. Moran-Thomas. 2009. Symptom: Technologies, social ills, subjectivities. *Annual Review of Anthropology* 38, no. 1: 267-88.
Biehl, J., and P. Locke. 2010. Deleuze and the anthropology of becoming. *Current Anthropology*.
Boellstorff, T. 2008. *Coming of Age in Second Life: An Anthropologist Explores the Virtually Human*. Princeton: Princeton University Press.
Caldeira, T. 2000. *City of Walls: Crime, Segregation, and Citizenship in São Paulo*. Berkeley: University of California Press.

Corin, E. 2007. "The 'Other' of Culture in Psychosis: The Ex-centricity of the Subject." In *Subjectivity: Ethnographic Investigations,* edited by João Biehl, Byron Good, and Arthur Kleinman, 273-314. Berkeley: University of California Press.

Declercq, F. 2006. Lacan on the capitalist discourse: Its consequences for libidinal enjoyment and social bonds. *Psychoanalysis, Culture & Society* 11, no. 1: 74-83.

Deleuze, G. 1997. *Essays: Critical and Clinical.* Minneapolis: University of Minnesota Press.

Deleuze, G. 2006. *Two Regimes of Madness: Texts and Interviews 1975-1995.* New York: Semiotext(e).

DelVecchio Good, Mary-Jo, Sandra Hyde, Sarah Pinto, and Byron Good. 2008. *Postcolonial Disorders.* Berkeley: University of California Press.

Derrida, J. 1981. "Plato's Pharmacy." In *Dissemination,* 61-171. Chicago: University of Chicago Press.

Doane, M. A. 2003. "Sublimation and the Psychoanalysis of Aesthetic." In *Jacques Lacan: Critical Evaluations in Cultural Theory,* 127-46. New York: Routledge.

Dumit, J. 2004. *Picturing Personhood: Brain Scans and Biomedical Identity.* Princeton: Princeton University Press.

Ecks, S. 2005. Pharmaceutical citizenship: Antidepressant marketing and the promise of demarginalization in India. *Anthropology & Medicine* 12, no. 3: 239-54.

Edmonds, A. 2007. "The poor have the right to be beautiful": Cosmetic surgery in neoliberal Brazil. *Journal of the Royal Anthropological Institute* 13, no. 2: 363-81.

Farmer, P. 2008. Challenging orthodoxies: The road ahead for health and human rights. *Health and Human Rights* 10, no. 1: 5-19.

Fassin, D., and R. Rechtman. 2009. *The Empire of Trauma: An Inquiry into the Condition of Victimhood.* Princeton: Princeton University Press.

Fischer, M. M. J. 2009. *Anthropological Futures.* Durham, NC: Duke University Press.

Fischer, M. M. J. 2007. "To Live with What Would Otherwise Be Unendurable: Return(s) to Subjectivities." In *Subjectivity: Ethnographic Investigations,* ed. João Biehl, Byron Good, and Arthur Kleinman, 423-46. Berkeley: University of California Press.

Foucault, M. 1979. *Discipline and Punish: The Birth of the Prison.* New York: Vintage Books.

Foucault, M. 1980. *The History of Sexuality, Volume I: An Introduction.* New York: Vintage Books.

Garcia, A. 2008. The elegiac addict: History, chronicity and the melancholic subject. *Cultural Anthropology* 23, no. 4: 718-46.

Geertz, C. 2000. "Common Sense as a Cultural System." In *Local Knowledge: Further Essays in Interpretive Anthropology.* New York: Basic Books.

Girard, R. 1996. *The Girard Reader.* New York: Crossroad.

Good, B., Subandi, and M. J. DelVecchio Good. 2007. "The Subject of Mental Illness:

Madness, Mad Violence, and Subjectivity in Contemporary Indonesia." In *Subjectivity: Ethnographic Investigations*, ed. João Biehl, Byron Good, and Arthur Kleinman. Berkeley: University of California Press, 243-72.

Harrison, J. E. *Epilogomena to the Study of Greek Religion*. Cambridge: Cambridge University Press.

Inhorn, M. 2003. *Local Babies, Global Science: Gender, Religion, and In Vitro Fertilization in Egypt*. New York: Routledge.

Jardim, L. B., M. L. Pereira, I. Silveira, A. Ferro, J. Sequeiros, and R. Giugliani. 2001. Machado-Joseph disease in South Brazil: Clinical and molecular characterizations of kindreds. *Acta Neurologica Scandinavica* 104: 224-31.

Jenkins, J. H., and R. J. Barrett, eds. 2003. *Schizophrenia, Culture, and Subjectivity: The Edge of Experience*. Cambridge: Cambridge University Press.

Kleinman, A. 2006. *What Really Matters: Living a Moral Life Amidst Uncertainty and Danger*. New York: Oxford University Press.

Lacan, J. 1972. "Del Discurso Psicanalitico" (Milan). Unpublished translation.

Lacan, J. 1989. "Science and Truth." *Newsletter of the Freudian Field* 3: 4-29.

Lacan, J. 1991. *Le Seminarie Livre XVII: L'envers de la psychanalyse*. Paris: Seuil.

Lakoff, A. 2006. *Pharmaceutical Reason: Knowledge and Value in Global Psychiatry*. Cambridge: Cambridge University Press.

Luhrman, T. 2000. *Of Two Minds: The Growing Disorder in American Psychiatry*. New York: Alfred A. Knopf.

Martin, E. 2007. *Biopolar Expeditions: Mania and Depression in American Culture*. Princeton: Princeton University Press.

Petryna, A. 2009. *When Experiments Travel: Clinical Trials and the Global Search for Human Subjects*. Princeton: Princeton University Press.

Petryna, A., A. Lakoff, and A. Kleinman. 2006. *Global Pharmaceuticals: Ethics, Markets, Practices*. Durham, NC: Duke University Press.

Pinto, S. 2008. *Where There Is No Midwife: Birth and Loss in Rural India*. Oxford and New York: Berghahn Books.

Rancière, J. 2004. Who is the subject of the rights of man? *The South Atlantic Quarterly* 102, nos. 2-3: 297-310.

Rajan, K. S. 2006. *Biocapital: The Constitution of Postgenomic Life*. Durham, NC: Duke University Press.

Rapp, R. 1999. *Testing Women, Testing the Fetus: The Social Impact of Amniocentesis in America*. New York: Routledge.

Reynolds Whyte, S. 2009. Health identities and subjectivities: The ethnographic challenge. *Medical Anthropology Quarterly* 23, no. 1: 6-15.

Rofel, L. 2007. *Desiring China: Experiments in Neoliberalism, Sexuality, and Public Culture*. Durham, NC: Duke University Press.

Scheper-Hughes, N. 2008. A talent for life: Reflections on human vulnerability and resistance. *Ethnos* 73, no. 1: 25-56.

Shaw, P. "From the Sublime to the Ridiculous: Lacan and Zizek." In *The Sublime,* 131-47. New York: Routledge.

Tsing, A. 2004. *Friction: An Ethnography of Global Connection.* Princeton: Princeton University Press.

Turkle, S., ed. 2008. *The Inner History of Devices.* Cambridge: MIT Press.

Whitmarsh, I. 2008. *Biomedical Ambiguity: Race, Asthma, and the Contested Meaning of Genetic Research in the Caribbean.* Ithaca, NY: Cornell University Press.

Zizek, S. 2006. "Jacques Lacan's Four Discourses." In: http://www.lacan.com/zizfour.htm (downloaded August 3, 2008).

PART FOUR

The Self and Emergence

Enigmatic Experiences: Spirit, Complexity, and Person

Catherine Keller

Now we see in a mirror, in an enigma, but then, person to person.

1 Corinthians 13:12

Usually, of course, 1 Corinthians 13:12 is rendered according to the King James Version: "Now we see in a glass darkly, but then, face to face."[1] This well-traveled Pauline sentence, placed in the midst of the teaching on "gifts of the spirit," emits a mysterious beauty in either translation. Nonetheless, in the familiar version, it suffers a triple loss of meaning. First, when the Greek word for "mirror" becomes "glass," a critical clue to the problem of human self-reflection, specularity, and projection is forfeit. In the same translational gesture, "enigma" *(ainegma)*, is then replaced by "darkness," sacrificing the coded complexity of an ancient verbal "riddle" to mere obscurity. The translators were at the same time sparing us the synaesthetic perplexity of "seeing" a "riddle" — and so they dissipate the metaphorical tension of the visual and the verbal. Third, "face," while a correct translation of *prosopon*, cuts off the promise of the fuller-bodied "person."

I do not mean to enter a conversation with Paul, let alone his myriad interpreters; I will not offer an exegesis of this too-well-known biblical text. I am, however, hoping that its hermeneutical puzzle may surprise us with a clue to a concept of the human person — a *theological* clue to a *trans-*

---

1. The NRSV offers: "For now we see in a mirror, dimly, but then we will see face to face. Now I know only in part; then I will know fully, even as I have been fully known."

disciplinary concept. Allowing for the entire history of Western self-consciousness that separates us from the Pauline context, without necessarily getting us a moment closer to his eschatological "but then," the verse may mirror to us the dilemma of our own self-conscious personhood.

Here is its clue: when I try to "see" the truth, I get in my way. My own image is reflected back to me. "I" — my presumptions, prejudgments, projections, sociolinguistic constructions — block my transparent view of any Other. But my own image is itself unclear. That self-mirroring Pauline icon of the mirror remains elusive. Indeed, the reflecting surface of most ancient mirrors looks more like a pond than like a silvered modern mirror, opaque to the back, objective to the front. Who all, what all, flicker across the surface? The mirror image already conveys, with a sense of partial prophecy, more than itself. In the promise of a disclosure of that "more," personhood already reflects an inescapable interdependence. The personal is always already the interpersonal. But the interpersonal is always already the transpersonal, more than personal, signifying the vast multiplicity of impersonal energies embodied in and crossing through each person. At the same time, the person is in transit, moving beyond itself, into as yet unfathomable relations — and getting in its own way all along.

Theology, however, does not monopolize even that motion into the transcendent future, and it does not even try — not, at least, if it is a transdisciplinary theology, polydox in its hermeneutics. But might we read the eschatological deferral ("but then") not as the standard guarantee of afterlife, but as the outer edge *(eschaton)* of personal emergence? Then we destabilize the standard icon of an ultimately visible divine Superperson, a God mirroring our own image back to ourselves. From the perspective of a present moment of becoming, the outer rim rightly appears "dark." But must this darkness be read as a mere opposite of light, as an empty nothingness? What if it has more the character of an excess, like Jean-Luc Marion's "saturated phenomenon," too complex to master epistemically? It may simply lie in the indifferent periphery of our consciousness. But this darkness becomes for us *enigma* when it engages our personhood.

In the first letter to the Corinthians, human personality, called into the intentional coexistence of a communal "body," actualizes its potentials, its "gifts," within the radically relational "spirit."[2] The text, of course, histori-

---

2. The mirror text is contained within the great chapter on love as the greatest of the gifts. Immediately prior to it is the elaboration of the metaphor of the body of Christ as comprised of multiple gifts interdependently participating in the same organism. "Now there are

cally precedes the doctrinal consolidation of the Holy Spirit as a "face" or "person," a *prosopon*, in the Trinity — and ipso facto the eventual Western notion of the human *persona* that would translate the *prosopon* of the Trinitarian debates. Let us here consider the spirit then not as itself a person, but as the field of interdependence, the very relationality, in which human persons in their interpersonality take place. "This singularly plural coexistence"[3] would then mark at once the irreducible uniqueness and the constituent multiplicity of any existent self. The person I see in the mirror — at once other and self — may signify the narcissism by which I reduce others to myself. Yet it discloses at the same time the entanglement of others in myself and myself in others: what I see I have already influenced.

In other words, the person is a *complex*: not something unitary and simple that has complexity or doesn't, but an effect of a vast multiplicity of embedded relations. Its complexity folds it in on itself dangerously and productively, rendering the boundary between self and its others always uncertain, shifting — enigmatic — and therefore rendering the self a puzzle to itself. Judith Butler puts this relational unknowingness succinctly: "Moments of unknowingness about oneself tend to emerge in the context of relations to others, suggesting that these relations call upon primary forms of relationality that are not always available to explicit and reflective thematization."[4] And so, in her marvelous parlance, "we undo each other." The self "comes undone" in encountering the frustration and the attraction — enigma indeed — of its own complex relationality. The enigma may generate at once more narcissism, more preoccupation with myself, with my fascinating, appalling person — who is she, who requires such constant attention? And at the same time it lures the self into the very emergence of self in and among its others, where the self becomes other than what it was. Like all complex, self-organizing systems, the person emerges in relation to its others. Those relations can be dissolved again and again, by ever-new ploys of self-absorption, into the inflated self manifest in the familiar preoccupations, therapies, and mirror-games of late-capitalist narcissism. Or the self may dissolve — with-

---

varieties of gifts, but the same Spirit; and there are varieties of services, but the same Lord; and there are varieties of activities, but it is the same God who activates all of them in everyone. To each is given the manifestation of the Spirit for the common good" (1 Cor. 12:4-7, NRSV).

3. Jean-Luc Nancy, *Being Singular Plural*, trans. Robert D. Richardson and Anne E. O'Byrne (Stanford, CA: Stanford University Press, 2000), 3.

4. Judith Butler, *Giving an Account of Oneself* (New York: Fordham University Press, 2005), 20.

out losing any of its selfishness — into a reductionist body inserted into an environment of determinate relations. Indeed, we might read the oscillation between the reduction and the inflation of the normative Western personality as symptomatic of a lost alternative, never quite found to start with: the haunting image of a personality at once free of its self and endlessly emerging.

Therefore, *emergent complexity* as the dynamic of spirit will suggest for the present exercise the enigmatic alternative to both the reduction and the inflation of the person. The spirit is at once mine and infinitely more than my own: it is psychosocial, it is grounded in the elements of the creation, and it is the spirit in which community dwells. Pneumatology, in other words, may embed that emergent interpersonality in an infinite field of interrelations. Or, perhaps more precisely, the redemptive action of the spirit is to disclose the transformative potentiality of that plenitude, that all-in-all.[5] In what follows, there appear five criteria for the emergence of a spirited self, not as steps in a finished argument, but as transdisciplinary potentialities or sites of the articulation of its becoming. The puzzling mirror of the person thus captures here five specific emergences: (1) counter-reductionist in its recourse to complexity theory, (2) pneumatological as a theological construction, (3) biblical in its theopoetic reading strategy, (4) feminist in its specular gender, and — as far as this complex of the person goes — (5) irretrievably enigmatic.

Counter-Reductionist Emergences

The problem of reductionism exists in a mutually reinforcing dialectic with that of absolutism; reductionist projects, founded on scientific secularism, attempt to deflate an inflated view of the person, exaggerated in its claims to autonomy and self-consciousness. Behind the modern inflations lurks the true target of the reductionist animus: the human person as created in the image of God the Person. But the problem of reduction has roots already in theology. As Feuerbach first drove the point home, the supernaturalism of the *imago Dei* sucks interest up and out of actual living persons: God the Fa-

---

5. "All in all" in 1 Corinthians suggests, as in 1 Corinthians 12:4-6, that (in my literal translation) "God is the same One Who *energizes* all in all"; the eschatological "all in all" of 1 Corinthians 15:28 is thus held in tension in "the body of Christ" with the interdependence of the many members, identified in terms of their divergent spiritual gifts.

ther *reduces* bodily existence to mere transient flesh, mere means to his transcendent ends. But that deflation is paradoxically inseparable from the earlier inflation, for which Pauline theology had its own cure. The diagnosis of the sin into which we are inextricably born at once exposes our interpersonal dependence and our hopeless self-ignorance. Thus the worst sin was theological arrogance, or "spiritual pride," as Luther, privy to the mirror-enigma, well recognized. But no notion of sin has protected theology from its own arrogance. Dogmatically over-secured, the doctrine of sin reduces the person to a puppet of God and Satan. So secular modernism reacts against the theological reduction, but opens itself to its own.

In other words, the inflation-deflation cycle operates *between* theology and science, but also *within* theology. Both reduction and inflation effect homogenizing simplifications. For the theological inflation depends upon reductive strategies. Wentzel van Huyssteen hits the nail on the head: "strategies which still claim theology's own 'internal logic' or self-authenticating notions of divine revelation as a basis for disciplinary integrity and then proceed to set up a dualism between naturalism and supernaturalism with a demand for a reductionist choice between these two."[6] The "logic of the One," as Laurel Schneider puts it, operates here in terms of the classical "simplicity" of the transcendent oneness of God, with its corresponding ideal of the rationally unified personhood. But it then transposes itself into the terms of the rational scientific subject, imposing the simplest unit of explanation, from the outside, upon its object. This ideal of simple unity has no biblical root, not even in the cosmopolitan Paul. It developed from Greek ontology into the hermeneutical medium for classical Christian orthodoxy, and thence into the modern deployments of static unitary Being that Continental philosophy exposes in secular texts as "ontotheology." Thus it may be salutary to seek clues to an alternative hermeneutical framework for spirited personhood not only in postmodern philosophies of complexity but also in postmodern science.

Specifically, complexity theory in the natural sciences represents one of the most powerful of the recent discourses — associated especially with the life sciences but running across multiple disciplines — that explicitly resist the heritage of scientific reductionism. It yields a rich discourse of "emer-

6. The proposal of a postfoundationalist "experiential accountability" as the "final and decisive move beyond fideist strategies" lies close to the heart of the present essay. J. Wentzel van Huyssteen, "Postfoundationalism in Theology and Science," in *Rethinking Theology and Science*, ed. Niels Henrik Gregersen and J. W. van Huyssteen (Grand Rapids: Eerdmans, 1998), 45.

gence" as the process whereby complex systems come to be. I have elsewhere engaged theories of the complexity of creation, as the emergence "at the edge of chaos" not just of biological life but of celestial systems. Emergence theory draws upon post-Newtonian principles of nonlinearity (unpredictability) and "extreme sensitivity to initial conditions" (the rippling relationality of the butterfly effect) that characterize what is called "chaos."[7] Descriptions of how the complexity of the universe, and life itself, has emerged from the chaos construe complex systems, including possibly that of the creation as a whole, as open systems. The biologist Stuart Kauffman, a pioneer of complexity theory, argues — against the reductionist rhetoric of the modern scientific legacy — that "biologists tell stories," that "stories are our mode of making sense of the context-dependent actions of us as autonomous agents." He defines the "strong form of reductionism" as "x is 'nothing but' y."[8] Emergence then marks the key operative alternative to reduction. Paraphrasing Hamlet, Kauffman counters the mechanistic habit that persists so far beyond its actual legitimacy: "The universe in its persistent becoming is richer than all our dreamings."[9] Or, in more technical language: "we cannot prestate the configuration space of a biosphere."

That configuration space may in theological translation appear as the field of interdependence in which persons and all their interdependents emerge, the space we call "spirit." The becoming it hosts is precisely our genesis. But to make such a theological move is precisely not to forfeit the ecological implications of that configuration space. For spirit, even when dogmatically intensified as the Holy Spirit, has for some time been recognized as hospitable to ecotheological attempts to deconstruct the anthropomorphism of God (as Father, as Son) while embedding the person in its relationship to all creatures.[10]

Theology has been attempting on many sides to repent of its insensitivity to the biosphere. Often it is our legitimate interest in the personal and the interpersonal, not to mention the divine persons, that has enabled a facile ac-

7. See my *The Face of the Deep: A Theology of Becoming* (New York: Routledge, 2003). My current project, *The Cloud of the Impossible: A Theology of Nonseparability,* finds itself enveloped in the folds of explication, implication, complication. For a nonscientist-friendly introduction, cf. John R. Gribbin, *Deep Simplicity: Bringing Order to Chaos and Complexity* (New York: Random House, 2004), 73.

8. Stuart Kauffman, *Investigations* (Oxford: Oxford University Press, 2000), 125.

9. Kauffman, *Investigations,* 134-35, 139.

10. Cf. *Ecospirit: Religions and Philosophies for the Earth,* ed. Laurel Kearns and Catherine Keller (New York: Fordham University Press, 2007).

quiescence in reductionist readings of the nonhuman creation. But reduction of the nonhuman has long issued in reduction of the human — not to a modest recognition of its own interdependence but to "nothing but" the central operator in the mechanisms of planetary competition, commodification, and exploitation. Indeed, the Western oscillation between inflated and reductive readings of human personhood — quite equally anthropocentric — seems now only to tempt eco-apocalyptic outcomes. So the potential for dialogue with the anti-reductionist sciences takes on ethical as well as theoretical urgency. For the planet's ecological emergency is surely based in large measure on the failure to appreciate biological emergence, and also on the failure to situate the person within its relationship to complex nonhuman systems.

When we gaze in that primordial mirror, do we ever only see an interplay of human and divine persons? After all, whether or not we attend to it, an entire transpersonal multiplicity of organs, cells, and pigments of animal flesh, fellow organisms, light waves, and atmospheres appears in any such glimpse. Isn't an earthly manifold mirrored enigmatically back at us, enmeshed in our own too-dominant *imago?*

Pneumatological Emergences

The coexistent becoming — *genesis* — of the creatures, supported by the theory of emergence, does not theologically imply a divine anthropomorphic Person, let alone inflated theologies of "intelligent design." Emergence is, however, of special interest to a theologian such as Philip Clayton, working at the intersection of panentheism and natural science: "Emergence theories presuppose that the project of explanatory reduction — explaining all phenomena in the natural world in terms of the objects and laws of physics — is finally impossible."[11] Clayton goes on to ask whether emergence can "help to make sense of the predicates of spirit or even deity" — with reference to the early Pannenberg's notion that in an important sense "God does not yet exist," to Schelling's notion of God as originally mere potential, and only gradually becoming actual in history *(Freiheitsschrift)*, and of course to Whitehead's "consequent nature of God," as the pole of divine becoming through interaction with all other becomings.[12]

11. Philip Clayton, *Mind and Emergence: From Quantum to Consciousness* (Oxford: Oxford University Press, 2004), 2.

12. Clayton, *Mind and Emergence,* 166-67.

When Clayton touches upon the familiar ambiguity of spirit as a level "beyond the level of mind" — is it the Holy Spirit or human spirit? — the idea of an "emergent spirit," divine or human, lets him pose the "model of the human person, understood as an integrated system of influences." In the "integrative state," the person has "affective as well as intellectual and social dimensions." Clayton can thereby account for the complexity symbolized traditionally by the dimensions of soul, mind, body, spirit, morality, and sociality, without rendering any of them separable substances or faculties. He draws a powerful inference. "Personhood may be an emergent quality of the natural world without being conceived as some specific mental 'thing.'"[13]

Such a rethinking of spirited personhood as emergent from the matrix of our transpersonally material — or better, embodied — relations encodes an alternative to materialist reduction. It will be part of any solution of the "riddle" of the mirror. But it also resists supernatural dualism, with its inflated human persons, in which one isolable "part" comprises an immaterial or Godlike substance. The person as a complex process of integration is then the specifically human materialization of an *open* system. And what makes it specifically human may lie precisely in the enigma of its mirror. For it remains our awareness of our own complex transpersonal becoming, our self-awareness *of and as* such processes, that at once confuses and humanizes us. But it is always some form of the self-mirroring, the reflection of our process to itself, that unfolds the specifically human complication, the self-conscious iteration that bears a memory and a future. It is, in other words, not spirit that makes me human; it is spirit that makes me alive, makes me a creature, might even in the ancient tradition of theosis or theopoeisis make me divine. But of course it makes for a spirited humanity — to the extent that we do not freeze out the spirit through a Cartesian self-objectification, an ego-reproducing certainty that severs the persona from its transpersonal collectivity.

Spirit would then not be identical with a person or part of a person, but would signify the transpersonal field of our emergence. Hence the importance of Michael Welker's hermeneutics of the "force field of the Spirit" as "open system."[14] My spirit is only "mine" inasmuch as I embody it; it is not "in" me as a faculty, a fuel, or a homunculus. Rather, I am "in the spirit." I do not possess it but may be "possessed" by it. Neither does it lie outside of me,

---

13. Clayton, *Mind and Emergence*, 197.

14. Michael Welker, *God the Spirit*, trans. John Hoffmeyer (Minneapolis: Fortress, 1994).

merely public or merely transcendent. Rather, it permeates my becoming; it flows — like the Johannine wind or water — through my vulnerability to the virtually infinite coexistences among which I emerge.

Person is not spirit but *spirited* — to the extent it remains inspired, conspiring with the pneumatic lure to greater complexity. Spirit does not guarantee a system of revelation but reveals itself as *system-opener*. But the opener is intrinsic to the relationality, not coming from the outside, as though our relations enclose us. This they do in the mode of inflation and reduction, of imposing egos and objectified others. But such dispiriting relations, while they often appear to block all vision beyond themselves, systemically obstruct the complex emergence of the person. For they radically simplify relations, sometimes even in the interest of absorbing complexity into an all-consuming self. The person hardens into its persona; the fluid mirror becomes the rigid mask.

So the system-opening spirit may appear metaphorically as the relation of relations, opening our relations to their own potential becoming, and thus kin to Augustine's Trinitarian figure of Spirit as love itself. Thus spirit resists the self-enclosure *(curvatio en se)*, indeed the closure, of the person — whether into a metaphysical substance (inflation) or a sociophysical function (reduction), whether into the narcissistic fixation on the mirror or the enclosure of the other as the mirror of myself. And the Cartesian subject, able to mirror himself *(sic)* back to himself as a transparent object, remains the epistemological temptation of a modern, still modern, consciousness. It forgets that its con/sciousness is knowing with itself but also with all its others, and that all disappears through the mirror into an eschatological infinity. But in the meantime the spirit may be that which relates our present, fractured multiplicity to an "all-in-all" we can know only "fragmentarily," *ek merous*.[15] The spirit does not fix or overcome the fragments. It would seem not to solve the enigma but to deepen it. For relations lived in that love open us vulnerably into one another. In Pauline parlance, they open like organs into and within the body of Christ, the great Corinthian text of which follows immediately upon the enigma of the mirror.

---

15. "For the expression *prosopon pros prosopon*, 'face to face,' cf. Gen 32:31. The temporal distance between the present and the age of vision is further indicated by *arti*, 'at present.' Verse 12b explains the figure in terms of indirectness, equivalent to imperfection, which is now expressed by *ek merous*, 'fagmentarily': cv. v. 9. *Ek merous* in turn is elucidated by the antithesis: 'perfect' knowledge (see v. 10) is knowledge *kathos kai epegnosthen*, 'even as I am known.'" Hans Conzelmann, *1 Corinthians: A Commentary on the First Epistle to the Corinthians*, trans. J. W. Leitch, Hermeneia (Philadelphia: Fortress, 1975).

Scriptural Emergences

Spirit as a specifically *biblical* dis/closure ought to have countered the odd selfishness of so much Christian piety, the fixation on my relation to Jesus, my God, my salvation. By the same token, spirit ought to have countered dissolution into flatly social identities. For "in the spirit," the singular gift of a particular person (in voice, prophecy, compassion, leadership) is intensified as charisma (1 Cor. 12–14). In the spirited emergence of difference within our own species, our gifts as differentiations of the gift of life ought to have opened the members of our species to each other in "adventures of the spirit" (Philip Clayton). Hence the mutual participation of "the body of Christ" may not have first had its exclusivist, self-enclosing connotations at all. In context it appears originally as an experiment in intentional community, disciplined and emergent. Yet the dispiriting personhood of the dominant subject seems to have appropriated the energies of the Christian body, often sealing it into itself, and its individuals into themselves. I am, of course, suggesting that the enigma of Western personality will not find solutions by simply shutting down the memory of that experiment. Rather, its reopening into polydox and pluralist complexity may offer the stronger subversion of Christian exclusivism. Buoyed up by recent retrievals of Paul by secular theorists such as Badiou and Zizek, and previously by the postmodern Talmud scholar Daniel Boyarin, we find a Paul, the "radical Jew," resistant to imperial power and ontological certainty. The embodiment of the early Christian community appears then as a strategy not for self-enclosed identities but for a transgressively wide, nonviolent mission across all the boundaries of human social groupings.

Is it going too far to hope that the pneumatological revival, in its transdisciplinary, transreligious width, will as Moltmann signals in *The Spirit of Life* also extend to human relations to the other species? The gifted creativity of the entire earth-collective is anticipated in the pneumatology of the biblical creation narrative, in the elemental "fluctuation of spirit on the face of the waters" (Gen. 1:2). All that is emerges at the edge of chaos — the deep. The spirit moving rhythmically mirrors the pulsing waters: a metaphor of the extreme sensitivity of initial conditions of chaos theory, as its contingent, unpredictable emergences yield the complex systems of our biosphere.

Almost immediately (Gen. 1:26ff.), the transpersonal spirit of the emergent creation gets narratively condensed and mirrored in the personifying (person-making) trope of coexistence encoded as *imago Dei*. The *spiritus creator* moves fluidly between the creator and creation and between the orders of creatures. Indeed, this enigmatic ambiguity of spirit-language, inconvenient for Trinitarian closure, leaves questions of its identity open. When is spirit only divine, when human? Don't the animals have *ruach/breath* as well? Is spirit a synonym for, or an emission of, "God"? Is it elemental immanence (breath-fire-water) or immaterial transcendence? Is it "it," "he," or "she"? Is the Holy Spirit someone other, more, or less than the Spirit of Life — or than God the Spirit? When is it radical intimacy (closer than I am to myself), when public witness (prophetic and pentecostal multilingualism)? Is there one Spirit, or are there many spirits? What (besides bad exegesis of 1 John) renders the multiplicity of spirits unholy?[16] This list of pneumatic ambiguities might multiply indefinitely, dissolving such arbitrary distinctions as Spirit versus spirits. The rich ambiguity of biblical pneumatology cannot be explained away as the leavings of vague and primitive traditions awaiting monotheistic discipline and Christian systematization. This enigmatic symbolic complex bears the narrative traces of the emergent complexity of the person. Spirit as its forcefield calls us out *(ek-klesia)* into an ever wider love, into a singular plurality that cannot be enclosed in a unitary self or a unitary dyad.

Michael Welker's hermeneutically founded exposition of "the public person of the spirit" demonstrates that pneumatological ambiguity does not dissolve within the biblical trajectory into moral relativism. The work of the spirit is disclosed in events of "justice and mercy." This is an animating and activating love, a force not deadened by public passivity or spiritual isolation. But it is the *person* who exercises agency, not the spirit as such. The spirit "pours out." We may *embody* the spirit. Personal agency should thus be understood not as an independent modern autonomy (reducing to relativism) and not as a dependent heteronomy disguised as theonomy (inflating to absolutism), but rather as a *cooperative autopoeisis*. Spirited selves emerge inasmuch as they participate in the system-opening *transpersonality of the spirit*. That flowing spirit, oceanic in depth, welling up as "the gift of God," has never been quite assimilable to God as metaphysical Person, or to one of Three Persons–One Substance, or to the analogous tripartite-faculty psy-

16. "Beloved, do not believe every spirit, but test the spirits to see whether they are from God." First John 4:1 is routinely misread to mean that the plurality of spirits is itself demonic, in opposition to the One Spirit. However, the next verse goes on to say "every spirit that confesses that Jesus Christ has come in the flesh is from God" — suggesting that indeed a multiplicity of spirits are capable of recognizing the incarnation, the fleshly rather than merely divine Jesus.

chologies. These were venerable attempts to protect the complexity of divine and human personhood against the pressure of their own logic of the One. Protection through enclosure and essentialization, however, locks down the system. It sabotages pneumatological personhood. The dogmatization of Father and Son language has literalized *prosopon* in the form of the three fixed faces of an immutable *substantia*. But the Holy Spirit was never quite a person, never really a face; she/he/it became in the West the "odd person out," who never quite fit the substance model — who cannot appear in the mirror.[17] If the Trinitarian dogma has tended toward a closed system, it has been trapped in the imaginary of two Guys and a Bird. Of course, the icon of the bird has great ecological promise — except when it signals subordination to the anthropomorphic Persons. The *filioque* was symptomatic of the problem. And the solution might not be to achieve Trinitarian equality by rendering Spirit yet another humanoid Person. Indeed, theologian Mark Wallace, writing the ecology of spirit, has sifted from biblical sources the Spirit's avian iconography as the trace of a pneumatological materiality — embodied not just in air, fire, and water but also in the earth: in the earthly body of the dove.[18]

In the open system of genesis, we conceive personhood as emergent precisely from its material-social relations to the rest of the planetary collective. Either our interpersonality in the Pauline body of Christ will now unfold mindfully, self-reflectingly, into the limitless interdependencies of planetary life, social and ecological, or we have reason to fear it will fold down into an ecclesial corpse on a dying planet. Not that the human species cannot in principle effect a just and sustainable future independently of Christianity. But it seems to be the case that the biblical narrative has so energetically entangled much of the planet, for good and for ill — ever spurred on by its Pauline genius — that the chances for that future will be better the more Christianity can be coaxed into a force of ecological renewal and pluralist justice. Within the Christian body it will come down always again to persons, spirited in their embodiment. And so we read them — biblically — as ecological transpersonalities, members not only of a church body, not only of a species body, but also of a planet body. Such complex emergence may be in our time the spirited alternative to an individual "born-again" of a disem-

17. On the theological, doctrinal, and patriarchal motive behind "Forgetting the Spirit," see Elizabeth Johnson, *She Who Is: The Mystery of God in Feminist Theological Discourse* (New York: Crossroads Continuum, 1994), 128-31.

18. Mark Wallace, *Fragments of the Spirit: Nature, Violence, and the Renewal of Creation?* (New York: Continuum, 1996; Harrisburg, PA: Trinity Press International, 2002).

bodied spirit, a person at once reduced and inflated, wasteful of the gifts of creaturely life. To see ourselves in the mirror may mean seeing ourselves for a moment as God would see us; but only as we imagine God, refracted through our constructed image of God, refracted in *imago Dei*. The mirror is not divine; it is not (contrary to some interpreters of Corinthians, for example) the spirit itself.[19] It is the shifting surface of the bottomless depth of the creation. If the spirit implicates in that infinity, our temptation will be to possess it as self-consciousness. But the temptation is the shadow of the gift of a profound, if always enigmatic, vision. The "self" reflected back to us in the very shadows of the mirror — inasmuch as it hints at the divine vision of us, would be me, frighteningly, all-in-all. And that would mean seeing ourselves implicated in, folded into, and responsible to our virtually infinite density of intercreaturely relations.

Gendering Emergences

Is it still, or again, too enigmatic to presume that such experiment in spirited embodiment as emergent personhood demands ongoing gender therapy? Personal coexistence is still systemically obstructed by the gyn-allergic reactions to the shared flesh, the feminized, queered, and occluded matrix/*mater* of life — and under the guise sometimes now of postfeminism, to feminist theory itself. Over decades, feminist theology revealed the synergy of divine and human gender-symbolism at the core of Christianity. If spirit-traditions of justice and mercy always threatened to overflow into the lives of women, doctrinal orthodoxy has usually closed the loopholes. "God" did not harden into the highest, the omnipotent, Being in abstraction from his masculinity. The men who constructed God in their own image sealed personhood into a straight masculine iconography. Yet for them also the potential for the spirited emergence of personhood claimed the imaginary of new birth. If that second birth, as a generation of feminist biblical and theological scholars made clear, carried the potential egalitarianism of the *imago Dei* of Genesis 1, it did so only at the expense of the material maternal womb. The Adam-

19. Unlike the Greek symbolizations of the mirror as clarity or self-knowledge, with its Gnostic developments, Paul resists the enthusiastic sense of any complete vision available in this world. Conzelmann notes that "Reitzenstein would offer the interpretation that the mirror is the pneuma, 'Spirit.' This is impossible. For Paul's point is the indirectness of our seeing the antithesis between present and future knowledge, and the latter is fullness of vision" (*1 Corinthians*, 228).

first tradition of Genesis 2 supervened in the cultivation of the normative Christian persona. Biblical patriarchy may be exposed or exceeded, but not erased. For millennia it has not been the generic human that blocks its own vision. It has been above all the normative male whose gaze gets in his own way — above all, and therefore reflecting himself to himself as divine. In itself the theopoeisis of the human becoming divine, in the mirror of divinity itself, might be the vision that liberates. But when this is a pale male divinity won at the expense of the less spiritual — i.e., less rational, and so less human — creatures, the mirror does truly darken.

In her classic *Speculum of the Other Woman*, Luce Irigaray meditates on the puzzling mirror. "For the optics of Truth in . . . its unconditional certainty, its passion for Reason, has veiled or else destroyed the gaze that remained mortal. With the result that it can no longer see anything of what had been before its conversion to the Father's law." Albeit without reference to the Pauline mirror, she circles close to its patriarchal problem. Irigaray has diagnosed the Platonic abandonment of the cave or earth-womb as a traumatic disconnection: "the pain of being blinded in this way, of being no longer able to make out, imagine, feel what is going on *behind* the screen of those/his ideal projections, divine knowledge: Which cut him off from his relations with the earth, the mother, and any other (female) by that ascent towards an all-powerful intelligibility."[20] The ontology at stake is, *ipso facto,* ontotheology. Irigaray's speculum appears as gynecological instrument, a tool to reduce women and magnify men, and as the "opaque and silent matrix of a logos immutable in the certainty of its own light."[21]

Inspired by Irigaray, along with a certain cosmological sense of connective emergence, my first work had recast personhood as neither separative (inflationary autonomy of male ego) nor soluble (deflating dependence of the corresponding female) but connective, and hence co-creative anthropologically as well as theologically. And I assumed that the Pauline mirror, with its eschatological anticipation of the transparent "face-to-face" with the allpowerful Father, has only helped to cut off those relations with the earth and those bodies who mirror it. Surely Christians have been blinded to their creaturely responsibilities by a light that they have opposed to the earthy, cavey darkness. The eschatological deferral — "but then" — meant to interrupt bogus certainties is twisted into their ultimate guarantor. We have pro-

---

20. Luce Irigaray, *Speculum of the Other Woman,* trans. Gillian C. Gill (Ithaca, NY: Cornell University Press, 1985), 362; her emphasis.

21. Irigaray, *Speculum of the Other Woman,* 144.

duced an unquestionable body of doctrinal certainty, with a critical mass of unquestioning Christians. Yet the questioners never ceased to emerge.

Nonetheless I am not proposing here that we break the Pauline mirror. It may be decoded as a critique of just such insentient certainty — and certainly of any pretense in our own lifetimes of attaining to "all-powerful intelligibility." But then we are *ipso facto* reading Paul against his own sexism (undeniable even if one can exegete away the worst bits as later additions) and so reframing his mirror.[22] In a way that would no doubt puzzle Paul; it is something that lay eschatologically far beyond, at least, *his* life. His mirror may now take on a depth possible only in the face-to-face with living others — even with "the Other, Woman."

No wonder such a dissident mystic and theologian as Marguerite de Porete would seize the image of the mirror as a subversive response, finding in it the God of love and therefore the divinity even of herself, a woman. She was burnt at the stake, along with most copies of her book, the *Miroir des Ames Simples.* For some decades a certain feminist mirror has circulated, in which women try to see themselves as women; but men, too, have found themselves anew, and so also their theology, in that gender-bending glass. Yet it is not now by clearing out masculinity, or any other embodied perspectival projection, but by recognizing it as such that spirited vision seems to be unfolding. In this enigmatic looking glass, gender cannot be separated from sex, and neither from the incarnate specificities of our racial, cultural, bodied transpersonalities.

Irigaray herself has another way of reading the mirror: "[I]f it is indeed a question of breaking (with) a certain mode of specula(riza)tion, this does not imply renouncing all mirrors. . . . But perhaps through this specular surface which sustains discourse is found not the void of nothingness but the dazzle of multifaceted speleology." She thus combines images of mirror and cave, eye and earth, surface and depth, luminosity and darkness. "A scintillating and incandescent concavity, of language also. . . . The recasting of their truth-value is already at hand."[23] An enigmatic mirror indeed: its disclosures are imminent, charged with a nonviolent apocalypse. Yet in reflecting its concavity in our own, feminist theologians no longer await any final face-to-face transparency. The reflecting surface evinces more complicated ripples, deeper faces, than

22. There exists a developing and nuanced history of feminist critiques and recuperations of Paul — cf. Bernadette Brooten, Elisabeth Schüssler Fiorenza, Antoinette Wire, and Melanie Johnson-DeBaufre.

23. Irigaray, *Speculum of the Other Woman,* 143.

even Irigaray could sustain. Its truth-value, which has long slipped through queerer mirrors, eluding feminine essentialism, does not cease to emerge. Gender is emerging entangled with sex, class, race, and ecology. Its difference appears as a facet, a face, in the bedazzling cave of language.

Enigmatic Emergences

"Already at hand," the shift, the millennial hope, the *basileia tou theou*, appears at the eschatological rim of vision — yet only among us, here and now, in and through and across our spirited interpersonalities. The incandescent concavity of language suggests the space-time curvature of the spirit, its forcefield of interactions enveloping what we can already say in what we cannot. The spirited interpersonality articulates its humanity in a knowing that remains inimical with certainty.[24] This knowing "in the mirror" displays us always to ourselves — in our ecologies, our genders, our manifold differences. In spirit and in truth, we do know "in part." Partiality is not self-erasure, as though we would no longer face our own image in the mirror, blocking — i.e., perspectivally constructing — everything else. To remain mindful of our own situation, our context, is to keep an eye on ourselves. We will still get in our own way, but at least we will notice that we do. Such critical self-knowing is not Cartesian self-objectification but its alternative, a spirited reflectivity. We might call its embodiment, to honor Paul, the *puzzling person*. Such a person may solve any specific puzzles, but not the puzzle of the mirrored self itself. Each answer deepens the riddle. For in encountering the relations that constitute us, we encounter the unknowable sources of ourselves — and of each other. And we realize that in our realizations we advance our knowledge — to new boundaries of unknowing.

Such a self has learned to live in what Trinh Min Ha calls "critical nonknowingness," or what Butler signifies as our "opacity" to ourselves. We are not therein relieved of responsibility for ourselves and our worlds, but of the burdens of bogus certainty. Instead, the very image of our self that limits our vision, that puzzles language, also displays our limits as *humus*, humble

---

24. For a multi-dimensional conversation on the relation of epistemic uncertainty to the discourse of knowing unknowability, see *Apophatic Bodies: Negative Theology, Incarnation, and Relationality*, ed. Chris Boesel and Catherine Keller (New York: Fordham University Press, 2010). On extending apophatic uncertainty to embodied persons, see also my "The Apophasis of Gender: A Fourfold Un/Saying of Feminist Theology," *Journal of the American Academy of Religion* 76, no. 4 (December 2008).

human earthflesh. But these limits also form the open stitches of our interconnectivity. The differences are the connections: they are the site of those gifts that can be received only in spirited coexistence.

Does the fullness of knowing — "face-to-face" — which is eschatologically promised, however, not after all suggest an ultimate revelation of the "all-powerful intelligibility"? Not in Paul. We "will know as we are known." This eschatology is embedded in a Hebrew epistemology: neither absolute and objective knowledge, nor knowledge dissolved in subjective relativism, but the startling divine entanglement in a *relational knowing*. Here, Emmanuel Levinas's eschatological ethics of the face-to-face may help to reread his fellow Jew's earlier version. "The idea of infinity, the infinitely more contained in the less, is concretely produced in the form of a relation with the face."[25] That relationship is not apocalyptically postponed until the end, but rather eschatologically anticipated now. A present opening takes the place of a future certainty. For a theological anthropology of the emergent person, the face that matters, the face of incarnation, materializes in the face of the neighbor, the lover, the alien — now. But (contra perhaps the tendencies of Levinas and Paul) this face appears with full mortal body attached.[26] Our personhood emerges even as we reflect upon it. It emerges from the chaos of our "extreme sensitivity to initial conditions" into specific complexity. Its vivid person-to-person encounters do not transcend but enrich the earthground of our creaturely coexistence. My face in the mirror comes entangled in others, human and nonhuman — the self that becomes other even as the others become selves. This is always the case. What is not frequent is our patient puzzling, our spirited reflection of this "plurisingularity." The singular plurality of the human cries out — in spirit — for a justice that will handle our risky, crowded interdependencies with care.

As we widen our peripheral vision, we learn and relearn to take responsibility for our own situated perspectives. But as the complexity of our relations grows, so do the challenges to the complex that is the self at any moment. The puzzle of personhood through time is not solved in time. But it may be deepened. Its projections, while inescapable, are also vectors of communication. They run to the infinite — not into a vague obscurity but into an unavoidable mystery that can be justly transcoded as "God." The divine is

---

25. Emmanuel Levinas, *Totality and Infinity: An Essay on Exteriority*, trans. Alphonso Lingis (Pittsburgh: Duquesne University Press, 1994), 196.

26. See Irigaray's response to Levinas: "Lovers' faces live not only in the face but in the whole body"; and Mayra Rivera's reading of both, in *The Touch of Transcendence: A Postcolonial Theology of God* (Louisville: Westminster/John Knox, 2007), 88-89.

thus left room to breathe — in spirit and in truth — perhaps indeed to emerge. Here, when theological language remains faithful to what it cannot ever quite say or know, eschatology does not promise a final certainty but an infinite unfolding. This is the tradition of apophatic theology, the "unsaying" that does not shut down language but recognizes the moving shadow of the unspeakable. It sees it; it refuses to occlude it, amidst the crowd and confusion of the mirror. Here the "brilliant darkness" of the sixth-century Dionysius the Areopagite seems to be mirrored in the dark bedazzlement of Irigaray's "incandescent concavity." But now the infinite of negative theology curves around the shape of a womb, down into the darkness of the deep — a darkness not opposed, as Nicholas of Cusa put it, to the light.

In other words, an "apophatic anthropology" will shadow any counter-reductionist project of emergent personhood.[27] But the unknowable fringes of the person do not melt into a unified totality or an abstract infinity; nor are they direct conduits upward to God. They do tie a person into the entire transpersonal complexity of the creation that gives one birth now and again. So what is unspeakable about you does not silence your spirited difference. You block your own view — of course, your image in the mirror is the enigmatic reflection of your perspective, which you cannot escape but only alter. Your puzzling permits the other to appear in this strange mirror of your own self-awareness, to appear as more, infinitely more, than yourself. But that other will appear at once constrained by your limits and sometimes able, in that moment, that quantum leap of knowing uncertainty, to move them.

The complexity that funds us will not cease to puzzle. For it becomes us. All that forms and deforms us comes entangled in its folds. We do not step outside of but embody its open-ended interpersonality. The person, then, appears — indeed, emerges — as a pneumatic complex. We see the riddles of its language; we speak the image in the mirror. Or we might collapse back into a mere mask of ourselves. As persons, irreducibly unique, overly sensitive, we emerge, if we do, at the edge of a chaos, on the face of a deep, in the word of an enigma.

27. "Like God who is incomprehensible because unlimited, humans might have a nature that imitates God only by not having a clearly delimited nature." Kathryn Tanner, "In the Image of the Invisible," in *Apophatic Bodies*, 121.

The Emergence of Self

James W. Haag, Terrence W. Deacon, and Jay Ogilvy

Starting Small

Rene Descartes' now legendary claim — "I think, therefore I am" — sets the challenge for a theory of self. Who or what is this "I" of which Descartes speaks? This is one of those irritating puzzles that perennially reemerges to challenge philosophers in every age. On the one hand, it is undeniable that the phenomenal experience of being a self is ubiquitous. On the other hand, the nature of this self we experience eludes typical forms of explanation.

In this chapter, we are concerned with the very possibility of explaining the existence of selves. Along this path, our current intellectual ethos typically leads us in one of two directions: either we follow David Hume and disavow any self over and above a set of mental and physical processes (the self is *a useful fiction*),[1] or we emphasize the experience of having a self and assume it to be a brute fact of the world (the self is *a phenomenological experience*). On the first path, which we can identify with eliminativism, the interpretation of our personal experiences as evidence of the existence of a separate subject that has these experiences is called into question. It is an inference from these experiences, not a fact in itself, and so could be mistaken. As

---

1. See D. Hume, *An Enquiry Concerning Human Understanding* (Amherst, NY: Prometheus Books, 1988).

The authors are grateful for extensive editorial feedback from Tyrone Cashman and discussion with Jeremy Sherman, Julie Hui, and Alok Srivastava.

Hume reminds us, there is no self to be found separate from these experiences, and so our projection of an entity that contains or possesses these is unjustified. On the second path, which takes its lead from Descartes and is articulated by various phenomenological paradigms, comes a focus on the first-person experience of having a self. This view maintains that first-person experiences are both ineffable and undeniably present, and this makes them unquestionably real and the ground for all other assessments of reality.

We believe that these two options force us into a false choice. This is because both approaches reflect a failure to adequately deal with issues of teleology. Eliminativist approaches deny the reality of teleological relationships, while phenomenological approaches assume it as an unanalyzable primitive. Selves are ultimately defined by their teleological properties. They are loci of agency directed toward the achievement of ends, they assign value to these consequences, and they must in some sense define an internal/external relationship, implicitly embodying a self-other representation. So the failure to resolve this issue of the origins and efficacy of teleological phenomena guarantees that the concept of self will pose irresolvable dilemmas and consequently remain ambiguous.

So beginning with Descartes' *cogito* is an ill-advised approach. It assumes what we must ultimately attempt to explain. And yet to deny its reality seems absurd. Subjective experience is both too special and too complex to serve as a starting point. It is too special because the sort of reflective cognition that Descartes accepts as undeniable became possible only after billions of years of evolution. It is not some general ubiquitous quality of things, even if it is our only window into the world. It is too complex because it is the product of an immensely subtle physical process taking place in the astronomically complicated and highly structured chemical-electrical living network that is a human brain. We believe that trying to make sense of something so nearly intractable as a first step is pointless. It is almost certainly one of the main reasons that discussions of self and of subjective experience have produced little progress in understanding. Descartes' question needs to be set aside until we can assess the problems of teleology and self at the simplest level possible, where it may be easier to dissect these issues and potentially build toward the question of subjective self incrementally.

So we will not begin by treating human consciousness as the only relevant exemplar, or as the singular appearance of the property of self in the cosmos. This does not, however, force us to find traces of self in stones and drops of water. Selves are associated with life. They are not only limited to organisms like humans with complex brains and subjective experiences, and indeed the self experienced by creatures with complex brains is in many ways derivative (or rather emergent from) the self of organism existence. It is not unusual to identify selves throughout the living world, from simple organisms to complicated humans. While these selves certainly have important qualitative and quantitative distinctions, they also share certain core features of what it means to be a self. We believe that much can be gained by exploring self at this more basic level before trying to tackle the problem in its most complex form.

Recognizing that even organisms as simple as bacteria have properties that qualify them as selves, in at least a minimal sense, suggests that self is not just a subjective issue. This allows us to at least temporarily bracket this troublesome attribute from consideration, while exploring certain more basic attributes. But in setting this issue aside we have not reduced out the most critical issue. Indeed, issues of teleology, agency, and representation, to mention a few, are still in need of explanation, and perhaps unpacking these challenging concepts in simpler contexts can provide clues to the resolution of some of these more complex issues. Nor have we reduced the problem to a merely scientific and physical issue. To the extent that only organisms — and not stones, clouds, streams, or even our most complex computing systems — are selves, it is clear that self is not a simple physical property and not just an issue of complexity alone. It is probably safe to say that four billion years ago there was no such thing as self in any form on this planet, and probably not anywhere in our solar system. Physical systems with this property emerged at some point, roughly coincident with the origin of life. The form of self that characterizes human subjectivity is a recent higher-order augmentation of this first transition, and so while this complex variant includes such radically different emergent properties as subjectivity and interiority, this phenomenal version of self should nevertheless reflect a common logic that traces to the original transition. We may thus gain a useful perspective on this problem, by stepping back from issues of subjectivity to consider the reasons we describe organisms as maintaining, protecting, and reproducing them*selves.*

The plan of this essay, then, is to first address the philosophical issue of teleology, to offer what we believe is an emergence-based account of the physical basis for true teleological relationships, then to apply this to a basic conception of organism self that addresses many of the component attributes we need to explain, and then finally offer a glimpse of how this way of addressing the issue may help resolve some of the more challenging and personal mysteries of being selves.

The Emergence of Teleological Phenomena

We believe that the primary reason that self poses such a philosophical problem is due to a historical failure to account for the existence of end-directed processes associated with self-behavior. Selves act (or behave) according to a purpose. They have functional components that serve ends and contribute to the integrity of the whole. And they are organized in such a way that achieving or failing to achieve these outcomes has a value. Selves are organized around "final causes" in Aristotle's terminology. Unfortunately, Aristotelian final cause has been treated as an illegitimate explanatory principle in philosophical discourse since the seventeenth-century Enlightenment. Philosophers since Spinoza, as we will mention below, have been adamant about the untenable assumptions implicit in teleology. Thus, the useful-fiction self and the phenomenological self correspond, respectively, to two dichotomous stances regarding the reality of teleological processes: (1) one can deny teleology in nature and use mechanistic terminology to describe such things as function or design (teleonomic arguments would be an example[2]), or (2) one can assume teleological processes and fail to provide an explanation for their existence and persistence. Are these the only options?

No. We believe that there is a middle ground: a scientific account that can explain how teleological processes in nature emerge from non-teleological antecedents. Although we agree that a direct mapping of phenomenal experience onto physical process is indeed impossible, this is not because of any deep metaphysical incompatibility, but rather because such an account skips over an essential mediating level of complex causal processes. In quasi-Aristotelian terms, we argue that a type of formal causality mediates the emergence of final causality from efficient causality. Instead of trying to reduce final causality to efficient causality (the Aristotelian term for the sort of causality studied in the physical sciences) or showing them to be ultimately incommensurable, we argue that this mediating domain of causal dynamics provides a necessary bridging domain between them. We argue that this intermediate domain of causal dynamics is constituted by processes that spontaneously generate and propagate form — often described as "self-organizing processes." These play a critical mediating role

---

2. See Ernst Mayr, "Teleological and Teleonomic: A New Analysis," *Boston Studies in the Philosophy of Science* 14 (1974): 91-117; Ernest Nagel, "Teleology Revisited: Goal-Directed Processes in Biology," *Journal of Philosophy* 74 (1977): 261-301.

between mechanistic and teleological accounts of causality, by virtue of the way they account for the spontaneous origin of dynamical constraints.

The concept of constraint, besides being a critical concept for defining information, also provides a negative way of defining order. Unlike concepts of order defined with respect to a model or an ideal form, describing a given phenomenon in terms of the constraints that it exhibits delineates form in terms of features *not* exhibited. Concepts of regularity and symmetry thus can be reframed in terms of the redundancy that is inevitable when other degrees of freedom or possible configurations are not expressed. The importance of constraint production, and by implication order production, is its contribution to the intrinsic asymmetry implicit in the notion of an end or goal, and the distinguishability of self from other, which is not defined by material properties alone.

Not only does the concept of constraint offer a way to define both structural and dynamical "form," it is the critical determinant of the capacity to do physical work, which the complexity scientist Stuart Kauffman usefully describes as the "constrained release of energy." The capacity to do work, in a physical sense, is critical to another intrinsic feature of self: agency.

We will thus identify self with *the intrinsic constraints that organize the physical work (e.g., of the brain or body of an organism) with respect to functional ends and the requirements of a system that confer this capacity.* To summarize the problem of self in Aristotelian terms, then, we will describe the self as a relationship among formal causes constituting the final causal processes that constitute experience. In this respect, self is effectively a system of self-perpetuating formal causes: a dynamical organization that includes the capacity to continuously maintain or reconstitute that form of organization in the face of intrinsic degradation and extrinsic disturbances.

A contemporary version of the Humean self is developed by philosopher Daniel Dennett. In his assessment, Dennett begins at a place not far from our own: "*Now* there are selves. There was a time, thousands (or millions, or billions) of years ago, when there were none — at least none on this planet. So there has to be — as a matter of logic — a true story to be told about *how there came to be* creatures with selves."[3] This approach to establish a sort of "proof of principle" echoes our attempt to find a minimal self. However, there are significant differences in Dennett's efforts as evidenced in his claim that basic biological selves are "just an abstraction, a principle of organization."[4] While

3. Daniel C. Dennett, *Consciousness Explained* (Boston: Back Bay Books, 1991), 413.
4. Dennett, *Consciousness Explained*, 414.

more complex, Dennett's commitment at the organism level to the useful-fiction self is echoed at the human level as well. While human selves are "nonminimal *selfy* selves," they remain a theorist's fiction: "Like the biological self, this psychological or narrative self is yet another abstraction, not a thing in the brain, but still a remarkably robust and almost tangible attractor of properties."[5] Of course, if a self is an abstraction, then there must be an interpreter capable of interpreting these phenomena in this way and if that interpreter must also be a self we are left with a vicious regress. There cannot be such a self. And if my self is no more than the collection of all these experiential episodes, whatever they are, then there is nothing more in addition to them to be a source of causal agency. This move to refer to selves as empty abstractions is rooted in two commitments: (1) any central command center in organisms or a "Cartesian Theater" in the human brain is impossible to locate, and (2) there is no way to account for causal changes enacted by an abstraction. We are in full agreement with the first commitment, but not the second. Despite its apparent problems, a variant of the concept of abstraction may, however, provide a clue to this form of causal influence.

This problem of "abstraction" is deeply rooted in some of the most basic assumptions of Enlightenment metaphysics. In their haste to reject Platonic forms, and to embrace a nominalistic materialism, where general principles and formal properties are only causally relevant when materially embodied in some specific substrate, Enlightenment thinkers inadvertently eliminated the possibility of conceiving of a bridge across this ontological gulf. This goes to the heart of the problem in a number of respects. Not only is self unable to be identified with any distinct physical material or energy; neither is the content of the thoughts or experiences of that self. How can what is not present influence what is?

In answer to this quite general criticism, we take a page from information theory. Information, as Claude Shannon defined it in a classic 1949 monograph on the topic,[6] is not something present; not a signal or sign or magnetic orientation of an iron fragment on a computer storage medium. Information is something removed: uncertainty. He demonstrated that information is measured in terms of how some medium used to convey it is constrained from exhibiting states that it could have been in. For example, when in 1775 Paul Revere saw two lanterns instead of one shining in the Old

---

5. Dennett, *Consciousness Explained*, 414.

6. Claude Shannon and Warren Weaver, *The Mathematical Theory of Communication* (Urbana: University of Illinois Press, 1949).

North Church in Boston, the uncertainty about British troop movements was eliminated. The fifty-fifty uncertainty of the day before was reduced by this either/or signal. No choice, no information. In this way information is a relationship to what is not exhibited. When a search party fans out into the woods to locate a lost child, the people who find nothing are contributing as much as the one discovering the child. Constraint refers to options, or degrees of freedom not realized — something not immediately present and not physically intrinsic. But even so, a constraint is something quite precise.

While treating self as an abstraction in the sense of a description or comparison leads to the conclusion that self cannot be a source of causal power, treating self as the source of constraint on the physical processes generated by an organism has precisely the attributes we require. To perform work and thus alter the physical state of things requires the constrained release of energy. The enclosure of an explosion by the piston and cylinder of an internal combustion engine or the diversion of a stream by a water wheel constrains the release of the energy of these processes so that it can be directed to achieve a desired physical change, like the movement of a vehicle or the grinding of grain. Constraint is, in this respect, exactly the sort of attribute that should be contributed by a self. If self is an abstraction in this sense — a form imposed upon the energetic processes of the world — it can introduce asymmetric causal properties such as are a necessary defining attribute of end-directedness. But we still need to explain the autonomy of this form: how it arises of itself to become a locus of asymmetrical causal influence.

The Persistence of *Telos*

Consider this phrase: "For Nature, like mind, always does whatever it does for the sake of something, which something is its end."[7] For Aristotle, this statement expresses an ostensibly unproblematic view of reality — one shared by many thinkers throughout history. The goal, or *telos,* of an action "causes" the instantiation of that very goal. When a carpenter builds a table, we recognize that the table was first represented in the carpenter's mind as an end. Tables are not the result of random, unintentional human actions. The seventeenth century brought with it a shift in worldviews, a move from the organic image of nature to a mechanistic alternative. The Aristotelian perspective domi-

---

7. Aristotle, *On the Soul,* in *The Complete Works of Aristotle,* 2 vols., ed. Jonathan Barnes (Princeton: Princeton University Press, 1998), Book II, Part 4.

nated thought until the Enlightenment. With the rise of modern science, many of the most influential thinkers of the age questioned its legitimacy (even its possibility). The melding of an atomistic metaphysics with Newtonian science — where causation is thought to occur only as collision-like interactions between very basic particles under determinate laws — collapses Aristotle's causal schema into efficient causation alone. Under this new mechanical philosophy of nature all matter is actual (i.e., nothing is potential), with its only attribute being extension in space. Appealing to the final state of an object is impossible (e.g., the chair from the carpenter's concept). As epitomized by Baruch Spinoza: "All final causes are nothing but human inventions."[8] This new worldview, as originally expressed by thinkers such as Descartes, Hobbes, and Boyle, which solidified the opposition to teleological explanations, continues to reign in philosophy and science to this day.

The future is literally "no thing" — how could it possibly be a cause? If science has drilled home any concept, it is that change is a function of the material and energetic features of the immediate contiguous past. In the case of the carpenter's intention, we recognize that it is a mental representation, and not some as-yet nonexistent future table that is the cause. But this sort of cause is equally troublesome. What sort of thing is this mental representation? It is not the complex neural state that represents it, and yet without this there would neither be a representation nor the organizing process that guides the carpenter's actions. Isn't the content of the carpenter's thought also an abstraction? Indeed, in the same sense that we considered above, we can say that the content is precisely what is not there, that which constrains the neurological activities that are present. And this means that these constraints are what enable this neural activity to do the work necessary to stimulate the controlled release of metabolic energy and coordinate the resulting muscle movements in the pursuit of this imagined end. Of course the self that we have described as a carpenter is not the neural activity and not even this content, but rather what generates this content. What could constitute the autonomy of this process?

In his effort to make philosophy compatible with the science of his day, Immanuel Kant focused considerable attention on the question of how science should regard teleology.[9] Like many others, Kant recognized that the

---

8. Spinoza, *Ethics,* trans. and ed. G. H. R. Parkinson (New York: Oxford University Press, 2000), 108.

9. Immanuel Kant, *Critique of Judgement, Part Two: Critique of Teleological Judgement,* trans. James Creed Meredith (Oxford: Clarendon Press, 1952), 18 (marginal pagination, 371).

mechanical explanations for nature seemed to leave something out. Specifically, he found machine analogies to be unsatisfying when biological phenomena are considered. Although Kant was a committed follower of the Newtonian worldview, he knew that to make sense of a purpose or end, it would have to be a *Naturzweck*, a natural end.

What status must be reached in order for a thing to be a natural end? Provisionally, Kant sets the minimum requirement: "A thing exists as a natural end *if it is both cause and effect of itself.*" To meet this requirement, Kant believes there are two principles that will allow us to establish a distinction between "natural ends" (as in, e.g., a living organism) and artificial "ends" (as in, e.g., a table). In the first principle, a thing is an end if its parts "are only possible by their relation to the whole." So, without the concept of the table in the carpenter's mind (the end), the legs of the table (the parts) are meaningless. Thus: "It is the product . . . of an intelligent cause, distinct from the matter, or parts, of the thing, and one whose causality . . . is determined by its idea of a whole made possible through that idea." However, there is a second principle that moves us beyond the realm of artificial ends to natural ends. Kant writes: "[T]he parts of the thing combine of themselves into the unity of a whole by being reciprocally cause and effect of their form." We have now eliminated the carpenter from the picture and stated that in order for this thing to still qualify as an end, its parts must "combine of themselves." For Kant, this combination is a type of *bildende Kraft* ("formative power"). While the table meets the first requirement of qualifying as an end, it fails as a natural end because one leg of the table does not produce another, nor does one table produce other tables. We agree with Kant that this is key to establishing the existence of a natural *telos*.

Self-Organization and Reciprocity

Kant notes that only a living organism is a natural end because it is the only phenomenon in the world that can be described as a *"self-formed being."* Kant states: "an organized being possesses inherent *formative* power . . . a self-propagating formative power." With Kant's notion of formative power comes the challenge of explaining how an organism is able to form itself. That is, in distinction from a machine in which there is an outside designer setting up the constraints by which the machine's function is determined, we need a way of having a similar process occur intrinsically, without the designer.

Organization is not the norm in the world. As the second law of thermodynamics tells us, left unattended, everything slips into disorder. We intuitively recognize that increasing organization or just preventing spontaneous disorganization from occurring takes outside effort. My desk doesn't organize itself; I must do the work to make the change. However, there are some physical processes that do spontaneously increase in orderliness over time. These are often described as self-organizing processes, though the invocation of this concept of "self" is potentially misleading in this context, since all that is meant is that the increase in order does not trace directly to any extrinsic cause. Examples of self-organizing processes include whirlpools, frost polygons, and snow crystals. These sorts of spontaneously regularized processes all, interestingly, are generated in systems under constant perturbation, but where these disturbances compound with one another in such a way as to increasingly correlate with one another. The process of becoming increasingly regular is a process of generating and spreading constraints. In the development of a whirlpool, for example, what begins as a disrupted flow of water becomes progressively symmetric in organization as different regions of noncircular flow tend to cancel one another's motions and regions of circular flow reinforce one another. What is important about such processes, from our perspective, is that the regularity develops over time as a result of biases of interaction among a vast many components compounding with one another. In this sense, the regularity that emerges is a function of intrinsic factors expressing themselves as a result of constant external disturbance. So long as the disturbing influence continues, the organizing effect is maintained,

It is not, then, a coincidence that the chemical processes that constitute living organisms are for the most part arranged in ways that produce self-organizing effects. The organism is in a constant state of renewal in which new organization is produced (formed and reformed) that allows it to maintain itself. At every moment an organism's material constitution is different, and yet its structural and dynamical organization remains within narrow variational limits, i.e., its organization is highly constrained. So although no new matter or energy is generated, an organism must continually generate and preserve constraints. In this respect it acts on its own behalf. This minimal persistent "self" that is the beneficiary of this formative process is not identified with the material or the energy of this process, but with the preserved organization and its capacity to organize work that preserves this capacity. What persists into future generations is not its "stuff" or its energy, but the constraints that constitute the organization of this stuff.

Consider a very simple organism like a bacterium. All parts of this organism are in a continuous state of turnover as it both responds to and resists thermodynamic dissolution while also compensating for a changing environment on which it depends for raw materials and energy. The molecular "parts" of this organism do not even enjoy any kind of existence *as* parts independent of this organization, since each is dependent on the interactions among others. So although the parts constitute the whole, the whole also generates each part.

This reciprocity is the essence of the special twist on the process of self-organization that constitutes an organism. It is not merely a self-organizing process, but a reflexively organized constellation of self-organizing processes, each of which contributes in some way to the conditions that make the others possible. So although each component self-organizing chemical process of an organism requires a constant introduction of molecules and energy to be able to sustain the generation of regularity, they need each other to generate the constraints that each requires in order to persist. These processes are, as Kant surmised, reciprocally both ends and means for one another, each process generating intrinsic constraints that promote the generation of other intrinsic constraints by other processes. In this way the constraint maintaining-propagating logic of the organism is in a sense a higher-order self-organizing dynamic among component self-organizing processes. It is by virtue of this higher-order stabilization of component constraint-generation processes that the global constraints constituting the reciprocity of the whole are not only preserved, but able to be reproduced. Reproduction is, in effect, simply an expression of this reflexively closed form-producing process. In this respect an organism is a means to produce itself as an end.

With this basic understanding, we are now in a position to ask: In what sense is the organism a self? If the organism is continually reproduced via synergistically interacting self-organizing processes, then defining self in substantive terms is problematic. Many self-organizing processes in living organisms are multiply realizable, that is, not limited to a single type of molecule or even any specific chemical reaction. So any search for the essential "stuff" of the organism will inevitably fail. Moreover, the organism is not even any single type of organized process, since these too can change over the course of a lifetime. Instead, the unit of continuity that is the self of an organism is the synergistic relationship between numerous self-organizing processes that constitutes this tendency to preserve the synergy. It is then this special reflexive organization of form — (constraint-)generating processes that determine the closure to formal influences — that we recognize as a kind of autonomy. Precisely because organized systems spontaneously tend to degrade, a system that actively regenerates and replaces its components and maintains their interrelationships intrinsically has itself as an end. As Kant suggested, when the end is the means and the means is the end a kind of intrinsic teleology comes into being.

Agency

Stuart Kauffman argues that the defining property of an organism is what he calls autonomous agency.[10] With a bit of unpacking, it is possible to see how this characterizes the kind of recursively organized system we have described above. He describes a system with this property as one that is "capable of acting on its own behalf." This phrase of course already presumes something like a self that acts and benefits from this action, but in the context of the description of organism we have been developing this can help us to more precisely analyze these critical features of self: autonomy and agency.

By using the term "act" he does not simply mean to undergo physical change. An act is goal directed, and it must have the capacity to change prevailing conditions. Additionally, it implies the production of work to initiate or counter some change. An action in this sense is therefore what we can describe as teleological work. As we have argued above, the teleological features of an organism emerge from the synergistic reciprocal closure of its component self-organizing processes. This most fundamental reflexive dynamic has an intrinsic directionality and end that both internal thermodynamic tendencies and extrinsic influences run counter to. It is in this respect that the reciprocity of these component self-organizing processes of an organism can be said to be an act with some function or end.

Something that can be a beneficiary of action is implicitly something that is organized to actively avoid being altered or degraded. A relatively inert physical object resists being altered but does not "act" to defend against this perturbation. A dynamical system with a relatively stable organization may also resist being perturbed, as does a whirlpool or a flame, but although it may change in response to disturbance, we would not want to describe this

---

10. Cf. Stuart Kauffman, *At Home in the Universe* (New York: Oxford University Press, 1995).

as acting on behalf of itself. A flame, for example, heats up its substrate to the point where it combusts and liberates more heat to raise the temperature of yet more substrate material. In this respect, a flame behaves in a way that maintains its present dynamical form. It has a self-organizing dynamic. But can we say that the flame behaves in such a way that benefits this form? Eventually, of course, it uses up its substrate and thereby undermines the conditions it depends on. We intuitively do not consider it to be acting or benefiting in any sense because its dynamical organization lacks the reflexivity that we have described for an organism. There is a reciprocity between the action of combustion and the requirements for combustion, but this is with respect to an extrinsic substrate. In other words there is no closure; no circularity of constraints; no means-end reciprocity intrinsic to this dynamic. Although life, like combustion, requires utilization of raw material and energy liberated from an extrinsic substrate in order to be able to continue to liberate more in the future, it is now in service of an intrinsic self-maintenant self-propagating dynamic. The dynamics of the flame lacks autonomous, internally reinforced determination of its form, and for this reason lacks a self and cannot be said to either act or benefit, even though it has a self-promoting dynamic.

The philosopher-cognitive scientist Mark Bickhard distinguishes these two forms of dynamic by describing a flame as self-maintenant and an organism as recursively self-maintenant, in the sense of maintaining its self-maintaining logic.[11] Again, as in the case of the term "self-organization," the use of the reflexive term "self" in these contexts does not smuggle in the concept of self as we are trying to explain it, but it does indicate the common circularity of effect that characterizes both sorts of phenomena. What we have shown is that a self, as we have applied it to the dynamics of organisms in general, is organized in a doubly reflexive way: in other words, reflexively organized reflexivity, and recursive recursivity of causality.

Such a system exhibits the property of autonomous agency because it does work to counter intrinsic and extrinsic influences that tend to be disruptive of this autonomy. Its capacity to be a locus of work, and therefore agency, derives from two features of this organization: the capacity to assimilate materials and energy from the surroundings and incorporate them into its reciprocal dynamics, and the capacity to generate and maintain dynami-

---

11. M. H. Bickhard, "Process and Emergence: Normative Function and Representation," in *Process Theories: Cross-Disciplinary Studies in Dynamic Categories*, ed. J. Seibt (Dordrecht: Kluwer Academic, 2003), 121-55.

cal constraints. As noted above, we can describe work as the constrained release of energy. This implies that what specifies different forms of work is
not the energy but rather the constraints that channel and organize its ex-
penditure. The reciprocity of the constraints generated by the component
self-organizing processes of an organism is in this respect the basis of its autonomy and its agency. By intrinsically generating, maintaining, and reproducing constraints on the flow of material and energy through it, an organism creates the capacity to originate specific forms of work that reflexively
reinforce this capacity.

Unpacking the assumption of autonomous agency in this way can help
to cast new light on one of the more troubling conundrums of metaphysical
philosophy: the problem of free will. Historically this riddle has been posed
in terms of a necessary contradiction between the notions of physical determinism and human agency. But as we have defined agency here it is not
merely causal determination, but rather a specific end-directed form of
work. An autonomous self, whether in the form of a bacterium or a reasoning human, is the locus of highly convoluted recursive processes that generate specific forms of work that are organized with respect to some aspect of
this autonomous circular dynamics and contrary to some pervasive condition or tendency extrinsic to this autonomous dynamics. This is in no sense
contrary to the deterministic cause-and effect-logic of the physical sciences,
but is instead only contrary to some specific local tendency, such as thermodynamic decay. Such tendencies are not deterministic in any strong sense.
The Second Law of Thermodynamics, for example, is a tendency — even if it
is an astronomically probable tendency — and at least locally it can be countered. Free will can in this respect be recast in terms of a minimally constrained capacity to initiate work aimed at modifying some otherwise prevailing tendency. Thus reduced to its essential features, it can be seen to be
entirely homologous with the concept of autonomous agency. As both autonomy and the flexibility to produce more diverse forms of work have increased over the course of biological evolution, so has the relative freedom
to interfere with the prevailing conditions of the world in ways that trace
their origin to intrinsically generated ends.

From Autonomous Agency to Subjectivity

We have argued above that the core property that links the selves of even the
simplest life forms with that seemingly ineffable property that characterizes

the human experience of self is a special form of dynamical organization: a doubly reflexive form-generating dynamics. Literally, this is the analogue of self-reference, a logical type violation, and it is not surprising that this feature is even the defining characteristic of reflexive reference in language. Articulating exactly how and why this feature is important for the constitution of a minimal physical self, such as an organism, has helped to unpack many of the assumptions that are implicit in all forms of self — like teleology, autonomy, and agency. It has not, however, provided an account of that most distinctive human attribute of self: its subjective experiential component. Although some might be tempted to ascribe a form of subjectivity to even simple organisms lacking nervous systems, even if this were so (which we doubt), it would only posit the existence of this property by fiat, and would do nothing to explain what difference having a brain contributes. While we argue that there is a common dynamical logic that is fundamental to all phenomena that we consider as having selves, this does not take into account the nested nature of neural dynamics within organism dynamics, and the additional complication that this complex, multilevel, multiply reflexive dynamic contributes. Thus, while we have argued that even the simplest bacterium can be said to be organized as a self, and exemplifies the emergence of teleological properties and autonomous agency, it is likely that the subjectivity we probably share with other species with complex brains involves higher-order properties emergent from these higher-order reflexive dynamics.

The value of starting small and simple in this analysis is that it has identified what appear to be very general organizational principles that should be relevant to self at whatever level and in whatever form it appears. Before we can apply these principles analogously to the case of human subjective experience and agency, it is necessary to consider what this nested logic of brains within bodies adds to the problem. The relevance of the sort of selfhood that characterizes living organisms, in general, to that more complex form of self that constitutes human subjective experience is made clear by the fact that although the unconsciousness of anesthesia can temporarily interrupt this experience, it can persist across such gaps, so long as the body remains alive and the brain is largely undamaged. Our worries about death, and our comparative unconcern with the state of unconsciousness, is clear evidence that we intuitively judge the self of Descartes' *cogito* to be subordinate to the self of life in general.

Rather than relying on introspection to provide us with a window on selfhood, agency, or subjectivity, we've chosen to construct an account of self that is based on simpler selves than those of humans. Now that we have that account in hand, we need to consider how the logic of this lower-order form of self might point the way toward features of subjectivity and the sense of interiority that is so distinctive of human consciousness.

Given the importance of the doubly reflexive form of dynamics that constitutes organism self, it seems reasonable to expect that something of this logic — instantiated at the higher level that brains provide — is relevant to the account of subjective self. With the evolution of ever more complex forms of organisms the recursive complexity of self has no doubt also grown, but the evolution of brains contributes more than merely a complexification of internal dynamics and of the work that an organism can initiate. It also provides a means to simulate these processes, in service of increasing their effectiveness and flexibility. Since the organism itself, its internal dynamics and its external relations, is also simulated by brains, additional logical-type violating loops of dynamics can come into play. On top of this, the capacity for recursive self-reflection aided by symbolic referential processes that have become uniquely available to humans introduces an even yet more convoluted possibility for reflexive causal relationships. These evolutionary innovations are distinctive rungs on the evolutionary ladder, where the discontinuous emergence of new levels of self punctuates the spectrum connecting humans to the simplest organisms. Rather than a continuous grayscale of degrees of self, the evolution of brains and of symbolic communication clearly marks transitions to higher-order forms of self-dynamics whose constituents are the self-properties of lower levels. So before we turn to the need for any metaphysical magic, it is worth attempting to understand what these further levels of reflexive dynamics might contribute.

The evolutionary framework suggests one further complication. The form of organization we have described as organism self has complexified and differentiated over evolutionary time. The evolutionary appearance of organisms with brains was, however, a special jump in levels, and ushered in an entirely novel emergent realm of self-dynamics. This is an important model to also keep in mind in our effort to explain subjective self. Since the function of a brain is in one sense to generate complex neural activity requisite to the complexity of a changing and unpredictable environment and the challenges it poses to the organism, the self-dynamics it produces is likely to be as undifferentiated as the dynamics of metabolic maintenance at some times and as differentiated as the complex stimuli and possible interactions required to engage in a complex interaction with other individuals with minds of their own in contexts that are unfamiliar. Indeed, moment-to-moment the level of differentiation of this dynamical synergy must rapidly change, developing from undifferentiated to highly differentiated forms of self in response to changing needs and extrinsic conditions.

The development of one's personal experience of self also has emerged in a process of differentiation. The self that is my entire organism did not just pop into the world fully formed. It began as a minimal undifferentiated zygote, a single cell that multiplied and gave rise to a collection of cells/selves that by interacting progressively differentiated into an embryo, a fetus, an infant, a child, and eventually an adult organism. Indeed, it is difficult to imagine subjective self just popping into existence fully differentiated. By the very nature of its thoroughly integrated and hierarchically organized form it would seem to demand a bottom-up differentiation in order to produce it. But if so, then it also suggests that the human subjective sense of self as well is only the final phase in the moment-to-moment differentiation from lower-level less-differentiated forms of self-dynamics.

Brains are, after all, organs that evolved to support whole organism functions critical to persistence and reproduction. They are not arbitrary general-purpose information-processing devices. Everything about them grows out of and is organized to work in service of the organism. Animal physiology is organized around the maintenance of certain core organism self-functions on which all else depends. Critical variables, such as constant oxygenation, elimination of waste products, availability of nutrients, maintenance of body temperature within a certain range, and so forth, all must be maintained or no other processes are possible. Sensory specializations, motor capabilities, basic drives, learning biases, emotional response patterns, and even rational reflection are ultimately organized with respect to these critical core variables. This suggests that the core undifferentiated form of subjective experience, from which all the more differentiated forms of experience emerge, is organized as are these core organism functions, and serves as a kind of seed from which complex forms of subjectivity differentiate.

So how might these special properties help explain why being an organism with a complex brain includes a form of reflexivity with a mode of reflexive organization that is also reflexively organized with respect to itself? Or to ask this in other terms, what is this locus that "feels" and from which agency not only emerges but to which it is also represented? Again we take our hint from the reflexive dynamical organization that constitutes even the simplest form of self. Since the teleology that distinguishes the agency of organisms from mere work is a product of the closed reciprocity of spontaneous form-generating processes, it is this higher-order dynamic that constitutes the self of the organism. Approaching the self-dynamics of brains from the same framework, we would have to say that there must be an analogous closure of dynamical activity with respect to which subjective agency emerges. Without such an origin, the agency of neural processes would inherit its teleological character only from organism self, but if in addition there exists an analogous reciprocal reflexive dynamics generated within the circuitry of the brain itself, there will also be a corresponding neurological source of this teleological orientation, only minimally subordinate to the teleology of the organism. The suggestion is that the subjective self is to be identified with this locus of neurological *telos,* a self-reinforcing reflexive process that serves as a reference dynamic against which all other dynamical tendencies and influences are contrasted as nonself. Though the minimal form of this dynamic may be as undifferentiated as the reciprocally organized metabolic processes that it depends on, its dynamically facile substrate also predisposes it to differentiate with respect to a complex environment of sensory "perturbations," present and remembered, as well as changing metabolic states.

The supra-individual symbolic tools made available to human brains add yet a further reflexive loop with respect to which teleological relationships can emerge and higher forms of agency can be generated. Because we humans can represent our worlds using symbols, which depend on a more abstract logical reciprocity and codetermination, we are capable of forms of work — e.g., the construction of narratives, the creation of obligations, obedience to principles, and so forth — not available to simpler forms of life. Thus it is not unusual for someone to identify with a self-narrative, or "higher purpose," and allow this to become a source of agency. Indeed, we might be tempted to ascribe the agency of supra-human selves like Jehovah or Allah to such a locus of teleology.

In conclusion, we have only briefly gestured toward a new way of understanding subjective self, but the picture of human "selfiness" that emerges from this account is neither Humean nor phenomenological. There is no ghost in the organic machine of the body, because the body is organized as a self of a lower order. There is no inner intender as witness to a Cartesian theater because the locus of perspective is a circular dynamic where ends and means, observing and observed, are incessantly transformed from one to the other. Instead, the logic of the mutual reciprocity of constraints creates a relational ontology with respect to which autonomy and agency, and their implicit teleology, can be given a concrete account.

Human subjectivity, when viewed through the perspective of this circular logic of form-generation, is not so much a "hard problem" in the sense of demanding highly sophisticated analytic and scientific tools to solve. It is rather a highly counterintuitive problem, because it requires that we abandon our search for a substantial self in favor of a self that is constituted by constraints, and constraints are not something present, but the boundary conditions determining what is likely. The complex and convoluted dynamical processes we believe to be the defining features of self at any given level are reciprocal limitations on dynamics, not the processes themselves nor the materials and energy that are their instantiation. So ultimately, this view of self shows it to be as nonmaterial as Descartes might have imagined and yet as physical and extended as the hole in the hub of a wheel, without which it would just be a useless disk.

Neurononsense and the Soul

Roger Scruton

We can conclude, from the most everyday observations, that the brain is more important than any other part of the animal organism in the production of mental states, and that it is — in that minimal sense — the "seat" of consciousness. Damage to the brain disrupts our mental processes; specific parts of the brain seem connected to specific kinds of thought, emotion, sensation, or desire; and the nervous system, to which we owe movement, perception, sensation, and bodily awareness, is a tangled mass of pathways, all of which end in the brain. This much was obvious to Hippocrates; and even Descartes, whose theory of the soul as an immaterial substance seems to locate the "seat of consciousness" outside the body altogether, acknowledged the special causal role of the brain in tying mind to body.

Paul Broca's identification of the third frontal lobe ("Broca's area") as governing the use of spoken language occurred in 1861, and set neurological research on a new path. Alexander Luria's studies of the effects of brain damage in soldiers during World War II confirmed the view that distinct mental functions are, with important reservations, assigned to distinct parts of the brain. The neural pathways through which information is passed from the eye to the occipital lobe have been identified by B. G. Cragg, M. Mishkin, and others in research published between 1969 and 1983. And recent advances in mapping brain functions through Magnetic Resonance Imaging have given rise to the view that we are getting constantly closer to explaining consciousness, to locating it as a physical process, and to removing the final mystery from the human condition, which is the mystery of the self.[1] Indeed, the conviction has arisen, not in brain science only, but in many fields of study previously conceived as "humanities," that neurobiology is destined to replace all the many vague studies of the human mind and its cultural by-products with precise neurological sciences, which will tell us how the brain produces moral judgments, social inclinations, aesthetic experiences, religious ecstasies, and emotional attachments — all without reference to anything that could conceivably deserve the name of "soul."

The trend was established in philosophy by Paul Churchland, with *Scientific Realism and the Plasticity of Mind,* published in 1979. Churchland argued that concepts such as that of the soul belong to a flawed "folk psychology," which will eventually be replaced by a cognitive neuroscience that makes mention only of biological processes and the computations that are carried out by them. Churchland's wife Patricia placed this idea at the center of the philosophy of mind with her 1986 book titled *Neurophilosophy,* a term that caught on and heralded the steady invasion of the humanities by the "neuro" virus. I have come across neuroethics,[2] neuroaesthetics[3] — even neuro-art history[4] — all enthusiastically proposed as the breakthroughs for which the "human sciences" have been waiting. Dartmouth College now has a McArthur Center for Law and Neuroscience, devoted to studying legal reasoning as a neurological process.[5] No doubt we will soon be seeing chairs in neurotheology and neuromusicology, not to speak of neurocookery, neurofootball, and (why not?) neuroalchemy too.

Yet, when you look more closely at these new sciences, you find that they have a tendency to divide neatly into two parts. On the one hand there is an analysis of some feature of our mental or social life — be it moral judgment, aesthetic experience, legal order, or religious faith — and an attempt to show its importance and the principles of its organization.

1. See, for example, Christof Koch, *The Quest for Consciousness: A Neurobiological Approach* (Englewood, CO: Roberts & Co., 2004).

2. There are 132,000 entries under this heading on Google, and countless institutes and branches of bioethics departments devoted to the topic.

3. There is a *Journal of Neuro-Aesthetic Theory,* now in its fourth issue, and an Institute of Neuroaesthetics at University College London, headed by Semir Zeki.

4. Discipline created by John Onians of the University of East Anglia, in *Neuroarthistory: From Aristotle and Pliny to Baxandall and Zeki* (New Haven and London: Yale University Press, 2008).

5. A major influence here being Michael Gazzaniga, whose book *The Ethical Brain* (Chicago: University of Chicago Press, 2005) summarizes his contribution to this area of research.

On the other hand, there is a set of fMRI readings, with interesting data concerning the areas of the brain that are activated in this or that kind of psychological state. Every now and then there is a shriek of "Eureka!" when it is shown that the very same area of the brain is active when, for example, a face is seen and when a face is imagined. But since there was no coherent description of the question to which this datum is supposed to suggest an answer, the cry dwindles quickly into silence. All that is left at the end of the venture into brain anatomy is a venture into brain anatomy, together with a bag of neurononsense, as I should like to describe it: a translation into the jargon of neuroscience of some highly contentious philosophical arguments. And I think there is a good reason why things turn out this way, and that it is worth rehearsing them, since they concern two features of the human condition that seem to stand in the way of any biological account of human nature. These two features are consciousness and first-person awareness. The first is a feature that we share with animals; the second is a feature that distinguishes us from everything else in nature.

There is a sense in which consciousness is more familiar to us than any other feature of our world, since it is the route by which anything at all becomes familiar. But this is what makes consciousness so hard to pinpoint. It is a way of knowing, but never the thing that is known. Look for it wherever you like; you encounter only its objects — a face, a dream, a memory, a color, a pain, a melody, a problem — but nowhere the consciousness that shines on them. Trying to grasp it is like trying to observe your own observing, as though you were to look with your own eyes at your own eyes without using a mirror. Colin McGinn has even argued that humans lack the cognitive capacities that will enable them to explain what he calls the "mystery" of consciousness — to understand, as he eloquently puts it, how "evolution converted the water of biological tissue into the wine of consciousness."[6] Such an inability to explain consciousness would itself explain why we produce only pseudo-explanations. We think in terms of the soul, the mind, the self, the "subject of consciousness," the inner entity that thinks and sees and feels and that is the real me inside. But, as is obvious, these traditional "solutions" merely duplicate the problem. We cast no light on the consciousness of a human being simply by redescribing it as the consciousness of some inner homunculus — be it a soul, a mind, or a self. On the contrary, by placing that

---

6. Colin McGinn, *The Mysterious Flame: Conscious Minds in a Material World* (New York: Basic Books, 2000), 13.

homunculus in some private, inaccessible, and possibly immaterial realm, we merely compound the mystery.

However, as Max Bennett and Peter Hacker have argued, this homunculus fallacy keeps coming back in another form.[7] Of course, the inner homunculus is no longer a Cartesian soul: as often as not it is the brain itself, which is described as "processing information," "mapping the world," "constructing a picture" of reality, and so on — all expressions that we understand, only because they describe conscious processes with which we are familiar. To describe the resulting "science" as an *explanation* of consciousness, when it merely reads back into the explanation the feature that needs to be explained, is not just unjustified — it is profoundly misleading, in creating the impression that consciousness is a feature of the *brain,* and not of the person whose brain it is. Hence Bennett and Hacker's description of this as the "mereological" fallacy — that is, the fallacy of explaining a property of a thing by attributing that very same property to one of its parts.

There is a view of the human condition that has increasingly many adherents among analytical philosophers, which goes something like this. We are organisms, situated in a world that acts on us and on which we act. Our brains have evolved to deal with the situations that we standardly confront, the most important and alarming of which are our encounters with our fellow human beings and other animals. In order to deal with these encounters we have developed a kind of proto-science of the mind, which Paul Churchland, Steven Stich, Daniel C. Dennett, and others call "folk psychology." This proto-science deploys concepts like belief and desire in order to provide rough-and-ready explanations of what others are up to. Belief and desire are two among many "intentional" states — states founded on representations that may or may not be true pictures of reality. Hence folk psychology is everywhere penetrated by the ideas of truth and falsehood, and by the reference to "intentional objects" — objects that may or may not exist, and which may or may not be as they are thought to be. Such objects have no place in real science, since they are not part of the material world, being representations in the mind of the observer. A real science of the mind would get rid of them, and therefore get rid of all those proto-scientific explanations of behavior in terms of belief and desire, which stand in the way of a real understanding of how the brain works. The work of philosophy is to prepare the way for this real science of the mind, and philosophers should be

7. Max Bennett and Peter Hacker, *The Philosophical Foundations of Neuroscience* (Oxford: Oxford University Press, 2003).

thinking about how to *replace* intentional concepts, not how to understand them.

That is a bit of a caricature, of course, and there is a kind of intermediate position in the writings of Daniel Dennett, who sees intentionality as a natural feature of information-processing systems — a feature that will survive translation into the terms of an adequate cognitive science.[8] But it seems to me that the idea of "folk psychology" as a proto-science, and one that could be replaced by a sophisticated theory of the nervous system, deeply misrepresents the way in which people relate to their environment and to each other. In his later writings Husserl introduced the concept of the *Lebenswelt* — the "life-world" — to denote the world in its *presented aspect,* the world as we perceive it, conceptualize it, and reflect on it in our ordinary encounters.[9] The world thus represented may not coincide with the world as science describes it. For it employs concepts that do not, and perhaps could not, feature in a scientific theory — a theory designed to *explain* the world, rather than to live in it. Science, as analytical philosophers often point out, deploys concepts of "natural kinds," concepts that "divide nature at the joints," and which can therefore feature in scientific laws, since they classify together those things that have a common explanation. (Examples: water, tiger, human being.) Ordinary human understanding deploys concepts of functional, artificial, and moral kinds, concepts that assemble objects according to our interests and not according to their causes. (Examples: table, ornament, person.) Note that in those examples "human being" occurs in the first list, "person" in the second. This is the root of the problem of personal identity.

The thesis that I touched on above holds that "folk psychology" is a kind of stopgap: an interim shot at science, which will be replaced as our knowledge increases. But this assumes two things: first, that our everyday classifications of mental phenomena deliver a *theory* of behavior; and second, that they are dispensable, so that we could replace them and still be familiar with the world in which we live. Neither of those assumptions is true. Of course, we are sometimes interested in explaining a person's behavior, and then, as like as not, we use concepts of belief and desire that the scientifically minded might hope to replace with something more rooted in neurological theory.

But could we replace such concepts and leave our world unchanged?

---

8. See Dennett's classic treatment in "Intentional Systems," in *Brainstorms* (Cambridge, MA: MIT Press, 1981).

9. See especially Edmund Husserl, *The Crisis of European Sciences and Transcendental Philosophy,* trans. D. Carr (Evanston, IL: Northwestern University Press, 1970).

This question leads us directly to the second feature of the human condition that stands in the way of a science of the mind: the feature of first-person awareness. Suppose I wonder why you have been avoiding me. I ask you a direct question, and you accuse me of betraying your confidences to a rival. I deny the charge, knowing it to be false, and ask you why you think it to be true. You recount the evidence and I refute it; your hostility disappears and we agree to work together to limit the damage. That kind of dialogue occurs all the time, and it is the way in which rational beings establish and build on their relations. It presupposes at every point that you and I both understand and make use of concepts like belief and desire. And it assumes that we each have *first-person knowledge* of our beliefs and desires — that we don't have to find out what they are but can summon them immediately and without evidence in response to the questions "why?" and "what?" Use of the first-person pronoun confers the ability to describe immediately, on no basis, and with a far-reaching immunity to certain kinds of error, the contents of one's present mental states. But this, as Wittgenstein has argued, is part of the deep grammar of the first-person case. Replace intentional concepts with the terms of neurological science, and first-person knowledge would vanish. We would all be equally hampered by the need to find out what was going on in our brains, and all such dialogue would disappear. With it would disappear the possibility of interpersonal relations, and with interpersonal relations would disappear language and all that has been built on it. In short, the neuroscience would be left with nothing of interest to explain. That is just one thought among many tending to the conclusion that our way of representing the *Lebenswelt* is not replaceable by the theory that explains it. Our world is a world of *appearances,* ordered by concepts that are rooted in dialogue, and therefore in the first-person perspective. But that perspective will not feature in the data of any science. There is no room in causal theories for terms like "I" and "thou," and it is precisely this that gives rise to the revulsion that we feel — or at any rate, ought to feel — when a philosopher "explains" human love, desire, longing, grief, and resentment in terms like these:

> The brains of social animals are wired to feel pleasure in the exercise of social dispositions such as grooming and cooperation, and to feel pain when shunned, scolded, or excluded. Neurochemicals such as vasopressin and oxytocin mediate pair-bonding, parent-offspring bonding, and probably also bonding to kith and kin.[10]

10. Patricia Churchland, "Human Dignity from a Neurophilosophical Perspective," in

Well might we protest that the *brains* of social animals feel neither pleasure nor pain; well might we protest at the reduction of "I-thou" relationships to forms of bonding that require neither first-person awareness nor even consciousness for their achievement. The author's style makes clear that all such protests are futile, since they belong to a language that she has put aside. All the same, if this is what it is to replace "folk psychology" by "neuroscience," one can only protest that neuroscience purchases its explanations at the cost of the facts.

Here it is useful to contrast two modes of understanding: science, which aims to explain appearances, and "intentional understanding," which aims to interpret them — i.e., to describe, criticize, and justify the human world.[11] Intentional understanding studies the world in terms of the concepts through which we experience and act on it — the concepts that define the intentional objects of our states of mind. The Kantian philosopher Wilhelm Dilthey coined the term *Verstehen* to refer to this kind of understanding — and the term has entered sociological usage through the writings of Max Weber. Intentional understanding engages directly with the world as we perceive it; but its aim is to incorporate the world as perceived into our plans and relations. It displays the world, to use Heidegger's idiom, as "ready to hand."

The concepts of our intentional understanding are not easy to analyze. They are embedded in feeling and activity, and are difficult to separate from the context of their use. Some of them — like the concept of the self — refer to features of the *Lebenswelt* that could not appear in a science of the mind, because they are essentially *perspectival*, tied to the way in which the world is represented, in the minds of creatures like us. Nevertheless, there are genuine, objective truths about the *Lebenswelt*, which we discover through philosophical analysis. Some call this analysis "phenomenology," rightly seeing the connection with first-person awareness, and the centrality of that awareness in building our shared social world. Others refer to the "analysis of concepts," often with little idea how they might explain what a concept is, and how the analysis of concepts differs from the investigation of generalities. In this area, however, where we are studying the structure of appearance, the

---

Human Dignity and Bioethics, essays commissioned by the President's Council on Bioethics, Washington, DC, 2008, 103.

11. Dennett writes in this connection of the "intentional stance" that he thinks may be adapted even to things like thermostats. By "intentional understanding," by contrast, I mean the kind of understanding that can form the basis of reciprocal exchanges between creatures with a first-person point of view.

phenomenological and analytical schools point to the same body of knowledge. The attempt to deepen our intentional understanding involves exploring the fabric of appearances, through which we understand the world as a sphere of action and an object of personal response.

People can be conceptualized in two ways, as organisms and as agents. The first way employs the concept "human being" (a natural kind); it divides our actions at the joints of explanation, and derives our behavior from a biological science of man. The second way employs the concept "person," which is not the concept of a natural kind, but *sui generis*. Through this concept, and the associated notions of freedom, responsibility, reason for action, right, duty, justice, and so on, we gain the description under which a human being is seen, by those who respond to him or her as a person. This "two conceptual-schemes" approach originates in Spinoza, but the profound insight on which it draws is that of Kant, in the Antinomies chapter of the first *Critique,* and in the second *Critique,* where he distinguishes the empirical self — part of the natural order and known as ordinary phenomenal objects are known, through the concepts of substance, cause, and so on — from the noumenal self, known in another way, through practical reason and the law of freedom.

Kant's way of putting the point often seems to lead to an ontological bifurcation, between noumenal and empirical self, the one outside nature, the other a part of it. Such a view creates far more problems than it solves; I therefore propose to distinguish *only* the two conceptual schemes, and the contrasting responses that are built upon them. In this I will be following a hint given by Peter Strawson, in his celebrated paper "Freedom and Resentment."[12]

In the normal case our response to another person is locked into the web of interpersonal dialogue and emotion. Each of us demands justification of the other, as in my example, and the resulting give-and-take of reasons is the root of social harmony. The concepts and conceptions that permit this are not just useful to us; they are indispensable. Without them we would not be persons at all, since we become persons precisely by learning the art of interpersonal dialogue. Anybody who has brought up a child knows this. Moreover, we should not assume that self-consciousness is a faculty that comes into existence simply as the organism develops. It is bestowed on us by language, by dialogue, and by the sense of ourselves as other than others and also other like them. In *The Phenomenology of Spirit* Hegel tells many interesting parables, one purpose of which is to show that the self

12. P. F. Strawson, *Freedom and Resentment and Other Essays* (London: Methuen, 1974).

is not an entity locked somewhere within the human envelope, but a by-product of social processes — of conflict, resolution, claim- and reason-giving — through which we come to be fully aware of our own agency, and able to take responsibility for our conduct in a society of moral equals. The logical status of Hegel's parables will always be questionable; but the truth that motivates them is indubitable: there is no such thing as the self — only the self-knowledge, accountability, and first-person perspective of persons, who obtain those attributes through their interaction with their kind. Having obtained them, however, they live in another world — a world in which self-awareness and reason-giving are the central facts.

Neurononsense arises when states of the whole person — in particular those mental states that belong within the sphere of self-consciousness, and which are bound up with the self-reference of the subject — are either attributed to some part of the person, such as the prefrontal cortex, or reduced to some process in the nervous system described without reference to the personal and interpersonal context. I earlier gave an example from Patricia Churchland. A more influential instance is Benjamin Libet's "proof" that actions we experience as voluntary are in fact "initiated" by brain events occurring a short while before we have the "feeling" of wanting, intending, or deciding on them.[13] The brain "decides" to do x, and the conscious mind records this decision some time later. The reams of neurobabble that this simple experiment has produced have been matched in other areas: in the evolutionary psychology of altruism, for example. But the fallacies on which the conclusion rests — the fallacies of assuming that an event in a *brain* is identical with a decision of a *person,* that an action is voluntary if and only if preceded by a mental episode of the right kind, that intentions and volitions are "felt" episodes of a subject that can be precisely dated in time — can be fully appreciated only when set in the context of the free-will debate, and the hasty thought that Libet's experiment in some way casts light on it. This illustrates a general principle: neurononsense gains a foothold when spoken in the vicinity of a real philosophical problem. Hence the discussion of aesthetic judgment is now invaded by the question of whether the appreciation of beauty is "hard-wired" in the human cortex, and if so, how you would design experiments to prove it.[14]

---

13. Benjamin Libet, "Unconscious Cerebral Initiative and the Role of Conscious Will in Voluntary Action," *The Behavioural and Brain Sciences* 8 (1985): 529-66.

14. See, for example, Denis Dutton, *The Art Instinct: Beauty, Pleasure, and Human Evolution* (London: Bloomsbury, 2009).

All such claims raise the question how the results of neuroscience might be integrated into a coherent conception of the human person — and one that would be true to our first-person experience as well as foundational to a real psychology. As things stand we seem to be faced with two incommensurate languages, presenting two distinct ontologies of the human condition, one about brains and bodily behavior, the other about people and their acts. Daniel Dennett believes that the "intentional stance" he has famously defended as a natural and explanatory response to information-processing systems, can be extended to brains and their parts, and that neuroscience is making headway precisely by adapting concepts from folk psychology. In this way, he believes, the "mereological fallacy" can be by-passed, and neuroscience used to develop genuine explanations of mental processes.[15] However, conspicuously absent from Dennett's treatment is any study of self-attribution and the first-person case, or a recognition of the difference that this makes to our ways of understanding and interacting with each other.

Traditional religious ways of thinking fudged the relation between the human animal and the human person through the doctrine of the soul. The problem with that doctrine is not that there is no such thing as a soul, but that we don't know what *kind* of thing it is — in particular to what ontological category it should be assigned. Descartes' view that the soul is a substance — in other words, an individual, subject of change, bearer of properties, surviving the body and so on — is untenable for the same reason that neurononsense is untenable, namely, that it locates mental processes elsewhere than in the thing that possesses them. That thing is the conscious, and self-conscious, person. Aristotle's rival view that the soul is related to the body as *form* to *matter* suggests that the soul is something like an organization and activity of the complete human being. This is perhaps nearer to the truth. Unfortunately, Aristotle explains the matter/form relation only through distant analogies — the relation between the bronze of a statue and the shape imposed on it, and that between the pupil of the eye and eyesight.[16] Aquinas adopted Aristotle's idea, while acknowledging the very real difficulties it places in the way of the Christian worldview, and while failing to explain Aristotle's analogies.

Aquinas is interesting for many reasons, however, and not least for his

15. Daniel Dennett, "Philosophy as Naïve Anthropology" in *Neuroscience and Philosophy: Brain, Mind and Language*, ed. Daniel Robinson (New York: Columbia University Press, 2008) — a fairly contemptuous response to the book by Max Bennett and Peter Hacker.

16. *De anima.* For some of the difficulties, see Bernard Williams, "Hylomorphism," in *Oxford Studies in Ancient Philosophy*, ed. M. J. Woods (Oxford: Clarendon Press, 1983-), vol. 4.

attempt to combine the Aristotelian theory of the soul as the "form" of the human being with the Roman-law theory of the human being as a person, as adopted by Boethius, who defined the person as an individual substance of a rational nature.[17] So we have a collection of obscure metaphysical ideas — form, individual, person, substance — from which to construct a theory of the rational agent. As is well known, Aquinas believed, on Aristotelian grounds, that the body is necessary to the individuation of the human being, and that therefore the resurrection of the body is an integral part of the promise of immortality. Between death and that moment of resurrection, however, there is a period of disembodied existence, in which the soul subsists as form alone — like a Platonic Idea. Aquinas was, I think, unsatisfied with this solution, which he fudges in the *Summa* and does not seem to return to elsewhere. Later thinkers followed Descartes, in identifying the soul as a mysterious inner something quite independent of the body, which survives the destruction of the body without any change to its essential nature. The science of neurophysiology, the behavioral sciences, and all other studies of the human body can tell us nothing about the Cartesian ego, which lies forever concealed from public observation, and the frequent result of this dualistic thinking is a radical skepticism: Why postulate the existence of this mysterious "inner" thing, when no science can ever make contact with it?

Descartes' theory of the soul-substance begins from the premise of self-consciousness, and it leads Descartes to the view that animals, since they are not self-conscious, do not have a soul, and are really automata. Aquinas, whose word for soul is the Latin *anima*, is inevitably led to see the soul from outside, as the thing that *animates* the body, the principle of life and movement, as was *psyche* for the Greeks. (For Aristotle, even a plant has a *psyche*.) The New Testament sometimes uses the old Greek term, but St. Paul, in his reflections on the relation between flesh and spirit, always uses the word *pneuma*, or "wind," as in Romans 8, no doubt because this is the Greek equivalent of the Hebrew *ruach*, used frequently in this connection in the Hebrew Bible. This word, too, has the implication that the soul is the principle of *movement* — that which sets the body in motion and directs it in its earthly tasks.

The Qur'an, by contrast, uses the ordinary Arabic word for self, which is *nafs* — a word that often functions simply as the reflexive pronoun. "The house itself" would be expressed as *al-bait nafsuha*, but without implying that the house has a *nafs*, or soul. The promise of immortality in the Qur'an

---

17. Boethius, *De duabis naturae*; Aquinas, *Summa Theologiae*, 1, 29.

is notoriously sensual and naïve; but it is an immortality promised to the *self,* the *I,* the *center of consciousness,* which appears in paradise or hell with its body intact — as though death had not occurred. The same emphasis on the inner reality of the human person permeates the Upanishads, and indeed is contained in the word normally used in those works for the soul, which is *atman.* The original meaning of this word was "breath," echoing *ruach* and *pneuma,* and coming down to us as German *Atem.* But *atman* became the standard Sanskrit word for the self, with a use similar to that of *nafs* in Arabic. In both Arabic and Sanskrit this points in the same direction as the neurononsense, finding the hidden core of the person in another entity (a self) that has all the personal attributes but without the inconvenient reality of a face and a smile.

What is needed is a theory of the soul that detaches the concept from the "inner self" idea, and endows it with a role in understanding the human being that will not be eroded by the advances of cognitive science. Such a theory is needed because, without it, we cannot say what distinguishes our form of life from the life of other social animals. That is what Aquinas thought that he had, in taking over the Aristotelian distinction between form and matter. Science studies the matter of the human being, which is the body; theology tells us about the form, which is the soul. And form is understood not by the exploration of material or efficient causes, but by the exploration of formal and final causes — to put it simply, by studying the goal toward which human life progresses, rather than the mechanism that drives it. Unfortunately, the matter/form distinction is no longer able to do the work that Aquinas hoped from it. It belongs to a style of science that, since Bacon and *The Advancement of Learning,* has progressively lost ground. Science today — and this is as true of empirical psychology as it is of chemistry — looks for quantitative laws uniting cause and effect, and mathematical theories that are related deductively to the empirical observations that refute or confirm them. Somebody who defended today the view that soul is related to body as form to matter would have to explain exactly what he means by this, and how it could be incorporated into a causal theory of human behavior. The task would not be an easy one.

The disconnection between neuroscience and intentional understanding can be witnessed in psychotherapy, which employs concepts familiar from the moral life, such as guilt, resentment, anger, and forgiveness, all of which presuppose a world of subject-object relations between entities with a first-person point of view. These concepts feature in experimental psychology only rarely, and usually accompanied by an excuse for using them and a promise that the science will soon be able to replace them with something more coherent. At the same time, when concepts like guilt, anger, and forgiveness appear in therapeutic practice they are often attached to some scientific or pseudoscientific theory that lifts them out of their normal use in brokering human relations, and attaches them to forms of explanation that seem forced and metaphorical. This is very evidently the case with Freud, who relies on our understanding of ordinary mental concepts, such as desire, love, anger, and guilt, while treating them as though they were the concepts of a latent scientific theory. We see how he is immediately led by this into elaborate metaphors, concerning the unconscious, the division of the mind into *Ich, Es,* and *Über-Ich,* and a pervasive hydraulic imagery. In Freud mental states and dispositions are pushed down, bubble up, break through, change direction, and so on, and are conceived in an old-fashioned reductivist way as "drives," or *Triebe* — the principal drive being the libido, from which our life-projects emerge as "outlets." (He later added a *Todestrieb,* or "death-drive," wrongly referred to as the "death-wish.")

Although Freud entertained the hope of transcribing all this into a neurophysiological theory, it is quite clear that no such theory would capture what he wanted to say. He could not have described his patients, or even begun his therapy, without using the everyday concepts of the mental. It was absolutely necessary to Freud, as it is necessary to all the theories that derive from him, to believe that he is describing the *desires* of his patients, their feelings of *guilt,* and their beliefs, whether or not conscious, about the actions and responsibilities of themselves and others. His threefold division of the mind is not a division at all, but a multiplication, each component being modeled on the human individual, with beliefs, desires, motives, and goals of its own. And Freud's theories are not constructed as scientific theories are constructed, by generalization from instances and experimental trial. By using our ordinary mental concepts the Freudian seems to be tied in to the pattern of *personal* relations that they presuppose — relations in which people do things, respond to things, criticize, resent, forgive, and so on. Of course, all this is supposed to go on at three levels — ego, id, and superego, to use the Latinisms of James Strachey. And the hydraulic theory is supposed to explain how mental contents get pushed around between those three contenders, and also directed away from their origins toward new objects and new goals.

It is not difficult to fault all this from the philosophical point of view. There is a fundamental mistake about intentionality involved in Freud's theory of *Besetzung,* or "cathexis," as Strachey translates it. A mental state can-

not switch from one intentional object to another and still be unprob-
lematically the same; and the explanation of someone's resentment of his
wife in terms of the unconscious survival of a resentment originally directed
at his mother is not an explanation at all, but the recognition of a similarity
that has yet to be explained. Our mental concepts do not work like that, and
by attempting to squeeze them into his hydraulic theory Freud inevitably
misrepresents both the condition of his patients and the possibilities of helping them.

Suppose you were to go back over the Freudian theories and ask yourself what a scientific explanation of the phenomena that he was studying
would really look like. Suppose, for example, you were to ask how a scientist
might explain the "incest taboo," as Freud calls it. Freud's theory begins from
a characteristic gesture of astonishment. Why is incest not just avoided but
forbidden? What explains the horror and the sense of pollution that cause
Jocasta to hang herself and Oedipus to stab out his eyes? Freud leaps at once
to his conclusion: that which is forbidden is also desired. And the horror is
needed because the desire is great. If it is so great it must be there in all of us,
repressed but simmering, seeking the channels through which to flow in
some disguised but virulent version.

A modern evolutionary psychologist, observing the facts, would draw
the opposite conclusion. Incest arouses horror not because we desire it but
because we don't. Why don't we? First, because incest undermines the relationships on which the home is built, and so impedes the transfer of social
capital; second, because communities that permit incest pay a genetic price.
Either way, the horror is there because societies that lack it *have all died out.*
That kind of evolutionary explanation is admittedly speculative; but it opens
the way to a more detailed biological theory, with the causal connections
properly spelled out — and in this it is the opposite of the Freudian theory,
which simply replaces one mystery with another, while making no *theoretical* advance whatsoever.

The Freudian story is a fiction, believed not because of its explanatory
power but because of its charm. On the other hand, the evolutionary theory
bypasses altogether the fact upon which Freud attempts to focus — which is
the state of mind of the subject, the nature of his horror, and the way in
which it is incorporated into his personal life. The theory of the incest taboo
that I have hinted at is partly genetic, partly a matter of group selection. I am
not saying that it is a true theory, and of course the idea of group selection is
deeply controversial among biologists. The point is that it does not use mental concepts at all: it doesn't explore the intentionality of our disgust at in-

cest, the nature of that disgust, or its place in our lives as persons. For the scientist it suffices that we are averse to incest, and the theory tells us that we are averse to incest since this aversion is an adaptation that has been selected for. That theory, if true, renders Freud's theory redundant, and also undermines the conclusion drawn by Freud, namely, that incest is something that we desire.

But we are likely to think that the evolutionary approach that I have adumbrated — whether expressed in terms of genetics or in terms of group selection — leaves something out of account, precisely because it has not been phrased in mental terms. It has somehow failed to tell us what the horror of incest really is, and failed to situate that horror in the mental life of the one who suffers it. Somehow the thing that interested Freud — the human mind — has dropped out of consideration altogether. You might try to build it back in, by means of a cognitive science that shows the intermediate links between the aversion toward incest and the action of avoiding it: but this would clearly advance us nowhere in understanding the thoughts and feelings of Oedipus and Jocasta on that fatal day. As like as not it would just be another piece of neurononsense, with lots of fMRI images connecting stories of incest with the puke centers of the brain.

Freud has taken the concepts that we use to *understand* each other, and tried to adapt them so as to construct a way in which to *explain* each other. He has tried to rewrite intentionality as a causal relationship, and to detach beliefs, desires, and emotions from their fundamental place in interpersonal relationships, attaching them instead to various quasi-hydraulic processes which are not, in any real sense, properties of the self-conscious person, and certainly not expressions of his first-person perspective. In doing this he has produced not a theory but a metaphorical redescription of the mind — one that might indeed be useful as a therapeutic tool, but only because it promotes its own special kind of interpersonal relationship between analyst and patient, and not because it explains how the patient came to think and feel as he does.

I think that the same pattern is exhibited by other schools of therapy — at least by those that have acquired any kind of following. The existential school of Ludwig Binswanger, and its vulgarization in the work of R. D. Laing; the Kleinian and Winnicottian theory of object relations; and the Jungian theory of the archetypes are all attempts to provide therapy by *rearranging personal relationships*. And they do this not by producing scientific theories, but by applying our ordinary mental concepts in metaphorical or extended ways. If they *did* try to produce explanatory theories, those theories would take a form that would be entirely useless in the therapeutic process. This is even true of "cognitive therapy," which — while it is obliquely connected to the aspirations of cognitive science — is in fact addressed directly to the beliefs, desires, and concepts of the patient. In persuading someone to see something as a mistake rather than a deliberate assault, as an expression of love rather than an expression of jealousy, and so on, we are simply extending the normal forms of human understanding, and the interpersonal reactions that are built on them. We are not stepping out of the realm of *Verstehen* into the realms of cognitive science. We are addressing the other as a person, and helping him to understand his personal relationships differently.

If we look now at the traditional concept of the soul, we will see that it developed precisely in order to engage directly with the interpersonal understanding that is the ground assumed by psychotherapy. The concept of the soul was meant to identify the target of those thoughts and emotions that are alive in our dealings with each other, and which require us to conceptualize each other's actions in terms of the subjectivity, self-consciousness, and freedom that they reveal. And it owes its durability to its capacity to unite certain features of our life as persons that seem to belong together, though we don't necessarily know how: the unity of the person, for example; freedom; the consciousness of self that underlies all our interchanges with each other; accountability and the distinction that we make between caring for the other as a subject, and using him as an object. All those things are summarized in the soul idea, which, even if it has metaphysical implications that go far beyond this, nevertheless enables us to get a handle on what is distinctive in our condition, and on the kind of relationships that are peculiar to us.

Now an "eliminative materialist" like Paul Churchland might take issue with what I have just said, arguing that the reality of the human being resides in his biological makeup: that he is nothing more than an organism, animated by a nervous system, which operates as an information-processing system analogous to a computer. Any explanation of what we are should therefore be phrased in terms of cognitive science, which explores human software, and neurobiology, which explores the hardware, or rather "wetware," in which that software is installed. Such an explanation, the critic might argue, would give a complete account of what we are; and of course it would not mention the soul idea, or any of those scientifically dispensable concepts like belief, desire, selfhood, or freedom, which belong to the scientifically fragile discipline of folk psychology.

An effective philosophical anthropology must set out to rebut that approach, and in particular the ontological narrowness that is expressed in it. I would suggest that we understand the person as an emergent entity, rooted in the human being, but belonging to another order of understanding than that explored by biology. Not all persons are human beings — there are corporate persons, and maybe supernatural persons and persons who belong to some other species. A human being is a person in something like the way that a painted canvas is a portrait or a pile of printed paper is a book.

"Emergence" is accepted in modern physics as part of the natural order. The laws governing the motion and transformation of large entities are not always reducible to the laws governing the motion and transformation of their parts: new orders of explanation emerge as we move up the scale of entities from quarks to galaxies. In referring to the person as an "emergent entity," however, I am not invoking the physicist's concept of emergence. Emergent entities in physics are governed by causal laws which, while irreducible to the laws governing the entities from which they "emerge," are nevertheless causal laws of the same logical kind, subsuming all relevant transformations under universal formulae. The laws through which we understand the human person, however, are of a different kind from the laws that govern his biological makeup. They do not import a higher-level causality but a higher-level understanding — the understanding that we owe to each other and is the foundation of interpersonal dialogue. They are, as Kant said, laws of freedom.

An analogy might help. When a painter applies paint to a canvas he creates a physical object by purely physical means. This object is composed of areas and lines of paint, arranged on a surface. When we look at the surface of the painting, we see those areas and lines of paint, and also the surface that contains them. But that is not all we see. We also see a face that looks out at us with smiling eyes. In one sense the face is a property of the canvas, over and above the blobs of paint; for you can observe the blobs and not see the face, and vice versa. And the face is really there: someone who does not see it is not seeing correctly. On the other hand, there is a sense in which the face is not an additional property of the canvas, over and above the lines and blobs. For as soon as the lines and blobs are there, so is the face. Nothing more needs to be added, in order to generate the face — and if nothing more needs to be added, the face is surely nothing more. Moreover, every process that produces just these blobs of paint, arranged in just this way, will produce just this face — even if the artist himself is unaware of the face. (Imagine how you would design a machine for producing Mona Lisas.)

Maybe personhood is an "emergent" feature of the human being in that way: not something over and above the life and behavior in which we observe it, but not reducible to them either. Once personhood has emerged it is possible to relate to an organism in a new way — the way of personal relations. (In like manner we can relate to pictures in ways that we cannot relate to something that we see merely as a distribution of pigments.) With this new order of relation comes a new order of understanding, in which reasons and meanings, rather than causes, are sought in answer to the question "why?" With persons we are in dialogue: we call upon them to justify their conduct in our eyes, as we must justify our conduct in theirs. Central to this dialogue are the two features — consciousness and the first-person perspective — which I earlier mentioned as seeming to lie beyond the reach of any science of the mind. Equally important are the concepts of freedom, choice, and accountability — concepts that have no place in the description of animal behavior, just as the concept of a human being has no place in the description of the physical makeup of a picture, even though it is a picture in which a human being can be seen.

The theory of personhood as an emergent feature of the human being raises the question of origins: When does the person come into being? This question is a topic in itself, and here I can only make a suggestion — one that corresponds to the old Aristotelian distinction (deployed repeatedly by Aquinas) between potential and act. The acorn is potentially an oak, though not actually. However, it belongs to the essence of the acorn that it should grow into an oak, and its oaken essence is contained within the acorn *ab initio.* Something similar might be said of the human embryo: that it has personhood *in potentia,* and that its personal essence is contained within it *ab initio.*

When I give a scientific account of the world, I am describing the way things are and the causal laws that govern them. This description is given from no particular perspective. It does not contain words like "here," "now," and "I"; and while it is meant to explain the way things seem, it does so by giving a theory of how they are. The self-conscious subject is in principle unobservable to science, not because it exists in another realm but because it is not part of the empirical world. It lies on the edge of things, like a horizon, and could never be grasped "from the other side," the side of subjectivity itself. Is it a real part of the real world? The question is surely wrongly phrased, since it misconstrues the deep grammar of self-reference and of the reflexive pronoun. When I refer to myself I am not referring to another *object* that is, as it were, hidden in the lining of the observable Roger Scruton. Self-reference is not reference to a Cartesian self, but reference to this thing, the thing that I am, namely, an object with a first-person viewpoint.[18]

18. See the argument of Thomas Nagel, *The View from Nowhere* (Oxford: Oxford University Press, 1986).

Hence we are not entitled to reify the "self" as a distinct object of reference. Nor can we accept — given the force of Wittgenstein's anti-private language argument — that our mental states exhibit publicly inaccessible features that somehow define what they really are. Nevertheless, self-reference radically affects the way in which people relate to one another. Once in place, self-attribution and self-reference become the primary avenues to what we think, intend, and are. They permit us to relate to each other as subjects and not as objects only: and that is what lies at the heart of the ideas of responsibility, accountability, guilt, praise, and blame.[19] By relating to another in this way, I come face to face with him: his essential being as a person "emerges" from his bodily reality, in the way that the face emerges from the colored blobs on the canvas. All of this is summarized in the soul idea — and it explains the connection between soul and person. The soul is the organizing principle of a self-conscious creature — that which implants in the human frame the activities and relations that endow him with individuality, personality, and will. If this organizing principle can survive the dissolution of the body in which it is exhibited, as religious people hope, then it is not as objects survive when taken from an envelope, but in the way that an image survives, when transferred from canvas to canvas.

In our endeavors to develop a viable concept of the human person, therefore, we should give up all the neurononsense and return to the fundamental idea of the human individual as a free and accountable agent, whose unique and unified self-consciousness is the primary means of access to the thing that he is. This does not require us to deny the truths of empirical psychology, neurobiology, and cognitive science; rather, it requires us to see those truths as belonging to another level of analysis, as the theory of pigments belongs to another level of pictorial analysis than iconology.

---

19. And also at the heart of the "second-person standpoint" eloquently defended by Stephen Darwall, as the core of morality. See *The Second-Person Standpoint: Morality, Respect and Accountability* (Cambridge, MA: Harvard University Press, 2006).

Persons at Home in the Universe: Openness, Purpose, and Transcendence

Philip A. Rolnick

> *What is it that breathes fire into the equations and makes a universe for them to describe?*
>
> Stephen Hawking

> *The mathematical descriptions of the physical world given to us by quantum theory presuppose the existence of observers who lie outside those mathematical descriptions.*
>
> Stephen Barr

> *Transcendence . . . is to a certain extent another name for the person.*
>
> Karol Wojtyla[1]

1. Stephen Hawking, *A Brief History of Time* (Toronto: Bantam Books, 1988), 174; Stephen M. Barr, *Modern Physics and Ancient Faith* (Notre Dame: University of Notre Dame Press, 2003), 238; Karol Cardinal Wojtyla, "The Person: Subject and Community," *Review of Metaphysics* 33 (1979-80): 282.

I would like to thank Alan Padgett, Jeffrey Wattles, Pavel Gavrilyuk, and Philippe Gagnon for their many helpful suggestions about this paper.

Introduction

Intellect and (free) will have long been considered to be two of the essentials of the uniqueness of human persons, but intellect and will need a universe home, an operating context in which persons can meaningfully exercise these attributes. Two extreme conceptions of the universe context, utter randomness and sheer determinism, would eliminate the possibility of meaningful human freedom. If things were truly random, without recognizable, repeatable patterns, neither the universe nor intellect could be formed. If things were truly deterministic, as they appeared to be in the wake of Isaac Newton (1642-1727), the universe would be so strongly ordered, so determined by law, that human freedom would be impossible. In determinism, "Every event is causally necessitated by antecedent events"; thus, "The facts of the past, in conjunction with the laws of nature, entail every truth about the future."[2]

Because it appeared to leave room only for matter, a common interpretation of classical physics spawned materialist, mechanical understandings of the self, in which intellect was reduced to the physics and chemistry of the brain. In 1997, when the computer program Deep Blue defeated world chess champion Gary Kasparov, mechanical constructs were given additional plausibility. The computer appeared to be making free choices but was actually following an intricate, predetermined program. Seizing upon this episode, some prominent materialist scientists have claimed that human choice is no more than a complicated program honed over long stretches of evolutionary time and hidden from those of us who think that we are thinking. And likewise with choosing.

Fortunately, some "plot twists" have taken place in mathematics and physics, and these developments have presented a picture more harmonious with freedom in human thought and action.[3] In what follows, from Gödel's

---

2. Michael McKenna, "Compatibilism," in *The Stanford Encyclopedia of Philosophy (Fall 2008)*, Edward N. Zalta, ed., URL = http://plato.stanford.edu/archives/fall2008/entries/compatibilism/.

3. "Plot twists" is taken from Barr, *Modern Physics and Ancient Faith*, 22-28. I am indebted to this seminal work.

Barr's five plot twists can be summarized as follows:

(1) The change from thinking of the universe as having a spatial center to the question of whether the universe had a beginning in time. The general contour of Big Bang theory is consonant with the biblical notion of a beginning in time, i.e., creation.

(2) Discovery of different levels and dimensions in physics has revivified the argument from design. Increasing unity, especially symmetry, has been uncovered within the beauty of formal laws.

theorems, to quantum physics, to the narrative-historical thread of human decisions, to what *person* means theologically, we will see that the universe is a suitable home for purposive, transcendent activities.

Gödel's Incompleteness Theorems and Polanyi's "Logical Gap"

Kurt Gödel (1906-1978) was an Austrian mathematician, logician, and philosopher whose work, especially in mathematics, ranks among the greatest discoveries of the twentieth century.[4] Gödel was a philosophical realist strongly opposed to materialism and any reductionist understanding of human intellect. Holding to a Platonic view of mathematics, he even opposed the idea that mathematics is our own creation. Most important for our purposes, his incompleteness theorems, published in 1931, imply that human intellect cannot be reduced to a rote program.

The first of these theorems proved that what is provable and what is true in arithmetic are not coextensive. Within arithmetic itself, the whole of arithmetic truth cannot be defined. Gödel showed that, in any consistent, formal mathematical system that includes at least arithmetic and simple logic, there are true statements, "formally undecidable propositions," that can neither be proved nor disproved using the rules of that system. His second incompleteness theorem proved that the consistency of a formal system itself is undecidable using the rules of that system.[5]

---

(3) With Copernicus's cosmology, humanity was dethroned from the center of the universe; however, cumulative discovery of "anthropic coincidences" intriguingly suggests that the universe was designed for creatures like us.

(4) Against the materialist assertion that the human mind is a machine, Barr cites two counterarguments: first, the ability to think abstractly, to think in universals; second, to know some truths as certainty and necessity. Furthermore, the theorem of Kurt Gödel (1931), as developed later by John Lucas (c. 1970) and Roger Penrose (1990s), argues against the human mind-as-computer theory.

(5) After Newton, many physicists believed that the universe was deterministic, and this determinism fit well into a materialist narrative. However, with the discovery of quantum physics in the 1920s, this most important piece of the materialist puzzle was removed.

4. I am drawing biographical material from Juliette Kennedy, "Kurt Gödel," in *The Stanford Encyclopedia of Philosophy (Winter 2008)*, Edward N. Zalta, ed., URL = http://plato.stanford.edu/archives/win2008/entries/goedel/.

5. See Barr, *Modern Physics*, 212-13. Systems can be either consistent or inconsistent. Gödel's theorem applies only to consistent systems. A system is inconsistent when it is possi-

The implication is that all such systems of mathematical thought need some assistance from *outside* the system. There is an openness in the mathematics itself and so also in the human mind that understands the mathematics. Although interpretations of Gödel's incompleteness theorems remain controversial, one implication is that mind is more than a machine.[6] Drawing upon the nonmechanical implications of Gödel's work, Michael Polanyi (1891-1976) developed an innovative understanding of how obstacles are creatively overcome in problem solving. Polanyi called this problem-solving process "crossing of a logical gap."[7] By definition, crossing a logical gap cannot be done solely by logic, for if the problem solver had the

---

ble, using the rules of that system, to prove both some proposition and its negation. Consistent systems have no such contradictions, but they do have at least one "undecidable" proposition. If any inconsistent statements can be proved, then all contradictory statements can be proved. For example, if, by a flawed setup, it can be proved that 1 = 0, then it is also possible to prove that 13 = 7.

(1) 1 = 0
(2) Multiply both sides by 6, then
(3) 6 = 0
(4) Add 7 to both sides, then
(5) 6 + 7 = 0 + 7
(6) 13 = 7

Bertrand Russell was asked by an interviewer if he could use the statement 2 = 1 to prove that he, Russell, was the pope. Russell responded without hesitation:

(1) Let a room contain two people, viz., Russell and the pope.
(2) Since 2 = 1, it is also true to say that there is only one person in the room.
(3) Since Russell is in the room, and the pope is in the room, and there is one person in the room, then Russell and the pope must be the same person. (The above proofs are, with slight alterations, taken from Barr, 212.)

6. For an argument that attempts to counter any nonmechanical implications of Gödel's theorems, one aimed especially at the interpretations of J. R. Lucas and Roger Penrose, see Stanislaw Krajewski, "On Gödel's Theorem and Mechanism: Inconsistency or Unsoundness Is Unavoidable in Any Attempt to 'Out-Gödel' the Mechanist," *Fundamenta Informaticae* 81 (2007): 173-81. For arguments defending the view that Gödel's theorems do imply that mind is nonmechanical, see J. R. Lucas, "Minds, Machines, and Gödel," in *The Modeling of Mind*, ed. K. M. Sayre and F. J. Crosson (Notre Dame: University of Notre Dame Press, 1963); and Lucas, *The Freedom of the Will* (Oxford: Oxford University Press, 1970), esp. 124-72. Also see Roger Penrose, *Shadows of the Mind: The Search for the Missing Science of Consciousness* (Oxford: Oxford University Press, 1994), 147-50.

7. Michael Polanyi, *Personal Knowledge: Toward a Post-Critical Philosophy* (Chicago: University of Chicago Press, 1962). See 123-30, 143, 150-51, 260-61, 367 et passim for "crossing a logical gap," and 118-19, 192, 259-61, and 273 for Polanyi's commentary on Gödel and its relation to Polanyi's theme of tacit knowing. In the remainder of this section, further page references to *Personal Knowledge* will be given parenthetically within the text.

logic, there would be no gap and no problem. Likewise, there can be no already known, preexisting, step-by-step procedure that would solve the problem. If such a procedure were known in advance, there would again be no gap.

Yet even though "the solution of a problem is something we have never before met," both ordinary problem solving and extraordinary acts of discovery do find new paths across a gap (126). Since formal logic or established procedures are insufficient to get across the gap, the solution will have to include an informal, intuitive component. When we search for a mislaid object, we are not clueless. We know what the object looks like and the likely regions in which to search. Analogously, when we are searching for a solution, "We are looking for it as if it were there, pre-existent" (126). A heuristic realism governs the quest across a logical gap (just as it does for a mislaid object), for if we did not believe that there was a solution, we would be unlikely to expend time and energy undertaking the search.

Borrowing from Henri Poincaré, Polanyi describes four stages of successful attempts to cross a logical gap: Preparation, Incubation, Illumination, and Verification (121). In mathematics, for example,

> The first active steps undertaken to solve a problem and the final garnering of the solution rely effectively on computations and other symbolic operations, while the more informal act by which the logical gap is crossed lies between these two formal procedures. However, the intuitive powers of the investigator are always dominant and decisive. (130)

The bookends of the process, computation and symbolic articulation, require intelligence, prior training, and skill. It is highly unlikely that a major discovery will be made without these. However, something more is needed. The "unremitting preoccupation" with the problem, the passionate desire to know, motivates taking pains to search into the unknown and energizes forward progress, especially during the Incubation stage (127). Elaborating upon Gödel, Polanyi notes, "The mathematician works his way towards discovery, by shifting his confidence from intuition to computation, and back again from computation to intuition, while never releasing his hold on either of the two" (260).

When we grope for a forgotten name, there is sometimes a point at which we think we almost have it. Likewise, in approaching a new solution, a kind of confident hope sometimes arises, as when a hunch propels us forward. But the creative, original, and nonmachine-like nature of the human mind is manifest in the "mental reorganization" that takes place in the moment of Illumination (367). The precise moment in which the mind grasps a solution is like the instant where the funny point of a joke hits us. The creative process is both active and passive, for there is a moment where the security of the old framework of thinking must be let go. This ability to go beyond (transcendence) older patterns and limitations in search of newer, more inclusive understanding is a key indicator of human uniqueness.

In the final stage of crossing a logical gap, Verification comes about as new insight brings about "new contact with reality."[8] Verification can be as ordinary as getting a stopped lawn mower to start or as monumental as the Wright brothers getting an airplane to fly. Once the logical gap is crossed, the method of solving the problem can then be articulated. Having achieved the far shore of a logical gap, the discoverer can then lay out insights and procedures that can be taught to and repeated by others.

The fact that problems get solved, that logical gaps can be crossed, indicates that the intelligibility inside the fabric of things is open to the intelligibility of the human mind. Gödel's incompleteness theorems and Polanyi's account of crossing a logical gap display two different kinds of openness. The former shows the openness of formal logic; the latter that formal logic is not sufficient to account for the human mind in the process of discovery. Crossing a logical gap requires openness to an unknown reality and faith that the unknown can become known. Its successful culmination is an act of self-transcendence.

Quantum Surprises: Indeterminism and the Measurement Problem

The development of quantum theory is one of the great scientific achievements of the twentieth century. Its success is apparent in the broad range that it covers, from atoms to the smallest known constituents of matter, quarks and gluons, a change of scale by a factor of about 10 million.[9] Quantum theory's predictive success, a crucial criterion of scientific plausibility, has been extremely high. Since its heyday in the 1920s, its leading discoverers — people such as Max Planck, Albert Einstein, Erwin Schrödinger,

---

8. "Contact with reality" is a vital theme of Polanyi's. See *Personal Knowledge*, 64, 104, 106, 124, et passim.

9. See John Polkinghorne, *The Quantum World* (Princeton: Princeton University Press, 1989), 1. Much of my account of quantum physics is indebted to this work.

Werner Heisenberg, Niels Bohr, Paul Dirac, and Louis de Broglie — have become legendary figures.

Quantum theory can be seen as indebted to past discoveries but also as a radically new way of conceiving matter. In the nineteenth century, Thomas Young demonstrated the wave character of light; Michael Faraday demonstrated the intertwined nature of electricity and magnetism; and James Clerk Maxwell's set of four equations summed up and interrelated what was known of electricity, magnetism, and light.

But new knowledge often leads to awareness of new problems, and when Rayleigh (John William Strutt) and James Jeans did experiments on radiation whose results made no sense, a new approach was needed. When exposed to radiation, ordinary bodies absorb some and reflect the rest; black bodies perfectly absorb radiation and then re-emit it. Rayleigh and Jeans naturally assumed that energy going into and out of their black body was continuous. With an insight that would give the new physics its name, Max Planck solved the radiation problem by conjecturing that energy going in and out could only do so in *discrete* packets, i.e., *quanta.* Quantum physics thus replaces the continuous with the discrete, the smoothly varying by a kind of ordered fitfulness. German mathematician Leopold Kronecker had once said that God made the integers and all else was man's work, and his quip appears to have some merit in regard to quantum theory.

Working in the larger world, classical, Newtonian physics could, for example, give an accurate account of a train's position and momentum. However, in the extreme tinyness of the quantum world, another surprise occurs. As Werner Heisenberg showed, in what is now known as the Heisenberg Uncertainty Principle, to the degree that, e.g., an electron's position is known, its momentum will not be known; to the degree that momentum is known, position will not be known. In John Polkinghorne's more colorful description, "If I know where an electron is I have no idea of what it is doing and, conversely, if I know what it is doing I do not know where it is."[10] There is an innate elusiveness to quantum entities that simply does not fit the determinism inspired by classical physics.[11]

10. Polkinghorne, *Quantum World,* 3.

11. Mathematically, the reasons for indeterminacy have to do with the noncommutative nature of quantum operators. In mathematics, an operator turns one vector into another. Mathematical operators are well suited to represent physical "observables," such as position, momentum, and energy. Ordinary number operations are often commutative, e.g., $8 \times 5 = 5 \times 8$. However, the quantum operators for position and momentum do not commute. This noncommutability means that there cannot be a state in which they both can be assigned

One of the strangest findings of quantum physics is the superposition principle. According to superposition, states (i.e., the details of motion) of quantum entities like electrons can be added to one another. The combined state exhibits probabilities that remain indeterministic until a measurement is taken. The surprise in superposition is not that states can be added, but that the combined states do not yield a middle position between the two component states; instead, they yield a certain probability of being either "here" or "there." In the famous double-slit experiment, where an electron is aimed at a screen with two slits and the passage of the electron is recorded on a second screen behind the first, the weird result is obtained that, under some circumstances, the electron passes through both slits — it is both "here" and "there."[12] Quantum particles, the most basic constituents of matter, retain a strange and irreducible indeterminateness.

In one of the benchmark achievements of quantum physics, an equation of Erwin Schrödinger provides a method of computing a physical system's changing probabilities over time. Over a period of time, the probable position of a particle like an electron (more technically, its "probability amplitudes," since the electron exhibits both particle behavior and wave behavior) can be computed with the Schrödinger equation;[13] once again, however, because of superposition, only relative probabilities of the particle's position, not certainty, can be obtained.[14]

The Schrödinger equation describes the rate of change of the probabilities in a smooth, continuous way — as long as there is no interference. However, taking a measurement dramatically interrupts the smooth rate of change. When experimentally interrogated, the quantum entity no longer superposes the two states "here" and "there," and what is called the "collapse of the wave packet" takes place with the definite realization of either "here" or "there." In this measurement event, a dramatic transformation takes

definite values, and our ability to measure all quantum components is thus restricted. For more detailed, technical explanation, see Polkinghorne, *Quantum World*, 24-29.

12. See Polkinghorne, "Which Way Did It Go?" in *Quantum World*, 34-43.

13. The amplitude of a quantum wave is its possibility; the probability is the possibility squared.

14. The nondeterministic nature of quantum phenomena was strongly supported by a theorem of John Bell that refutes deterministic, local theories. "Locality" means that no influence can be transmitted faster than the speed of light. See Bell, "On the Einstein-Podolsky-Rosen Paradox," *Physics* 1, no. 3 (1964): 195-200; for commentary and a helpful explanation, see James T. Cushing, "A Background Essay," in *Philosophical Consequences of Quantum Theory: Reflections on Bell's Theorem*, ed. James T. Cushing and Ernan McMullin (Notre Dame: University of Notre Dame Press, 1989), 1-24.

place: the indeterminate becomes determinate, and the superposition of multiple possibilities collapses into one actuality. Every act of measurement entails the collapse of the wave packet from its potential states into one of them.[15] The observer radically affects the quantum observation.

If we transition, mutatis mutandis, to the world of middle-sized objects, an episode from my own experience may serve to illustrate how, by an act of measurement, the observer becomes involved in the observation. By invitation of a friend, I once attended a banquet where some famous and powerful individuals were present. During the pre-dinner cocktail hour, I was rather deeply engaged with a man about some theological issues. In the midst of what I thought was a good conversation, his attention was suddenly and irrevocably turned, as a klieg light came on and one of the famous ones walked by, followed by a videographer. At first I was mildly irritated at having our conversation interrupted; then it occurred to me that something instructive was going on. Our little world of those at the banquet had suddenly been intruded upon by a kind of measurement — a recording that was then and there opening our previously closed system to a larger world. But in effecting this opening, the klieg light/video measurement was unquestionably changing behaviors within the system. As the videographer with the klieg light moved through the room tracking the famous ones, I observed that numerous conversations were disturbed. Perhaps it is not so strange that human beings would change their behavior when being observed, but it remains puzzling and somewhat mysterious that quantum entities should do so.

Schrödinger, de Broglie, and Einstein emphatically did not like the uncertainty and probability of quantum physics. Schrödinger went so far as to say: "If we are going to stick with this damn quantum jumping, then I regret that I ever had anything to do with quantum theory." Einstein, rather than give up his preference for a universe of strictly determined and therefore knowable causality, claimed to prefer being "a cobbler, or even an employee in a gambling house, than a physicist." Later, in a letter to Max Born, he infamously claimed that "God does not play dice." In the late 1920s, Einstein and

---

15. How to understand the role of the observer who takes the measurement is one of the most controversial and mysterious aspects of quantum theory. There are at least four ways to interpret the collapse of the wave packet: (1) the idea that an idealist interpretation such as Bishop Berkeley might have made; (2) the Copenhagen Interpretation, where there is a transition from small to large systems, and the measuring apparatus is always seen as part of the experiment; (3) the thesis that the collapse may have occurred at the interaction of matter and mind, where consciousness enters; (4) the many worlds hypothesis. Each one has its difficulties. See Polkinghorne, *Quantum World*, 63-68.

Bohr had a series of exchanges in which Einstein tried to dismantle the uncertainty principle. To each of Einstein's proposed objections, Bohr was able to defend the theory. Indeterminacy and uncertainty prevailed.[16]

The quantum realm is neither randomly chaotic nor overly determined and causally closed; rather, it is at once orderly and open. In short, it provides the kind of context that intellect and will need in order to operate freely. Prediction, which is the ideal of the physical sciences, still works well in the larger world because minuscule quantum fluctuations have a propensity to cancel each other out. However, in regard to quantum entities, even with complete knowledge of the present state of a physical system, quantum theory forbids in principle that everything about the future behavior of the system could be known. The quantum realm is not only open to our interventions, disruptive as they prove to be, but also to its own unpredictable but creative interactions. Robert Russell sees that its

> surprise events radically change the history of the system involved. Atoms decay; they do not "reassemble" on their own. When nuclei fuse and emit light, they become an entirely different kind of nucleus. Particles annihilate and pair produce. Particles don't just change their properties, they are transformed: the old perishes, the new is born, and the event of transformation is a surprise. Quantum physics reveals that nature is full of surprise: deterministic causal explanation falls short of the reality being revealed, and the world is radically changed and transformed at each quantum event.[17]

All theology needs from physics is compatibility, not proof, and the surprisingly open context of the quantum world provides it.

In attempting to understand something in mathematics, physics, or indeed to learn anything new, the one who seeks to know is attempting to discover what *is*. Wanting to know what is the case, whether we are talking about God or any level of created being, St. Thomas Aquinas (1225-1274) states: "Being is the proper object of the mind."[18] Similarly, John Polking-

---

16. Polkinghorne, *Quantum World*, 53-55.

17. Robert John Russell, "Quantum Physics in Philosophical and Theological Perspective," in *Physics, Philosophy, and Theology: A Common Quest for Understanding*, ed. Robert J. Russell, William R. Stoeger, S.J., and George V. Coyne, S.J. (Vatican City State: Vatican Observatory, 1988), 356.

18. Aquinas, *Summa Theologica* I.5.2 (New York: Benziger, 1947). For an account of how analogy works theologically, see Philip A. Rolnick, *Analogical Possibilities: How Words Refer to God* (New York: Oxford University Press, 1993).

horne more recently asserts: "Epistemology models ontology."[19] Every scientific researcher tacitly presupposes the existence of what is being sought. Scientists do not spend years of concentrated research seeking what they do not believe exists. The very pursuit of science is a tacit indicator of great metaphysical confidence — that something is there to be understood and that it is intelligible to the human intellect — just as a theologian would expect to find in a creation that arises from *logos* (John 1:1-3).

As humanity cumulatively seeks to expand its understanding of the way things are, the universe encountered displays both lawful stability and probabilistic dynamism. In this material context so eminently suited for human intellect and will, the universe and its human inhabitants are moving through time as an unfolding narrative. From the moment of the Big Bang, the cosmos and all that is in it is historically shaped. Given the historical shape of things, let us now turn to consider persons in history.

Enacting Decisions — Persons in History

Like our universe home, personal life is inherently historical. Just as the intrusion of an observer's measurement brings about the collapse of the wave function, so too does a human decision "collapse" various possibilities into a clearly defined datum — into a past event. The arrow of time only moves one way.[20] Past events remain fixed. History, constituted in the stark asymmetry between past and future, is the moving context of human freedom. Like the quantum underlay of our home in the physical universe, history, as it moves forward, is neither random nor completely determined; it is the open arena in which purpose may be freely and intelligently pursued. What we value and what we abhor are played out in this arena.

The irreversible sequence of temporal events urges us to take historical reality seriously: a deed done cannot be undone; a word spoken cannot be unspoken. Nonetheless, unlike the strict fixity of material events, as where two nuclei fuse or a lion eats its prey, the understanding of past events can be

19. John Polkinghorne, *Serious Talk: Science and Religion in Dialogue* (Harrisburg, PA: Trinity Press International, 1995), 81.

20. Similar to the use of imaginary numbers, in quantum theory time can be *conceived* as reversible. For an accessible explanation, see http://www.higgo.com/quantum/laymans.htm. For a more thorough study, see J. G. Muga, R. Sala Mayato, and I. L. Egusquiza, eds., *Time in Quantum Mechanics*, Lecture Notes in Physics, vol. 734 (New York: Springer, 2008).

cast in a new light. We cannot change what happened, but we can and often do change our understanding of what happened. We can even change our attitude about what happened, and in a mark of human uniqueness, when necessary, we can ask or receive forgiveness. While the arrow of time proceeds unidirectionally, individual and community understanding has no such inexorability. Flexibility of thought is another indicator of the freedom of human intellect — and its accompanying responsibility.

A community's understanding of the broad range of the settled data of the past constitutes a repository, a base from which new efforts may be launched. Without this historical repository kept in trust and narrated by the community, present meaning would be denuded. Nikolai Berdiaev contends that "to forget the past . . . would be equivalent to a state of insanity in which mankind would live only upon the rags of time, in its torn instants without any coordinating principle."[21] Neither science nor religion can function without its past. In science, Einstein could not have discovered relativity if his community had not first trained him in mathematics. In religion, Jesus' prayer, "Our Father . . . hallowed be thy *name*," creatively builds upon the long Hebrew tradition of respect for the name of God.

Data alone do not constitute a human past. We need a "coordinating principle" to tell us what the data mean and how they might form a purpose for our present and future orientation. Every narration is a condensation that attempts to graph lived historical data along the axis of meaning. Like the actual lives of individuals and community, narrated histories can deconstruct if they lose their sense of purpose by which data is filtered and focused into a meaningful whole.

In a basic sense, history is what we live. We do not merely write histories; each of us *is* a history being "written" in the fabric of reality as our lives unfold. Our most basic identity and all of its components are historically shaped.

History is punctuated with events that benchmark the flow of time with meaningful and memorable interactions. Character is tested and forged in these events, which become the stuff of memory in calmer, more reflective times. The ancient Greeks had two terms for time: *chronos* and *kairos*. *Chronos* indicates the normal, clocklike passage of time; *kairos* indicates critical time, time of requisite decision and action, the time of event. Decisive and definitive events interrupt the smooth flow of *chronos* with meaning-laden

---

21. Nikolai Berdiaev, *The Meaning of History*, trans. George Reavey (London: Geoffrey Bles, Centenary Press, 1936), 73; punctuation slightly altered.

kairos, and thus time takes on meaningful contours. An eventless human life makes a dull narrative, which is to say that it makes for a rather uninteresting life. As novelist John Steinbeck saw, "Eventlessness has no posts to drape duration on. From nothing to nothing is no time at all."[22]

In Jewish and Christian faith, divine action penetrates history, so that history becomes the context in which God's transcendence and immanence are interlaced and revealed. As dramatic events bring the Babylonian Captivity to an unexpected close, God proclaims through the prophet Isaiah: "Behold, I am doing a new thing; now it springs forth, do you not perceive it?" (Isa. 43:19). Christianity takes the Hebraic emphasis on history to heightened levels in its understanding of Christ's incarnation: "But when the fullness of time had come, God sent his Son, born of a woman" (Gal. 4:4). In this unique event, clarified truth arrives as the divine Son arrives. It is a measurement event, an intervention that benchmarks all of human history, past and future, a singularity that opens the chronological to the kairotic whenever and wherever this event is confronted anew. The corollary to the belief that God became incarnate and lived among us is that human history is not causally closed to the divine.

If human history can play host to the divine, then alertness to our own historical possibilities is called for. Every moment and epoch of our lives, every category by which we measure time, has a certain potential. As we attempt to actualize the potential of our situation, our performance leaves a double inscription, an inscription that marks the world around us and an inscription in our own soul, the personal repository of achievement and failure.[23]

The freshness of each historical moment is guaranteed by its finitude, by the certainty that it will end. Every human activity comes to an end, whether it be childhood, a conversation, a family meal, or a college career. This recurring eschatology asks that we be alert to each possibility, for the character of our narrative, that is, our character, is forged in historical performance. One of the most important things to be said about human life is that it ends. Whether that end comes as personal demolition or as another sort of opening is more a matter of faith than argument, but how we decide this question casts a certain light over experience and differently orients us toward all our endings.

22. John Steinbeck, *East of Eden* (New York: Penguin Books, 1986), 73.

23. For a creative treatment of inscription that differs from but is harmonious with my own, see Ernst M. Conradie, "Resurrection, Finitude, and Ecology," in *Resurrection: Theological and Scientific Assessments,* ed. Ted Peters, Robert John Russell, and Michael Welker (Grand Rapids: Eerdmans, 2002), 277-96.

Person, Purpose, and Transcendence

Although there were pre-Christian glimpses into the concept of *person,* its sustained development really took off during the Trinitarian and Christological controversies of the fourth and fifth centuries. No one was looking for a concept of person; rather, solutions to the relations of Father, Son, and Spirit were sought; and then later, how the human and divine natures of Christ were related. The incipient notion of person arose as the church groped its way toward solving these complex problems.[24] Although the church first applied *person* to God, analogous applications to humans inevitably followed and have continued to the present day and to the writing of this present volume.

Three clear gains about the notion of person can be garnered from the ancient church controversies: *person distinguishes, relates,* and *unifies.* Although conceived as equals, the Son is not the Father, and the Spirit is not the Son. Hence, *person distinguishes.* At the same time, *person relates,* because, e.g., there can be no Father without a Son. Hence, the distinctions and relations are co-implicative. *Person unifies* because each of the Father, Son, and Spirit is perfectly unified with the infinite entirety of the divine nature, so that there is one nature, substance, or essence with three Persons.[25] The unity was stressed to counter the logical objection of tritheism. Likewise, in the Christological controversy, the church's solution was that Christ is one person who unifies the two natures, divine and human. Hence, the important distinction between person, which is unique, and nature, which is common.

Drawing upon these theological developments, we can, after making the necessary adjustments, apply them to basic human self-conceptions. To get at the meaning of how *person distinguishes* among humans, we must first distinguish person from individual. The pencil lying on my desk is an individual thing. It comes from a box of twelve, from a larger unit of 144, and so on. It is designed to be fungible, i.e., replaceable by any other individual pencil in the box. What makes it valuable is its dependable commonality, its common pencil nature. However, in contrast to the pencil, it would insult human uniqueness to say that a husband, child, or best friend could be re-

24. For an account of the development of the concept of the person, see Philip A. Rolnick, *Person, Grace, and God* (Grand Rapids: Eerdmans, 2007), esp. "Person: Etymological and Historical Development," 10-57.

25. For clarification of nature, substance, and essence, see Rolnick, *Person, Grace, and God,* 19-20.

placed upon malfunction or expiration. Each human person, and *a fortiori* each relationship, is nonfungible. Particularity valorizes relationship because the content of a relationship, what is said, felt, or done, is largely a function of interactive freedom. Human love depends upon treasuring particularity. Each person is an ultimate stopping point, an end in itself that cannot be adequately understood without respecting its singular reality. Individuals can be looked at as a part of a whole or as the instantiation of a species, and patterns do indeed form; but looking in this direction, whatever the gains of biological or sociological understanding, necessarily obscures the reality of the person.

Persons possess an inherent excess, something that is neither determined by laws of cause and effect nor violates those laws. To conceive of a best friend or spouse as the result of physics, chemistry, biology, and perhaps a dose of social conditioning, reduces sacred particularity to commonly held nature. It is not the case that we may never consider the natural components of those whom we love, only that love does not limit itself to such considerations.

That *person relates* is empirically apparent. Every human child, at least biologically, is born of a father and a mother; most of us have siblings; all of us have ancestry that can in principle be traced back to human origins. Moreover, we not only have common ancestry with other biological species, we also have common ancestry with every particle of matter that has emerged since the Big Bang. From a theological perspective, being related to God has the ethical corollary that we bear a familial relation to all other persons, as implied in the first two words of Jesus' prayer, "Our Father." In addition to these given relationships, freely chosen relationships like friendship especially highlight particularity.

That *person unifies* is contingent and relative in the human case. In classical theism, God's unity is a state of being; but for us, unification is a task to be undertaken throughout life. Unity or its absence is an indicator of how well someone is doing. Of those doing well, it is commonly heard, "she has it together." Of those doing poorly, "she is falling apart."

A relatively unified person typically has a clear sense of purpose. According to William Temple (1881-1944), onetime Archbishop of Canterbury, "Purpose is the highest and most distinctive mark of personality."[26] But purpose admits of levels. Purpose can be limited to evolutionary survival, or when survival is no longer a problem, to pleasure. These levels, however, fall

---

26. William Temple, *The Nature of Personality* (London: Macmillan, 1915), 71.

under what is common to species and genus; they do not attain the particular and distinctive — the personal. At this point the debate about human uniqueness takes a decisive turn, for the denial of anything beyond the biological and natural world, i.e., the denial of the transcendent, is the agenda that Nietzsche set and a good part of postmodernism followed.[27]

Belief in God and belief in the possibility of human transcendence are strongly correlative. The very appellation "God" minimally indicates one who transcends the world but, in the three great monotheistic faiths, is also capable of involvement with it. To believe in God is to believe that universe systems are not ultimately closed, that each level or system, including the universe as a whole, makes sense by its openness to something beyond it. When humans are said to be created "in the image of God," human identity is being defined by something that greatly exceeds our current status. Dynamism, movement toward God, is implied in being made in the image of God. To pursue what have traditionally been called the "transcendentals," the true, good, and beautiful, is to pursue manifestations of the intellect and will of God in our own sphere of activity.

The actualization of transcendent potentials distinguishes human persons. If indeed there is anything unique about humanity, if there are persons and not merely individual members of *Homo sapiens*, it is because we do not live by bread alone. We are both like and unlike other species. The likeness has been amply documented by biology since Darwin. The unlikeness is that there is something urging us to go beyond our own nature. As Aquinas puts it: "The ultimate purpose of a rational creature exceeds the capacity of its own nature."[28] Seeking more than bread alone, Plato suggests that human beings are "nourished" when they "behold the plain of truth," and Jacques Maritain exhorts us to "feed upon the transcendentals."[29]

In the domain of personal purpose, the true, good, and beautiful pro-

27. See Friedrich Nietzsche, *Beyond Good and Evil*, in *The Philosophy of Nietzsche*, trans. Helen Zimmern (New York: The Modern Library, 1937), 160, § 230, where Nietzsche calls for a return to *"homo natura."* For a fuller account of the denial of transcendence, see Rolnick, *Person, Grace, and God*, 94-120.

28. Aquinas, *Compendium theologiae*, I.143, n. 285, in *Opuscula theologica*, vol. 1, ed. Raymundi A. Verardo, O.P. (Turin and Rome: Marietti, 1954), 68; my translation.

29. Plato, *Phaedrus* 248e, in *The Collected Dialogues of Plato*, ed. E. Hamilton and H. Cairns (Princeton: Princeton University Press, 1961); Jacques Maritain, *The Person and the Common Good*, trans. John J. Fitzgerald (Notre Dame: University of Notre Dame Press, 1966), 64.

30. Karol Cardinal Wojtyla, *The Acting Person*, trans. Andrzej Potocki, ed. Anna-Teresa Tymieniecka (Dordrecht and Boston: D. Reidel, 1979), 155.

vide what Karol Wojtyla (John Paul II) calls "absolute points of reference."[30] The fate of the human person hinges on the issue of transcendence. It is not too much to say, as does Wojtyla, that "transcendence . . . is to a certain extent another name for the person."[31] Absent the possibility of transcendence, the point of speaking of persons would be lost.

In those whose lives are unconcerned with the possibilities of truth, goodness, and beauty, there is something mean, ignoble, and sometimes even "inhuman."[32] It is highly pejorative to say of someone, "He's a real animal." When the upper and uniquely human dimensions have been suppressed, there remains little to be admired.

The possibility of the transcendentals is also the possibility of love, for the content of love is the true, good, and beautiful. Whether considered as *agape, philia,* or *eros,* the existence of love and of the transcendentals is mutually determinative. The opposites of the transcendentals, falsehood, evil, and ugliness, are unfortunately common in human relations, but these three are so relationally offensive precisely because they are experienced as love's negation.

Concluding Reflections

In the interdisciplinary spirit of this anthology, I have tried to show that different levels of reality are both ordered and open to human and divine persons. In physics, the shift away from classical certainties to quantum probabilities describes a world that is fitting for free will. Quantum mechanics provides the Goldilocks context for human intellect and freedom — not too random and not too deterministic. As Stephen Barr observes:

> There is nothing in the laws of nature or in the character of physics as they exist today which is logically incompatible with free will . . . the determinism which reigned in physical science for almost three centuries, and which seemed to leave no place for freedom, has been overthrown.[33]

In mathematics, Gödel's incompleteness theorems, especially as developed

---

31. Wojtyla, "The Person: Subject and Community," 282.

32. For an argument that holds that only humans can be "inhuman," see Robert Spaemann, *Personen: Versuche über den Unterschied zwischen 'etwas' und 'jemand'* (Stuttgart: Klett-Cotta, 1996), 16.

33. Barr, *Modern Physics,* 184.

in Polanyi's crossing a logical gap, suggest that the human mind characteristically goes beyond a rote program. Gödel, using impeccable and rigorous logic, demonstrated that truth is not confined to demonstration. In history, we again encounter a reality that is neither determinately fixed nor random. Rather, history is open to purposive human action, and, in Christian belief, to divine action.

Just as the narrative of one person's life is embedded within family, ethnic, national, and denominational narratives, the entire human narrative is embedded within the underlying narrative of the natural world. To hold that persons in some vital ways transcend the known laws of the universe in no way violates those laws. Law is the necessary base from which something greater may be attempted. Ultimately, human uniqueness depends upon the reality of the transcendent. Should we become convinced that nothing is or could be transcendent, we would have to accept Richard Rorty's dismal assessment that "[w]e are just complicated animals."[34]

There is something deadening, something slowly suicidal, in reductionist accounts of the human person. All such reductionisms are sophisticated ways of betting against oneself. Isn't there something anti-evolutionary in pursuing such avenues of thought?

In human endeavors and relationships, at least in good ones, we desire to experience something more than mere exchange, tit-for-tat. We have a propensity to love and enjoy appropriate excess. We somehow know that great symphonies are not merely following acoustical laws; great friendships are not based on keeping a balanced account of credits and debits. Human love and enjoyment can manifest generosity, a qualitative leap beyond necessity. In this realm of generosity, human uniqueness can be detected among the complexities of cause-and-effect patterns, probabilities, and the transcendent applications of intellect and will. Systems at every level show themselves to be open to higher levels, and human persons can be open to divine values and the God in whom these values ultimately reside.

34. Richard Rorty, "Putnam and the Relativist Menace," *Journal of Philosophy* 90, no. 9 (September 1993): 458.

List of Contributors

The Editors

J. Wentzel van Huyssteen is the James I. McCord Professor of Theology and Science at Princeton Theological Seminary. He specializes in interdisciplinary and philosophical theology and teaches a wide array of courses and seminars in the broader field of theology and science. In 2004, Wentzel van Huyssteen delivered the Gifford Lectures at the University of Edinburgh in Scotland. In this lecture series he explored the interdisciplinary dialogue between theology and paleoanthropology, and questions of human uniqueness, by focusing on the meaning of prehistoric European cave paintings as some of the oldest surviving expressions of human symbolic activity. The Gifford Lectures were published in the United States of America by Wm. B. Eerdmans Publishing Company, and in Europe by Vandenhoeck & Ruprecht, Germany, as *Alone in the World? Human Uniqueness in Science and Theology*. His current research focuses on the impact of Darwinian evolution on theological anthropology, and specifically on the evolution of sexuality, morality, language, music, and religion.

Erik P. Wiebe currently holds three positions in Evanston, Illinois, where he lives with his wife, Kate, and three children. Erik is a PhD candidate in theological ethics at Garrett-Evangelical Theological Seminary; Research Intern at the Stead Center for Ethics and Values; and Director of Worship and Discipleship Formation at the First Presbyterian Church of Wilmette. His research and work continually prompt further questions regarding the nature of personhood, the implications of embodied anthropology for moral theology, and the constructive resources of the sciences in ministry.

The Contributors

JUSTIN L. BARRETT is senior researcher at the University of Oxford's Centre for Anthropology & Mind and a lecturer in the Institute of Cognitive and Evolutionary Anthropology. He is a research fellow of Regent's Park College, Oxford. He specializes in the cognitive science of religion, psychology of religion, and cognitive approaches to the study of cultural phenomena. His research interests and activities range from the origins of religion in human prehistory to the origins of religion in children, and also include general considerations of how humans understand nonhuman agents, virtue development, and cognition of the visual arts.

ERIC BERGEMANN, PhD, MBA, MFT, is the Director of Professional Education and Training at the Mindsight Institute. He is also a licensed psychotherapist in private practice in Los Angeles and is passionate about exploring the intersection of neuroscience, contemplative practice, and psychotherapy.

JOÃO BIEHL is Professor of Anthropology and Co-Director of the Program in Global Health and Health Policy at Princeton University. Biehl is the author of the award-winning books *Vita: Life in a Zone of Social Abandonment* (University of California Press, 2005) and *Will to Live: AIDS Therapies and the Politics of Survival* (Princeton University Press, 2007). He is also the co-editor of *Subjectivity: Ethnographic Investigations* (University of California Press, 2007). His current research explores the social impact of large-scale treatment programs in resource-poor settings and the role of the judiciary in administering public health.

EMMA COHEN is a postdoctoral researcher in the research group for Comparative Cognitive Anthropology at the Max Planck Institute for Psycholinguistics (Nijmegen, The Netherlands), and a visiting researcher in the Department of Comparative and Developmental Psychology at the Max Planck Institute for Evolutionary Anthropology (Leipzig, Germany). Her research interests concern the evolutionary and cognitive foundations of social and cultural phenomena, especially cultural transmission, recurrence, and variability. She has researched and written on a range of widespread cultural concepts and practices, including spirit possession, witchcraft and sorcery, divination, person-body reasoning, and afterlife beliefs, and has also developed projects on group processes in human sociality.

PAMELA COOPER-WHITE is Ben G. and Nancye C. Gautier Professor of Pastoral Theology, Care and Counseling at Columbia Theological Seminary, Decatur, GA, and recipient of the American Association of Pastoral Counselors' 2005 national award for "Distinguished Achievement in Research and Writing." She holds PhDs from Harvard University and the Institute for Clinical Social Work, Chicago, and is the author of *Many Voices: Pastoral Psychotherapy and Theology in Relational Perspective* (2006), *Shared Wisdom: Use of the Self in Pastoral Care and Counseling* (2004), and *The Cry of Tamar: Violence Against Women and the Church's Response* (1995). An Episcopal priest and pastoral psychotherapist, Dr. Cooper-White is a clinical Fellow in the American Association of Pastoral Counselors. She is former Co-Chair of the Psychology, Culture, and Religion Group of the American Academy of Religion, and currently serves as Publications Editor of the *Journal of Pastoral Theology*.

TERRENCE W. DEACON is Professor of Anthropology and Neuroscience at the University of California, Berkeley. He is author of *The Symbolic Species: The Coevolution of Language and the Brain* (W. W. Norton, 1998), which synthesizes much of his work on human brain and language evolution. His current work focuses on the mechanisms underlying the emergence of major synergistic innovations in evolution. His forthcoming book, entitled *Incomplete Nature: How Mind Emerged from Matter* (2011), outlines a new theory of what he calls "emergent evolution" and proposes a general mechanism underlying the origins of information in biology, from its emergence at the dawn of life to its transformation into mental and ultimately symbolic form in the evolution of humans.

DEANIE EICHENSTEIN was born and raised in Los Angeles and is an intern at the Mindsight Institute. She is currently finishing her undergraduate studies at Sarah Lawrence College, concentrating in psychology and its sociopolitical implications. She aspires to build a clinical practice in psychology.

JAMES W. HAAG is Lecturer in Philosophy at Suffolk University in Boston. He is author of numerous publications on science, philosophy, and religion, including the book *Emergent Freedom: Naturalizing Free Will* (Vandenhoeck & Ruprecht, 2008). Haag is currently co-editing the *Routledge Companion to Religion and Science* (due out Spring 2011) and is co-chair of the Science, Technology, and Religion Group of the American Academy of Religion.

JAN-OLAV HENRIKSEN is Professor of Systematic Theology and Philosophy of Religion at (MF) Norwegian School of Theology, Oslo, Norway. He is also director of the interdisciplinary Norwegian research school Religion Values Society, and Professor of Religious Studies at Agder University, Kristiansand, Norway. Henriksen specializes in research on contemporary theology and how to articulate the Christian faith in the present cultural and philosophical conditions, and much of his scholarly work is, accordingly, on the boundary between theology and philosophy.

IAN HODDER is Dunlevie Family Professor in the Department of Anthropology at Stanford University. His main interests are archeological theory and method, with particular reference to the understanding of material culture ethnographically, historically, and prehistorically. In order to pursue these interests he has excavated at Çatalhöyük in Turkey since 1993.

CATHERINE KELLER is Professor of Constructive Theology in the Theological School and the Graduate Division of Religion of Drew University. She is the author of *On the Mystery: Discerning Divinity in Process; God and Power: Counter-Apocalyptic Explorations; Face of the Deep: A Theology of Becoming; Apocalypse Now & Then: A Feminist Guide to the End of the World;* and *From a Broken Web: Separation, Sexism and Self.* She has co-edited *Process and Difference: Between Cosmological and Poststructuralist Postmodernism,* as well as several Transdisciplinary Theological Colloquium volumes (Fordham Press), the most recent being *Apophatic Bodies: Negative Theology, Incarnation and Relationality.*

BARBARA J. KING is Chancellor Professor of Anthropology at the College of William and Mary. For many years, she studied monkey and ape behavior, seeking to understand primate social learning and communication through dynamic systems theory. Now she writes books and articles about the evolutionary and cultural history of animal-human relating.

JAY OGILVY taught philosophy at Yale University; University of Texas, Austin; and Williams College before taking up contract research and consulting, first at SRI International (formerly Stanford Research Institute), and then with a firm he co-founded, Global Business Network. He is the author or editor of seven books and over fifty articles.

PHILIP A. ROLNICK is Professor of Theology at the University of St. Thomas in St. Paul, Minnesota. He is the author of *Analogical Possibilities: How Words Refer to God* (Scholars Press, 1993, now with Oxford University Press) and *Person, Grace, and God* (Eerdmans, 2007). Besides his work in theories of analogy and personhood, he has been researching the interaction of science and theology. He is currently writing a theology of evolution and Big Bang cosmology.

HELENE TALLON RUSSELL is Associate Professor of Theology at Christian Theological Seminary in Indianapolis. She is on the board of Process and Faith at Claremont. She earned a PhD in philosophy of religion and theology at Claremont Graduate University, studying under Marjorie Suchocki. Russell has previously taught at Allegheny College, Albertson College of Idaho, and Claremont McKenna College. She is the author of *Kierkegaard and Irigaray: Multiplicity, Relationality, and Difference* (Mercer University Press, 2009). She has also written scholarly articles and given presentations at the American Academy of Religion and at the Center for Process Studies on various topics, and she has written for the Human Rights Campaign's "Out in Scripture Project" (http://www.hrc.org/scripture/).

CALVIN O. SCHRAG is the George Ade Distinguished Professor of Philosophy Emeritus at Purdue University. He has served on the faculties of the University of Illinois, Northwestern University, Indiana University, and Stony Brook University. A graduate of Yale and Harvard, Fulbright Scholar at Heidelberg and Oxford, Guggenheim Fellow at Freiburg, and founding editor of the international journal *Continental Philosophy Review,* he is the author of ten books and numerous book chapters and journal articles, many of which have been translated into a score of foreign languages. His specialization includes theory of knowledge, philosophy of the social sciences, and philosophy of religion.

ROGER SCRUTON is a scholar at the American Enterprise Institute, Visiting Professor at the University of Oxford, and Fellow of Blackfriars Hall, Oxford. He has written widely on philosophy, architecture, music, and culture, and is well known as a public intellectual fighting futile battles in defense of civilization. He is currently arming himself against neurononsense.

MAXINE SHEETS-JOHNSTONE is an independent, highly interdisciplinary scholar whose publications span philosophy, psychology, evolutionary biology, dance, and cognitive science and whose undergraduate/graduate degrees and postdoctoral studies span the same disciplines, plus French and comparative literature. She has an ongoing Courtesy Professor appointment in the Department of Philosophy at the University of Oregon, where she taught periodically over a period of ten years in the 1990s. Her current research is on xenophobia, a strong thematic that emerged in the course of one of her recent books, *The Roots of Morality.*

DANIEL J. SIEGEL, MD, is clinical professor of psychiatry at the UCLA School of Medicine, co-director of the UCLA Mindful Awareness Research Center, and executive director of the Mindsight Institute. A graduate of Harvard Medical School, he is the co-author of *Parenting from the Inside Out* and the author of the internationally acclaimed professional texts *The Developing Mind, The Mindful Brain, Mindsight,* and *The Mindful Therapist.* Dr. Siegel keynotes conferences and presents workshops throughout the world. He lives in Los Angeles with his wife and two children.

ELLEN STREIT is a junior at the University of Southern California majoring in neuroscience with a minor in peace and conflict studies. She plans to pursue a career in child neuropsychology, working with children both abroad and at home. She is an intern at the Mindsight Institute and currently lives in Los Angeles.

MARJORIE HEWITT SUCHOCKI is Professor Emerita at Claremont School of Theology, where she held the Ingraham Chair in Theology, and also served as Dean. Her specialty is process theology, in which she has published a number of books. Since her retirement her interests have turned to theology and film; she serves on international ecumenical juries at film festivals, directs the Whitehead International Film Festival, and has written *Sin and Cinema: Violence and Redemption in Film and Theology* (forthcoming).

IAN TATTERSALL is a curator in the Division of Anthropology of the American Museum of Natural History in New York City. Over the last four decades his research has focused mainly on the biology of Madagascar's lemurs and on human evolution, and he has carried out fieldwork in numerous locales worldwide. Most recently, he has been concerned with systematics within the hominid family, and with the emergence of modern humans in both anatomical and behavioral contexts.

JENNIFER THWEATT-BATES holds a PhD in theology and science from Princeton Theological Seminary and is currently an adjunct instructor at New Brunswick Theological Seminary. Her research interests focus on the nexus of epistemology, science, technology, and theological anthropology, specifically regarding constructions of the human and the posthuman.

LÉON TURNER is a senior research associate in the Psychology and Religion Research Group at the Faculty of Divinity, University of Cambridge, where he teaches the psychology of religion and issues in science and religion. His primary research interests center upon the relationship between philosophical anthropology, theological anthropology, and the human sciences, particularly psychology.

HETTY ZOCK is KSGV Professor in Spiritual Care and Senior Lecturer in Psychology of Religion at the University of Groningen, The Netherlands. She earned her MDiv and PhD at the University of Leiden, and worked for ten years as a minister in the Dutch Reformed Church. She has been teaching psychology of religion since 1994 and spiritual care since 2000. Her primary works have focused on Erik H. Erikson's contribution to the psychology of religion, spiritual care and meaning-making from the perspective of psychology of religion, and psychological studies of popular cultural phenomena such as Harry Potter. Her academic interests include contemporary psychoanalysis and identity theory; the relation between art, religion, and meaning; and spiritual care in a secularized, globalized context.

Index of Names

Index of Subjects

absolutizing finitude, 260
abstraction, 323-25
agency, 55, 64-67, 108-9, 112-19, 159, 164-66, 171, 174, 236-37, 245, 247-48, 253-55, 311, 320-21, 323-24, 330-37
agricultural societies, 53-54
Akineton (drug), 277, 285, 293
apophaticism, 318
attentive onlooker, 199, 205-11
attunement, 88, 94
autonomy, 54, 64, 111, 125, 130, 147-48, 245-48, 252-53, 304, 311, 314, 325-27, 330-37

Big Bang theory, 358n.3, 367, 371
bottom-up processing, 90, 92-94. *See also* cortex
Brutus (chimpanzee), 73-74, 77

Çatalhöyük, Turkey: burial practices in, 56-67; houses in, 56-67; increasing individuation within, 64-66; and the relation to things, 58; tools in, 62-63
character, 128, 148-49, 153-55, 158, 167-68, 172, 219, 237, 368-69
Christian theology, 1-3, 125, 129-37, 143-44, 160-62, 253-55, 266-72, 301-7, 349, 366

cognitive mechanisms, 106-8, 112-14, 117-20
collective self-identity. *See* self
communication, between species, 71-72
Communion, 141-42
complexity theory, 87, 304-7
consciousness, 1-3, 8-18, 34-37, 44, 83-84, 119, 153, 167, 177, 192-97, 199-203, 205-8, 211-12, 214, 223, 230, 232-33, 243, 247, 261, 276, 302, 304, 320, 334, 338-41, 344-46, 348-49, 355-56, 365n.15
constraint, 323, 325-32, 336-37
cortex, 91-96, 346
counterreductionism, 304-7
creation, 157, 267-70, 306-7, 310-13, 367

dance, 192
Deep Blue (computer), 358
desire, 83, 92, 116, 144-45, 153-54, 161, 213, 228, 247, 253, 255, 256-72, 273-76, 278-82, 293-94, 341-43, 350-53
diachronic experience, 127-29, 134, 163, 166n.3, 172, 178, 212
Dissociative Identity Disorder, 112n.3, 145
dividuals. *See* self, as partible
dualism, 85, 109, 118-19, 154